BREAKING THROUGH

Understanding Sovereignty and Security in the Circumpolar Arctic

Edited by Wilfrid Greaves and P. Whitney Lackenbauer

Globalization, climate change, and increased geopolitical competition are having a profound impact on the Arctic, affecting how we understand both sovereignty and security within the region. In *Breaking Through*, a diverse group of emerging and established scholars investigate Arctic sovereignty and security, rarely examined together, and present a theoretically robust study of Arctic sovereignty and security in both historical and contemporary contexts.

Throughout the volume, readers will discover fresh perspectives on under-studied dimensions of Arctic sovereignty, including environmental changes, foreign and security policies, and how Indigenous peoples interact to produce different meanings of sovereignty and security in the Arctic. Drawing on extensive primary and secondary research, *Breaking Through* offers important and timely conclusions for policymakers, advocates, scholars, and students.

WILFRID GREAVES is an assistant professor of international relations at the University of Victoria.

P. WHITNEY LACKENBAUER is the Canada Research Chair (Tier 1) in the Study of the Canadian North and a professor in the School for the Study of Canada at Trent University.

Breaking Through

Understanding Sovereignty and Security in the Circumpolar Arctic

EDITED BY WILFRID GREAVES AND
P. WHITNEY LACKENBAUER

UNIVERSITY OF TORONTO PRESS
Toronto Buffalo London

© University of Toronto Press 2021
Toronto Buffalo London
utorontopress.com
Printed and bound by CPI Group (UK) Ltd, Croydon, CR0 4YY

ISBN 978-1-4875-0486-1 (cloth)   ISBN 978-1-4875-3105-8 (EPUB)
ISBN 978-1-4875-2352-7 (paper)   ISBN 978-1-4875-3104-1 (PDF)

Library and Archives Canada Cataloguing in Publication

Title: Breaking through : understanding sovereignty and security in the
   circumpolar Arctic / edited by Wilfrid Greaves and P. Whitney Lackenbauer.
Other titles: Breaking through (2021).
Names: Greaves, Wilfrid, 1984–, editor. | Lackenbauer, P. Whitney, editor.
Description: Includes index.
Identifiers: Canadiana (print) 20200408720 | Canadiana (ebook) 20200409247 |
   ISBN 9781487523527 (softcover) | ISBN 9781487504861 (hardcover) |
   ISBN 9781487531058 (EPUB) | ISBN 9781487531041 (PDF)
Subjects: LCSH: Arctic regions – Strategic aspects. | LCSH: Arctic regions –
   International status. | LCSH: Jurisdiction, Territorial – Arctic regions. |
   LCSH: Arctic regions – Foreign relations. | LCSH: Sovereignty.
Classification: LCC UA880 .B74 2021 | DDC 355/.0330113 – dc23

This book has been published with the help of a grant from the Federation for
the Humanities and Social Sciences, through the Awards to Scholarly Publications
Program, using funds provided by the Social Sciences and Humanities Research
Council of Canada.

University of Toronto Press acknowledges the financial assistance to its
publishing program of the Canada Council for the Arts and the Ontario Arts
Council, an agency of the Government of Ontario.

**Canada Council   Conseil des Arts
for the Arts   du Canada**

ONTARIO ARTS COUNCIL
CONSEIL DES ARTS DE L'ONTARIO
an Ontario government agency
un organisme du gouvernement de l'Ontario

Funded by the   Financé par le
Government   gouvernement
of Canada   du Canada

Canadä

Contents

BREAKING THROUGH

Understanding Sovereignty and Security
in the Circumpolar Arctic

Understanding Sovereignty and Security in the Circumpolar Arctic: An Introduction

WILFRID GREAVES AND P. WHITNEY LACKENBAUER

The transformation of the circumpolar Arctic region since the early 1990s has been nothing less than extraordinary. Seldom in history has any part of the world undergone such tectonic shifts across so many different aspects of its politics, economy, society, and ecology. The apparent end of the superpower rivalry between the United States and post-Soviet Russia allowed for a realignment of Arctic politics away from Cold War militarism, leading to the establishment of the Arctic Council and to rapid growth of a dense network of political organizations working to foster regional cooperation. The increasing integration of the Arctic into the global marketplace created new opportunities for economic investment in polar industries, driven particularly by global demand for natural resources such as fossil fuels, minerals, and fish, as well as commercial interest in destinational tourism and the potential viability of polar shipping routes. The dramatic impacts of human-caused climate change on the Arctic environment, most notably by the precipitous reduction in summer sea ice cover, have also propelled rising economic interest in the region. These new Arctic dynamics represent a fundamental shift in the relationships among circumpolar states, peoples, non-governmental organizations, and the natural environment, compounding the already dramatic impacts of geopolitics and modernization experienced over the course of the twentieth century. In a few short years, life at the top of the world has changed radically, and the breadth of these changes requires reflection to comprehend their implications and to chart a path for the future.

The responses by states, international organizations, sub-state actors, and non-governmental organizations – as well as outside observers such as scholars and journalists – to these myriad regional changes have renewed interest in the core political concepts of sovereignty and security and their distinct features in the Arctic region. The confluence of climate change and the end of the Cold War led the Arctic states to reconsider their Arctic interests in light of the changing geopolitical and physical environment, generating a wave of new official foreign and security policies that continue to emphasize (in many cases) Arctic states' central preoccupation with defending their Arctic territory and sovereignty. Other actors, most notably Indigenous peoples through their self-governing institutions and representative organizations, have articulated conceptions of security and sovereignty in the region that both support and challenge the priorities identified by Arctic states. Their various understandings of security and sovereignty reveal both similarities and differences, as well as apparent contradictions. Overall, significant variations among different representations of sovereignty and security in the Arctic reinforce that the meaning and application of these concepts remain contested.

What Are (Arctic) Sovereignty and Security?[1]

Sovereignty and security are among the most widely used – and misused – concepts in current debates around global and domestic politics. What do they actually mean? Neither security nor sovereignty has an objective definition; rather, each is an inherently political and contested concept whose various definitions are based on underlying normative commitments that have significant impacts on people and their political communities.[2] The question of what or whom is to be considered sovereign and as worthy of being secured brings to light societal values and theoretical biases, and its answer indicates whose voices and views we think should be represented within our politics. These definitions are especially relevant in the circumpolar region, which – as a comparatively "new" region for inter-state politics that also possesses some unique defining characteristics – is susceptible to challenges to mainstream definitions of both concepts. For some Arctic stakeholders and rightsholders, the meanings of sovereignty and security in the region have expanded or shifted owing to the intersection of economic and cultural globalization, climate change, and greater recognition and implementation of the rights of Indigenous peoples. Political actors have actively contested and redefined these concepts to suit their interests. These changes, and their implications for Arctic politics, are still unfolding, but their effects are already significant and undeniable. Below, we discuss the conceptual ties that bind sovereignty and security together.

Since the start of the modern political era, often associated with the Peace of Westphalia in 1648, global politics has increasingly been defined by the principle of sovereignty. Sovereign power constitutes the modern state; in the words of pioneering sociologist Max Weber, sovereignty means to possess a monopoly on the legitimate use of organized force in a given territory.[3] In addition to constituting the state as a form of political organization, the exercise of sovereign power was necessary to protect individuals from threats of violence within a bounded space. Since the power to defend individuals primarily resided with the state, and the primary threat of mass violence originated in other states, security become associated with the maintenance of the sovereign territorial state, the use of state-authorized violence, and the distribution of power and interests within the international system of states.[4] The modern origins of sovereignty and (national) security in the Westphalian era are inextricably linked through establishing a system of territorially bounded, juridically equal political units engaged in relations of competition and conflict, with the wellbeing of individuals fundamentally tied to the survival and prosperity of their respective states.

Given its centrality to global politics, sovereignty has been a long-standing target of critique within International Relations. In particular, constructivist scholars have drawn attention to sovereignty's contingent nature and co-constitution with ideas and norms about political authority and the nature of the international system.[5] Others have been pointedly critical; Charles Tilly compared sovereign states to gangsters,[6] and Stephen Krasner famously defined the international system of sovereign states as one of "organized hypocrisy" because it is premised on principles that, in practice, are frequently violated, notably non-aggression and non-interference in the domestic affairs of other states.[7] Moreover, as an expression of the highest form of political authority within a given community, sovereignty is not a property exclusively reserved for territorially bounded states. States have always coexisted with other forms of political organization in the world,[8] including both more traditional and more modern forms of governance. Some scholars, such as Biersteker and Weber, take a constructivist approach, acknowledging space for non-state sovereigns by defining sovereignty as "a political entity's externally recognized right to exercise final authority over its own affairs."[9] There are, in fact, different types of sovereignty, and an exclusive emphasis on state sovereignty obscures the contestation over sovereignty among different actors and over different aspects of intra-state politics.

Historically, sovereignty in the Arctic referred to the consolidation of political control over distant northern regions by the southern capitals of circumpolar states and tended to focus on perceived foreign threats to territory, maritime boundary disputes, and control over natural resources. As discussed in chapters 1 and 2 of this book, sovereignty in the Arctic has conformed with the Weberian definition of sovereignty as monopoly on the use of coercive force through effective control over territory. Thus, for example, the legal status of the Northwest Passage and ownership of the rock known as Hans Island have figured prominently in discussions of Canadian Arctic sovereignty, while other countries have focused on control over other polar straits such as Russia's Northern Sea Route; on unconventional political jurisdiction, such as Norway's Svalbard Archipelago; and on determining extended marine territories under the United Nations' *Convention on the Law of the Sea*. The interpretation and application of Arctic sovereignty has varied across circumpolar states and sometimes within them. For instance, there is a vigorous historiographical debate between scholars who see the Cold War bilateral relationship over Arctic sovereignty and security between Canada and the United States as inherently conflictual,[10] and those who emphasize more cooperative, functional relationships predicated on mutual respect and the benefits of "agreeing to disagree" on divergent legal views.[11] In some ways, these debates persist to the present day. But despite the warnings and concerns of some journalists and other analysts (as Landriault examines in chapter 3), sovereignty issues between Arctic states are generally managed in an orderly and non-confrontational way.

Setting aside the symbolic value and national attachment to certain Arctic geographies, notably the North Pole, what lies behind states' interests in asserting and expanding their Arctic sovereignty is a desire for the greatest possible future economic benefits from Arctic resources.[12] At stake are shipping lanes, fisheries, and hydrocarbons, the latter estimated to be 90 billion barrels of oil (13 per cent of undiscovered global resources) and 46 trillion cubic metres of natural gas (30 per cent of undiscovered global resources).[13] Major conflicts are unlikely, given that doubt remains about the viability of developing these resources, the majority of which are believed to lie in undisputed sovereign territory.[14] Even so, the link between sovereignty assertion and energy resources is clear. "Issues of Arctic energy and development and Arctic sovereignty are linked," Benoit Beauchamp and Rob Huebert suggest. "When no one was talking about actually developing Arctic resources, the many sovereignty issues could be and were ignored."[15] In practice, many boundary and status-of-waters disagreements continue to be managed or sidelined, though the stakes involved in the symbolic politics of Arctic territory have grown now that resource extraction has become a greater possibility. Though all Arctic states continue to emphasize the absence of conventional military threats in the region and reaffirm their commitments to peaceful resolution of Arctic disputes, many national governments have also constructed Arctic resources as central to their national economic interests.[16] Thus, while there is little evidence that the warming environment will directly result in inter-state violence, the opening of the Arctic has led to a renewed emphasis on military activity, and the prospect of resource wealth has raised the stakes for states asserting and defending their Arctic sovereignty claims.

These traditional narratives of Arctic sovereignty have been disrupted by growing recognition of the rights of Indigenous peoples to self-determination and by the devolution of political powers to northern and sub-state governments, including Greenland, Nunavut, and northern Scandinavia. While political devolution falls well short of independence or statehood for the Arctic's Indigenous peoples, their empowerment represents a significant political consensus that, to borrow Inuit leader Mary Simon's memorable phrase, "sovereignty begins at home."[17] Arctic states cannot separate their claims to territory and authority over vast Arctic geographies from the rights and political agency of the peoples who inhabit the region. For states, this roots Arctic sovereignty claims in the prior occupation of Arctic Indigenous peoples. In turn, for these peoples, sovereignty is rooted in their daily activities, which serves to reduce the emphasis on abstract political claims by distant central governments. In the contemporary Arctic, Indigenous leaders argue that sovereignty is best understood by reflecting on the views of Arctic inhabitants, rather than focusing on borders, bombers, and battleships.[18] In the twentieth-century Arctic, the application of state sovereignty typically focused on military defence, especially the protection of national borders and the assertion of state sovereignty over Arctic lands and waters. During the Cold War in particular, security in the Arctic was inseparable from nuclear deterrence and the bipolar rivalry between the American and Soviet superpowers, a conception whose legacy persists in various ways (see Greaves in chapter 5, Sergunin in chapter 6, and Østhagen in chapter 8).

The tensions between these various accounts of sovereignty have been mirrored with respect to the concept of security. Emma Rothschild persuasively argues that security in the early modern era was seen "as a condition both of individuals and of states … a condition, or an objective, that constituted a *relationship* between individuals and states or societies."[19] Because of the anarchic structure of the international system, preserving the state necessarily came first in order to secure the welfare of the people. The idea of security evolved significantly during the revolutionary period of the late eighteenth and nineteenth centuries, when the understanding of the sovereign state as the provider of security for individuals shifted toward an emphasis on the state itself as the object to be protected.[20] Security came to be practically synonymous with *national*

security: on a state's sovereign right to defend its territory, political institutions, and populations against violent threats to its survival and core
interests.

The reconceptualization of security is thus tied to the changing dynamics of sovereignty as the ordering principle of global politics and
the international system and to the emergence of new, often non-state,
political actors exercising diverse forms of agency within global politics. In the postwar period, scholars began to "redefine security," arguing that conventional national security discourse did not capture
the full range of emerging security issues.[21] Writing in 1952, Arnold
Wolfers was among the first to observe the mutability of security, noting that "when formulas such as 'national interest' or 'national security' gain popularity they need to be scrutinized with particular care.
They may not mean the same thing to different people. They may not
have any precise meaning at all."[22] Wolfers was ahead of his time, but
in the last two decades of the twentieth century, scholars increasingly
recognized that security has no given meaning: it is a social construct
whose substantive content is ascribed by social actors. Drawing on the
insight that there can be no objective meaning for inherently normative concepts such as "democracy," "freedom," or "justice," Steve Smith
argues that security is also a contested concept whose basic meaning
is a matter of inherent dispute. "No neutral definition is possible," he
argues, because "any meaning depends upon and in turn supports a
specific view of politics ... All definitions are theory-dependent, and
all definitions reflect normative commitments."[23] Smith thus echoes a
basic tenet of critical theorizing, that "theory is always *for* someone,
and *for* some purpose."[24] Arguing that security should be understood
as *national* security exposes prior views about states and the behaviour
of rational actors under conditions of structural anarchy that reveal
preferences for how politics should be conducted.[25] This may be how
security was largely defined in the past, but it need not be how it is
defined in the future.

The dominant account of national security was increasingly contested
after the 1970s because of theoretical and empirical shifts in global politics. As the Cold War dragged on and as states and people around the
world found themselves confronted by serious challenges unrelated to
the bipolar balance of power or the risk of nuclear conflict, the understanding of security as inherently tied to the state and organized violence came under increasing challenge. Various actors sought to alter,
undermine, or reappropriate how security was understood and pursued
at the individual, national, and international levels. In the West, the anti-
nuclear peace research community sought to frame the existence and

potential use of nuclear weapons as a source of insecurity rather than viable protection against the Soviet threat.[26] Scholars and practitioners of development emphasized the critical situation of the global poor and many states in the "Third World," as well as the indirect costs of prioritizing military expenditures over social investments.[27] The women's movement and independence for the remaining European colonies in Asia, Africa, and the Americas inspired feminist, critical, and postcolonial approaches that directly challenged dominant frameworks of security, seeking to radically reorient the subjects and contexts of security by inquiring into the lived experiences of women, children, minorities, and other subaltern groups.[28] Environmentalists, invoking the local, national, and global impacts of military and economic activities on the environment, began observing the need for certain ecological conditions to be maintained in order for conditions of security to be sustainable.[29] The conception of "national" security as inherently state-, military-, and Western-centric was widely disputed as these alternatives gained greater prominence (see Rob Huebert in chapter 4 and Gunhild Hoogensen Gjørv in chapter 10 for different perspectives on this debate). These alternative narratives of security demonstrated that, far from having a given meaning tied to military defence of the sovereign state, "security" varies according to national and social context and has been reimagined at different points in history.

The meaning of security in the Arctic has changed in recent decades; indeed, the Arctic has been a site for all of the factors (listed above) that have driven changing assessments of security: Cold War political transformations, the anti-nuclear peace movement, discourses of decolonization and the "Fourth World" (Indigenous peoples residing in poverty within the comparative wealth of developed countries), feminism, and (most of all) human-caused environmental change resulting in the wide-scale transformation of ecosystems and the human and non-human communities that rely upon them. During the Cold War, the Arctic suffered from a dichotomy whereby its overmilitarization as a buffer between competing superpowers resulted in an underpoliticization from which it has still only partly emerged.[30] The geopolitical conditions that transformed the Arctic "first into a military flank, then a military front or even a 'military theatre'" restricted the development of effective political institutions.[31] The end of the Cold War thus altered the geopolitical context that had kept the Arctic frozen in a state of superpower competition, stifling opportunities for regional development and necessitating the deployment of substantial military resources to the region. This political shift has interacted with the changing environment to affect the security of Arctic states in at least three ways: it has catalysed regional cooperation; it has made the Arctic more accessible to state and commercial actors, raising the stakes for outstanding boundary disputes and resource development; and it has contributed to the emergence of various unconventional security issues, such as illegal shipping, smuggling, irregular migration, and even terrorism, in increasingly accessible Arctic waters. The latter issues have attracted high-level concern and informed training scenarios for some armed forces.[32]

The post–Cold War period has also given risen to alternative understandings of security that emphasize the economic, social, cultural, and environmental concerns of *people* rather than states. Broader and deeper conceptions of security that reflect new and distinct types of threats and that encompass peoples and communities are often grouped together within the general framework of human security issues.[33] Many analysts and government stakeholders now include health, housing, economic sustainability, community vitality, food and water systems, ecosystem resilience, linguistic practice, and cultural identity as unconventional security issues (Petra Dolata discusses the distinct politics of energy security in chapter 9, and Natalia Loukacheva and Frank Sejersen provide different perspectives on food security in chapters 11 and 12, respectively).[34] This reflects the widespread acknowledgment that long-standing issues related to pollution, chronic ill health, and personal and community well-being – all the result of traumatic processes of colonial assimilation and economic globalization across the region – have not been sufficiently addressed or have even grown more severe, particularly for circumpolar Indigenous peoples.[35] Terry Audla, former president of Inuit Tapiriit Kanatami (the national Inuit organization in Canada), has asserted that "the insecurities that Inuit face as a result of our living, over three or four generations, in what has been a firestorm of cultural change," mean that "while some insecurities have abated, new ones have arisen and some old ones have taken on new forms."[36] Environmental changes have amplified these chronic challenges to Arctic life, reshaping natural and social systems and threatening to "exceed the rate at which some of their components can successfully adapt."[37]

As Audla's statement intimates, ethnicity and indigeneity also condition human security in the Arctic. Changes to the physical landscape have directly affected the subsistence practices of Indigenous peoples on their traditional territories, undermining multi-generational knowledge of weather and climate, changing animals' migration patterns, and compelling new methods of hunting and gathering.[38] Indigenous peoples' identities and cultural practices are predicated on close relationships to the natural environments of their ancestral territories, with the consequence that environmental degradation leads inexorably to loss of culture and identity.[39] For Inuit, this relationship is exemplified by the reduced quality and availability of traditional country foods, including game, fish, and berries. "To hunt, catch, and share these foods is the essence of Inuit culture," the *Arctic Climate Impact Assessment* observed. "Thus, a decline in [country foods] … threatens not only the dietary requirements of the Inuit, but also their very way of life."[40] Accidents associated with changing ice conditions and unpredictable weather patterns also threaten Inuit lives, given that Inuit are a maritime people whose communities are predominantly coastal; indeed, some communities travel by sea or not at all.[41] High rates of suicide among Inuit are associated with uncertainty about gender roles in changing conditions, with young men "not seeing a future for themselves as hunters and contributors to their community and at the same time not fitting into the cash employment structures that are becoming the dominant lifestyle."[42] This bleak expectations are driven by interactions between colonialism, rapid cultural change, and environmental change that limit opportunities for subsistence living and impede the acquisition, practice, and celebration of cultural skills.[43] Higher rates of male suicide, in turn, place a disproportionate economic burden on surviving female relatives to provide for their families. The links between issues like suicide, cultural change, and environmental transformation point to the multitude of insecurities facing people and communities. Thus, human security issues highlight the connections between material and non-material threats, offering a broader framework to interrogate "security" than more traditional, state-centric definitions.

Clearly, sovereignty and security are important social constructs. But both are inevitably contested, because defining either requires committing oneself to a particular configuration of politics and society. They may exist in particular dominant forms but be inherently subject to contestation; moreover, both are being increasingly challenged as various non-state actors have advanced alternative claims to sovereignty and security. The understandings of sovereignty and security in the Arctic discussed in the existing research and in this book are heterogenous, and reflect perspectives that can support the existing structure of security as national security and sovereignty as reserved for territorial states, or advance alternative subjects and objects for consideration as security- and sovereignty-relevant within the international system. In so doing, these different accounts can serve distinct sets of interests and result in vastly different material and normative outcomes for states, peoples, and other human communities. These distinctions are clearly in evidence in the case of sovereignty and security in the circumpolar Arctic.

Seeking Better Understanding

Given these multitudinous understandings of security and sovereignty, it is challenging to know how to move toward a better understanding of these foundational concepts. In this book, we suggest that Arctic scholars can help bridge the gap between different understandings of sovereignty and security by generating theoretical and policy insights that reflect a diversity of perspectives from around the region. This book was inspired by a gathering of more than forty researchers and analysts from Canada, the United States, and Europe at the University of Toronto in January 2016 for a workshop on "Understanding Sovereignty and Security in the Circumpolar Arctic." The origins of this workshop are reflected in the contributions to this volume. The authors are Canadian, Norwegian, Danish, German, and Russian – or hybridized variations of multiple national identities. They write from the perspectives of scholars and expert observers of the Arctic with institutional and professional affiliations around the North Atlantic region.

In this volume, we have attempted to incorporate reflections on sovereignty and security from states across the circumpolar region, with particularly strong empirical reflections on Canada, Norway, and Russia. While this focus is, in some respects, limiting, there are good reasons why the framing concepts of sovereignty and security employed here are particularly suited to the study of these states. As discussed by Lajeunesse (chapter 2), Greaves (chapter 5), and Østhagen (chapter 8), Canada and Norway have distinctive foreign policy inheritances in the Arctic that have typically been framed in terms of both sovereignty and security issues. This is particularly the case with non-traditional security issues, such as those related to human and environmental security, that have been prominent since the early 1990s, as well as ongoing legal–political disputes pertaining to jurisdiction and territorial control over unusual Arctic geographies such as Svalbard and the Northwest Passage, respectively. By contrast, the United States has never particularly conceived of itself as an Arctic state, and sovereignty and security have been peripheral, at best, to Iceland, Finland, and Sweden's pursuit of their Arctic interests. Russia is central to questions of regional security, both in its own right, as discussed by Sergunin (chapter 6), and in terms of its construction as the primary antagonist in the Arctic policies of many of its neighbours, as Huebert (chapter 4), Greaves (chapter 5), Lackenbauer (chapter 7), and Østhagen (chapter 8) demonstrate. Russia's Arctic security policies and practices are deeply implicated in those of its middle-power Arctic neighbours. We regret that there is no chapter that reflects a deeper engagement with other relevant regional issues such as

Greenland's contentious relationship to full sovereignty from Denmark, or indeed, other dimensions of Indigenous sovereignties in the region. As with any scholarly work, this one has limitations, and while the contributors discuss a broad array of historical and contemporary cases from across much of the circumpolar region, the focus remains primarily on Arctic states, with other types of political actors underrepresented.

Nonetheless, based on this workshop and other recent scholarship, we identify five points that we believe are crucial for understanding sovereignty and security in the contemporary Arctic and that inform the contributions to this edited collection:

1 In a modern and a rapidly changing Arctic, security and sovereignty must also encompass environmental, economic, social, and cultural issues. Climate change is especially important. As President Obama noted at a climate change conference in Alaska in August 2015, climate change "will define the contours of this century more dramatically than any other [issue]."[44]

2 We must stop thinking of the Arctic as a single holistic place. All eight Arctic states have released new Arctic foreign policy and security strategies in response to the changing climate, but each state's sovereignty and security issues are shaped by geography, ecology, culture, and national interests. Each country experiences the Arctic differently and assigns it a different symbolic importance. Consequently, the Arctic is constructed differently within each country's respective policies.

3 Arctic governments and Arctic peoples may have different understandings of sovereignty and security. Arctic states typically prioritize military defence, natural resource extraction, and territorial expansion, whereas people living in the Arctic tend to prioritize social, economic, ecological, and cultural threats to their communities. At the same time, citizens generally agree on which issues matter most, whether they live north or south of the Arctic Circle. Global warming and other environmental issues are overwhelmingly viewed as the greatest threats, according to the second *Arctic Security Public Opinion Survey*, conducted in 2015.[45] Economic, social, and cultural issues followed, and traditional national security issues ranked at the very bottom.

4 The perspectives of the Arctic's original inhabitants must be included in policy-making. In particular, the voices of those who experience the most acute or chronic threats to their survival and well-being should be heard. This includes Indigenous peoples, whose experiences of threats are very different from those of settler populations

or newcomers and whose claims to Arctic territory often underpin the contemporary sovereignty of Arctic states. Furthermore, policy-making must factor in gendered forms of insecurity, where threats disproportionately affect one group over others. For example, women experience high rates of intimate-partner and domestic violence, and young men are more likely to attempt suicide.

5 Communities and households must be empowered to address issues of Arctic sovereignty and security. Governments, militaries, and constabulary forces, as well as regional organizations such as the Arctic Council, remain essential to providing security and promoting sovereignty. But these concepts must extend deeper to encompass communities, families, and individual households. We must examine the ways in which government policies, cultural and social pressures originating in the south, and the contributions of industrialized states to global climate change threaten security within Arctic homes and communities, and find ways to mitigate these.

We contend that security in the rapidly changing Arctic region can no longer be exclusively about military threats and dangers and that sovereignty cannot fixate on the rights of states to the exclusion of those of Indigenous communities or regional and global governance. Deepening and broadening our understanding of sovereignty and security can help reduce vulnerability and increase the resiliency of Arctic societies in the face of compounding, and accelerating, social and environmental changes.

In chapter 1, historian Peter Kikkert outlines the sociopolitical and legal debates associated with state claims to polar sovereignty in the first half of the twentieth century. Situating debates around the legal status of Arctic sovereignty in relation to the Antarctic as well, he explores how lawyers and state officials understood the definition and function of polar sovereignty, particularly in geographic areas that lacked permanent Indigenous inhabitants. His chapter examines the problem of how to apply a body of rules and practices for territorial acquisition that is ambiguous, underdeveloped, and open to interpretation and modification so as to reflect the unique conditions of the polar regions. Kikkert's chapter offers a historical perspective on how sustained legal ambiguity and the uncertainty it inspired defined the polar legal landscape and had a profound impact on state policies and activities that continues to this day in the Arctic.

In chapter 2, another historian, Adam Lajeunesse, looks at conventional diplomatic discussions between Canada and the United States over sovereignty beginning in the mid-1950s. Situating his discussion in a Cold War continental defence context, Lajeunesse examines how Canada's Department of External Affairs began to consider its legal and political position vis-à-vis the waters of Canada's Arctic Archipelago. Were these sovereign Canadian waters, and, if they were, on what basis? He documents the internal debates that took place about this question over the following twenty years as successive Canadian governments struggled to establish a realistic and coherent sovereignty position. Instead of describing a monolithic Canadian viewpoint, he observes competing schools of thought about what External Affairs sought to achieve during this period and what its motivations may have been.[46] In the end, he confirms that a "gentlemen's agreement" between Canada and the United States quietly evolved during the Cold War that avoided conflict over legal principles. A "don't ask, don't tell" system allowed both parties to maintain their respective political positions, facilitated smooth defence cooperation, and avoided political confrontation between two close allies.[47]

Chapter 3 focuses on media representations of Arctic sovereignty and security. The media play a vital role in spreading political knowledge and informing citizens, so it is crucial to study the messages and ideas expressed in the popular media to evaluate whether they are contributing to a sound, evidence-based conversation. To this end, political scientist Mathieu Landriault analyses opinion pieces published in Canadian newspapers during Arctic sovereignty "crises" between 2005 and 2007 to discern how commentators characterized Arctic relations and anticipated the Arctic's future. Basing his chapter on three episodes that generated high levels of public attention (the 2005 Hans Island dispute between Canada and Denmark, the 2005–6 USS *Charlotte* transit incident between Canada and the United States, and the 2007 Russian flag event between Canada and Russia), Landriault reveals that most experts and editorialists displayed a high level of alarmism and spread counterfactual premises. This narrative, which described Canadian Arctic sovereignty and security as fragile and threatened, culminated in 2007 with the rise of what was defined as a credible and imminent threat: Russia. The author observes that these alarmist sentiments preceded the Conservative Party leadership's incorporation of the idea of an increasingly hostile Arctic into government discourse; clearly, then, the news media in did much to shape public and political opinion.

In chapter 4, veteran political scientist Rob Huebert begins with the core question of what security means in an Arctic context, noting a sharp division between analysts who adopt traditional or military security studies (also known as strategic studies) frameworks and those who embrace expanded definitions that also focus on human, environmental, gendered, health, and food security. In this chapter, he mounts a defence of traditional security, suggesting that the Arctic is no longer a region of "exceptional" peace and cooperation and that forces of international competition have returned. "This is not about conflict *over* the Arctic," he insists, "but is about the Arctic being a central element of the defence interests of the Arctic states, and increasingly of non-Arctic states such as China." In his view, a traditional security theoretical approach remains essential if we are to understand the re-emergence of state-based military actions in the North. He cautions against excessive weight being placed on critical security approaches.

In the first of four detailed empirical chapters examining Arctic states' security and defence policies, political scientist Wilfrid Greaves examines the dominant historical and contemporary meanings of Arctic security in Norway, focusing especially on the post–Cold War redefinition of security in the High North. While Norway emphasized *de*securitizing Russian relations immediately following the Cold War, the more recent High North Initiative has served to heavily securitize the Arctic region within Norwegian national security discourse and policy. In chapter 5, Greaves argues that despite many changes in global and European politics, Russia and the extraction of Arctic resources remain the key pillars of Norway's official understanding of security in the Arctic in both recent and historical contexts. Drawing upon scholarship on Norwegian foreign and security policy, as well as primary analysis of Norwegian government policy documents and related texts, he concludes that security is the central concept for Norwegian policy in the Arctic, and he agrees with Østhagen (chapter 8) that Norway's Arctic security interests have been constructed around the threat of Russian instability and/or invasion, as well as the control and extraction of petroleum, which is fundamental to the Norwegian economy and the maintenance of its social welfare system.

In chapter 6, Russian international affairs professor Alexander Sergunin explores how Russia's Arctic security policies and actions can be evaluated in more positive terms. Drawing on and translating government documents, Sergunin offers the perspective that Russia is a country that wants circumpolar security and stability and that is open to international cooperation in the High North; its intentions are inward-focused and defensive, aimed principally at the protection of the country's sovereign rights and legitimate interests. Unlike in the Cold War era, when the Arctic was a zone of confrontation between the Soviet Union and NATO, Moscow now sees this region as a platform for international cooperation. Analysing Russian threat perceptions and security doctrines since 2008, Sergunin suggests that Russia perceives no serious hard security threats to the Arctic and has elevated the economic, environmental, and social dimensions of the soft security agenda to much greater importance. Accordingly, he contends that military power now serves new functions, such as protecting Moscow's economic interests in the region through expansion of the energy, mining, infrastructure, communications, and other sectors. In contrast to the fears expressed in other Arctic capitals, Sergunin argues that Moscow has subordinated its international strategy in the region to its domestic needs; this has generated powerful incentives for the Russian leadership to opt for cooperative behaviour in the Arctic and to seek solutions to regional problems via negotiations, compromises, and strengthened governance mechanisms.

In chapter 7, Canadian Studies professor Whitney Lackenbauer examines how Canada's Conservative government under prime minister Stephen Harper conceptualized and mobilized Arctic sovereignty and security in its political discourse between 2006 and 2015 and, in turn, how the Canadian military articulated these concepts in Arctic policy and implementation plans during those years. By interrogating the government's "speech acts" over its entire decade in office, Lackenbauer reveals a shift from early "use it or lose it" rhetoric predicated on conventional state-based threats to Canadian sovereignty toward more comprehensive definitions of security that dominated after 2008. He observes that in implementing this broad political direction, the Canadian Armed Forces downplayed conventional military threats to the region and articulated its role in term of a whole-of-government context that deliberately avoided "militarizing" Arctic sovereignty. The broader Northern Strategy framework placed more emphasis on the human dimensions of sovereignty. Having analysed sovereignty and security as contested concepts that can change over time, and having examined both political rhetoric and policy outcomes, Lackenbauer suggests that the Harper government's approach to Arctic security ultimately yielded a situation in which the military assumed an appropriate, supporting role that legitimized the primacy of "soft" security and safety threats over conventional military ones.

Chapter 8 builds on the discussion of traditional and non-traditional approaches to security but adjusts the empirical lens to compare and contrast Norwegian and Canadian approaches to security and national defence. These two countries that have been at loggerheads over NATO's role in the Arctic. Political scientist Andreas Østhagen asks why their security interests diverge in the region and what this entails for the circumpolar North as a "security region" writ large. In his careful study, he discerns a clash of interests between Norway and Canada that stems from a fundamental difference in their respective approaches to Arctic security: Norway's push for a more active NATO in the Arctic reflects its geographic proximity to and relationship with Russia, whereas Canada's wariness of an explicit Arctic role for NATO (which it sees as a *European* security alliance) reflects a different set of core Arctic security interests that are less state-centric and more rooted in North American relationships. Østhagen concludes that the growing trend toward examining and studying the Arctic as *one* security region does not hold. Instead, he suggests that the Arctic is best understood in security terms as a series of sub-regions where the predominant security variable (from a state perspective) is a resurgent Russia rather than the melting sea ice.

Over the past fifteen years, the linkages between Arctic sovereignty, security, and energy resources have generated an intense debate about the future for peace and stability in the circumpolar North. Engaging with current theoretical discussions, historian Petra Dolata's assessment of the recent history of energy security in the Arctic deconstructs the simplistic assumption that the Arctic is energy-rich and will play an important role in global energy markets. In chapter 9, she contests the supposition that energy figures prominently in the strategic considerations of Arctic states. Instead, she observes that there are many Arctics with different geological, political, historical, and cultural trajectories affecting resource activities and governance. Furthermore, local understandings of both resource extraction and energy more generally differ from elite discussions of energy security. Thus, the distinction between local and national narratives is extremely important in understanding how energy and security interact in the region. Dolata cautions against using the wrong concepts when analysing insecurities in the Arctic, which "do not link well to international, geopolitical understandings of energy security ... If they have to be considered as security issues at all, then these have to do a lot more with environmental, economic, and human security of those living in the Arctic."

In chapter 10, political scientist Gunhild Hoogensen Gjørv applies a critical and gender International Relations lens to the question of security and insecurity in the Arctic, investigating whether there is a perception-based Arctic exceptionalism "bubble" that is immune to, or untouched by, the inequalities and insecurities that persist across the region. In identifying what is meant by human security, she explains that these perspectives contest "trickle-down" notions of security from the state to individuals and communities, which assume that a secure state means secure people within it. She emphasizes that it is critical to ensure that gaps in security – between different peoples, or between peoples and their states – are identified, recognized, and examined for ways in which those gaps can be reduced. Certain segments of Arctic populations continue to experience insecurities, including marginalized Indigenous peoples who have lived in the Arctic for millennia and peoples new to Arctic shores. Understanding their insecurities means analysing security issues across levels of analysis, with a focus on how security relates to the everyday lives of people living in Arctic states. This chapter outlines dominant security discourses in the Arctic and explains the relevance and importance of intersectional human security approaches that encourage researchers to re-evaluate the meaning of Arctic and Nordic exceptionalism.

In chapter 11, political science and legal scholar Natalia Loukacheva shifts the focus from traditional to non-traditional security ideas and actors through a case study approach to food security. Examining food as a human rights issue in Nunavut in Canada's Eastern Arctic, where most of the population is Inuit, she investigates how questions of food security are affected by global and local pressures and are linked to a sovereignty discourse. Socio-economic inequalities and poor community health indicators, which are inextricably linked to food security, make it a vitally significant political topic for Nunavummiut. Furthermore, by extending her analysis to look at the international dimensions of food security from Inuit perspectives, she reveals how this issue is intertwined with a broad array of political and legal issues, including the assertion of sovereignty, social justice, and the recognition and implementation of Inuit rights.

In chapter 12, anthropologist Frank Sejersen looks at "the transformative power of "'security'-talk," exploring how defining and addressing security issues is a productive act that entails revisiting and renegotiating scales, causalities, and subjects. He sees security thinking as a particular kind of world-making that both transcends and reproduces existing ideas of what constitutes sovereignty, community stability, and contemporary understandings of the good life. He argues that security thinking sets up a transformative space for society because it invites newness to enter the scene. In imagining "future bads" – as security thinking forces us to do – people confront their own "future selves" and, in the process, "rethink and rescale constituent parts of society and identities." Security discussions thus constitute an act of cultural translation, where something may be lost and something may be gained. Applying the idea of transformative space to issues related to climate change in Alaska and food security in Canada, Sejersen grapples with themes of temporality, agency, and the relationships between "contemporary self" and "future self" (as "other"). In this provocative contribution, we are reminded to move beyond the typical security question of *how* we should deal with risks to also ask *who* we wish to become when dealing with these risks.

In the Afterword, Wilfrid Greaves reflects on the future of sovereignty and security in the circumpolar region. Drawing on recent developments in Arctic politics and security that affirm the sovereignty of polar states across a variety of issue areas, he outlines three pathologies related to how security has been defined and pursued by Arctic states. These pathologies – remilitarization, the continued extraction of fossil fuels, and the constrained inclusion of Indigenous peoples within regional governance – have significant consequences for the current and future conditions of security, in the circumpolar world and globally. They suggest the limitations of security discourse and practice; they also exemplify the ongoing obstacles that exist when it comes to producing sustainable conditions of security, and responsibly exercising sovereignty, for peoples, communities, and states across the Arctic.

NOTES

1 Parts of this introduction are adapted from Wilfrid Greaves and P. Whitney Lackenbauer, "Arctic Sovereignty and Security: Updating Our Ideas," Arctic Deeply.org (2016), https://www.newsdeeply.com/arctic/community/2016 /03/23/arctic-sovereignty-and-security-updating-our-ideas.

2 Steve Smith, "The Contested Concept of Security," in *Critical Security Studies and World Politics*, ed. Ken Booth (Boulder: Lynne Rienner, 2005), 27–8.

3 Max Weber, "Politics as a Vocation," in *From Max Weber: Essays in Sociology* [1919], trans. and ed. H. Gerth and C. Wright Mills (New York: Oxford University Press, 1946), 78.

4 Barry Buzan and Lene Hansen, *The Evolution of International Security Studies* (Cambridge: Cambridge University Press, 2009).

5 Thomas Biersteker and Cynthia Weber, eds., *State Sovereignty as Social Construct* (Cambridge: Cambridge University Press, 1996).

6 Charles Tilly, "War Making and State Making as Organized Crime," in *Bringing the State Back In*, ed. Peter Evans, Dietrich Rueschemeyer, and Theda Skocpol (Cambridge: Cambridge University Press, 1985), 169–87.

7 Stephen D. Krasner, *Sovereignty: Organized Hypocrisy* (Princeton: Princeton University Press, 1999).

8 Hendrik Spruyt, *The Sovereign State and Its Competitors: An Analysis of Systems Change* (Princeton: Princeton University Press, 1994).

9 Biersteker and Weber, *State Sovereignty as Social Construct*, 12.

10 See Shelagh Grant, *Sovereignty or Security? Government Policy in the Canadian North, 1936–1950* (Vancouver: UBC Press, 1988); Grant, *Polar Imperative: A*

History of Arctic Sovereignty in North America (Vancouver: Douglas and McIntyre, 2010).

11 See, for example, Ken Coates, P. Whitney Lackenbauer, Bill Morrison, and Greg Poelzer, *Arctic Front: Defending Canada in the Far North* (Toronto: Thomas Allen, 2008); P. Whitney Lackenbauer and Peter Kikkert, "Sovereignty and Security: The Department of External Affairs, the United States, and Arctic Sovereignty, 1945–68," in *In the National Interest: Canadian Foreign Policy and the Department of Foreign Affairs and International Trade, 1909–2009*, ed. Greg Donaghy and Michael Carroll, 101–20 (Calgary: University of Calgary Press, 2011); P. Whitney Lackenbauer and Peter Kikkert, "The Dog in the Manger – and Letting Sleeping Dogs Lie: The United States, Canada, and the Sector Principle, 1924–1955,'" in *International Law and Politics of the Arctic Ocean: Essays in Honour of Donat Pharand*, ed. Suzanne Lalonde and Ted McDorman, 216–39 (Leiden: Brill, 2014); and Adam Lajeunesse, *Lock, Stock, and Icebergs: The Evolution of Canada's Arctic Maritime Sovereignty* (Vancouver: UBC Press, 2016).

12 Jeffrey Mazo, "Who Owns the North Pole?" *Survival* 56, no. 1 (2014): 61–70.

13 Donald L. Gautier, Kenneth J. Bird, Ronald R. Charpentier, Arthur Grantz, David W. Houseknecht, Timothy R. Klett, Thomas E. Moore, et al., "Assessment of Undiscovered Oil and Gas in the Arctic," *Science* 324, no. 5931 (2009): 1175–9.

14 Kathrin Keil, "The Arctic: A New Region of Conflict? The Case of Oil and Gas," *Cooperation and Conflict* 49, no. 2 (2014): 162–90.

15 Benoit Beauchamp and Rob Huebert, "Canada's Sovereignty Linked to Energy Resources in the Arctic," *Arctic* 61, no. 3 (2008): 342.

16 Leif C. Jensen and Pål Wilter Skedsmo, "Approaching the North: Norwegian and Russian Foreign Policy Discourses on the European Arctic," *Polar Research* 29, no. 3 (2010): 439–50; Leif C. Jensen, "Seduced and Surrounded by Security: A Post-Structuralist Take on Norwegian High North Securitizing Discourses," *Cooperation and Conflict* 48, no. 1 (2012): 80–99.

17 Mary Simon, "Inuit and the Canadian Arctic: Sovereignty Begins at Home," Journal of Canadian Studies 43, no. 2 (2009): 250–60.

18 Simon, "Inuit and the Canadian Arctic"; Inuit Circumpolar Council (ICC), *A Circumpolar Declaration on Sovereignty in the Arctic* (2009), https://www.itk.ca/publication/circumpolar-declaration-sovereignty-arctic.

19 Emma Rothschild, "What Is Security?," *Daedalus* 124, no. 3 (1995): 61. Emphasis in original.

20 Buzan and Hansen, *The Evolution of International Security Studies*, 22–30; Rothschild, "What Is Security?," 61.

21 Lester Brown, *Redefining National Security*, Worldwatch Paper 14 (Washington, D.C.: Worldwatch Institute, 1977); Richard H. Ullman, "Redefining

Security," *International Security* 8, no. 1 (1983): 129–53; Jessica Tuchman Mathews, "Redefining Security," *Foreign Affairs* 68, no. 2 (1989): 162–77.

22 Arnold Wolfers, "'National Security' as an Ambiguous Symbol," *Political Science Quarterly* 67, no. 4 (1952), 481.

23 Smith, "Contested Concept of Security," 27–8.

24 Robert W. Cox, "Social Forces, States and World Orders: Beyond International Relations Theory," *Millennium: Journal of International Studies* 10, no. 2 (1981): 128. Emphasis in original.

25 Stephen M. Walt, "The Renaissance of Security Studies," *International Studies Quarterly* 35, no. 2 (1991): 211–39.

26 Johan Galtung, "Violence, Peace, and Peace Research," *Journal of Peace Research* 6, no. 3 (1969): 167–91; Arthur Westing, *Weapons of Mass Destruction and the Environment* (London: Taylor and Francis, 1977); David Cortright, *Peace: A History of Movements and Ideas* (New York: Cambridge University Press, 2008).

27 Amartya Sen, *Poverty and Famines: An Essay on Entitlement and Deprivation* (New York: Clarendon Press, 1982); Peter Worsley, *The Three Worlds: Culture and World Development* (London: Weidenfeld and Nicholson, 1986); Jacques Fontanel, "The Economic Effects of Military Expenditure in Third World Countries," *Journal of Peace Research* 27, no. 4 (1990): 461–6.

28 Carol Cohn, "Sex and Death in the Rational World of Defence Intellectuals," *Signs: Journal of Women in Culture and Society* 12, no. 4 (1987): 687–718; Jean Bethke Elshtain, *Women and War* (New York: Basic Books, 1987); Gayatri Chakravorty Spivak, "Can the Subaltern Speak?," in *Marxism and the Interpretation of Culture*, ed. Cary Nelson and Lawrence Grossberg (London: Macmillan, 1988); J. Ann Tickner, "Hans Morgenthau's Principles of Political Realism: A Feminist Reformulation," *Millennium* 17, no. 3 (1988): 429–40; Cynthia Enloe, *Bananas, Beaches, and Bases: Making Feminist Sense of International Politics* (Berkeley: University of California Press, 1990).

29 Richard Falk, *This Endangered Planet: Prospects and Proposals for Human Survival* (New York: Random House, 1971); Norman Myers, "The Environmental Dimension to Security Issues," *The Environmentalist* 6, no. 4 (1986): 251–7; Norman Myers, "The Environment and Security," *Foreign Policy* 74 (1989): 23–41.

30 Carina Keskitalo, "International Region-Building: Development of the Arctic as an International Region," *Cooperation and Conflict* 42, no. 2 (2007): 187–205 at 194.

31 Lassi Heininen, "Circumpolar International Relations and Geopolitics," in *Arctic Human Development Report*, ed. Neils Einarsson et al. (Akureyri: Stefansson Arctic Institute, 2004), 218.

32 Michael Byers, *Who Owns the Arctic: Understanding Sovereignty Disputes in the North* (Vancouver: Douglas and McIntyre, 2009), 16–18; Meagan Fitzpatrick, "Arctic Military Exercise Targets Human-Smuggling 'Ecotourists,'" *CBC News*, 24 August 2012, http://www.cbc.ca/news/politics/arctic-military-exercise -targets-human-smuggling-ecotourists-1.1166215.

33 UNDP, *Human Development Report 1994: New Dimensions of Human Security* (New York, 1994).

34 Gunhild Hoogensen Gjørv, Dawn Bazely, Maria Goloviznina, and Andrew Tanentzap, eds., *Environmental and Human Security in the Arctic* (New York: Routledge, 2014).

35 Wilfrid Greaves, "Arctic In/Security and Indigenous Peoples: Comparing Inuit in Canada and Sámi in Norway," *Security Dialogue* 47, no. 6 (2016): 461–80.

36 Terry Audla, "Inuit and Arctic Security," in *Nilliajut: Inuit Perspectives on Security, Patriotism, and Sovereignty*, ed. Scot Nickels (Ottawa: Inuit Tapiriit Kanatami, 2013), 8.

37 Intergovernmental Panel on Climate Change (IPCC), *Climate Change 2014: Impacts, Adaptation, and Vulnerability* (Geneva, 2014), 3.

38 Yvon Csonka and Peter Schweitzer, "Societies and Cultures: Change and Persistence," in *Arctic Human Development Report*, 47–53.

39 Chris Cocklin, "Water and 'Cultural Security,'" in *Human Security and the Environment: International Comparisons*, ed. Edward A. Page and Michael Redclift (Northampton: Edward Elgar, 2002), 159.

40 Arctic Climate Impact Assessment (ACIA), Impacts of a Warming Arctic (Cambridge: Cambridge University Press, 2004), 94.

41 Inuit Circumpolar Council–Canada, *The Sea Ice Never Stops: Circumpolar Inuit Reflections on Sea Ice Use and Shipping in Inuit Nunaat* (Ottawa, 2014); James D. Ford, Ashlee Cunsolo Wilcox, Susan Chatwood, Christopher Furgal, Sherilee Harper, Ian Mauro, and Tristan Pearce, "Adapting to the Effects of Climate Change on Inuit Health," *American Journal of Public Heath* 104, no. S3 (2014): e9–e17.

42 ACIA, *Impacts of a Warming Arctic*, 157.

43 Michael J. Kral, "The Weight on Our Shoulders Is Too Much, and We Are Falling," *Medical Anthropology Quarterly* 27, no. 1 (2013): 63–83.

44 Barack Obama, "Remarks by the President at the GLACIER Conference – Anchorage, AK," 31 August 2015, https://obamawhitehouse.archives.gov/the -press-office/2015/09/01/remarks-president-glacier-conference-anchorage-ak.

45 Munk-Gordon Arctic Security Program, *Rethinking the Top of the World: Arctic Public Opinion Survey*, vol. 2 (2015), http://gordonfoundation.ca/resource /rethinking-the-top-of-the-world-arctic-public-opinion-survey-vol-2-2.

46 Other scholars have made this observation, including P. Whitney Lackenbauer and Peter Kikkert, eds., *The Canadian Forces and Arctic Sovereignty:*

Debating Roles, Interests, and Requirements, 1968–1974 (Waterloo: Laurier Centre for Military Strategic and Disarmament Studies / WLU Press, 2010); and Lackenbauer and Kikkert, "Sovereignty and Security."

47   Lajeunesse's description of this "don't ask, don't tell" system builds upon the "agree to disagree" framework elaborated by Franklyn Griffiths and Whitney Lackenbauer, among others. See, for example, Griffiths, "The Shipping News: Canada's Arctic Sovereignty Not on Thinning Ice," *International Journal* 58, no. 2 (2003): 257–82; Lackenbauer, *From Polar Race to Polar Saga: An Integrated Strategy for Canada and the Circumpolar World* (Toronto: Canadian International Council, 2009); Griffiths, Rob Huebert, and Lackenbauer, *Canada and the Changing Arctic: Sovereignty, Security and Stewardship* (Waterloo: Wilfrid Laurier University Press, 2011); and Lackenbauer and Huebert, "Premier Partners: Canada, the United States and Arctic Security," *Canadian Foreign Policy Journal* 20, no. 3 (2014): 320–33.

1 In Search of Polar Sovereignty, 1900–1959

PETER KIKKERT

A flurry of activity in the polar regions during the first decade of the twentieth century illuminated the many blank spots on the Arctic map and penetrated the little-known Antarctic continent one small parcel at a time. As these expeditions explored new lands (or ice) they raised their national flags and held elaborate ceremonies claiming large areas. For international lawyers, these acts raised the question: what would happen when states decided they wanted these polar areas and supported their acts of exploration with official claims? And what about the states that already had?

Following Robert Peary's announcement in 1909 claiming the North Pole for the United States, three prominent international lawyers – James Brown Scott, Thomas Willing Balch, and René Dollot (who used the pseudonym René Waultrin) – published their thoughts on polar territorial claims. Several lawyers had already written about the legal status of Svalbard; the opinions of Scott, Balch, and Dollot represented the first attempts to clarify the judicial nature of polar sovereignty more generally.[1]

The two Americans, Balch and Scott, offered a simple response: the same legal requirements for territorial acquisition that applied in the more temperate areas of the world should be applied to the polar regions. The doctrine of effective occupation, they argued, demanded that a claimant state physically occupy or make use of the area. Both lawyers insisted that no state could claim unoccupied land (or worse, unexplored polar land) or justify annexing a vast territory by visiting or occupying a small part of its coast – critiques that applied to many existing polar claims.[2] Here they echoed the opinion of Thomas Baty, a British international lawyer who had recently reviewed the Svalbard situation and argued that "it is impossible to annex the twenty-third largest island of the world by putting up a fish-curing house in one corner." In Baty's opinion, the occupation of one polar island in a larger group could not confer sovereignty over the entire archipelago, and the establishment of a polar outpost "could not carry with it more than a reasonable adjacent zone."[3] Adopting similar opinions, Scott and Balch both concluded that most of the Arctic and Antarctic remained unoccupied and should be considered *terra nullius* – a "no man's land" belonging to no state.[4]

French lawyer and internationalist René Dollot expressed a far different view. He explained that "a desert is not administered like a metropolis, a glacial island like an African Bazaar," and insisted that the rules of acquisition must be tailored to the unique conditions of the polar regions. "In these territories one must reduce the indispensable formalities, reduce them to the strict minimum," he asserted. "To assure oneself of the legitimacy of the discovery, to regularize the possession, to protect it against strangers, such are the fundamental principles."[5] While Balch and Scott demanded settlement to secure polar claims, Dollot suggested that the requirements of international law could be relaxed for the polar regions and their "indispensable formalities" reduced.

In the decades that followed the publication of Scott, Balch, and Dollot's legal opinions in 1909 and 1910, international lawyers, officials serving states with interests in the polar regions, and other experts contemplated these two approaches, adding a wide array of opinions, adaptations, novel concepts, and competing principles to the evolving discourse on terrestrial polar sovereignty. This chapter explores how these lawyers and officials defined and understood the function of polar sovereignty, particularly in regions where there were no permanent Indigenous inhabitants.[6] They grappled with the problem of how to apply a body of rules and practices for territorial acquisition that they found ambiguous, underdeveloped, and open to interpretation to the unique conditions of the polar regions, and they pondered whether the rules could and should be modified. This legal ambiguity and the uncertainty it fostered defined the polar legal landscape and had a profound impact on state policies and activities that continues to be felt in the Arctic and Antarctic today.

A Bipolar Understanding

In the first decades of the twentieth century, many state officials and international lawyers understood polar sovereignty within a bipolar framework. Scholars' fixation on a single nation's experience or international interactions regarding one of the poles has obscured the historic legal development of a bipolar world. Transnational legal concepts and arguments evolved and took on different meanings as they flowed from one pole to the other and across the borders of the polar claimants. State officials and international lawyers understood that legal developments and state practices in the Arctic could have a dramatic impact on the Antarctic, and vice versa. When they pondered the uncertainties of polar sovereignty in the first half of the twentieth century, they viewed the Arctic and Antarctic as a conjoined legal space whose two parts suffered from the same problems and demanded similar solutions. Hume Wrong, Canada's Ambassador to the United States, made this point in 1946: "It now seems probable that the Antarctic area rather than the Arctic will provide the field for working out general rules of international law."[7]

Reports prepared by state officials such as the US State Department's 1926 study "Territorial Sovereignty in the Polar Regions" and the 1946 Foreign Office statement "The Necessity of Physical Occupation as a Means of Securing Sovereignty in the Polar Regions" attempted to set out general legal principles applicable to both regions.[8] State officials often sought legal arguments or opinions that could affect or set a precedent for their own territorial claims. British and Commonwealth officials, for example, consistently shared information on how to strengthen and defend their claims in the Arctic and Antarctic, an effort embodied by the Polar Committee, formed in 1930 by member-states of the British Empire.[9] In the 1940s, Oscar Pinochet de la Barra, an international lawyer and one of the architects of Chile's polar strategy, drew heavily on Canada's Arctic strategy to support his country's Antarctic claims.[10] This bipolar approach to sovereignty continued through the 1940s and 1950s. In 1952, Brian Roberts, leading polar expert in the British Foreign Office, still wondered "whether any formula could be found for having one rule in the Arctic and another in the Antarctic; or must any rule apply equally to both areas[?]"[11]

"Far from Settled": Polar Sovereignty and the Ambiguous Principles of Territorial Acquisition[12]

In the first half of the twentieth century, sustained legal uncertainty was the most powerful force shaping international law for the polar regions. Ever since Columbus's first voyage in 1492, popes, jurists, and empires have constructed legal arguments to justify Europe's territorial expansion and seizure of land often occupied by Indigenous peoples, most notably using the doctrines of discovery, cession, occupation, and conquest. While there was "remarkable stability in these doctrines," Andrew Fitzmaurice observes, "they were subjected to ceaseless reinterpretation."[13] States and jurists adjusted the law of nations to suit a wide range of legal and political circumstances, and no clear, absolute formula for territorial acquisition emerged. The rules proved incredibly flexible and expendable in shifting historical, geopolitical, and geographical contexts, especially in what Lauren Benton has characterized as "anomalous legal space" within which European officials struggled to determine the nature of sovereignty. These difficult-to-define spaces inspired "spatial variations" of imperial control that forced states to conceive of new ways to conceptualize sovereignty and its relationship to international law.[14] The tangled web of juridical writings and state practices made the legal regime on territorial acquisition anything but black-and-white.

The growth of Europe's formal empires at the end of the nineteenth century, particularly in Africa, relied upon multiple legal justifications in support of imperial sovereignty, especially arguments based on effective occupation, prescription, and contiguity. The doctrine of effective occupation proved the most important of these justifications. "The word 'occupation' itself is ... a legal term of art," explained legal scholar Humphrey Waldock in 1948. "It is the Latin *occupatio* meaning appropriation, not occupation in its sense of 'settling on' ... [I]t means, in international law, the appropriation of sovereignty."[15] Jurists, however, spilled much ink debating the level and kind of state activity the doctrine demanded.[16] State practice also endorsed prescription or adverse possession, that is, the idea that sovereign rights held over a long period could perfect a territorial title, no matter how defective.[17] Contiguity held that the effective occupation of part of a region entitled a state to all of it.[18] Even as these legal constructions appeared to become more consistent and cohesive in scholarly accounts, lawyers and states consistently found room for interpretation and exception.[19] The arbitration and judicial settlement of territorial disputes brought little clarity as jurists sought to establish which state had a stronger title rather than "formulate generally applicable rules."[20] State practice and legal treatises offered few guidelines for how states could apply these principles to establish sovereignty over uninhabited areas and harsh environments.

Historians who examine state claims in the polar regions have largely overlooked or bypassed this convoluted legal environment, which served as the key context in which state officials and international lawyers began to draw the Arctic and Antarctic into the realm of international law. Those who studied polar sovereignty in the early twentieth century understood that the legal foundations in their field were weak. In 1920, Canadian Loring Christie, armed with a law degree from Harvard and ample experience as legal adviser to prime ministers Robert Borden and Arthur Meighen, noted the confusion in international law about the "concrete steps" required to obtain perfect title.[21] In early March 1925, the Australian National Research Council (ANRC), investigating an Australian Antarctic claim, highlighted that international law did not "lay down any general rule for deciding the ownership of uninhabited or savage lands."[22] A year later, the US State Department concluded that the principles of international law on territorial acquisition had not yet been "definitely established" by state practice. International legal practice lacked a "clearly specified or decisive manner in which 'occupation' becomes 'effective,' even in the temperate regions."[23]

Scholars often point to the *Palmas Island* (1928), *Clipperton Island* (1931), and *Eastern Greenland* (1933) cases – all of which dealt with state title over uninhabited or sparsely populated territory – as pivotal decisions that brought immediate clarity to the international law of territorial acquisition.[24] Certainly, many commentators in the international legal community at the time recognized the potential impact of these cases on polar territorial claims, particularly the ruling of the Permanent Court of International Justice (PCIJ) in the *Eastern Greenland* case. Norway's challenge that Denmark had not done enough to effectively occupy Eastern Greenland inspired many to believe that the case would "define the law, now unsettled," for the acquisition of territory.[25] After the court released its decision recognizing Denmark's sovereignty over the territory, some lawyers and state officials pointed to the ruling to argue that a template now existed to secure territorial title in the Arctic and Antarctic – a template that required a modest amount of state activity in uninhabited and environmentally challenging regions.[26]

For most practitioners, however, the judicial nature of polar sovereignty remained ambiguous. After it was released in 1933, various legal experts questioned the value of the *Eastern Greenland* decision as a precedent. Commentators pointed to the multitude of variables that had complicated the case: the role played by foreign recognition; the length of time involved; the careful balancing of legal values carried out by the court; the court's failure to lay out the acts required to create and maintain a right to sovereignty; and the existence of a dissenting opinion and separate opinions in the ruling that could play an important role in future cases.[27] In light of these factors, Charles Cheney Hyde, a professor of international law and former solicitor at the US State Department, concluded that the decision "may perhaps be deemed to lack the significance otherwise to be assigned to it as an enunciation of legal principle concerning" the acquisition of territorial sovereignty.[28] The *Eastern Greenland* ruling reflected a common problem with the PCIJ's decisions: they were often too specific and focused on the particular circumstances of each case to establish general principles of international law.[29] No one could predict with any certainty how the arguments, conclusions, and opinions of the *Eastern Greenland* decision would be applied to future polar disputes.

State officials who researched polar claims recognized that shades of grey continued to surround the requirements of effective occupation and the rules of territorial acquisition. After reviewing all three cases in 1935, William Roy Vallance, who worked in the US State Department's Office of the Legal Adviser, lamented that international law had "not very definitively established" the steps necessary for a state to make a successful territorial claim.[30] A few years later, Frank Debenham, the co-founder and director of the Scott Polar Research Institute, advised the Foreign Office that "there being no such thing as a formal code of international law with respect to countries which are uninhabitable, claims to polar lands rest upon a variety of evidence, every one of which is open to debate and may be upset on other grounds."[31]

Over the next two decades, state officials and legal experts continued to express concern over the law's ambiguity. In 1944, a legal adviser with Canada's Department of External Affairs noted that "there may be some doubt whether Canada is actually extending enough jurisdiction throughout lands already discovered to make her claim to those territories unquestionable ... Precise information as to what constitutes 'control and administration' is scarce."[32] In the postwar years, legal advisers in the British Foreign and Colonial Offices could not determine exactly how much the local environment could modify the doctrine of effective occupation.[33] In 1946, the US State Department admitted that it was struggling to find a set of "clear legal principles" on how to acquire polar territory,[34] and in 1952, a departmental legal expert observed that these rules were "far from settled."[35] Richard Casey, Australia's Minister for External Affairs, complained there was "no general agreement on what suffices" to make a claim in the polar regions.[36]

For these officials, the rules for territorial acquisition remained unclear. How much uninhabited or sparsely populated territory could a state claim to occupy through a settlement or an administrative post? How continuous and permanent did state control have to be? While the three legal cases had suggested that state control was not a constant requirement for every nook and cranny, countries still struggled to determine the limits that an international court or an arbiter would place on this allowance in future disputes. How much foreign recognition did the law require to secure a claim? More important than the questions left unanswered was the knowledge that the doctrine of effective occupation had been malleable and expendable in the three cases. That malleability kept the door open for claims based on previous arguments in support of contiguity, symbolic annexation, and periodic visits.

It was more than just the requirements of effective occupation that confused state officials. They also worried about how those requirements might evolve. Every lawyer understood that international law was mutable, and Huber's intertemporal theory had stressed the impact that changes in the law could have on territorial claims. While arbitrating the *Palmas Island* case in 1928, Huber had distinguished between the creation of a right and the maintenance of a right, which suggested that states had to keep up with legal and technological developments if they hoped to maintain their title over time.[37] By implication, no state title could be considered perfected for all time, particularly if a country's occupation had not been continuous or if it had exercised control and administrative functions inconsistently.[38]

Huber's theory of intertemporal law has faced criticism since he released it in 1928. Legal scholars argue that its application would "encourage spurious claims and ... foster widespread uncertainty as to title to territory" and threaten the stability of the international legal order.[39] For state officials involved in polar claims, Huber raised troublesome possibilities. Foreign Office legal advisers reiterated on several occasions when studying polar sovereignty that international law was "not static": "You can acquire sovereignty in 1926 in accordance with the law of 1926, but if you wish to maintain it in 1946 you must fulfill the requirements of the law of 1946."[40]

Time brought new ideas about the law as well as technological advances that opened up the polar regions to human activity like never before, thus changing legal expectations and requirements. Judge Dionisio Anzilotti's dissenting opinion in the *Eastern Greenland* case captured this sentiment when it argued that "natural conditions prevailing in Greenland and their importance changed appreciably as a result of technical improvements in navigation which opened up to human activities a part of that country, especially the East coast, which previously, although known, had been practically inaccessible." Due to the impact of technological changes, "the question of Danish sovereignty over Greenland presented itself in a new light."[41] Officials responsible for state claims in the Arctic and Antarctic had to consider the impact that long-range aircraft, mechanical vehicles, advanced icebreakers, and stations that allowed people to overwinter relatively comfortably in the harshest conditions might have on requirements related to territorial acquisition and occupation. Concern over how the law might evolve in the decades that followed Huber's ruling in the *Palmas Island* case only increased the tension and confusion regarding the anomalous legal space of the polar regions.

State Policy in an Anomalous Legal Space

The legal ambiguity infusing the polar regions drove state officials and lawyers to seek creative legal arguments and develop new approaches in support of territorial claims. In 1929, Canadian diplomat Lester B.

Pearson argued that the Arctic's harsh and unique conditions, "unlike any visualized by international lawyers in the past," called for new rules and practices.[42] In 1933, Samuel Whittemore Boggs, geographer of the US State Department and its leading expert on polar territorial claims, echoed Pearson's notion when he noted that the differences between the polar regions and more temperate zones "create problems which appear to require special development of international law."[43] Fifteen years later, the department's legal adviser Jack Tate advised that "if polar regions are to be subject to sovereignty, there must be an evolution of the law in the nature of a relaxation of the minimum requirements of effective occupation."[44] Argentinian and Chilean officials were adamant that it was not "possible to apply to polar regions the usual juridical standards for the acquisition of public domain," and Chilean experts argued that there should exist a special legal regime of "modern polar international law."[45] Likewise, Vladimir Leont'evich Lakhtine, secretary-member of the Committee of Direction of the Section of Aerial Law for the Soviet Union, argued that the "triple formula" of territorial acquisition – discovery, occupation, and official notification – could not be applied to the Arctic and Antarctic.[46]

State officials and international lawyers contemplating a new legal regime for the polar regions had to decide how far to push the boundaries of international law. Some insisted that the requirements of effective occupation should be loosened for uninhabited polar spaces; others asserted that discovery and symbolic acts should play a greater role; still others, that contiguity and other geographic arguments should hold more weight. Pearson believed that the sector principle represented the best "practical solution" to the problem of polar sovereignty.[47] British diplomat Laurence Collier wrote in early 1930 that "the most recent history of territorial claims in the Arctic is really the history of the development of what is now known as the 'Sector Principle.'"[48] The British applied this principle when expanding their claim to the Falkland Islands Dependencies (FID) in 1917 and to carve out the Ross Dependency for New Zealand in 1923. Canada applied it in 1925 to its polar regions, followed by the Soviet Union (1926), Australia (1933), France (1938), Chile (1940), and Argentina (1942) in various contexts.

During the interwar years, British and Commonwealth officials constructed the most elaborate legal foundation for the sector principle. Together, they located the basis of the principle in treaty law and contiguity, insisting that sectors flowed out of a state's control over the coastline and other points of access to a polar hinterland – a new version of the doctrine of effective occupation suited to the polar regions. They insisted that in the harsh polar environment, control could consist of the occasional visit by state officials, administrative acts, the issuing of licences to foreigners operating in the claimed area, legislation and, in the Canadian context, a small number of occupied police posts.[49]

As polar empires expanded, many state officials embraced the sector principle as a simple and cost-effective solution to a complex and anomalous legal space. This approach would set aside difficult questions about settlement, state administration, and undiscovered territory. Soviet international lawyer T.A. Tarcouzio explained that to safeguard against any potential discoveries by Western aerial expeditions, Russian officials had adopted the position that "irrespective of the nationality of the discoverers or explorers, sovereignty to lands discovered automatically vests with the state within whose sphere or sector or 'terrestrial gravitation' the land is found."[50] Like the Soviets, Chilean and Argentinian officials emphasized that only countries that were direct geographical neighbours to a polar territory could use the principle; in doing so, they were targeting the British claim in the Falkland Islands Dependencies. Their Antarctic sectors flowed out of the doctrine of contiguity ("contiguidad"), and they argued that the Antarctic was simply a prolongation of South America via the Andean range. Both sides used terms such as "geographically dependent," "geographical unity," and "hinterland," echoing earlier statements found in Canadian legal assessments with regard to the Arctic Archipelago.[51] Unlike the Soviets, Chilean officials asserted that the sector principle granted states a preferential right to sovereignty, not full legal title, though it also imbued their acts of sovereignty with greater legal strength than those completed by non-neighbouring states.[52]

Supporters of the sector principle maintained that it could serve as the basis of a new bipolar legal regime for resolving territorial claims – a convenient solution to a problem that traditional international law had been unable to solve in the anomalous legal space of the polar regions. To meet the day's emerging requirements, the international legal system needed to change and adapt, legal scholar Roscoe Pound argued in 1923.[53] An obvious example in that decade was the burgeoning body of law created to address international aerial navigation, embodied in international agreements such as the Convention on Aerial Navigation (1919) and the Warsaw Convention (1929). If an original body of law could be developed to deal with aerial navigation – a new problem demanding novel legal solutions – why not for the polar regions?

This line of reasoning led many international legal experts and state officials, particularly in Britain and the Commonwealth, to believe by the 1930s that the sector principle was on the verge of acceptance as a customary rule of law.[54] Experts also based their positive assessment of the sector principle's legal status on the sustained silence of the international community – especially of the United States. Officials took that silence as tacit acquiescence to the principle. Customary international law generally reflects the conduct approved or tolerated by the powerful (and especially a powerful state directly influenced by the new rule), and the sector principle did affect the Americans, given their interests in the Arctic and Antarctic.[55]

Faced with a growing number of polar territorial claims, in 1924 the US State Department adopted the Hughes Doctrine, which demanded the physical settlement and utilization of polar lands as a prerequisite for territorial acquisition.[56] This approach reflected the arguments of Balch and Scott, as well as the legal treatise of John Bassett Moore, an international lawyer and past adviser to the department, which stated bluntly that "[t]itle by occupation is gained by discovery, use and settlement."[57] In a note to Norway, Hughes explained that the US position demanded that discovery be followed by physical settlement. The "formal taking of possession" had "no significance" beyond heralding "the advent of the settler," which he implied might be impossible in parts of the polar regions.[58] Under the doctrine, official declarations, occasional visits, temporary camps, and a semblance of control did not allow a country to acquire sovereignty over polar territory.

With the US legal position in hand, Norway began to maintain publicly that the level of occupation required in the polar regions should not be significantly reduced; rather, it should be "permanent and efficient" (although Norway's 1939 claim to Queen Maud Land was couched in such ambiguous language that many concluded it was a sector claim).[59] American uncertainty over how the rules of territorial acquisition applied to the polar regions, however, led to confusion, indifference, and official silence on matters of polar sovereignty. The confusion is evident in American officials' appraisals and the selective manner in which they asserted their country's perceived rights. They struggled with what to do about the sector principle, how to apply the Hughes Doctrine, and whether the United States should challenge the polar claims of other states or support potential US claims. Throughout the 1930s and 1940s, State Department officials even considered adopting less rigorous requirements designed specifically to establish polar sovereignty – a formula for territorial acquisition that officials labelled "constructive occupation." The department defined the doctrine as "a combination of exploration, repeated visits, and maintenance of semi-permanent stations, but rejects as inapplicable to polar regions the standard concept of occupation."[60] According to this American conception of polar sovereignty, aerial overflights and temporary scientific activities carried significant legal weight.[61]

Sustained indecision on the legal requirements of polar sovereignty led Washington to choose silence when faced with the growing number of territorial claims in the Arctic and Antarctic, even though the State Department drew up multiple official challenges. In 1925, officials wrote a protest disputing Canada's claim to the Arctic Archipelago, arguing that "the recognized rules of international law require the establishment and maintenance of an effective occupation of new lands as a prerequisite to the acquisition of sovereignty" and that the Canadians had not done so on "some of the islands."[62] Four years later, Under Secretary of State Joshua Rueben Clark, a prominent American lawyer who served in the Solicitor's Office for many years, wrote up a broad challenge to existing polar claims, disputing any solution to the problem of polar sovereignty that did not involve actual settlement and use.[63] The United States, however, chose not to issue these challenges or others like them. While diplomatic factors influenced these decisions, so too did confusion over the strength of the US legal position.

Finally, in November 1934, US officials reserved their rights in New Zealand's Ross Dependency sector, telling the British that they could not recognize sovereignty in the absence of "occupancy and use."[64] President Franklin D. Roosevelt proved a strong proponent of the Hughes Doctrine. To bolster US legal rights in the Antarctic he pushed for the establishment of the official United States Antarctic Service Expedition (USASE) in 1939–41, "to prove ... that human beings can permanently occupy a portion of the Continent winter and summer."[65]

While the ambiguity that marked the polar legal landscape had fostered new approaches and ideas about polar sovereignty, it also amplified the impact of the Hughes Doctrine. Without clear guidelines for establishing sovereignty, territorial disputes hinged on which state displayed the stronger title. With the American espousal of the Hughes Doctrine and rejection of a polar legal regime based on the sector principle, most claimant states recognized the need for widespread permanent occupancy and use to secure title to polar territory – especially if they hoped to gain recognition from the increasingly powerful United States. Nothing illustrates the impact of the American legal position more than how it changed the thinking of the legal advisers at the British Foreign Office. The American position, coupled with challenges in the Falkland Islands Dependencies from Chile and Argentina, led these experts to emphasize the need for permanent scientific bases and "practical use,"[66] such as surveys and maps, a meteorological service, geological exploration, scientific expeditions, and sledging patrols.[67] By the early 1950s, the legal advisers had started to view the British claim in the FID not as a sector, but as pockets of sovereignty emanating from these bases and patrols and supported by scientific research.

Given the ambiguity and complexity of the law, states recognized that official foreign recognition – particularly from powerful states such as the United States and Britain – offered the only sure way of securing sovereignty. As a result, states had to determine whether to aggressively seek international recognition and risk inspiring official foreign rejection, or quietly strengthen their position and hope that in time other countries would consider it unchallengeable. This dilemma, and the search for alternatives, would shape state polar policy deliberations for decades. Denmark pursued foreign recognition of its sovereignty over Greenland between 1915 and 1921, forging agreements with several major powers, including Britain[68] and the United States (in return for agreeing to sell the Danish West Indies).[69] In a risky gamble that paid great dividends in the *Eastern Greenland* case, the Danes agreed to recognize Norwegian sovereignty over Svalbard in return for verbal recognition of their sovereignty over Greenland – the *Ilhen Declaration*.[70] Other states looked for ways to solicit or even trick states into tacit (unspoken or inferred) acquiescence. Britain, for instance, always provided consent and offered to help foreign expeditions entering its polar claims whether they had sought permission or not.[71] Likewise, the Argentinians, who had run a weather station on Laurie Island in the South Orkneys since 1904, insisted that Argentina's sovereignty in its Antarctic sector was "tacitly recognized by all those who availed themselves of the Argentine meteorological services of the Orkneys."[72]

Other states quietly strengthened their claims and hoped that at some point other governments would consider them unassailable or that the passage of time would bring tacit acquiescence. Canberra, for example, placed a great deal of faith in the "lack of opposition by other nations" to its claim, which "has generally been accepted as recognition and acceptance" of Australia's sovereignty.[73] While some Canadian officials contemplated asking the United States to officially recognize Canada's sovereignty over the Arctic Archipelago at several points in the first half of the twentieth century, most understood that the Americans would reject this request in light of the Hughes Doctrine. The Canadians chose caution and were rewarded for their patience when Cold War exigencies led the United States to recognize Canadian sovereignty over the islands in 1946. In doing so, the United States was quietly conceding to Canada what it was not prepared to acknowledge in international law more generally: a more relaxed interpretation of effective occupation and ownership of territory in polar regions than the Hughes Doctrine allowed.[74] No matter how a state achieved foreign recognition, in the anomalous legal space of the polar regions it remained the only dependable and sure method through which to secure sovereignty.

The Americans' recognition of Canada's sovereignty settled the last potential source of a large-scale terrestrial territorial dispute in the Arctic (for more on the Canada–US Arctic relationship, see Adam Lajeunesse in chapter 2). In sharp contrast, the Americans refused to recognize any Antarctic claims. Despite a clear focus on physical presence and use, a specific formula for polar sovereignty remained elusive. Attempts to clarify the rules culminated in 1955 with Britain's failed attempt to settle its dispute with Argentina and Chile over the FID at the International Court of Justice. In the absence of an ICJ judgment on the principles of territorial acquisition in the Antarctic, the region remained an anomalous legal space – a key factor in the creation of the Antarctic Treaty. In a sense, recognition of claims finally brought the Arctic to legal stability, while *non*-recognition of claims achieved a similar result for the Antarctic. The tangle of claims and rights, the disputes, and the uncertainty that non-recognition inspired in the Antarctic eventually drove states toward the legal stability offered by a multilateral treaty that could freeze these problems in time.

The Search for Sovereignty Continues

The history of polar sovereignty in the first half of the twentieth century highlights how much international law and its ambiguity shaped states' behaviour in the Arctic and Antarctic. The same unique polar environment that made the application of traditional rules so difficult also gave the law added importance. States struggled to display a preponderance of power, or even a modicum of control, that would clearly indicate state ownership over the harsh, uninhabited polar spaces. Legal arguments and justifications provided a significant (and inexpensive) tool for polar claimants looking to support territorial claims in which they had little physical presence. Without a clear formula for territorial acquisition, state officials and legal experts could formulate creative arguments in defence of territorial title and craft multiple versions of polar sovereignty.

Anthony Carty and Richard Smith have argued that legal advisers usually operate in the context of decided policy and that their job generally involves checking and rechecking the application of the law in order to strengthen existing strategies.[75] In state deliberations on the polar regions, however, legal considerations often guided decision-making, decided internal debates, and created policy. The advice offered by legal advisers had a profound impact on the formation of national polar policies and on the broader bipolar legal landscape. The legal analysis they offered explains Canada's establishment of police posts on uninhabited islands where there was no one to police, state support of polar science, permanent human inhabitation of the Antarctic continent, and how states approached foreign recognition. In the complex legal space of the polar regions, their ideas mattered.

Legal assessments and evolving understandings of sovereignty continued to shape the polar regions in the second half of the twentieth century. In the Antarctic, legal uncertainty about terrestrial territorial claims lies dormant, just under the surface of the treaty. Indeed, the assertion and maintenance of territorial sovereignty is as much an issue today as in the pre-treaty years. As legal scholar Donald Rothwell observes, "sovereignty was and still remains one of the principal reasons for human endeavour in Antarctica."[76] Claimant states continue to support bases and scientific research programs in their sectors in order to maintain their sovereign rights through permanent presence and use. The motto of Argentina's Esperanza Base captures the sentiment best: *Permanencia, un acto de sacrificio* (Permanence: An Act of Sacrifice).

In the Arctic, disputes over maritime domain and continental shelves intensified after the 1950s as states grappled with a new body of ambiguous rules and principles. Although the Law of the Sea has managed this uncertainty, instability remains, particularly over the legal status of the Northwest Passage. While Canada views the Northwest Passage as internal waters, the United States contends it is an international strait. Over the past decades, Canadian officials have had to utilize creative legal arguments to defend their position on the Northwest Passage, consider how far to push the boundaries of the Law of the Sea, and decide whether they should seek official US recognition.[77] As the impacts of climate change continue to intensify in the Arctic, the legal uncertainty around the status of the passage will grow. Arguments about ambiguous legal principles, ranging from the validity of Canada's straight baselines to the amount of use required to make an international strait, will increase in importance. In this context, legal uncertainty will continue to leave its century-old mark on the polar regions.

NOTES

1 See James Brown Scott, "Arctic Exploration and International Law," *American Journal of International Law* 3, no. 4 (1909): 928–41; Thomas Willing Balch, "The Arctic and Antarctic Regions and the Law of Nations," *American Journal of International Law* 4, no. 2 (1910): 265–75; René Waultrin, "Le *probleme de*

la souverainete des poles," *Revue Générale de Droit International Public* 16 (1909): 649–60. Dollot also had an earlier article that largely dealt with Spitsbergen. Waultrin, "La question de la souveraineté des terres arctiques," *Revue Générale de Droit International Public* 15 (1908): 78–125, 185–209, 401–23.

2 Balch, "The Arctic and Antarctic Regions," 269.

3 Thomas Baty, "Spitzbergen," *Law Magazine and Review* 33 (1907): 83–8; Baty, "Arctic and Antarctic Annexation," *Law Magazine and Review* 37 (1912): 326–8.

4 Scott, "Arctic Exploration and International Law," 941.

5 Waultrin, "Le *probleme de la souverainete des poles,"* 659.

6 Randall Lesaffer, "International Law and Its History: The Story of an Unrequited Love," in *Time, History, and International Law,* ed. Matthew Craven, Malgosia Fitzmaurice, and Maria Vogiatzi (Leiden: Martinus Nijhoff, 2007), 35.

7 Hume Wrong to Lester B. Pearson, 30 December 1946, LAC, RG 25, vol. 2145, file A-2/2–10, pt 1.

8 Department of State, Division of Western European Affairs, "Territorial Sovereignty in the Polar Regions," 6 August 1926, 14–15, NARA, RG 59, CDF 1910–29, box 7156, file 800.014.

9 The name change was made in February 1930. Polar Committee, 25th Meeting, 11 February 1930, NAA, A981, ANT 4 PART 9.

10 Oscar Pinochet de la Barra, *La Antártica Chilena* (Santiago: Imprenta universitaria, 1948).

11 Note by Brian Roberts, 14 November 1952, National Archives, FO 371/100885.

12 James Bonbright to Mr Matthews, G, 15 July 1952, NARA, RG 59, CDF 1950–4, box 3066, file 702.022 / 7-1552, Antarctic.

13 Andrew Fitzmaurice, "Discovery, Conquest, and Occupation of Territory," in *The Oxford Handbook of the History of International Law,* ed. Bardo Fassbender and Anne Peters (Oxford: Oxford University Press, 2012), 840.

14 Lauren Benton, *A Search for Sovereignty: Law and Geography in European Empires, 1460–1900* (Cambridge: Cambridge University Press, 2010), 28–9.

15 C.H.M. Waldock, "Disputed Sovereignty in the Falkland Islands Dependencies," *British Yearbook of International Law* 25 (1948): 317n2.

16 See, for instance, Martti Koskenniemi, *The Gentle Civilizer of Nations: The Rise and Fall of International Law, 1870–1960* (Cambridge: Cambridge University Press, 2001), 121–55.

17 Vaughan Lowe, *International Law* (Oxford: Oxford University Press, 2007), 145.

18 Hans Kelsen, "Contiguity as a Title to Territorial Sovereignty," in *Rechtsfragen der internationalen Organisation: Festschrift für Hans Wehberg,* ed. Walter Schätzel and Hans-Jürgen Schlochauer (Frankfurt am Main: Klostermann, 1956),

200–10. Also called proximity, propinquity, hinterland, adjacency, continuity, geographic unity, region of attraction.

19 Milos Vec, "From the Congress of Vienna to the Paris Peace Treaties of 1919," in *The Oxford Handbook of the History of International Law,* ed. Bardo Fassbender and Anne Peters (Oxford: Oxford University Press, 2012), 672.

20 Georg Schwarzenberger, "Title to Territory: Response to a Challenge," *American Journal of International Law* 51, no. 2 (1957): 309.

21 Memorandum from L.C. Christie, Legal Adviser, to Prime Minister, Ottawa, "Exploration and Occupation of the Northern Arctic Islands," 28 October 1920, in *Documents on Canadian External Relations* (DCER), vol. 3, 1919–25 (Ottawa: Queen's Printer, 1977), 534.

22 Orme Masson on behalf of the Australian National Research Council, Memorandum on Australian Sector of the Antarctic and recent French claim to administer Adélie Land, NAA, A981, ANT 4, Part 3.

23 Department of State, Division of Western European Affairs, "Territorial Sovereignty in the Polar Regions," 6 August 1926, NARA, RG 59, CDF 1910–29, box 7156, file 800.014/Arctic.

24 For such analysis of the *Eastern Greenland* case, see, for example, Gordon W. Smith, *A Historical and Legal Study of Sovereignty in the Canadian North,* ed. P. Whitney Lackenbauer (Calgary: University of Calgary Press, 2014), 313–20; Janice Cavell and Jeff Noakes, *Acts of Occupation: Canada and Arctic Sovereignty, 1918–25* (Vancouver: UBC Press, 2010), 246–7, 260; Shelagh Grant, *Polar Imperative: A History of Arctic Sovereignty in North America* (Vancouver: Douglas and McIntyre, 2010), 193, 242; David Day, *Antarctica: A Biography* (Oxford: Oxford University Press, 2013), 239; Gillian Triggs, *International Law and Australian Sovereignty in Antarctica* (Sydney: Legal Books, 1986), 30–1.

25 Lawrence Preuss, "The Dispute between Denmark and Norway over the Sovereignty of East Greenland," *American Journal of International Law* 26, no. 3 (1932): 487.

26 See, for example, J.S. Reeves, "George V Land," *The American Journal of International Law* 28, no. 1 (January 1934): 119; and Anonymous, "The Legal Status of Eastern Greenland," *Geographical Journal* 82, no. 2 (1933): 151–6. For examples of state legal appraisals that analyse and assess these three cases, see Law Officers of the Foreign Office and Colonial Office, Paper B on the Legal Authorities, 12 January 1947, National Archives (NA), FO 371/61288; and E.R. Hopkins, Legal Adviser for External Affairs, Legal Aspects of Sovereignty in the Canadian Arctic, 22 January 1949, LAC, RG 2, vol. 122, file A-25.

27 Judge Dionisio Anzilotti offered the dissenting opinion, while Walther Schücking and Wang Chung-hui offered the separate opinions.

28 Charles Cheney Hyde, "Acquisition of Sovereignty over Polar Areas," *Iowa Law Review* 19, no. 293 (1933–34): 287n3.

29 Stephen C. Neff, *Justice among Nations: A History of International Law* (Cambridge, MA: Harvard University Press, 2014), 356.

30 William Roy Vallance, The Legal Adviser, Department of State, to Mr. R. Walton Moore, 30 March 1935, NARA, RG 59, CDF 1930–9, box 4520, file 800.014 Antarctic/79.

31 Frank Debenham, Director of the Scott Polar Research Institute, Memorandum on the Australian Sector of the Antarctic, 21 August 1937, National Archives of Australia (NAA), A981, ANT 2, Part 1, "Antarctic Control Australian Sector," pt 1.

32 Memorandum for the Legal Adviser, 21 May 1944, LAC, RG 85, vol. 268, file 1003–6-1.

33 Law Officers of the Foreign Office and Colonial Office, Paper B on the Legal Authorities, 12 January 1947, NA, FO 371/61288.

34 Department of State, Polar Regions: Policy and Information Statement, 1 July 1946, NARA, RG 59, CDF 1945–9, box 4073, file 800.014 Antarctic 7–146.

35 James Bonbright to Mr Matthews, G, 15 July 1952, NARA, RG 59, CDF 1950–4, box 3066, file 702.022 / 7-1552, Antarctic.

36 R.G. Casey, Minister for External Affairs, to Cabinet, "Antarctic: Position Regarding Claims," NAA, A4926/1039/Antarctic – position regarding claims – Decision 1214.

37 Island of Palmas Arbitration, Award of 4 April 1928, 2 *UNRIAA*, 845.

38 T.O. Elias, "The Doctrine of Intertemporal Law," *American Journal of International Law* 74, no. 2 (1980): 292.

39 Martin Dixon, *Textbook on International Law*, 7th ed. (Oxford: Oxford University Press, 2013), 167. See also Anthony D'Amato, "International Law, Intertemporal Problems," in *Encyclopedia of Public International Law*, vol. 2, ed. Rudolf Bernhardt (Amsterdam: North Holland, 1992), 1234–6.

40 Law Officers of the Foreign Office and Colonial Office, Paper B on the Legal Authorities, 12 January 1947, NA, FO 371/61288.

41 Dissenting Opinion of M. Anzilotti, *Eastern Greenland (Denmark v. Norway)* (1933) Permanent Court of International Justice (PCIJ), Series A-B, No. 53, 84.

42 John English, *Ice and Water: Politics, Peoples, and the Arctic Council* (Toronto: Allen Lane, 2013), 64.

43 S.W. Boggs, Department of State, Office of the Historical Adviser, "The Polar Regions: Geographical and Historical Data in a Study of Claims to Sovereignty in the Arctic and Antarctic Regions," 113–14, 21 September 1933, NARA, RG 59, CDF 1930–9, Box 4522, file 800.014, Arctic/31.

44 Jack E. Tate (L) to Mr Hickerson (EUR), "Procedure and Steps to Assert Antarctic Claims," 28 June 1948, NARA, RG 59, CDF 1945–9, file 800.014, Antarctic/6-2848.

45 See, for instance, Speech Concerning the Grounds of Chile's Claim to Antarctica Delivered to the Senate by the Minister for Foreign Affairs, Raúl

Juliet Gómez, 21 January 1947, in W.M. Bush, ed., *Antarctica and International Law: A Collection of Inter-State and National Documents*, vol. 2 (New York: Oceana, 1982–1988), 334; Barra, *La Antártida Chilena*. See also Juan Carlos Rodriguez, *La República Argentina y las Adquisiciones Territoriales en el Continente Antárctico* (Buenos Aires: Imprenta Caporaletti, 1941).

46 V.L. Lakhtine, "Rights over the Arctic," *American Journal of International Law* 24, no. 4 (1930): 710.

47 English, *Ice and Water*, 64.

48 Laurence Collier, Memorandum Respecting Territorial Claims in the Arctic to 1930, 10 February 1930, NA, DO 35/167/7, Territorial Claims in the Arctic.

49 See, for instance, Imperial Conference, 1926, Committee on British Policy in the Antarctic, Minutes of the First Meeting of the Committee, Dominions Office, 10 November 1926, NAA, M4794, 1/17, pt 1; Report by Committee on Polar Questions, Imperial Conference, 1930, NAA, A981/ANT 4, pt 8.

50 T.A. Taracouzio, *The Soviet Union and International Law* [1935] (New York: Macmillan, 1972), 56–7.

51 See Warwick Chipman, Canadian Ambassador, Buenos Aires, to the Secretary of State for External Affairs, 8 January 1947, LAC, RG 25, vol. 3843, file 9091–40, pt 1. For arguments using contiguity and the sector principle, see Appendix VIII, The Case for Argentine Territorial Claims in the Antarctic, Territorial Claims in the Antarctic, Research Department, Foreign Office, 1 May 1945, NAA, A4311, 365/8; José Carlos Vittone, *La Soberanía Argentina en el Continente Antárctico* (Buenos Aires: El Ateneo, 1944); Raul Martinez Moreno, *Soberenía Antárctica Argentina* (Tucumán: Universidad Nacional de Tucumán, 1951).

52 Barra, *La Antártida Chilena*, 111–13, in Bush, *Antarctica and International Law*, vol. 2, 355–6. British officials had always feared that Argentina and Chile would utilize the sector principle to claim territory in the Antarctic, which is why they insisted that all polar sectors emanated from discovery and control of a polar coastline and not from simple geographical proximity.

53 Roscoe Pound, *Interpretations of Legal History* (Cambridge: Cambridge University Press, 1923), 1.

54 See, for instance, Imperial Conference, 1930, Committee on Polar Questions Report, NA, DO 35/167/7; and Comments of Foreign Office legal adviser William Eric Beckett to Percival Molson, 16 January 1948, LAC, RG 25, vol. 3843, file 9092-A-40, pt 1.

55 M.C.W. Pinto, "Making International Law in the Twentieth Century," *International Law FORUM du droit international* 6 (2004): 141.

56 Gordon G. Henderson, "Policy by Default: The Origin and Fate of the Prescott Letter," *Political Science Quarterly* 79, no. 1 (1964): 76–95; H. Robert Hall, "The 'Open Door' into Antarctica: An Explanation of the Hughes Doctrine," *Polar Record* 25, no. 153 (1989): 137–40.

57 John Bassett Moore, *A Digest of International Law*, vol. 1 (Washington, D.C.: GPO, 1906), 258.

58 Charles Hughes to Norwegian Minister, 2 April 1924, *FRUS*, 1924 (Washington, D.C.: GPO, 1939), 519–20.

59 See, for instance, Expose of M. Arne Sunde, 12 December 1932, *Eastern Greenland (Denmark v. Norway)* (1933) PCIJ, Series C, No. 66, Pleadings, Oral Statements and Documents, 3154–8. On Norway's Antarctic claim, see J.S. Reeves, "Antarctic Sectors," *American Journal of International Law* 33, no. 3 (1939): 519–21.

60 OIR Report, 4436, Map Intelligence Division, Office of Intelligence Collection and Dissemination, State Department, "Basis for Possible U.S. Claims in Antarctica," 12 September 1947, NARA, RG 59, CDF 1945–9, box 4074, file 800.014, Antarctic.

61 Hugh Cumming, Division of European Affairs, Department of State, American Policy Relating to the Polar Regions, 28 July 1938, NARA, RG 59, CDF 1930–9, box 4520, file 800.014 Antarctic/126.

62 Suggested Draft Note to the British Embassy, Department of State, Division of Western European Affairs, 16 September 1925, NARA, RG 59, CDF 1910–29, box 7156, file 800.014.

63 Anna O'Neill, Assistant to the Secretary of State, Memorandum to Accompany Reply to British Embassy's Note No. 526, 17 November 1928, 28 February 1929, NARA, RG 59, CDF 1910–29, box 7156, file 800.014, Antarctic/4.

64 Cordell Hull, U.S. Secretary of State, to R.C. Lindsay, British Ambassador, Washington, 14 November 1934, Document NZ14111934, in Bush, *Antarctica and International Law*, vol. 3, 67.

65 President Roosevelt to Acting Secretary Welles, 7 January 1939, NARA, RG 59, file 800.014, Antarctic; Roosevelt to Byrd, 1939, quoted in Peter Beck, *The International Politics of Antarctica* (London: Croom Helm, 1986), 27.

66 Territorial Claims in the Antarctic, Research Department, Foreign Office, p. 140, 1 May 1945, NAA, A4311, 365/8.

67 Margaret Anstee, Minute, 17 May 1950, NA, FO 371/81131.

68 Laurence Collier, Memorandum Respecting Territorial Claims in the Arctic to 1930, 10 February 1930, NA, DO 35/167/7, Territorial Claims in the Arctic.

69 See, for instance, Charles Callan Tansill, *The Purchase of the Danish West Indies* (Gloucester: Peter Smith, 1966).

70 Malgosia Fitzmaurice and Olufemi Elias, *Contemporary Issues in the Law of Treaties* (Utrecht: Eleven International, 2005), 13–16.

71 See, for example, British Ambassador to the United States to the Secretary of State, 17 November 1928, Document NZ17111928, in Bush, *Antarctica and International Law* 3, 60–1.

72   Warwick Chipman, Canadian Ambassador, Buenos Aires, to Secretary of State for External Affairs, 8 January 1947, LAC, RG 25, vol. 3843, file 9091–40, pt 1.

73   P.G. Law, Officer in Charge, Antarctic Division to the Secretary, Department of External Affairs, 29 June 1950, NAA, A1838, 1495/3/2/1, pt 1.

74   See P. Whitney Lackenbauer and Peter Kikkert, "The Dog in the Manger – and Letting Sleeping Dogs Lie: The United States, Canada and the Sector Principle, 1924–1955,'" in *The Arctic Ocean: Essays in Honour of Donat Pharand*, ed. Suzanne Lalonde and Ted McDorman (Leiden: Brill, 2014), 216–39.

75   Anthony Carty and Richard Smith, eds., *Sir Gerald Fitzmaurice and the World Crisis: A Legal Adviser at the Foreign Office, 1932–1945* (The Hague: Kluwer Law International, 2000).

76   Donald Rothwell, "Sovereignty and the Antarctic Treaty," *Polar Record* 40, no. 1 (2010): 17.

77   See P. Whitney Lackenbauer and Peter Kikkert, "Archipelagic Analogues? Indonesian Baselines, Canadian Arctic Sovereignty, and the Framing of Mental Maps, 1957–62," *International Journal of Canadian Studies* 50 (2014): 227–52; and Adam Lajeunesse, *Lock, Stock, and Icebergs: A History of Canada's Arctic Maritime Sovereignty* (Vancouver: UBC Press, 2016).

2 The Gentlemen's Agreement: Sovereignty, Defence, and Canadian–American Diplomacy in the Arctic

ADAM LAJEUNESSE

In June 1949, Frederick Varcoe, Canada's Deputy Minister of Justice, received a letter from Deputy Minister of Mines and Resources C.W. Jackson concerning a forthcoming American resupply voyage to the Joint Arctic Weather Stations in the Queen Elizabeth Islands. In it, Jackson noted with concern that questions regarding the legal status of Canada's Arctic waters were arising with increasing frequency and that his department could find no evidence of any firm ruling on the subject.[1] Given the steady growth in the number of American ships being used to establish and maintain a growing assortment of Cold War defence projects, Jackson felt that a clarification of Canadian sovereignty was important. Deputy Minister Varcoe was, however, at a loss for a clear answer.

The problem faced by the Canadian government in the late 1940s was that it remained uncertain as to how it might claim sovereignty over Arctic waters. Since the nineteenth century, successive Canadian governments had treated the water and ice within the Arctic Archipelago as their own, though none ever attempted to formalize that arrangement with a direct claim to sovereignty. International law made a formal assertion difficult, while the possibility of a challenge to any such action from the United States, the world's dominant maritime power, remained a serious and persistent concern.[2]

The fact that so many US naval and Coast Guard vessels were required to establish and resupply joint defence projects in the Canadian North placed Canada in a difficult position. To allow this activity to continue as though Canada had no sovereignty over the waters in question would effectively abdicate ownership. But openly asserting sovereignty would risk the rejection of that claim by a US government whose principled policy at the time was to challenge almost any assertion by states to maritime control beyond the then established three-mile territorial limit.[3] Such a political conflict would damage bilateral relations and imperil vital joint defence cooperation. Finding itself between a rock and a hard place, Canada required a more creative solution.

What emerged from this dilemma was a diplomatic framework as simple as it was clever. Alternatively described as a "modus vivendi" by the Advisory Committee on Northern Development in 1969 and a "gentlemen's agreement" by Prime Minister Joe Clark in 1979, this framework for Arctic cooperation involved an implied American promise to abstain from any open challenge to Canada's Arctic claims, provided that Canada never confront the United States with a clear statement of sovereignty, or demand recognition of that sovereignty.[4] In the early 1950s this framework governed American icebreaker and defence operations in the Arctic Archipelago – such as the establishment of the Joint Arctic Weather Stations and the Distant Early Warning (DEW) Line. These missions were essential to continental defence but politically sensitive, given the still uncertain nature of Canadian sovereignty at the time.[5] In the 1960s, American submarines began to operate in the Northwest Passage, exploring routes that they would continue to use until the end of the Cold War (at least).[6] Like the icebreakers before them, these vessels forced the two countries into the balancing act of enabling vital defence activities while sidestepping the awkward political questions surrounding transit rights, ownership, and the status of the Northwest Passage itself.[7]

This system of Arctic "don't ask, don't tell" evolved throughout the Cold War, adapting itself to different types of defence operations and different circumstances. Still, the essence of this implicit agreement remained the same, namely, a willingness to shy away from the sovereignty elephant in the room to focus on more practical matters. In so doing, both parties maintained their respective political positions, ensured smooth defence cooperation, and (for the most part) avoided political confrontation throughout the Cold War.

Defining Canadian Sovereignty

In the early Cold War, the question of Arctic maritime sovereignty was a difficult file to address. From a legal perspective, Canada's position was tenuous. Its internationally accepted territorial sea measured only three miles from *terra firma*, and a state's right to extend its sovereignty beyond that was extremely limited.[8] Canada's options for officially laying claim to Arctic waters were therefore constrained by the legal framework of the time. This shifted somewhat in the early 1950s, with the international Court of Justice (ICJ) decision in the *Anglo-Norwegian Fisheries Case*, which recognized a state's right to enclose archipelagoes within straight baselines as internal waters – meaning that those waters were considered to be under the complete sovereignty of the state.[9]

Despite this new precedent, basing Canadian sovereignty on straight baselines was far from straightforward. Only one year after the ICJ's ruling, the Interdepartmental Committee on Territorial Waters advised the Privy Council Office that the applicability of this system of delineation to the Arctic Archipelago remained "ambiguous."[10] The exact allowable length of baselines had not been laid out in 1951; however, it was no small consideration that Norway's lines stretched from only a few hundred yards to a maximum of 44 miles, while Canada's would need to be considerably longer.[11] A preliminary survey done for the Minister of Mines and Technical Surveys in 1956 placed the total baseline length at 2,902 miles, with the largest enclosed section being McClure Strait at 130 miles across.

Canada's ability to claim the waters as "historic," a crucial factor in Norway's case, also remained uncertain since Canada's history of exercising authority over the waters in question was sporadic at best. The Inuit had long used the ice for hunting and transportation, but these activities only reinforced the Canadian claim to the specific areas of Inuit activity, leaving out some of the waters farther west and north.[12] Canada could also point to a series of naval expeditions, such as the voyages of Captain Joseph-Elzéar Bernier and the Eastern Arctic Patrols; but these expeditions were few in number and spread across a region the size of Europe.

So, the government of Prime Minister Louis St Laurent adopted a very cautious approach. In July 1956, the cabinet took the important step of defining its Arctic maritime claim as those waters within straight baselines surrounding the Arctic Archipelago.[13] The following month, the Privy Council Office circulated a letter to all government departments informing them of Canada's principled decision to "lay claim to sovereignty over the waters of these channels." It also instructed the bureaucracy to take no action, and make no public statements, that might prejudice a future Canadian claim. Still, these were internal communications. The exact extent and basis of Canada's claim was never made public, and those baselines remained a decision in principle, one that was neither legislated nor announced.

This extreme caution stemmed from the government's fear that any attempt to make this new policy official would be challenged by the United States. Since the eighteenth century, US governments have resisted attempts by other states to limit the freedom of the seas, and that remained a cornerstone of US government policy during the Cold War. In 1951, the US Department of State addressed the specific question of sovereignty over ice in a directive that read: "Nor could the Arctic seas, in our view, be made subject to 'territorial' sovereignty of any state even though they might contain ice areas having some characteristics of land ... The US position is that the Arctic seas and the air spaces above them, in so far as they are outside of accepted territorial limits, are open to commerce and navigation in the same degree as other open seas."[14]

There was no question within Department of External Affairs that the United States would refuse to accept straight baselines or any assertion of Canadian sovereignty outside of its three-mile territorial sea. It was equally understood that an explicit American rejection of Canadian sovereignty would have serious legal and political consequences. Legally, it would risk international arbitration; politically, it would sour relations and create discord at a time when joint defence projects needed to be maintained and a unified front presented to the Soviet Union.

Managing the ever-expanding joint defence operations in the Arctic waters was therefore an awkward affair. As Canada's Arctic policy remained ambiguous, any activity had to be managed to protect the country's position by ensuring that the United States respected (or least appeared to respect) Canadian sovereignty, all without ever being able to state explicitly what that sovereignty entailed. In response to this predicament, a new framework for joint defence operations gradually emerged. Within this system the Canadian government consciously avoided asking its American counterpart for an explicit recognition of Canadian sovereignty. The Americans, for their part, obliged the Canadians by simply avoiding the issue. What emerged was the unspoken gentleman's agreement that, in the words of the Advisory Committee on Northern Development (ACND), allowed "each country [to maintain] its position while refraining from asserting it in such a manner as to embarrass the other publicly.[15]

Don't Ask, Don't Tell

This framework was an effective enabler of joint defence cooperation because it worked in both US and Canadian interests. Both nations recognized that maintaining good bilateral relations and continuing their continental defence projects was more important than settling unresolved law-of-the-sea issues. By carefully managing the conversation, the two governments were able to reserve their relative legal positions while avoiding the political drama that would have accompanied an open fight over the status of the Arctic waters.

While this diplomatic framework remained unspoken and unofficial, it was well understood by both sides. A 1954 US Embassy report to the State Department conveys that attitude very clearly:

Although the US has not recognized these claims [to the Arctic waters] it has also refrained from challenging them. In view of our primary objective of gaining and maintaining Canadian support for our hemispheric defense projects – which extend in the Arctic – and of Canadian sensitivities with respect to that region … [w]e doubt that it would be appropriate to urge upon the Canadians a policy which would, in effect, diminish whatever validity their claims to Arctic waters may have.[16]

Avoiding the issue also exempted the US government from making an uncomfortable choice of its own. Challenging Canadian maritime claims in the region might have caused catastrophic political fallout with a vital ally while recognizing them would have directly contradicted the long-established American position on freedom of the seas. Ironically, Washington found itself in as difficult and sensitive a position as Canada. Thus, by not asking the United States to recognize its Arctic sovereignty, the Canadian government was allowing the Americans to avoid their own no-win situation.

The best example of this practice involved the maritime elements of the Distant Early Warning Line (DEW) construction project. Between 1955 and 1958, the United States sent out two large convoys each year to the eastern and western Canadian Arctic to undertake hydrographic and beach surveys, support operations, and site construction. Most of this work was done by the US Navy's amphibious forces, with American contractors doing the on-site construction. Major support operations were carried out in 1956 and again in 1957, though the largest effort was made during the initial push in 1955. During that summer, more than 100 American ships were working in the Arctic.[17]

The Canadian government closely monitored the sealift regulations that oversaw wildlife treatment, pollution, hunting and firearms, marine discharge, and American interactions with the local Inuit. Vessel courses were monitored and approved by Canada, and deviations drew protest from External Affairs. Yet despite all this activity and regulation, at no point was the issue of maritime boundaries ever clarified, nor was the basis of this jurisdictional authority. This elegant arrangement allowed both Canada and the United States to interpret the situation in the manner most convenient to each.

Canada took this control over American shipping as an implicit recognition of Canadian sovereignty. In a 1957 speech to the House of Commons, Prime Minister St Laurent highlighted what he considered the Americans' implicit acceptance of Canadian ownership. For each resupply voyage to the Arctic, the US Navy was required to apply for a waiver from certain provisions of the Canada Shipping Act. St Laurent told the

House that it was uncertain "whether we can interpret the fact that they did comply with our requirements that they obtain a waiver ... as an admission that these are territorial waters, but if they were not territorial waters there would be no point in asking for a waiver."[18]

Washington, however, viewed these Canadian regulations and requirements in a very different light. While the US Navy consistently requested permission before sending vessels into the Arctic, even referring to the Northwest Passage as "Canadian territorial waters," its interpretation of these agreements, and even the term "Canadian territorial waters," differed greatly.[19] In requesting permission to enter "territorial waters," the US government could argue that it was referring only to the three-mile strip around the Canadian mainland and each individual Arctic island. Since every American expedition passed within these boundaries at some point, Washington interpreted these requests and regulations as applying only to Canada's internationally recognized territorial sea and not to operations in the Arctic as a whole.

In 1955, Jean E. Tartter, Third Secretary at the US Embassy in Ottawa, wrote to the State Department to inform it that, whatever the Canadians might believe, the United States was not actually acknowledging Canadian claims to the polar ice when it requested clearance for vessels to proceed through the Arctic Archipelago more than three miles from land. Alluding to the standard clearance given to American icebreakers to transit Canadian waters during the 1954 Beaufort Sea Expedition, he wrote, "but this was only to travel in Canadian territorial waters *without specifying what these might be.*"[20]

Similarly, the waivers for which the United States applied in order to resupply the DEW Line were seen in a different light. While St Laurent interpreted these requests in the broadest possible sense, the US Navy saw only the letter of the agreement. They did not recognize Canadian authority over Arctic waters; their only intent was to satisfy certain Canadian regulations related to coastal shipping. In fact, they waived only Part 13 of the Canada Shipping Act for American vessels moving Canadian goods between Canadian ports.[21] For example, the relevant sections of the waiver for the 1955 DEW Line sealift read:

His Excellency the Governor General in Council, on the recommendation of the Minister of National Revenue and the Minister of Transport and under authority of section 287 of the Customs Act and section 673 of the Canada Shipping Act, is pleased to declare and doth hereby declare that the provisions of section 671 of the Canada Shipping Act relating to the use of vessels in the Canadian Coasting Trade, shall not apply to the US Government-owned vessels.[22]

The United States was not asking permission to enter the Arctic waters *per se*, it was only requesting an exemption from section 671 related to cabotage (trade or navigation within a state's coastal waters). Since some of the supplies being shipped out of Boston that year were Canadian in origin, these cabotage laws technically applied.

Throughout this process, the Department of External Affairs understood perfectly well that the US Navy did not consider these waivers or requests to enter "Canadian territorial waters" as an actual recognition of Canadian sovereignty. But that was less important than the fact that the Americans continued to act in a manner that Canadian governments could interpret as respecting Canadian sovereignty. As such, American voyages continued to be authorized on what External Affairs described as "the unstated assumption that territorial waters in that area means whatever we may consider to be Canadian territorial waters, whereas the US does likewise."[23]

Early Submarine Voyages

Throughout the 1950s, maintaining this gentleman's agreement was made easier by the fact that American operations always fell under the umbrella of continental defence, and the ships involved were destined for defence sites on Canadian territory. This meant that American vessels had to enter Canada's three-mile territorial limit, allowing Canada and the United States to comfortably and quietly disagree on the nature of American requests. Also, those ships rarely transited the entire Northwest Passage, instead sailing to stations in Canada and returning home along the same route.

Submarines were different. These vessels were not travelling to Canadian territory, and while navigating the Northwest Passage they did not need to enter Canada's three-mile territorial sea. This made it more difficult to request similar arrangements as those governing the surface traffic.[24] Submarine voyages were therefore managed somewhat differently, though still within the same general framework.

Since there was still no reason for the United States to challenge Canadian sovereignty outright, and every reason to seek Canadian cooperation in northern defence, the first such voyage – the 1960 transit of the USS *Seadragon* – proceeded as a joint operation with significant Canadian input and assistance. In August 1960, the submarine passed from east to west through the Parry Channel. Canadian documents indicate that the Americans requested "concurrence" in advance of the voyage.[25] This concurrence was not the same as permission, though it was an ambiguous enough term that both countries could interpret it as they saw fit. External Affairs considered it to be a request to transit (of sorts) and believed it strengthened Canada's sovereignty.[26] The State Department, on the other hand, felt that no such recognition had been given.[27]

As was standard practice, both parties deliberately avoided the issue of sovereignty. After *Seadragon*'s voyage, the submarine's captain was instructed to avoid discussing the subject with reporters; if the question of "internal versus territorial waters" should arise, he was to refer the matter back to the Department of the Navy. Just as importantly, the captain was told to avoid answering any questions about whether Canadian clearance had been requested for the passage.[28]

In 1962 the US Navy deployed a second boat through the Northwest Passage: the USS *Skate*, which followed *Seadragon*'s route in reverse, from west to east. This operation worked in much the same way as *Seadragon*'s two years earlier, with Canada "formally notified" of *Skate*'s plans. External Affairs recognized that this was not a transit request *per se*, but it was close enough that it could be seen as one and therefore strengthen Canada's position.[29] As with the resupply missions of the 1950s, the US Navy could tell itself it had not requested Canadian permission to transit, while Ottawa could (and did) interpret the situation quite differently.

The SS *Manhattan* Rocks the Boat

This framework remained in place throughout the 1960s and was made easier by the end of US submarine operations in the Arctic after the voyage of the *Skate*, largely owing to a shortage of deployable submarines as the US Navy conducted a major safety overhaul of its fleet.[30] The Soviet military's transition from strategic bombers to intercontinental ballistic missiles (ICBMs) during the 1960s likewise lessened the Americans' strategic interest in the North by rendering the DEW Line largely obsolete. This reduced the US presence and interest in the Arctic and led to a certain amount of complacency within External Affairs, which soon found itself far more focused on maritime disputes on Canada's Atlantic and Pacific coasts.[31]

This calm was dramatically interrupted in 1969 when Humble Oil announced the planned transit of the Northwest Passage by its ice-strengthened supertanker, SS *Manhattan*. The voyage was intended to test the feasibility of shipping oil through the region from newly discovered fields at Prudhoe Bay in Alaska to refineries on the US eastern seaboard. Initially, the Canadian government was very much in favour of the operation. From Ottawa's perspective it was a no-lose scenario: either *Manhattan* would establish a shipping route that Canadian companies could then leverage as they developed hydrocarbon deposits in the Mackenzie Delta, or, if the voyage failed, a pipeline might be built from

Prudhoe Bay down the Mackenzie Valley – which Canadian companies could also use to their advantage.[32] Cooperation was the order of the day, and political questions continued to be set aside, as in years past. The traditional diplomatic approach, whereby neither party raised the matter of sovereignty, would be maintained, and the issue would not be forced.[33]

At the time, there was little reason to believe that decades of functional cooperation would not continue, especially since *Manhattan*'s voyage had never been intended as any sort of a challenge. Technically, the real danger to Canadian sovereignty was the tanker's escort, the US Coast Guard icebreaker *Northwind*. Prior to the voyage, the Canadian government made a low-key suggestion to the State Department that the United States request permission for *Northwind's* transit, but the request was refused.[34] This refusal hardly came as a surprise, but it was not seen as derailing the broader operation. The US Coast Guard had a long history of working in Canada's northern waters without incident, and there was little reason to think that this transit would be any different.

Much to the chagrin of Prime Minister Pierre Trudeau and his government, the *Manhattan* voyage was very different from the previous decade's resupply missions and even the two submarine voyages of the early 1960s. The sheer size of the supertanker, the dramatic nature of its transit, and the prospect of many more like it appearing in the North was enough to warrant more publicity than past operations. The fact that the *Manhattan* experiment might lead to the establishment of a major petroleum shipping route through the Arctic's sensitive waters added another new and important element to the equation as the spectre of pollution in the country's pristine northern environment raised a great deal of public concern.

By the end of 1969, the Liberal government found itself besieged on all sides as Arctic sovereignty became the national *cause célèbre*. The *Globe and Mail*, the *Toronto Star*, and the *Toronto Telegram* all published editorials demanding an outright declaration of sovereignty. The same suggestions were coming from the northern territories and even from within the Liberal Party itself. The predominantly Liberal Standing Committee on Indian and Northern Affairs issued its report to Parliament in December 1969, calling on the government to make official its long-deferred (and only vaguely implied) claims to the waters of the Arctic Archipelago.[35]

Even in the face of this pressure, the Liberal government never seriously considered such direct action, so real was the old fear that an American challenge would bring the issue to court.[36] Ivan Head, then special assistant to the prime minister with responsibility for advice on foreign policy, remarked in 1971 that Canada had no choice but to refrain from any such overt declaration. In Head's words, "it would be better to be silent than to speak out and be knocked down."[37] Instead of an outright declaration of sovereignty, Canada sought to push the question aside once more by relying on a more functional approach to maritime pollution. The answer was an expansion of the country's territorial sea (from three to twelve nautical miles) and a unilateral declaration of a 100 nautical mile pollution prevention zone. These actions were considered less extreme and, therefore, less likely to elicit a real challenge, but they still represented a significant departure for Canadian policy. The assertion of a twelve-mile territorial sea was in line with the general global movement toward that limit; however, the pollution prevention legislation was clearly outside of international law. The new Arctic Waters Pollution Prevention Act (1970), which established this pollution prevention zone, was denounced by the US government as illegal but pushed forward by the Trudeau government nonetheless as a means of assuaging an agitated public while neatly sidestepping the issue of sovereignty.[38]

The *Manhattan* incident was the first clear break from the old framework, which demanded that the precise definition of Canadian sovereignty remain ambiguous. That break could hardly have been avoided, given the publicity surrounding the voyage, which brought the legal disagreement to the surface in an extremely uncomfortable way for both parties. After the *Manhattan* voyage, neither government could go back to the comfortable ambiguity of the 1950s and 1960s. While it dodged the political and legal perils of legislating straight baselines, the Canadian government was forced to clarify its position on sovereignty, and soon thereafter it stated with greater clarity that it considered the Northwest Passage to be historic internal waters.[39] The United States, for its part, was drawn into stating publicly that it recognized no Canadian rights beyond the three-mile territorial sea.[40]

The parameters of the legal dispute were now out in the open; even so, the two governments made every effort to maintain the spirit of cooperation that had defined the 1950s. The public spat over the Northwest Passage was soon pushed behind closed doors as External Affairs and the State Department worked to find some kind of equitable resolution. A broad "Arctic Treaty," which would have ensconced the AWPPA within a multilateral framework, failed in 1971 because of Soviet suspicion of American motives.[41] More successful was the Canadian–American initiative to legitimize coastal state jurisdiction over ice-covered waters by adding an article on the subject to the UN *Convention on the Law of the Sea* (Article 234).[42] During these talks, US and Canadian negotiators neatly sidestepped the question of sovereignty, to the point that the Canadian delegation felt the need to remind the Americans in April 1976 that Canada did still intend to claim the waters of the Arctic Archipelago as internal "at an appropriate time."[43]

Fitting Under-Ice Defence into the Equation

In the years following the *Manhattan* imbroglio, the military significance of the Arctic waters, which had waned in the 1960s, began to increase once again. By the mid-1970s, the Soviet Navy had grown into a formidable blue-water fleet, with a powerful nuclear submarine arm and an expanding Arctic capability. The Soviet arsenal of modern nuclear attack and ballistic missile submarines (SSNs and SSBNs) had expanded dramatically, leading analysts to worry that Canada's Arctic channels would be used either as missile-firing stations or as transit routes into NATO's Atlantic sea lanes.[44]

Canada responded by establishing listening arrays in the Arctic to detect and track any such incursions. This long-term project was led by the Defence Research Establishment, which occasionally relied on American equipment and technical expertise.[45] Beginning with the deployment of test buoys in 1969, these systems involved American and Canadian agencies working together to quietly defend the same Arctic waters which were then the subject of such controversy and dispute. While the politicians argued in public, the two militaries continued their long-standing practice of sidestepping political and legal disagreements to ensure that vital defence work continued unimpaired.

It was Canada that deployed and managed these arrays but testing and calibrating them required American nuclear submarines. Thus, the US Navy was asked to deploy its attack boats in the same waters where *Manhattan* and *Northwind* had caused such an uproar. How exactly these voyages were undertaken remains classified. Most likely it was in a similar spirit to the submarine operations of the early 1960s. No permission was sought by the United States, but Canada was involved in various capacities, some of which were managed through the Permanent Joint Board of Defence and labelled joint operations.[46] Whether that cooperation existed within a formal system or on a more *ad hoc* basis is unknown, but also largely irrelevant. Existing defence arrangements from the 1950s allowed American vessels to enter Canadian waters (and vice versa) without formal diplomatic clearance, and that was likely enough to allow defence planners to set aside the question of sovereignty yet again.[47]

The *Polar Sea*

Continued cooperation between the Canadian and US navies and research establishments was possible in the 1980s because their work was so secretive. As with the *Manhattan*, the system was derailed only when a public crisis forced the question of sovereignty back onto the agenda.

This arose in 1985 when the US Coast Guard icebreaker *Polar Sea* transited the Northwest Passage without requesting the permission of the Canadian government.[48] And, as had been the case in 1969, public pressure forced the dispute into the open once more.

This public attention forced the issue and Prime Minister Brian Mulroney's Conservative government decided that the time was right for an official declaration of sovereignty. As such, the waters of the Arctic Archipelago were officially declared historic internal waters, delineated by newly drawn straight baselines. As was the case in 1970 with the AWPPA, this move generated public protest in the United States, but this was short-lived, and the matter was soon pushed behind closed doors to prevent too much damage to the bilateral relationship. A strong partnership between Mulroney and his counterpart, US President Ronald Reagan, coupled with an ongoing American feud with the International Court of Justice and the increasing acceptance of straight baselines in international law, gave Canada the leverage to move forward with its claim in a way that had not been politically possible in the 1970s or earlier.[49]

Despite the State Department's willingness to meet the Canadian claim with only low-level protests, a solution was still needed to allow American icebreakers into the Northwest Passage without setting off another crisis. Years of difficult negotiations followed during which External Affairs sought to convince the Americans to break with their long-standing policy while State Department negotiators sought to mollify the Canadians with something short of full recognition.[50] By 1987, it was clear that Canada could no longer tolerate American surface vessels in those waters without its consent. The United States, for its part, clearly refused to request such consent. The two sides had reached an impasse.

Ultimately a solution was found: a return to the purposeful ambiguity that had defined Canadian–American agreements in the 1950s – an agreement that both sides could interpret differently to suit their respective requirements. This time the issue of "consent" was linked to scientific research. Under the UN *Convention on the Law of the Sea*, research on a state's continental shelf could only be undertaken "with the express consent of and under the conditions set forth by the coastal state."[51] If the United States agreed to request consent to transit in order to (actually or ostensibly) conduct scientific research, then both nations could secure what was most important to them. Canada had its political victory, since Mulroney could legitimately claim that the Americans were requesting Canadian permission to transit. Meanwhile, the Americans could say that such permission did not represent recognition of Canadian sovereignty, since conducting research along the way necessitated such a request under accepted international law.

The Canadian interpretation of this framework (later styled the Agreement on Arctic Cooperation) was made clear by Minister of Foreign Affairs Joe Clark, who, in a speech to the House of Commons in January 1988, said: "As a result of that agreement, the United States now acknowledges and has a legal obligation to seek Canada's permission before there is a transit through the Northwest Passage." Clark did not say that the Americans had an obligation to request permission before conducting research; rather, they had to do so before transiting.

The Americans naturally preferred to emphasize the research element. In the words of American negotiator David Colson:

> Canada got us to use the word consent, which was a word we did not wish to use but we felt that in the context in which we were dealing – where we had decided to use the icebreaker operations to do scientific research on every voyage through the Northwest Passage – that research was something that we didn't have to do, that we would do on our own volition. By conducting scientific research we were bringing ourselves within Canadian jurisdiction as we would recognize it and so it was appropriate to use the word consent.[52]

In managing American operations in the Northwest Passage in this manner, both states were able to claim that their fundamental requirements were being met. Each side understood that the other interpreted the agreement very differently, but that was not the point. What mattered was that both governments were able to continue to operate in the North, unconstrained by concerns of fomenting a political crisis.

Conclusion

The gentleman's agreement between Canada and the United States regarding the status of Arctic waters survived in different permutations from the late 1940s until the end of the Cold War and beyond. Never an actual agreement, it was more a loose framework within which Canadian–American Arctic defence activities were managed. It evolved with the times and adapted to different circumstances, but at its core, it represented a willingness on the part of both nations to sidestep the question of sovereignty so as to enable smooth and effective cooperation. Icebreaker and supply ship operations in the 1950s, and submarine voyages from the 1960s to the 1980s, were kept at arm's length from the legal/political question of sovereignty. This involved crafting operational agreements that were purposefully ambiguous when it came to matters of permission and transit rights. Both surface and subsurface operations were undertaken as joint defence projects, and these missions often continued uninterrupted during periods of political tension and dispute.

When this framework broke down in the face of a dispute, both governments were quick to push their disagreement, and the question of sovereignty itself, behind closed doors. That was the case in the aftermath of the *Manhattan* transit in 1969 and that of *Polar Sea* in 1985. Once the nature of the dispute was public and ambiguity became difficult to maintain, the two states relied on the secrecy of submarine operations and the joint nature of continental defence to continue sidestepping the legal disagreement looming in the background.

Since the 1940s, both governments recognized that actually resolving the legal issue at the heart of this running dispute was beyond them, since doing so would require one country to compromise a sacrosanct policy position. Canada could not surrender its sovereign rights in the Arctic and the United States could not compromise on what it viewed as an important precedent affecting the freedom of the seas. Instead, this gentleman's agreement, as a framework for northern operations, presented Canada and the United States with the next best thing: decades of cooperation, largely uninterrupted by the political imperatives to either defend principled positions on sovereignty or the freedom of the seas. This was the genius of Canadian–American diplomacy, and a testament to the closeness of the relationship and the level of trust between the two militaries and foreign services during the Cold War.

NOTES

1   C.W. Jackson to F.F. Varcoe, 3 June 1950, LAC, RG 85, vol. 750, file 4419, pt 6.

2   Adam Lajeunesse, *Lock, Stock, and Icebergs: The Evolution of Canada's Arctic Maritime Sovereignty* (Vancouver: UBC Press, 2016), chs. 1–2.

3   On this see, for instance, the assessment from the Canadian Ambassador to Washington: Letter from J.S. Nutt to Jean-Louis Delisle, 17 November 1958, LAC, RG 25, vol. 7118, file 9057–40, pt 8.

4   On the ACND, see Memorandum for Cabinet, 20 March 1969, LAC, RG 12, vol. 5561, file 8100–15-4-2, pt 1. On Joe Clark, see Arctic Waters Panel meeting, 27 June 1979, LAC, RG 12, vol. 5561, file 8100-15-4-2, pt. 3.

5   On this uncertainty see, for example, the statement by Hume Wrong to A.D.P. Heeney, 14 June 1946, LAC, RG 25, vol. 3347, file 9061-A-40, pt 1. For an introduction to the extensive literature on this period, see Ken Coates, P. Whitney Lackenbauer, Bill Morrison, and Greg Poelzer, *Arctic Front: Defending Canada in the Far North* (Toronto: Thomas Allen, 2008); P. Whitney Lackenbauer, ed., *Canada and Arctic Sovereignty and Security: Historical Perspectives* (Calgary: Centre for

Military and Strategic Studies / University of Calgary Press, 2011); and Adam Lajeunesse and Lackenbauer, eds., *Canadian Armed Forces Arctic Operations, 1945–2015: Historical and Contemporary Lessons Learned* (Fredericton: Gregg Centre for the Study of War and Society, 2017).

6 Evidence of American submarine transits ends in the mid-1980s, though it is very likely that operations continued past that point and up to the present. On these operations, see Adam Lajeunesse, "A Very Practical Requirement: Under-Ice Operations in the Canadian Arctic, 1960–1986." *Cold War History* 13, no. 4 (2013): 507–24.

7 See, for example, Donat Pharand, *Canada's Arctic Waters in International Law* (Cambridge: Cambridge University Press, 1988); Rob Huebert, "A Northern Foreign Policy: The Politics of Ad Hockery," in *Diplomatic Departures: The Conservative Era in Canadian Foreign Policy, 1984–93*, ed. Nelson Michaud and Kim Richard Nossal (Vancouver: UBC Press, 2001), 84–99; and Ted McDorman, *Salt Water Neighbors: International Ocean Law Relations between the United States and Canada* (New York: Oxford University Press, 2009).

8 For a fuller description of a state's right to extend sovereignty over certain areas deemed "historic waters," see Donat Pharand, "The Arctic Waters and the Northwest Passage: A Final Revisit," *Ocean Development and International Law* 38, no. 1 (2007): 5–13.

9 Straight baselines are lines drawn from headland to headland; within such areas, all waters to landward are under the sovereign authority of the state.

10 Memorandum for Head of Legal Division, 1952, LAC, RG 2, series 8, vol. 236, file T-30-1-C.

11 Pharand, "The Arctic Waters," 22.

12 David Vanderzwaag and Donat Pharand, "Inuit and Ice: Implications for Canadian Arctic Waters," *Canadian Yearbook of International Law* 21 (1983): 69.

13 Memorandum from Legal Division, 12 July 1968, LAC, RG 25, vol. 15729, file 25-4-1.

14 US Department of State, *Foreign Relations of the United States*, "Department of State Policy Statement," *Polar Regions*, vol. 1, 1 July 1951, 1724.

15 Memorandum for Cabinet, 20 March 1969, LAC, RG 12, vol. 5561, file 8100-15-4-2, pt 1.

16 Ernest de W. Mayer, Counselor of Embassy, to William C. Herrington, Department of State, 11 August 1954, NARA, RG 84, entry UD 2195C, box 8.

17 US Navy Electronics Laboratory, *The Sourcebook on Submarine Arctic Operations*, 27 April 1966, NHH, Waldo K. Lyon Papers.

18 Canada, House of Commons, *Debates*, 6 April 1957, 22nd Parliament, 5th session, 3186.

19 US Embassy to Secretary of State for External Affairs, 19 December 1949, LAC, RG 25 vol. 5737, file 17.E (s).

20   Jean E. Tartter, Third Secretary of the US Embassy, Ottawa to the Department of State, 10 March 1955, NARA, RG 84, entry UD 2195C, box 26. Italics added.

21   R.B. Bryce, "Waiver from the Canada Shipping Act," 12 July 1956, NARA, RG 84, entry UD 2195C, box 45.

22   G. Ignatieff, Under-Secretary of State, External Affairs, to Mr Mayer, Counselor, US Embassy, Ottawa, 3 June 1955, NARA, RG 84, entry UD2195C, box 24.

23   Memorandum, 29 July 1958, LAC, RG 25, file 9057-40, pt 7.

24   Memorandum by John Diefenbaker, "Canadian Position in Relation to Arctic Waters; Passage of USS Seadragon," 21 May 1960, DHH, MG 01/XII /C/125, Defence, 1952–62, vol. 56.

25   Memorandum from Under-Secretary of State for External Affairs to Secretary of State for External Affairs, 10 June 1960, *Documents on Canadian External Relations*, vol. 27, no. 665.

26   Ibid.

27   On the American refusal to recognize Canadian sovereignty in connection with the voyage, see Memorandum by John Diefenbaker, "Canadian Position in Relation to Arctic Waters; Passage of USS Seadragon," 21 May 1960, DHH, MG 01/XII/C/125, Defence, 1952–62, vol. 56.

28   Naval Message from CHINFO to USS *Seadragon*, September 1960, NARA, RG 59, entry 5298, box 13, Bureau of European Affairs: Country Director for Canada, Records Relating to Military Affairs, 1942–1966.

29   Memorandum from the Deputy Minister of Defence to the Undersecretary of State for External Affairs, 18 July 1962, LAC, RG 25, vol. 11, file 9057-40.

30   For more, see Lajeunesse, *Lock, Stock, and Icebergs*, 119–20.

31   For more on these disputes see ibid., 123–8.

32   Cabinet Conclusions, 11 September 1969, LAC, RG2, Privy Council Office, series A-5-a, vol. 6340.

33   Memorandum for Cabinet, 20 March 1969, LAC, RG 12, vol. 5561, file 8100-15-4-2, pt. 1.

34   Edgar Dosman, "The Northern Sovereignty Crisis," in *The Arctic in Question*, ed. Edgar Dosman (Toronto: Oxford University Press, 1976), 39.

35   John Kirton and Don Munton, "The Manhattan Voyages and Their Aftermath," in *Politics of the Northwest Passage*, ed. Franklyn Griffiths (Montreal and Kingston: McGill–Queen's University Press, 1987), and Canada, House of Commons, *Debates*, 22 January 1970, 28th Parliament, 2nd session, 2721.

36   Kirton and Munton, "The Manhattan Voyages," 76.

37   Record of Meetings Held in the Department of External Affairs to Discuss the Proposed Multilateral Conference on Safety of Navigation and Prevention of Pollution in Arctic Waters, 11–12 February 1971, LAC, RG 25, vol. 15732, file 25-5-5-CDA-5.

38 Talking points for Ambassador Johnson, 20 March 1970, LAC, RG 2, series A-5-a, vol. 6359.

39 See, for instance, Telegram from External Affairs to Canadian Embassy, Washington, 5 July 1976, LAC, RG 12, vol. 5561, file 8100-15-4-2, pt. 2.

40 Ibid., 47.

41 Record of Meetings Held in the Department of External Affairs to Discuss the Proposed Multilateral Conference on Safety of Navigation and Prevention of Pollution in Arctic Waters, 11–12 February 1971, LAC, RG 25, vol. 15732, file 25-5-5-CDA-5.

42 The United States agreed to this provision in exchange for Canadian support for the straits regime, which Washington considered crucial for guaranteeing transit passage through international straits around the world. For more, see Lajeunesse, *Lock, Stock, and Icebergs*, 208–12.

43 Memorandum for ministers, "Status of the Canadian Archipelagic Waters," 5 October 1979, LAC, RG 12, vol. 5561, file 8100-15-4-2, pt 3.

44 Harriet Critchley, "Polar Deployment of Soviet Submarines," *International Journal* 34 (Autumn 1984): 842; John Honderich, *Arctic Imperative: Is Canada Losing the North?* (Toronto: University of Toronto Press, 1987), 92.

45 For a full account see Lajeunesse, *Lock, Stock, and Icebergs*, ch. 10.

46 Ibid.

47 PJBD Recommendation 52/1, NARA, RG 59, General Records of the Department of State, PJBD, subject file 1940–59, box 6.

48 The *Polar Sea*'s voyage was operational in nature and in no way designed to challenge Canadian sovereignty. Before it became a political issue, the Canadian Coast Guard had concurred in its transit and agreed that it would be made without prejudice to either state's legal position. For the most detailed history, see Rob Huebert, "Steel, Ice, and Decision-Making: The Voyage of the Polar Sea and Its Aftermath: The Making of Canadian Northern Foreign Policy," unpublished PhD diss., Dalhousie University, 1993.

49 See Lajeunesse, *Lock, Stock, and Icebergs*, ch. 11.

50 For details see ibid., 272–5

51 United Nations, *Convention on the Law of the Sea*, Pt XIII, Section 3, Article 245.

52 David Colson, qtd in Christopher Kirkey, "Smoothing Troubled Waters: The 1988 Canada–United States Arctic Co-operation Agreement," *International Journal* 50, no. 2 (Spring 1995), 415.

3 Arctic Security and Sovereignty through a Media Lens: From a Pile of Frozen Rocks to the Bottom of the Sea

MATHIEU LANDRIAULT

The concepts of sovereignty and security may be conceptualized differently; one focuses on physical security and the assertion of sovereignty through military presence and human occupation, the other on economic development and environmental stewardship. In the circumpolar region, various political, social, and economic actors can also construct these two central concepts differently. So far, most scholarly attention has been devoted to how national governments have represented this region, focusing on sovereignty assertion policies and operations. In addition, a welcome effort has been made recently to dissect how non-governmental actors perceive Arctic security and sovereignty. For example, many experts have furthered our understanding of Inuit perspectives,[1] and those of non-governmental organizations such as Greenpeace and the World Wildlife Fund, with regard to these two concepts.[2] This chapter furthers this scholarly enterprise by exploring how another key non-governmental actor, the media, have popularized certain understandings and images of Arctic sovereignty and security.

Canadian newspapers have always played an important role at key times in building social pressure to compel the federal government to defend the Canadian Arctic; this brings to mind, in particular, the 1969 *Manhattan* transit and the 1985 *Polar Sea* incident (see Lajeunesse, chapter 2). More recently, Whitney Lackenbauer blamed "muckraking academics and journalists" for popularizing an "outdated rhetoric and thinking" rooted in alarmism about a soon-to-be polar race of competing state interests.[3] The alarmist discourse on Arctic sovereignty that dominates in the Canadian media seems plausible at first glance. However, this assertion needs to be supported by empirical evidence, which this chapter provides.

More specifically, this chapter focuses on opinion texts published in Canadian newspapers. I view the opinion pages of Canadian newspapers as a forum where a great diversity of experts have a voice. On those pages, academics, ex-bureaucrats, and NGO leaders, as well as editorial writers (who do not sign their work), share views and issue recommendations in specific policy domains. These opinion texts all have an interpolative function, meaning they try to compel readers or governments to act.[4] Furthermore, by acting as knowledgeable authorities on these matters, authors of opinion texts are participating in the construction of popular understandings of issues and locations about which the vast majority of citizens have limited knowledge. By defining the intentions of foreign actors and interpreting specific incidents, opinion-page contributors are instrumental in defining threats and laying out solutions to them. The importance of such a role is heightened in times of crisis, when complexity is typically reduced and simplifications are many.[5]

This chapter examines editorial-page reactions to three Arctic security and sovereignty crises. All three were unforeseen, involved Canadian Arctic sovereignty directly or indirectly, and generated considerable media attention. All three unfolded between July 2005 and August 2007. Two databases were utilized to gather opinion texts. Sixteen anglophone newspapers were reviewed using the Canadian major dailies database, and nine newspapers (five francophone and four anglophone) were studied through the Eureka database.[6]

A First Crisis: Hans Island

The first crisis involved Canada and Denmark. The two countries signed a delimitation treaty in 1973, establishing a dividing line between Greenland and Canada's Arctic Archipelago. However, ownership of Hans Island, a tiny island in the middle of the Nares Strait, was not allocated.[7] Both countries would visit the island in subsequent years.[8] Denmark conducted military reconnaissance of the island in 2002, 2003, and 2004, raising concerns in the Canadian press and among some Arctic scholars. The most vocal of these commentators, Rob Huebert (see chapter 4), called the Danish expeditionaries "modern day 'Vikings,'" stressing that their visits "highlight[ed] the problem of Canada's ability to know and defend its interests in the north."[9] The *National Post* was the most active newspaper on this issue, providing extensive coverage in March and April 2004 and referring to Denmark as a "petite, aggressive European nation." Political pressure was exerted by the opposition parties, with Stockwell Day, the then Conservative Party's foreign affairs critic, leading the charge by labelling the event a challenge to Canadian sovereignty.[10]

Table 3.1. Distribution of Opinion Texts by Date and Identity of Authors from 26 July to 22 September 2005

Date	Number of Texts	Identity of Authors
26 July	1 text	1 in-house contributor
27 July	1 text	1 in-house contributor
28 July	5 texts	5 in-house contributors
29 July	1 text	1 in-house contributor
30 July	2 texts	2 in-house contributors
31 July	3 texts	3 in-house contributors
1 August	2 texts	1 in-house contributor, 1 guest editorial
2 August	2 texts	1 in-house contributor, 1 guest editorial
3 August	3 texts	3 in-house contributors
7 August	1 text	1 in-house contributor
8 August	1 text	1 in-house contributor
16 August	1 text	1 in-house contributor
19 August	1 text	1 guest editorial
21 August	1 text	1 in-house contributor
21 September	1 text	1 in-house contributor
22 September	1 text	1 in-house contributor

Note: In-house contributors are considered to be either editorials (unsigned and written by a member of the editorial team in anglophone newspapers, signed by an editorialist in francophone publications) or columns.

The actual crisis over Hans Island unfolded in the summer of 2005. On 13 July, Canadian soldiers landed on the island to plant the Canadian flag and erect an *inukshuk*. Canada's Minister of National Defence, Bill Graham, made a helicopter visit a week later, on 20 July. The Danish frigate HDMS *Tulugaq* responded by departing from Greenland, reaching Hans Island on 4 August 2005; however, its crew did not disembark there. On 9 August 2005, both parties agreed to negotiations at the UN with the goal of peacefully resolving the issue. At the time, the International Court of Justice was still viewed as dispute resolution mechanism.[11] On 19 December 2005, the two countries agreed to suspend further actions concerning Hans Island in order to focus on negotiations.

This crisis generated significant media coverage; twenty-three opinion pieces (editorials, columns, and guest editorials) were published between 20 July and 22 September. As Table 3.1 indicates, media attention was concentrated in the ten days following Canada's patrol. In-house contributors focusing on Hans Island, especially editorials written by editorial teams, helped turn the event into a crisis.

Regarding content, these documents were permeated with terms minimizing the importance of both Hans Island and Graham's actions. A comparison of the written editorials indicates that all of their arguments were structured similarly. Indeed, in thirteen of these texts, Hans Island was described variously as "a pile of frozen rocks,"[12] as "a lonesome dot of land in the high, high, high Arctic,"[13] or as one of the closest things to Hell on Earth.[14] In like manner, ten editorials attempted to minimize Graham's visit, saying for example that his "little stroll on Hans Island ... sounds more like a scene from a Gilbert and Sullivan operetta than a serious attempt at sabre-rattling."[15] Others used more colourful metaphors to describe the conflict, comparing it to "two bald men fighting over a comb,"[16] or describing the quarrel as "being a case of two mice that roar at each other."[17] Only one editorial noted how "Graham's decision to use a helicopter to set foot on this disputed territory carried personal as well as diplomatic risks."[18]

The general approach was, first and foremost, to label the visit as one of little consequence. As described in one editorial, of "all the issues the federal government finds in its overcrowded inbox, the fate of Hans Island must rank near the bottom."[19] However, the importance of this issue was greatly emphasized in many other texts. Denmark was not portrayed as a threat in itself; it was, rather, the strategic nature of Hans Island that was framed as a sign of upcoming global changes.

Although Hans Island has little to do with these dynamics, ten editorials cited the impact of global warming on the Arctic as the main reason for the emergence of this crisis and for the growing interest in this region. As Bernard Descôteaux wrote, "the warming of the Arctic gave a brand new geopolitical dimension to a dispute that did not require immediate resolve, and this until we were hit with the realisation that the Arctic lands could potentially revert to their lush green origins, just as we are reminded with the word 'Greenland.'"[20] This phenomenon would consequently impart more importance to Hans Island, owing to its proximity to natural waterways: "nobody has cared very much before, but now that global warming is making northern water passages, mining and oil-drilling more feasible, other countries are eyeing that territory."[21]

According to these accounts, global warming had triggered a race for natural resources and an increase in maritime traffic in the region. Indeed, the race for natural resources was mentioned in eleven of the editorials, and the increase in maritime traffic in ten. The *National Post* noted that "this country must start taking its northern land claims seriously: Valuable mineral deposits are being discovered in the area."[22] *The Gazette* followed suit: "now ... with global warming threatening to make

Arctic shipping and resource development ever more feasible, both countries are rethinking their positions."[23]

Interestingly, the very description of the threats looming over Canada in relation to Hans Island led us to worry about countries other than Denmark. For example, an editorial in *The Gazette* stated that "the stakes at Hans Island are low and a settlement should prove possible. But across the whole Arctic, the stakes might prove to be much higher."[24] As such, some opinion texts identified many countries as threats to the Canadian Arctic sovereignty: "It is widely understood that American, Russian, British and perhaps even North Korean submarines frequently sail into those waters unnoticed."[25] The intent attributed to the Canadian government followed a similar path: "Ottawa's move might not have been intended as a provocation to Copenhagen, but rather as a warning to all other capitals that Canada is at home in the Arctic."[26] Clearly, Denmark was not the principal concern here. Following this logic, inaction or being too soft would result in a powerful message to the rest of the world that Canada would not stand up for its Arctic.

The dominant opinion stance was one that considered the Hans Island conflict with Denmark as a test of Canada's Arctic capabilities, focusing on the importance of the message that it would likely send to the other Arctic countries, namely the United States. The menace clearly established itself as a potential loss of prestige, or even as setting a dangerous precedent toward our neighbours to the south.

Hence, the issue of international prestige was raised in different editorials, linking Arctic action (or inaction) to the Canadian mission in Afghanistan. The editorial team at the *Sudbury Star* expressed: "[T]his is the kind of mission [Afghanistan] that buys international respect … International respect will be harder still to pursue if Canada proves unable to assert sovereignty over its own territory."[27] The final query to Raymond Giroux's editorial demonstrated this anxiety surrounding prestige and international respect, especially from Washington: "[I]f Canada is unable to deal with Denmark, how will it manage to work with George W. Bush's friends?"[28] A similar point was made in an opinion piece by Steven Edwards published in the *National Post* linking Hans Island to concerns over the Northwest Passage and the Beaufort Sea maritime boundary between Canada and the United States: "Canada must reject Denmark's claims if it is to have any leverage against the United States … Canada could lower its chances of owning the debate by opening discussions on offers and debating – rather than asserting – its sovereign rights."[29] From this perspective, Hans Island may have constituted "a test case on sovereignty claims along the Northwest Passage."[30]

The Hans Island crisis was about sending a direct message to Denmark and an indirect one to the United States. A similar narrative envelops the argument of many different editorials: the domino theory. In this scenario, the loss of a portion of the Arctic would foreshadow the loss of even larger parcels of land on Arctic territories where Canadian sovereignty was already well established. Here, the *National Post* stated the following: "absent such clear signals as this, Canada risks seeing its broader nordic jurisdiction eroded – not just by Denmark, but also by the United States."[31] The editorial added that there was also "the humiliation Canadians would feel if we were forced to seek the permission of foreign powers to use sea lanes that once belonged to us."[32] This discourse was seconded in an editorial in the *Ottawa Citizen*: "today, it may just be the Danes on Hans Island, but next week, it could be Mackenzie King Island flying the Stars and Stripes."[33] The *Citizen* spoke of the geographical carving up that Canadians might have to witness, powerless, given the limited amount of resources invested in the territory.

This observation led not so much to blaming Denmark for Danish claims over the island, but to blaming Canada's lack of a coherent and durable Arctic policy. As such, out of the twenty-one editorials studied, seventeen voiced the request that the Canadian government implement more concrete measures and initiatives to better assert Canadian Arctic sovereignty. Recommendations for a more sustained investment in the Arctic steered in a precise direction: a reinvestment in the military was mentioned in half the editorials studied (11), while four authors raised the use of radar, satellites, or unmanned aerial vehicles (UAVs). These fields were most commonly referred to in the context of this claim for Arctic activism. Scientific and social issues (well-being of northern populations, economy, health) were raised twice and once, respectively.

A Second Crisis: USS *Charlotte*

A second crisis episode arose a few months after the Hans Island incident. The US submarine USS *Charlotte* passed through Arctic waters in November 2005. The trip lasted nearly a month, with the boat journeying through the Bering Strait before cruising in Arctic waters. The submarine made it to the North Pole on 10 November before heading south to the east coast of the United States. The vessel did not have to surface at any point during the trip, for it is nuclear-powered.[34] In fact, it only surfaced once, at the North Pole, crashing through sixty-one inches of ice in the process. The precise itinerary followed by the *Charlotte* is not clear, but the shortest route to the North Pole would have involved navigating in the vicinity of Canadian territorial waters near Ellesmere Island in the Nares Strait.[35] The submarine would then have headed southeast, crossing the Davis Strait to reach the coast of the United States a few days later. Suspicions were that the *Charlotte* had entered Canadian waters on its way from the North Pole to the American East Coast.

Table 3.2. Distribution of Opinion Texts by Date and Identity of Authors from 21 December 2005 to 22 February 2006

Date	Number of Texts	Identity of Authors
21 December	1 text	1 guest editorial
22 December	1 text	1 guest editorial
23 December	1 text	1 in-house contributor
24 December	1 text	1 guest editorial
28 December	1 text	1 in-house contributor
30 December	1 text	1 in-house contributor
5 January	1 text	1 in-house contributor
7 January	1 text	1 guest editorial
11 January	1 text	1 guest editorial
24 January	1 text	1 guest editorial
28 January	8 texts	8 in-house contributors
29 January	1 text	1 in-house contributor
30 January	2 texts	2 in-house contributors
2 February	1 text	1 in-house contributor
11 February	1 text	1 guest editorial
22 February	1 text	1 guest editorial

The *National Post* made public news of this transit on 19 December 2005, that paper having obtained information as well as still frames from a video taken by the American submarine, showing its sailors emerging from the vessel to stroll on the ice at the North Pole. This event instantaneously became an issue in the Canadian federal election campaign that had begun on 29 November (the election would be held on 23 January 2006). This crisis differed from the one over Hans Island. It was not sparked by a move on Canada's part, nor did it require an immediate response to a move by the United States; the *Charlotte* had returned a few weeks before the news of its activities was made public. Furthermore, submarine passages are not assertions of sovereignty, nor are they considered "traffic" in international law. Thus, very few consequences for Canadian sovereignty can be drawn from such an incident.

The number of opinions published during and after this event was similar to what we found for the Hans Island crisis. However, the event unfolded in two phases (see Table 3.2). Revelations were first made public in the *National Post* on 19 December 2005. This was followed by a verbal exchange between newly elected prime minister Stephen Harper and the US Ambassador to Canada on 25 January 2006, which reignited the incident. In total, twenty-four opinion texts were gathered from between 19 December 2005 and 26 February 2005 from the newspapers examined (see Table 3.2).

The immediate responses to the news of the *Charlotte*'s passage were, in retrospect, quite scant. During the electoral campaign, academics already cognizant of the issue were among the first to comment. Michael Byers was interviewed for an article in the *National Post* that revealed the American submarine's passage. He sounded the alarm bell by stating that the voyage could threaten Canadian claims over hundreds of thousands of square kilometres of the North, including the Northwest Passage: "This is very important – it's crucial ... Any unauthorized passage could have a serious effect on our claim."[36] He added that hydrocarbon resources might be lost to Canada if foreign ships were allowed in Canadian waters without government consent. In response to Byers, Rob Huebert took a somewhat different view, expressing doubts about the importance of the *Charlotte*'s voyage and suggesting that it did not constitute a threat to Canadian Arctic sovereignty.[37]

Overall, the passage of the *Charlotte* served as a reminder that Canada needed to increase its presence in the Arctic and improve its surveillance and control capacities there. The issue was not addressed *per se*, but rather was used to detail a body of threats currently looming over the Arctic and to underscore the importance of this region for Canadians. In terms of the former, authors attempted to list a comprehensive inventory of threats to the Arctic, paying little attention to the passage of foreign submarines and downgrading that issue to one of lesser importance. In this way, the American threat was raised, but it was framed in the context of the Canada–US dispute over the Northwest Passage. The American challenge to Canada's ownership of it was deemed a significant threat in seven of the twenty-six texts studied.

Nevertheless, the discussion of Arctic security in the articles surveyed for this chapter extended far beyond the threat that the Americans posed to encompass non-state threats and hypothetical scenarios as well. These included terrorist attacks (5 mentions), oil spills and other environmental disasters (10), and the possible loss of ownership of the Arctic's natural resources (6). To these, Byers added that "a cruise ship in distress would require an expensive and possibly dangerous rescue mission. An international shipping route along Canada's third coast could also facilitate the entry of drugs, guns, illegal immigrants and perhaps even terrorists, as well as providing an alternative route for illicit shipments of weapons of mass destruction or missile components, vessels in distress, arrivals of illegal immigrants, drug trafficking, as well as weapons of mass destruction."[38]

Yet the fears ignited by the Hans Island crisis were not reignited by the controversy over the *Charlotte*. Many opinion texts from a few months earlier had expressed a core idea that Canada should send other nations a strong signal in relation to Hans Island, because any timidity toward the Danes could weaken Canada's position in regard to its other claims over the Arctic and could give the impression that Canada had no interest in defending its Arctic. Yet none of the authors who wrote about the *Charlotte* crisis even suggested that the American incursion had been spurred by a timid Canadian reaction to the Hans Island dispute.

Twenty-two of the twenty-four opinion pieces on the Arctic were published after 22 December, the day the Conservative Party's campaign promised new military investments in the Arctic, including three armed icebreakers, an underwater detection system, and a deepwater docking facility. These texts focused on the American incursion as well as on the merits (or lack thereof) of the Conservatives' pledges concerning Arctic sovereignty.

The comments made after the Conservatives' announcement were largely positive, with only two texts deeming the plan dangerous and ill-informed. Eleven articles offered an opinion on the Conservative agenda; eight of them viewed its proposals as steps in the right direction. These authors noted that "Harper's campaign promise, costly though it would be to fulfill, at least serves to remind us that we have an issue up north, one which demands attention."[39] The mere mention here of the Arctic as a territory of importance is worthy of note: "[Harper] has done us a service in raising the need for a proactive policy on our Arctic archipelago."[40] Favourable opinions were the norm, even when questions were raised about the costs of keeping these promises. Even if they amounted to more than $1 billion, Saskatoon's *StarPhoenix* wrote, "the Conservative leader is on the right track about asserting Canadian sovereignty over our northern land mass and Arctic Ocean approaches."[41] The *Globe and Mail* opined that "[the Conservative platform] is a tall and highly expensive order, one that may have to take second place to other priorities. But Mr. Harper has drawn a commendable line."[42] Other texts described the Conservatives' plan as "a reasonable step,"[43] and "the most determined approach" since the 1950s as far as the Arctic was concerned.[44]

A Third Crisis: To the Bottom of the Sea

In late July and early August 2007, an expedition led by Russian nationals dropped a Russian flag on the ocean floor at the North Pole. This expedition included an icebreaker as well as a research vessel, the latter having departed from Murmansk in late July 2007. On 1 August, two mini-submarines reached the seabed below the North Pole at a depth of 4300 metres.

Table 3.3. Distribution of Opinion Texts by Date and Identity of Authors from 28 July 2007 to 22 September 2007

Date	Number of Texts	Identity of Authors
28 July	2 texts	2 in-house contributors
29 July	1 text	1 guest editorial
30 July	1 text	1 in-house contributor
3 August	2 texts	2 in-house contributors
4 August	2 texts	2 in-house contributors
5 August	1 text	1 guest editorial
6 August	3 texts	3 in-house contributors
7 August	3 texts	3 in-house contributors
8 August	3 texts	2 in-house contributors, 1 guest editorial
9 August	2 texts	1 in-house contributor, 1 guest editorial
10 August	4 texts	1 in-house contributor, 3 guest editorials
11 August	1 text	1 guest editorial
12 August	4 texts	4 in-house contributors
13 August	1 text	1 in-house contributor
14 August	3 texts	3 in-house contributors
16 August	1 text	1 in-house contributor
20 August	1 text	1 guest editorial
21 August	2 texts	1 in-house contributor, 1 guest editorial
25 August	1 text	1 in-house contributor
22 September	1 text	1 guest editorial

This expedition, led by Arthur Chilingarov, a member of the Duma (the Lower House of the Russian legislature), was carried out as part of a research mission aimed at validating Russian sovereignty claims over the continental shelf. Chilingarov had secured a mix of public and private financing in order to carry out the expedition.[45] Russian scientists aimed to collect sediments from the seabed in order to prove that the continental shelf under the Arctic Ocean was the natural extension of the Eurasian landmass.

It was this crisis that drew by far the most media attention. A total of thirty-nine opinion pieces were printed between 28 July 2007 and 22 September 2007 in the major dailies studied. In contrast to the second crisis, this one received steady media coverage throughout the period (see Table 3.3). In fact, both left-leaning (*Toronto Star*) and right-leaning (*National Post*) newspapers had published editorials about this issue even before the actual incident unfolded. Also, more experts also expressed opinions about this crisis that about the two previous ones.

In most of these texts, descriptions of the Russian mission to the North Pole were coloured by a few recurring themes. In close to 36 per cent, the Russian action was described as a media stunt, as mere symbolism, in hopes of minimizing the achievement. As the *Globe and Mail* wrote, the "claims on the North Pole [were] more an act of theatre than of science or sovereignty."[46] Similarly, *Le Devoir* stated that it was "true that the gesture is symbolic and that it has no decisive legal ground/carries no decisive legal weight."[47] Also, the Russian mission was mostly framed as a spectacle for a nationalist audience: "The Russian expedition was a show put on primarily for the folks back home ... a symbol of national pride in the achievement of a significant feat."[48] Though the Russian actions were defined as largely symbolic and of minimal scientific importance, commentaries deemed the consequences to be tremendous. They generally described the Russian mission as having unleashed irresistible forces upon the Arctic region. They set out two basic global dynamics: a race for the Arctic, and the Arctic as a battleground.

The first prevailing idea was that the Russian actions had been part of a race between states for control or ownership of a part of the Arctic and, in particular, its natural resources. Russia, according to many authors, had just launched a scramble for Arctic territory – to be more precise, for the natural resources there (and not just for seabed mineral resources). In this context, the placing of the flag had sounded "a warning note to Canada and others that Russia plans to be at the forefront of the race for the enormous deposits of minerals that could lie under the ocean, as well as for rights to shipping lanes and fishing rights."[49] Historical analogies were offered so as to compare this new "scramble" to similar events in the past. Hence, some compared it to the colonial scramble for Africa that had unfolded in the late nineteenth century. The *Gazette* declared that "the scramble is on again, only this time it's for the oil, minerals and fish of the newly melting Arctic Ocean, not the minerals and other wealth of 19th-century Africa."[50] Victoria's *Times Colonist* offered the same idea: "these days, oil, gas and mineral claims are even more important, so that national ownership of an adjoining sea bed can confer extraordinary wealth. We have something like the old colonial scramble for Africa."[51] Another academic author, in an attempt to link the growing interest in the Arctic to the colonization of the American continent beginning in the fifteenth century, claimed that a "new race to explore, conquer and acquire another 'new world' is on."[52]

This concept of a "race" then latched itself to the second dominant concept, which was broached multiple times: the Arctic as a battleground. The first imagery of a battle for the Arctic was published on 8 August, less than a week after the Russians dropped their flag. It was subsequently mentioned in more than one third of all opinion texts published after that date. On 8 August, law professor Eric Posner dubbed the Arctic "a new battleground at the top of the world."[53] Mario Roy of *La Presse* pushed the concept further still by assigning responsibility for this battle to one party: "we obviously have recognized the elements involved in what we could call the Arctic battle, initiated in a spectacle-like manner by the Russians."[54]

The concept of a "struggle," present or future, was closely linked to that of a battle. For example, *The Province* wrote of a process that was already in motion, of a "struggle for control of one of earth's final frontiers."[55] Historical benchmarks were weaved into this "struggle for the Arctic," with some authors mobilizing terms such as "a new, truly cold war"[56] and "a new Great Game."[57] These concepts reintroduced the geopolitical realities of an earlier time. Furthermore, that the Arctic would be partitioned among the major powers was deemed inevitable: "at some point, Russia, the U.S. and other countries will carve up the Arctic into mutually exclusive economic zones."[58] Additionally, commentators suggested that Canadians should "prepare themselves for a hard, lengthy struggle with Russia over the Arctic in years to come."[59] In an even more pessimistic tone, the *Calgary Herald* predicted that the Russian mission would "suspend the peace dividend until further notice. And Canada, along with the rest of NATO, will embark on a costly rediscovery of their alliance's original purpose."[60]

According to others, there was no ongoing battle or struggle yet – though it would come. Political scientists Stéphane Roussel and Samantha Arnold asserted that while there was no actual battle at present, signals of an upcoming one were blinking. In their assessment, various elements were feeding a logic of conflict among the main governments of the region – even if, for the time being, the exploitation of Arctic resources, as well as newly emerging threats, remained in the realm of theory rather than reality.[61] Similarly, the *Times Colonist* spoke of a battle over the northern territory that might be "about to turn into a free-for-all."[62]

Having identified these two dominant ideas – a scramble for the Arctic, and the Arctic as a battleground – it should come as no surprise that the overall description of the Russians was neither flattering nor positive. The Russian bear metaphor resurfaced often in Canadian media coverage, particularly after the North Pole flag drop. Some authors employed the Russian mission as a bridge to frame that country in a traditional role, one in which conflicts were integral to its behaviour on the world scene. Eric Posner claimed that "it [was] re-emerging as a global troublemaker,"[63] while others perceived a return to the Russian foreign policy of the tsars and Leonid Brezhnev, during which Russia attempted "to alter the balance of power in the Kremlin's favour by keeping the U.S. and its allies busy with small to medium-sized provocations around the world."[64]

Similarly, several editorials depicted Russia as a straightforward menace, an aggressor. "This Russian stunt was an act of purposeful aggression against our own national interest and the interests of all civilized nations," one reporter declared.[65] Another described Russia as a "rival"[66] attempting to make "aggressive territorial claims."[67] Media coverage insisted that Russia was displaying strong intransigence and a sense of entitlement, as well as pride in the notion that the Arctic had always been Russian.[68] The presumed elevation of the Russian threat in the Arctic concerned many commentators. Lorne Gunter in the *Edmonton Journal* used the term "troubling" to describe the situation, given that Canada possessed no means of countering this expansion of Russian sovereignty in the Arctic.[69] In this sense, many opinion pieces agreed with the principle raised by Prime Minister Harper that Canada had to use its sovereignty or (potentially) lose it. One journalist suggested that "possession of a territory translated into 8/10 of sovereignty rights in international law. Indeed, if one can't physically occupy a territory, they probably don't own it."[70]

However, a small minority of texts attempted to ease the fears and reduce the perceived importance of the Russian threat (8 of the 44 texts). These authors urged Canada to view Russia as a partner, considering it necessary to seek compromise without recourse to militarization.[71] This concept of a partnership cradled a vision in which the two countries would be able to create an inseparable bond and "command three-quarters of the northern latitudes of the Earth."[72] This minority of authors also underscored that the Russian flag drop had been quite normal and that Canada would have done the same if it had the capabily to do so.

Conclusion

This study does not assume that the ideas expressed in these opinion texts have been transferred whole into public policy or translated into real-life events: talking about potential conflicts does not *cause* conflicts. That would be a simplistic assessment of how ideas can influence perceptions of complex realities, especially considering that the opinions studied were expressed in the media. This study does contend that authors of opinion pieces in daily newspapers constitute an influential elite and can influence Canadians by spreading specific interpretations of what Arctic sovereignty and security mean and how both can be strengthened. As this chapter has demonstrated, most of these contributors pushed the interpretation that Canada faced an looming Arctic threat. They helped articulate these incidents as crises, thus injecting them into the Canadian political agenda. Indeed, political scientist Franklyn Griffiths called several of the scholars who published during these three crises as "academic purveyors of polar peril."[73]

Editorialists and columnists can also be viewed as purveyors of polar peril. They authored the great majority of opinion texts published on the Hans Island and *Charlotte* incidents. Right-wing publications, particularly newspapers owned by CanWest Global (such as the *National Post*, the *Ottawa Citizen*, and the *Gazette*), as well as the *Winnipeg Free Press*, were the most vocal participants in this coverage, helping to frame the events as crises. The three incidents discussed in this chapter had many similarities: they were all unexpected, they all squared Canada against a foreign government, and they all dealt with Arctic sovereignty and security issues. Most editorials expressed alarmist ideas about Canadian Arctic sovereignty and security. Support for a "use it or lose it" approach – a trademark of the Harper government's initial Arctic stance – can be detected after the Hans Island episode. The presentation of the Arctic as a unitary space that Canada could lose as a result of this modest dispute, through a domino effect spreading to the entire Arctic Archipelago, underscored the supposed urgency of the situation and compelled the Canadian government to act in defence of its Arctic sovereignty. Hence, the "use it or lose it" principle and alarmist assessments in general found societal support prior to their incorporation into partisan and governmental discourses.

Moreover, editorialists and external contributors (particularly scholars) overwhelmingly promoted a militaristic approach to addressing Arctic sovereignty issues. A reinvestment in military resources to stand up for Canadian Arctic sovereignty proved to be the dominant proposed solution in all three crises. The fact that very few voices (3 out of 13) questioned the Arctic plan detailed by the Conservative Party during the 2005–6 electoral campaign is striking, particularly in light of the vague pricing put forward by the CPC for the announced investments.

These crises were portrayed either as direct (the Russian flag) or indirect (Hans Island, USS *Charlotte*) challenges to Canadian sovereignty. The Russian flag crisis brought forward a different type of threat: Russia was viewed as a menace to be combated head-on, vigorously and without compromise (unlike the United States). This last crisis provides a striking example of threat inflation, a disproportionate reaction. First, no party, including Russia, purported that flag-dropping was a legitimate way to assert sovereign rights to a specific territory. Second, if the incident sparked a race, it was more akin to a marathon than a 100-metre dash. The Arctic battle image suffers from a similar overstatement, especially when compared to the nineteenth-century scramble for Africa. The long and onerous legal process for demarcating continental shelf claims through a UN commission orients state behaviours toward orderly, rule-based mechanisms.

Dire assessments about an imminent scramble and struggle for Arctic resources have proven to be wild exaggerations. Even the rise of the Russian threat in the Arctic region seems blown out of proportion, given that Russian aggression in Ukraine and Syria has not significantly eroded positive circumpolar relations.[74] Accordingly, this study of opinion texts serves as a cautionary tale on how *not* to react to sovereignty crises. Alarmist commentators with elite access to popular media outlets should refrain from oversimplifying small incidents and hypothetical developments as international crises.

NOTES

1   Frances Abele and Thierry Rodon, "Inuit Diplomacy in the Global Era: The Strengths of Multilateral Internationalism," *Canadian Foreign Policy Journal* 13, no. 3 (2007): 45–63; Jessica Shadian, *Rethinking Westphalian Sovereignty: The Inuit Circumpolar Council and the Future of Arctic Governance*, Walter and Duncan Foundation, Working Papers on Arctic Security no. 8 (2013).

2   Timo Koivurova, "Alternatives for an Arctic Treaty – Evaluation and a New Proposal," *Review of European Community and International Environmental Law* 17, no. 1 (2008): 14–26; Carina Keskitalo, "International Region-Building – Development of the Arctic as an International Region," *Cooperation and Conflict* 42, no. 2 (2007): 187–205.

3   P. Whitney Lackenbauer, *From Polar Race to Polar Saga: An Integrated Strategy for Canada and the Circumpolar World*, Foreign Policy for Canada's Tomorrow No. 3 (Toronto: Canadian International Council, 2009), 1.

4   Sean Hier and Joshua Greenberg, "Constructing a Discursive Crisis: Risk, Problematization, and Illegal Chinese in Canada," *Ethnic and Racial Studies* 25, no. 3 (2002): 490–513.

5   Peter Suedfeld, "Bilateral Relations between Countries and the Complexity of Newspapers Editorials," *Political Psychology* 13, no. 4 (1992): 601–11.

6   For the first category, the newspapers are the *Calgary Herald, Edmonton Journal, The Gazette, The Globe and Mail, Kingston Whig-Standard, Regina Leader Post, National Post, The Ottawa Citizen, The Province, Saskatoon StarPhoenix, Sudbury Star, Times-Colonist, Toronto Star, The Vancouver Sun, The Windsor Star, Winnipeg Free Press.* For the second category, the titles are *L'Acadie Nouvelle, Le Droit, La Presse, Le Soleil, Le Devoir, The Guardian, The Daily News, The Telegraph-Journal,* and *The Telegram.*

7 Christopher Stevenson, "Hans Off! The Struggle for Hans Island and the Potential Ramifications for International Border Dispute Resolution," *Boston College International and Comparative Law Review* 30, no. 1 (2007): 266.

8 For the comprehensive list, see Stevenson, "Hans Off!"

9 Rob Huebert, "Return of the Vikings," *The Globe and Mail,* 28 December 2002, A17.

10 Adrien Humphreys, "Danes Summon Envoy over Arctic Fight," *National Post,* 30 March 2004, A1.

11 Stevenson, "Hans Off!"

12 Bernard Descôteaux, "Les Canadiens débarquent," *Le Devoir,* 1 August 2005, A6.

13 "Carolyn Parrish's Behaviour Beastly," [Editorial] *Edmonton Journal,* 25 July 2005), A14.

14 Benoît Beauchamp, "Why We Always Pick on the Little Guy," *Calgary Herald,* 2 August 2005, A6.

15 "Graham's Hans-on Diplomacy," [Editorial], Montreal *Gazette,* 27 July 2005, A18.

16 William Neville, "Blair's Track Record Hurting Him," *Winnipeg Free Press,* 29 July 2005, A11. Print.

17 "Arctic Tussle" [Editorial], *Winnipeg Free Press,* 22 September, 2005, A13.

18 "Graham Earns Hans Down Win with Move" [Editorial], *Saskatoon Star-Phoenix,* 28 July 2005, A12.

19 "Intrigue in the High Arctic" [Editorial], *Sudbury Star,* 2 August 2005, A10.

20 Descôteaux, "Les Canadiens débarquent," A6.

21 "Hans Off Our Island!" [Editorial], *Ottawa Citizen,* 26 July 2005, A10.

22 "Graham's Small Steps for Sovereignty" [Editorial], *National Post,* 28 July 2005, A16.

23 "Graham's Hans-on Diplomacy," A18.

24 "Graham's Hans-on Diplomacy," A18.

25 "Intrigue in the High Arctic,"A10.

26 Descôteaux, "Les Canadiens débarquent," A6.

27 "Intrigue in the High Arctic,"A10.

28 Raymond Giroux, "Le retour des Vikings," *Le Soleil,* 3 August 2005, A13.

29 Steven Edwards, "How to Win Islands and Influence Superpowers," *National Post,* 21 September2005, A12.

30 Henry Srebrnik, "A Backgrounder on Canada and Hans Island: Is It Worth Fighting For?," *The Guardian,* 19 August 2005, A7.

31 "Graham's Small Steps."

32 "Graham's Small Steps."

33 "Hans Off."

34 "Nuclear-Powered Sub Can Remain Submerged Indefinitely," *National Post,* 19 December 2005, A10.

35 Chris Wattie, "U.S. Sub May Have Toured Canadian Arctic Zone," *National Post,* 19 December 2005, A1.

36 Wattie, "U.S. Sub."

37 Rob Huebert, "U.S. Subs Do Not Threaten Our Sovereignty," *National Post*, 21 December 2005, A16.

38 Michael Byers, "Ottawa Must Act Quickly to Assert Sovereignty in Arctic," *Winnipeg Free Press*, 7 January 2006, A15.

39 "Harper Looks North, Not South" [Editorial], *The Gazette*, 28 January 2006, A30.

40 David Watts, "Rediscovering the Northwest Passage," *Edmonton Journal*, 11 January 2006, A19.

41 "Arctic Platform a Positive Sign" [Editorial], *Saskatoon StarPhoenix*, 30 December 2005, A10.

42 "Harper Speaks Up for Canada's Arctic" [Editorial], *Globe and Mail*, 28 January 2006, A22.

43 "Talking Sense on Defence" [Editorial], *The Gazette*, 28 December 2005, A28.

44 "Harper Is Right to Defend Canada's Claim in the Arctic" [Editorial], *The Province*, 29 January 2006, A20.

45 C.J. Chivers, "Eyeing Future Wealth, Russian Plant Flag on the Arctic Seabed, below the Ice Cap," *New York Times*, 3 August 2007, A8.

46 "Pushing ahead on the Arctic Seabed" [Editorial], *Globe and Mail*, 3 August 2007, A14.

47 Guy Taillefer, "L'or noir du Pôle nord" [Editorial], *Le Devoir*, 6 August 2007, A6.

48 "Merely Claiming the Arctic Isn't Enough to Further Canada's Stake" [Editorial], *Vancouver Sun*, 8 August 2007, A10.

49 "Enough Symbols: Time to Deal on Arctic" [Editorial], *The Gazette*, 6 August 2007, A14.

50 "Enough Symbols."

51 David Warren, "An act of Aggression against Canada: Russia's Reckless Pursuit of Northern Resources Must Be Countered Quickly" [Editorial], *Times-Colonist*, 8 August 2007, A12.

52 Robert Miller, "Finders Keepers in the Arctic?" [Editorial], *Regina Leader-Post*, 9 August 2007, B10.

53 Eric Posner, "Cold-Weather Allies: A U.S. Scholar Argues that Ottawa and Washington Must Co-operate to Thwart Russia's Arctic Ambitions," *National Post*, 8 August 2007, A15.

54 Mario Roy, "La bataille de l'Arctique," *La Presse*, 10 August 2007, A15.

55 "Canada Must Do All It Can to Play Catch-up in Warming Arctic" [Editorial], *The Province*, 12 August 2007), A20.

56 Pierre Bergeron, "Ne pas perdre le Nord," *Le Droit*, 13 August 2007, 12.

57 "U.S. Lagging in Race to North Pole" [Editorial], *Toronto Star*, 25 August 2007, A6.

58 Posner, "Cold-Weather Allies."

59 John McCannon, "Russia's Drive for the Arctic: A Heartfelt Conviction That It Alone Is the Arctic's True Master Lies at the Heart of Modern Russia's National Identity," *Ottawa Citizen*, 10 August 2007, A13.

60 "Russian Bear on the March: Kremlin Keeping U.S., Allies Busy with Run of Provocations" [Editorial], *Calgary Herald*, 12 August 2007, A12.

61 Stéphane Roussel and Samantha Arnold, "Veillée d'armes sur l'Arctique," *La Presse*, 16 August 2007, A19.

62 "Canada Must Push Arctic Claims: Sovereignty Battle over Northern Territory May Be about to Turn into a Free-for-All" [Editorial], *Times-Colonist*, 12 August 2007, D2.

63 Posner, "Cold-Weather Allies."

64 "Russian Bear on the March."

65 Warren, "An act of Aggression."

66 "Canada Must Do All."

67 "Canada's Arctic Stake."

68 McCannon, "Russia's Drive for the Arctic."

69 Lorne Gunter, "Russian Sovereignty Claim Troubling: Canada Must Assert Itself Aggressively and Quickly in the Arctic" [Editorial], *Edmonton Journal*, 3 August 2007, A16.

70 "The Russians Are Coming."

71 Émilien Pelletier, "Il faut démilitariser l'Arctique" [Editorial], *Le Devoir*, 10 August 2007, A9.

72 Christopher Westdal, "Don't Demonize Putin" [Editorial], *Globe and Mail*, 21 August 2007, A15.

73 Franklyn Griffiths, *Towards a Canadian Arctic Strategy: Foreign Policy for Canada's Tomorrow No. 1* (Toronto: Canadian International Council, 2009), 26.

74 Kari Roberts, "Why Russia Will Play by the Rules in the Arctic," *Canadian Foreign Policy Journal* 21, no. 2 (2015): 112–28.

4 Understanding Arctic Security: A Defence of Traditional Security Analysis

ROB HUEBERT

Any discussion of Arctic security inevitably leads to a discussion of what security *means*. Specifically to this chapter, what does it mean for the Arctic? How is it understood, and what does that understanding mean for the region? These seemingly straightforward questions have generated significant debate among Arctic analysts. At the heart of that debate is a divide between *traditional* or *military* security studies (also known as strategic studies) and *expanded* security studies, which encompass such categories as human security, environmental security, gendered security, and health security. At one level, this debate is about the best analytical means of understanding Arctic security in the current international system. However, there is another consideration that complicates the discussions about which of these approaches best explains the new Arctic security environment. For some commentators, the choice is not just about understanding the system; it is also about influencing the security environment itself. For these participants, it is not just about deliberating on the best theoretical approaches to apply; it is also about demonstrating that choosing a traditional/narrow understanding of security serves a political process of legitimizing the existing state system. This is then assumed to prevent a proper understanding of Arctic security, which in turn results in the marginalization of many of the voices of people who live in the Arctic. Thus, the issue becomes not only that a traditional/narrow understanding of Arctic security results in a faulty intellectual approach, but also that this very understanding is part of the problem.

Efforts to delegitimize a particular intellectual approach instead of attempting to show it is wrong or incapable of explaining the various factors that now shape the Arctic security environment threaten a robust debate. It may well be that an overly narrow understanding of security misses important elements of the new Arctic security environment. It is also possible that such an approach is inappropriate for understanding the current international system. In the practices of scholarly thought, however, it is generally accepted that the means of determining such evaluations can only come about as proponents of the various approaches debate and discuss their differing understandings of security and thereby determine the best means of proceeding. To dismiss one side of the discussion as mere *politics* is to delegitimize the efforts of those who use such an approach, thereby blocking them from even engaging in the overall debate.

There are two serious consequences here. First, efforts to delegitimize a specific approach can have a chilling effect within the newer academic community. Emerging scholars never want to think of themselves as being a source of the problem, which can happen when they employ a narrow understanding of Arctic security. The second issue pertains to the outcomes that emerge when a narrow understanding of Arctic security is employed. What if an approach should not have been ignored or excluded from the general debate? What if it could have provided insights and understandings regarding the current Arctic security environment? What if it is right on some issues? If it is not included or if it is delegitimized, could key elements of Arctic security be missed?

This chapter addresses two key questions: What is the case against using traditional security to understand the Arctic security environment? And what contribution could a traditional security framework make?

Traditional/Narrow Security

To answer these questions, it is necessary to establish what is meant by a traditional/narrow security framework. This terminology reflects the vigorous debate that developed within the field of strategic studies and security at the end of the Cold War. As Greaves and Lackenbauer discussed in their introduction to this book, with the end of military and political rivalry between the Soviet Union and NATO, led by the United States, many scholars began to question the various forms of realism that had long dominated the discussion of how international security was to be understood. The debate in the early 1990s between Stephen Walt and Edward Kolodziej brought out many key issues.[1] Debates developed over the utility of the realists' focus on the state (or, in the case of the neo-realists, the system) and their near total focus on military issues and hence military-based security. Into this debate entered other scholars such as Keith Krause and Michael Williams, who argued for a broadening and deepening of the concept of security.[2] There were significant calls to move beyond simply examining the state, as well as calls by many to focus on sub-state actors including (but not limited to) the individual. These authors also called for an expansion of the topic issues covered within studies of international security to address issues pertaining to human security, environmental security, and gendered security, to name a few, and not just military security.[3]

At the same time, the debates initiated by Anatol Rapoport and Philip Green during the Cold War were revisited.[4] These writers had criticized the writings of security scholars such as Herman Kahn and Henry Kissinger, who attempted to examine issues pertaining to nuclear war.[5] Kahn's and Kissinger's attempts to address the possibility of thermonuclear war in a rational way, notwithstanding that such a war might kill tens if not hundreds of millions of humans, were viewed by Green and Rapaport as increasing the possibility of such an event occurring and therefore as immoral. In the post–Cold War era, writers identified with critical security studies such as Martin Shaw and Wyn Jones picked up many of the arguments put forward by Green and Rapoport.[6]

The response of realists like Hedley Bull was that it was irresponsible *not* to examine what nuclear war would actually mean to humanity, because the development of these weapons systems was proceeding regardless.[7] In their view, it would be immoral *not* to consider all of the elements surrounding a possible nuclear war so that decision-makers could make the most rational decisions. This echoes the writings of Carl von Clausewitz, who had argued that war must be studied precisely because it *is* so terrible.[8] But the question remained – was the act of studying nuclear war in a realist framework an immoral act in itself? The vigorous discussion that continues to this day indicates that this debate has not been settled.[9]

The next question is, what are the main elements of the narrow or traditional security approach? There is a wide literature on this subject, and space limitations prevent a thorough consideration of all of the elements of the modern understanding of the term, but certain key elements can be identified. First, it remains rooted in the theoretical framework of realism. Many supporters of this approach point out that while realism remains the dominant approach to considering traditional security, it has modified some of its more dogmatic elements from the Cold War era. Traditional security still focuses on states' actions and efforts to maintain security through military power. However, as Lawrence Freedman puts it: "[T]here is room for a non-dogmatic realism that would acknowledge the significance of non-state actors, the impact of social, economic, cultural, and local political factors on state behaviour, the importance of values and mental constructs, and can be sensitive to the epistemological issues raised by presumptions of objectivity."[10] He goes on to say that the second element of the new thinking about traditional understandings of security continues to focus on armed forces. This includes the use of force to achieve state objectives for the defence of the state but also actions that can be seen as going beyond the state as means for "improving the human condition."[11]

Let us accept the basic review provided by Freedman as a sound basis for understanding current thinking. The following observations can now be made about traditional security studies. They still focus on the actions of states and their armed forces to achieve policy objectives. This means they focus on understanding the impact of military actions on the international system. However, other actors beyond the state are now accepted as important players in the overall security of the international system. There is a continuing assumption that actors within the system will often act in a negative manner that threatens the security of states. This suggests in somewhat reductionist terms that there is a continued acceptance of the darker elements of human nature. However, it is difficult to find many supporters of this approach who explicitly make this point.

Having briefly outlined the elements of what is meant by the term traditional security studies, it is now time to return to the two key questions of this chapter. First, what is the case against using traditional security to acquire an understanding the modern Arctic security environment? Second, what can the employment of a traditional security framework contribute?

Understanding the Issue

Over the past two decades, Arctic security has developed into one of the most important issues facing the international system. Previously, the Arctic had been seen as a pristine and peaceful part of the world that had somehow escaped the conflicts and competitions found everywhere else. Arctic "exceptionalism" developed as a means of understanding the cooperative behaviour of all the Arctic states as well as the many non-Arctic states that had begun to develop their own interests in that region at the end of the Cold War. Most leading Arctic analysts, such as Franklyn Griffiths,[12] Oran Young,[13] P. Whitney Lackenbauer,[14] Timo Koivurova,[15] Rolf Tamnes and Kristine Offerdal,[16] and Michael Byers,[17] have written extensively on the cooperative nature of the international Arctic security environment. In one manner or another all have argued that the Arctic is an exception to the normal pressures and demands of the larger international system. Factors such as its geographic isolation meant that the Arctic states were able to put aside their base self-interests and cooperate for the greater good of both their national interests and those of the entire Arctic region. By this sort of assessment, the Arctic is an example of how cooperation works. Thus, international bodies such as the Arctic Council have been able to focus their attention on the pursuit of scientific understanding, and on the empowerment of the northern Indigenous peoples, so that they can pursue shared policies toward sustainable development. The Arctic Council is the only international body that has given special standing to the northern Indigenous peoples. It has done so by devising the category of Permanent Participants and guaranteeing them seats at all negotiations. This seems to have further strengthened the argument that the Arctic is an exceptional region.[18] There is also a general acceptance among these authors that the Arctic states understand the lack of utility of using military force to achieve their objectives.

This perception that the Arctic is exceptional has caused many to ponder the meaning of international security there. Questions have re-emerged regarding whether traditional security is adequate or helpful in understanding today's Arctic. Building on the debates within strategic studies and security studies, many of these commentators and analysts have sought new understandings of what security means in terms of the Arctic. Some, such as Gunhild Hoogensen Gjørv,[19] Lassi Heininen,[20] and Wilfrid Greaves,[21] have attempted to expand the concept to include elements such as environmental and human security. Others point to the need to focus on cultural security, with a focus on the well-being of the northern Indigenous peoples.[22] Still others have argued for a gendered understanding of security.[23] Others suggest that there is a need to reconsider some of the epistemological assumptions that inform traditional understandings of international security and move away from its positivist elements to refocus on security as a largely social construct.[24] There is no question that all of these approaches and considerations are valid. In any field, the essence of a healthy debate is normally found in a proliferation of understandings of its key ontologies, epistemologies, and focuses. Understanding Arctic security is no different.

When proponents of an expanded definition of security engage those who propose that it is necessary to retain a field that addresses the issue of traditional security, there is a tendency to set up traditional security as a straw man that is then easily discarded. These authors have a strong tendency to resort to the writings of critics of traditional security. The common approach is to turn to the works of Buzan and colleagues, who have pioneered the development of securitization to provide an understanding of international security.[25] Seldom do we see used the writings of realists such as John Mearsheimer[26] and Colin Gray,[27] even though their works provide the theoretical foundations for current traditional security studies. Thus, the theoretical basis of narrow or traditional security tends to be presented through the lens of critiques of this approach. On the rare occasions when realists are cited, it is inevitably a precursory mention without any explanation of realist understandings of the concept.[28]

A more significant problem is the embedded normative assumptions that colour efforts to engage in debate. Echoing the arguments of Rapoport and Green, many proponents of an expanded understanding of Arctic security suggest that traditional understandings of security not only need to be challenged but also are part of blocking progress toward a more cooperative Arctic. Often, the analyst who utilizes a traditional security approach is said to be engaging in a scholarly *and* political act. As stated by Hoogensen Gjørv (see chapter 9), "when security analysts 'observe' acts of security or security moves, the analyst has immediately contributed to the politics of the process by recognizing (or not recognizing) an actor as a security actor and a securitizing move as being successful or not."[29] In other words, the focus of security analysts helps to shape the actual security environment that they are examining. By focusing on issues related to competition rather than cooperation, they are both validating and creating the conditions in which the core actors will act in a competitive manner.

The implication of this understanding of traditional security is clear. Not only do critiques of traditional security contend that this approach is too narrow and misses many key issues and actors, but the very act of taking such an approach is *morally* problematic, for it confirms the existing power structure that ultimately threatens the human security of the individuals within the Arctic system. Thus it is no mere academic debate between different understandings of Arctic security; it is also a debate in which traditional security analysts themselves become part of the "problem." This argument then goes on to suggest that an analytical framework that fails to include the core issues of human security or environmental security or any of the other expanded security approaches will lead to policies that cause policy-makers to ignore these elements. In effect, the traditional security understandings with their emphasis on state security will be favoured, resulting in policies that focus on military and foreign policy rather than on policies that serve the people of the region.

A second element of this argument is that there has been a significant expansion of the understanding of Arctic security since the end of the Cold War. There is a growing community of scholars who utilize the expanded understanding of Arctic security. In the eyes of some of these analysts, however, the problem remains that "popular and official security discourses still tend to focus on state-centric security issues, ignoring or downplaying the wants and fears of Arctic residents."[30] Thus, despite the efforts of this academic community, the public and governments of the region remain wedded to a more traditional understanding of security in the region, resulting in the neglect of the local inhabitants' security needs. The suggestion is that those with the "power" to apply the traditional basis of security, with its focus on the state and military competition, maintain a hold over both government officials and the public.

Critics of the traditional security approach argue that it is too narrow to properly explain or account for the current Arctic security environment. The Arctic had been a site of strong tensions when the dangers of nuclear war were extreme, but the core issues that led to that danger have been resolved.[31] Throughout the Cold War, the Arctic had been the site of the some of the most dangerous confrontations in that conflict. The geographic realities of the Cold War and the harsh logic of nuclear deterrence were such that the bulk of the strategic nuclear forces of the Soviet Union and the United States were arrayed across the Arctic.[32] For deterrence to work, each side needed to convince the other that should one side launch a nuclear strike, the other would both have the capability and intent to respond. This knowledge would keep either side from launching in the first place, thereby guaranteeing the "cold" peace between the two sides. The two main belligerents were the Soviets and the Americans, which meant that the nuclear-armed warheads, carried by land-based missiles, submarines, and long-range bombers, would have to fly over the Arctic to strike their designated targets. This meant that the military forces maintained in the region needed to be credible and to carry the most destructive weapons known to humankind.

Key to the Arctic's role in the Cold War security environment was that the deployments and expansion of the Soviet and NATO forces were not about seizing territory in the Arctic (northern Norway being the exception) but about employing the Arctic as a critical transit point for the vast forces arrayed to preserve nuclear deterrence – and as a battleground in a total war if deterrence failed. However, this stand-off prevented any form of cooperation in the region.[33] When the Cold War ended, the need to maintain such weapons systems was understood also to have ended. Thus, in 1989 the Arctic began to undergo a substantial demilitarization.[34] The military forces that had dominated the region were dismantled or substantially reduced. This reduction further strengthened the argument that the Arctic was a new zone of cooperation.

This transformed discussions about international Arctic security: the focus shifted from traditional military security to environmental and human security.[35] To cement the new era of cooperation, the former antagonists moved to create new forms of governance that would allow new forms of

cooperation. Thus, under the leadership of Finnish and Canadian officials, the Arctic Environmental Protection Strategy (AEPS) was created.[36]
This brought together the eight Arctic states – the Soviet Union (now Russia), the United States, Canada, Norway, Iceland, Denmark (for Greenland), Sweden, and Finland – to develop a joint understanding of the
environmental problems facing the region. At the same time, Canadian
officials succeeded in ensuring that northern Indigenous peoples were
recognized and given specific and separate seats at the table. The Inuit
of Canada, Alaska, Greenland, and Russia, the Saami of Scandinavia, and
the Russian northern Indigenous peoples were all welcomed. As this body
morphed into the Arctic Council in 1996, the cooperative efforts to understand and respond to the region's environmental problems meant that
the entire region was increasingly held up as an example to the entire international system on how cooperation could be successfully employed.[37]

What seemed to truly mark the end of the traditional understanding
of military security in the region occurred when the United States, Norway, and the Britain – and, later, Canada – came together to provide
substantial resources (in the billions of dollars) to help the Russian government safely decommission most of its Cold War–era nuclear-powered
and -armed submarine fleet.[38] The dissolution of the Soviet Union had
left its successor state, the Russian Federation, in economic straits so dire
that it was unable to properly dispose of many of its older submarines.
They had been left to literally rot in northern Russian ports, where they
posed an increasing danger both to Russia and to its northern neighbours, in the form of a nuclear meltdown or spill (or both).[39] Overall, it
was clear why so many of the leading experts in the field came to accept
that the Arctic had emerged as an "exceptional" region characterized by
threats to environmental and human security and by responses to them.

Some analysts, however, such as Borgerson[40] and myself,[41] have not accepted the view that the Arctic is exceptional or that the application of
a traditional security framework has contributed to competition and/or
tensions in the region. Instead, this school of thought argues that there
is nothing intrinsically different between the Arctic and any other region
of the world. Rather, the region's relative isolation and extreme climate
have left states unable to pursue their self-interests in a normal manner.
Thus a façade of cooperation has developed. The reality is that, as soon as
they can, the Arctic states will allow their national interests prevail when it
suits their agendas. There is nothing "exceptional" about the Arctic, and
to think otherwise raises the real danger of ignoring or dismissing security
threats when they do arise. This is not to suggest that the achievements
in cooperation that were achieved in the immediate post–Cold War years
were unimportant. Environmental cooperation and the empowerment of

the North's Indigenous peoples have been considerable achievements. The central argument of the Huebert/Borgerson school of thought, however, is that as the Arctic becomes more "like" the rest of the world, developments there will begin to include *competition* as well as cooperation. According to this school of thought, the return of traditional security concerns in the region is likely to be triggered by resource development and the concomitant geopolitical implications. With the dissolution of the Soviet Union, the emergent state of Russia had been temporarily weakened, but there are few indications that its desire to continue as a "great power" has weakened as well or that its long-term national interests have become perfectly aligned with those of the Western states. Thus as new resources are discovered in the region and the means to exploit them are developed, the focus on protecting the environment is likely to be complemented and perhaps even replaced by competition over those resources.

Neither school of thought initially appreciated the impacts of climate change. After the Cold War, commentators assumed that the Arctic would remain an isolated region where the permanent ice cover meant that only the northern Indigenous peoples would be truly comfortable living there. The cooperation that developed during this era provided evidence to alter this view. An international study of the Arctic region gave rise to a truly global understanding of the impact that climate change was having on the entire world, and specifically on the Arctic, and of the speed of that impact. The Arctic Climate Impact Assessment (ACIA), commissioned by the Arctic Council in the early 2000s, established that world temperatures were rising at an unprecedented rate and would fundamentally change the region.[42] At the heart of this transformation was the melting of the permanent ice cap – an observation that initially met with disbelief but is now accepted as reality. This in turn has led to an understanding that the Arctic is becoming accessible to the outside world to a degree that no one had ever thought possible.

Thus the return of geopolitics to the region is understood as linked to the development of its resources, which is being accelerated by the warming Arctic. Russia's economic prosperity hinges on its exploitation of its natural gas and oil resources, and as Russia has regained its prosperity, it has regained its strength.[43] There are two main locations for these resources. The more established region is around the Caspian Sea; the newer sources are in the north. Thus, as Russia has moved to recover economically, it has moved northward. Vladimir Putin's consolidation of power and his intention to return Russia to "great power" status has thus accelerated the return of geopolitics to the Arctic. Until 2014, however, Russia's renewed strength did not seem to weaken the argument that the Arctic remained an exceptional region in terms of international cooperation.

The Ukrainian crisis of 2014 catalysed the return of "great power" geopolitics to the Arctic. Seemingly unconnected to the Arctic, the crisis crystalized the growing divide between the Americans, Canadians, Norwegians, and Danes on one side and Russia on the other. The fall of the pro-Russian government of Viktor Yanukovych and its subsequent replacement by a pro-Western government resulted in Russian forces seizing parts of the eastern Ukraine and the Crimean Peninsula. The use of military force to redraw European borders led to the Western states imposing sanctions on Russia. Relations between Russia and the other Arctic states have deteriorated significantly since then.

The Return of Hard Politics and the Need for a Traditional Understanding of Arctic Security

There have been efforts to maintain Arctic regional cooperation since 2014, and there have been some significant successes at this, such as the Arctic Ocean Fishing Agreement reached in 2017.[44] But the conflict has illustrated that three core processes were largely ignored until the crisis demonstrated that the region had lost much of its "exceptional" status. These forces have brought the Arctic back under the ambit of military security in the conduct of international relations. These forces existed before the 2014 crisis, but as long as political cooperation had dominated the region, most observers either ignored or did not understand their significance. With the deterioration of relations as a result of the Ukraine crisis, these forces have become apparent to all.

First, the Arctic remains vital to national security for both Russia and the United States. For the Russians this means protecting their nuclear deterrent, which is still based primarily in their Arctic region. While many commentators had assumed that the Russians had abandoned nuclear deterrence as the key to their security, a reading of their core security policies and an examination of their defence expenditures throughout the 2000s demonstrate that this is not true. Russian defence documents produced after the Cold War always listed the maintenance of nuclear stability, aka nuclear deterrence, as their principal defence requirement.[45] Throughout the 1990s and into the 2000s, despite their economic collapse, the Russians persevered in their efforts to rebuild the submarine element of their deterrent. They encountered significant setbacks in the development of their most modern nuclear-armed submarine-launched missile. The fact that they persevered demonstrates their determination to rebuild and maintain their nuclear deterrent.

Likewise, many observers suggested that Russia's resumption of long-range bomber patrols in the Arctic in August 2007 was for domestic audiences and should not be seen as marking a return to the challenges of the Cold War.[46] In 2008, there were similar dismissals of the Russia's decision to resume patrols by its nuclear-powered and -armed submarine fleet (SSBN). The long timelines that the Russian armed forces faced in rebuilding this capability strongly suggest that they never lost sight of the importance of military force in the Arctic for their security. As long as relations remained good with the West, Russia's efforts to rebuild its deterrent – primarily through its Northern Fleet and bomber command – could be ignored. When relations worsened, however, it became clear that Russia had significantly rebuilt its northern capabilities to the point that it now can be considered the regional hegemon in terms of military power.[47] This means that despite the best efforts of most Arctic security analysts to move away from a focus on state-based hard power in the region, the Russian government is still moving ahead with that agenda. So it is important not to ignore that Russia is determined to use military power to achieve its core objectives.

Second, as Russia has moved to strengthen its Arctic military capabilities, so have the West's Arctic states, largely through the NATO and NORAD alliances. Canada and the United States have been developing means to modernize NORAD with a focus on improving its surveillance capabilities.[48] At the same time, Canada, Norway, Denmark, Iceland, and the United States are developing means to strengthen the alliance's ability to protect it northern flanks.[49] Further complicating this development are the closer relations that are now developing between the NATO alliance and Finland and Sweden.[50] While neither state is a full member, both have dramatically increased their military cooperation with NATO. In part, this has been spurred by increased Russian military actions that are violating their air and maritime spaces.

Space limitations preclude a detailed examination of NATO's relationship to the Arctic, but there is evidence that some NATO countries, such as Norway, concluded that Russian military expansion in the region demanded a NATO-based response.[51] Other NATO states, such as Canada under Stephen Harper, were concerned that any indication that NATO was expanding into the Arctic would cause the Russians to feel that they were being encircled, so they did not initially approve of such moves.[52] The Canadian government under Justin Trudeau has been abandoning this reluctance, and its 2017 defence policy signalled a willingness to consider a stronger NATO presence in the Arctic.[53] Meanwhile, the most recent US strategic document identifies Russia and China as the most direct threats to American security.[54] Before this, in the aftermath of the 9/11 attacks on the United States, the Americans had consistently identified terrorist organizations as the greatest threat. All of this demonstrates the importance of utilizing a state-based analysis of the military measures that are now taking place.

Third, since 2014, China has begun developing its military capability in the region. While these efforts are currently low-level, they do represent a new security development. Thus, in 2015 a five-ship Chinese naval task force sailed around the Aleutian Islands and into the Bering Sea.[55] At the same time, the Chinese navy made its first official visit to Finland, Sweden, and Denmark.[56] In 2017, a three-ship task force held joint exercises with Russian forces and China's one icebreaker sailed through the Canadian Northwest Passage.[57] Clearly, China is now beginning the challenging task of learning how to deploy to the region. In January 2018, the Chinese issued an Arctic policy document, which focused on demonstrating to the greater international community the cooperative nature of Chinese actions in that region.[58] But it is important to note that the Chinese government seldom issues documents that provide detailed considerations of their policy. The fact that the Chinese took the effort to produce and disseminate this policy document is a clear indication of how seriously they take their involvement in the region.

Conclusion

The Arctic is no longer a region of "exceptional" peace and cooperation. Instead, there are indications that the forces of international competition have returned. This is not about conflict *over* the Arctic, but *is* about the Arctic being key to the defence interests of the Arctic states, and increasingly of non-Arctic states such as China. Serious questions need to be asked in order to understand how the changing international security environment will affect the Arctic region. Those questions can only be addressed through a traditional security theoretical approach.

The lack of traditional security analysis did not stop state-based military actions in the North from re-emerging. A review of the existing literature on Arctic security throughout the post-Cold War era demonstrates that very few analysts employed that theoretical framework. Only a handful of analysts, such as myself and Borgerson, have embraced this approach; the literature has largely and explicitly rejected it. It is difficult to understand why, if a realist-based traditional security understanding amounts to a political act, so few realist understandings caused the Arctic to return as a geopolitical space of strategic importance. If the writings of Borgerson and others are so powerful, the critical theorists who contend that this is a political act need to explain how. They need to explain more clearly how the writings of so few can be so powerful in influencing the system.

Changes in the international system since 2014 have resulted in a significant spillover of traditional security issues into the Arctic region. This is not to suggest that the region is returning entirely to the dangers of the Cold War era, but traditional security affects it, and that impact must be analysed accordingly. The recent agreement on commercial fishing in the central Arctic Ocean affirms that cooperative forces remain at work that can be explained through an expanded security framework. Likewise, pressing issues related to the societal, gendered, and individual frameworks of security need to be understood. Nevertheless, issues related to the state use of military power are still explained best using traditional security analysis.

NOTES

1   Stephen Walt, "The Renaissance of Security Studies," *International Studies Quarterly* 35, no. 2 (1991): 211–39; Edward Kolodziej, "Renaissance in Security Studies? Caveat Lector," *International Studies Quarterly* 36, no. 4 (1992): 421–38.

2   Keith Krause and Michael Williams, "Broadening the Agenda of Security Studies: Politics and Methods," *Mershon International Studies Review* 40, no. 2 (1996): 229–54.

3   Alan Collins, ed., *Contemporary Security Studies*, 4th ed. (Oxford: Oxford University Press, 2016).

4   Antol Rapoport, *Strategy and Conscience* (New York: Harper and Row, 1964); Philip G. Green, *Deadly Logic: The Theory of Nuclear Deterrence* (Columbus: Ohio University Press, 1966).

5   Herman Kahn, *Thinking about the Unthinkable* (New York: Horizon Press, 1962); Henry Kissinger, *Nuclear Weapons and Foreign Policy* (New York: Harper and Row, 1957).

6   Martin Shaw, *War and Genocide: Organized Killing in Modern Society* (Cambridge: Polity Press, 2003); Richard Wyn Jones, *Security, Strategy, and Critical Theory* (Boulder: Lynne Rienner, 1999).

7   Hedley Bull, "Strategic Studies and Its Critics," *World Politics* 20, no. 4 (1968): 593–605.

8   Carl von Clausewitz, *On War* (Princeton: Princeton University Press, 1976).

9   Colin Gray, *The Future of Strategy* (Cambridge: Polity Press, 2015).

10   Lawrence Freedman, "Does Strategic Studies Have a Future?" in *Strategy in the Contemporary World: An Introduction to Strategic Studies*, 5th ed., ed. John Baylis, James Wirth, and Colin Gray, 386 (Oxford: Oxford University Press, 2016).

11   Ibid., 387.

12   Franklyn Griffiths: *The Arctic as an International Political Region*, No. 3, Science for Peace/Samuel Stevens (1988); *Defence, Security, and Civility in the Arctic Region* (Reykjavik: Nordic Council's Arctic Conference, 1993); *Environment in the US Security Debate: The Case of the Missing Arctic Waters* (Washington, D.C.: Woodrow Wilson International Center for Scholars, 1997).

13   Oran R. Young: *Arctic Politics: Conflict and Cooperation in the Circumpolar North* (Hannover: Dartmouth College Press, 1992); "Governing the Arctic: From Cold War Theater to Mosaic of Cooperation," *Global Governance: A Review of Multilateralism and International Organizations* 11, no. 1 (2005): 9–15; "Building an International Regime Complex for the Arctic: Current Status and Next Steps," *Polar Journal* 2, no. 2 (2012): 391–407.

14   P. Whitney Lackenbauer: *From Polar Race to Polar Saga: An Integrated Strategy for Canada and the Circumpolar World* (Toronto: Canadian International Council, 2009); "Mirror Images? Canada, Russia, and the Circumpolar World," *International Journal* 65, no. 4 (2010): 879–97.

15   Timo Koivurova, "Limits and Possibilities of the Arctic Council in a Rapidly Changing Scene of Arctic Governance," *Polar Record* 46, no. 2 (2010): 146–56.

16   Rolf Tamnes and Kristine Offerdal, eds., *Geopolitics and Security in the Arctic: Regional Dynamics in a Global World* (New York: Routledge, 2014).

17   Michael Byers: *Who Owns the Arctic? Understanding Sovereignty Disputes in the North* (Toronto: Douglas and McIntyre, 2010); *International Law and the Arctic* (Cambridge: Cambridge University Press, 2013).

18   Mary Simon, "Inuit and the Canadian Arctic: Sovereignty Begins at Home," *Journal of Canadian Studies* 43, no. 2 (2009): 250–60.

19   Gunhild Hoogensen Gjørv, "Virtuous Imperialism or a Shared Global Objective? The Relevance of Human Security in the Global North," in *Environmental and Human Security in the Arctic*, ed. Gunhild Hoogensen Gjørv, Dawn Bazely, Martina Goloviznina, and Andrew Tanentzap, 58–80 (New York: Routledge, 2014); Gunhild Hoogensen Gjørv and Maria Goloviznina, "Introduction: Can We Broaden Our Understanding of Security in the Arctic?," in *Environmental and Human Security in the Arctic*, 1–14; Gunhild Hoogensen, Dawn Bazely, Julia Christensen, Andrew Tanentzap, and Evgeny Bojko, "Human Security in the Arctic – Yes, It Is Relevant!," *Journal of Human Security* 5, no. 2 (2009): 1–10.

20   Lassi Heininen: "Globalization and Security in the Circumpolar North," in *Globalization of the Circumpolar North*, ed. Lassi Heininen and Chris Southcott (Fairbanks: University of Alaska Press, 2010): 221–64; "'Politicization' of the Environment: Environmental Politics and Security in the Circumpolar North," in *The Fast-Changing Arctic: Rethinking Arctic Security for a Warmer World*, ed. Barry Zellen (Calgary: University of Calgary Press, 2012): 35–55.

21   Wilfrid Greaves: "For Whom, from What? Canada's Arctic Policy and the Narrowing of Human Security," *International Journal*, 67, no. 1 (2012a):

219–40; "Insecurities of Non-dominance: Re-theorizing Human Security and Environmental Change in Developed States," in *Natural Resources and Social Conflict: Towards Critical Environmental Security*, ed. Mathew A. Schnurr and Larry A. Swatuk (New York: Palgrave, 2012b): 63–82; "Securing Sustainability: The Case for Critical Environmental Security in the Arctic," *Polar Record* 52, no. 6 (2016): 660–71.

22 Jessica Shadian, *The Politics of Arctic Sovereignty: Oil, Ice, and Inuit Governance* (London: Routledge, 2014).

23 Stephanie Irlbacher-Fox, Jackie Price, and Elana Wilson Rowe, "Women's Participation in Decision Making: Human Security in the Canadian Arctic," in *Environmental and Human Security in the Arctic*, ed. Gunhild Hoogensen Gjørv, Dawn Bazely, Martina Goloviznina, and Andrew Tanentzap (New York: Routledge, 2014): 203–30.

24 Kamrul Hossain, Gerald Zojer, Wilfrid Greaves, J. Miguel Roncero, and Michael Sheehan, "Constructing Arctic Security: An Inter-disciplinary Approach to Understanding Security in the Barents Region," *Polar Record* 53, no. 1 (2017): 52–66.

25 Buzan Barry, Ole Wæver, and Jan de Wilde, *Security: A New Framework for Analysis* (London: Lynne Rienner, 1998). See also Gunhild Hoogensen Gjørv and Marina Goloviznina, "Can We Broaden Our Understanding of Security in the Arctic?," in *Environmental and Human Security in the Arctic*, ed. Hoogensen Gjørv, Dawn Bazely, Marina Goloviznina, and Andrew Tanentzap (London: Routledge, 2013), 1.

26 John Mearsheimer, *The Tragedy of Great Power Politics*, 2nd ed. (New York: W.W. Norton, 2014).

27 Colin Gray, *Modern Strategy* (Oxford: Oxford University Press, 1999).

28 See for example Hossain et al., "Constructing Arctic Security," 53.

29 Hoogensen Gjørv and Goloviznina 2014, 2.

30 Hossain et al., "Constructing Arctic Security," 62.

31 Young, "Governing the Arctic."

32 Sanjay Chaturvedi, "Arctic Geopolitics Then and Now," in *The Arctic: Environment, People, Policy*, eds. Mark Nuttall and Terry Callaghan, 441–58 (Edmonton: CRC Press, 2000).

33 Young, "Governing the Arctic."

34 Ronald G. Purver, "Arctic Security: The Murmansk Initiative and Its Impact," in *Soviet Foreign Policy: New Dynamics, New Themes*, ed. Carl G. Jacobsen, 182–203 (London: Palgrave Macmillan, 1989).

35 Hoogensen Gjørv et al., eds., *Environmental and Human Security in the Arctic*.

36 Rob Huebert, "New Directions in Circumpolar Cooperation," *Canadian Foreign Policy* 3, no. 2 (1998): 37–57.

37 Koivurova, "Limits and Possibilities."

38 Margaret Blunden, "The New Problem of Arctic Stability," *Survival* 51, no. 5 (2009): 121–42.

39 Sherri Goodman, "Changing Climates for Arctic Security," *Wilson Quarterly* (Summer 2017), https://wllsonquarterly.com/quarterly/into-the-arctic /changing-climates-for-arctic-security.

40 Scott G. Borgerson: "Arctic Meltdown: The Economic and Security Implications of Global Warming," *Foreign Affairs* 87, no. 2 (March–April 2008): 63–77; "The Coming Arctic Boom," *Foreign Affairs* 92, no. 4 (July–August 2013): 76–89.

41 Rob Huebert, "Canada and the Newly Emerging International Arctic Security Regime," in *Arctic Security in an Age of Climate Change*, ed. James Kraska, 193–217 (Cambridge: Cambridge University Press, 2011); Robert Huebert, Heather Exner-Pirot, Adam Lajeunesse, and Jay Gulledge, *Climate Change and International Security: The Arctic as a Bellwether* (Arlington: Center for Climate and Energy Solutions, 2012).

42 ACIA, *Impacts of a Warming Climate: Arctic Climate Impact Assessment* (Cambridge: Cambridge University Press, 2004), 144.

43 Ekaterina Klimenko, *Russia's Arctic Security Policy: Still Quiet in the High North?* (Stockholm: Stockholm International Peace Research [SIPRI], 2016).

44 CBC, "Historical Agreement: Canada Signs High Arctic Commercial Fishing Ban," *CBC News North*, 1 December 2017, http://www.cbc.ca/news/canada /north/high-arctic-fishing-ban-1.4428360.

45 Russia, *Principles of State Policy in the Arctic to 2020* (Security Council of Russia: 2008), http://www.scrf.gov.ru/documents/98.html. It should be noted the Russia did not publicly release the document on its webpage until March 2009. It should also be noted that some accounts refer to the document as the *Foundations of State Policy in the Arctic to 2020*. There is also no official English version: several have been released, but they differ slightly from one another. See also Russia, Decree of the President of the Russian Federation, *Russia's National Security Strategy to 2020*, 12 May, 2009, no. 537 (С Т Р А Т Е Г И Я национальной безопасности Российской Федерации до 2020 года). (For an English translation see http://rustrans.wikidot.com /russia-s-national-security-strategy-to-2020).

46 Frédéric Lasserre, Jérôme Le Roy, and Richard Garon, "Is There an Arms Race in the Arctic?," *Journal of Military and Strategic Studies* 14, nos. 3–4 (2012): 1–56.

47 Katarzyna Zysk, "Military Aspects of Russia's Arctic Policy: Hard Power and Natural Resources," in *Arctic Security in an Age of Climate Change*, ed. James Kraska, 85–106 (New York: Cambridge University Press, 2011).

48 Andrea Charron and James Fergusson, "Beyond NORAD and Modernization to North American Defence Evolution," Policy Paper (Canadian Global Affairs Institute: May 2017).

49 Kristian Åtland, "North European Security after the Ukraine Conflict," *Defense and Security Analysis* 32, no. 2 (2016): 163–76.

50 Finland, *The Effects of Finland's Possible NATO Membership: An Assessment* (April 2016).

51 Paal S. Hilde, "The 'New' Arctic – the Military Dimension," *Journal of Military and Strategic Studies* 15, no. 2 (2013): 130–53.

52 Helga Haftendorn, "NATO and the Arctic: Is the Atlantic Alliance a Cold War Relic in a Peaceful Region Now Faced with Non-military Challenges?," *European Security* 20, no. 3 (2011): 337–61.

53 Canada, *Strong, Secure, Engaged* (Ottawa: Department of National Defence), http://dgpaapp.forces.gc.ca/en/canada-defence-policy/index.asp.

54 United States, *Summary of the 2018 National Defence Strategy of the United States of America: Sharpening the American Military's Competitive Edge* (Washington, D.C.: Department of Defence, January 2018, 2.

55 Missy Ryan and Dan Lamothe, "Chinese Naval Ships Came Within 12 Nautical Miles of American Soil," *Washington Post*, 4 September 2015), https://www.washingtonpost.com/world/national-security/chinese-naval-ships-came-within-12-nautical-miles-of-american-soil/2015/09/04/dee5e1b0-5305-11e5-933e-7d06c647a395_story.html.

56 Shannon Tiezzi, "China's Navy Makes First-Ever Tour of Europe's Arctic States," *The Diplomat*, 2 October 2015, http://thediplomat.com/2015/10/chinas-navy-makes-first-ever-tour-of-europes-arctic-states.

57 Tyler Rogoway, "Chinese Naval Group to Sail the Baltic Sea at the Same Time as Russian Armada," *The Drive*, 19 July 2017, http://www.thedrive.com/the-war-zone/12656/chinese-naval-group-in-baltic-sea-at-same-time-as-russias-biggest-sub-and-cruiser.

58 Xinhuanet, *China's Arctic Policy*, January 2018, http://www.xinhuanet.com/english/2018-01/26/c_136926498.htm; P. Whitney Lackenbauer, Adam Lajeunesse, James Manicom and Frédéric Lasserre, *China's Arctic Ambitions and What They Mean for Canada* (Calgary: University of Calgary, Press, 2018).

5 National Security and the High North: Post–Cold War Arctic Security Policy in Norway

WILFRID GREAVES

Norway has long considered its northern territory a core national interest, but in the post–Cold War period it has been constructed as a highly securitized domain of public policy, with multiple phenomena identified as relevant to national and regional security. This chapter examines the Norwegian government's understanding of security as it relates to its Arctic region, the "High North." The first section situates the High North and provides a brief overview of its relationship to Norwegian society and national identity. The second section describes the widening and deepening of Norway's foreign and security policy after the Cold War, which culminated in a new High North Initiative in 2006. The third section argues that the meaning of Arctic security for the Norwegian state can be synthesized into two main pillars: geographic proximity to Russia, with associated concerns over possible Russian aggression; and securing territorial control over maritime areas in order to facilitate hydrocarbon resource extraction.

Overall, this chapter examines the dominant historical and contemporary meanings of Arctic security for the Norwegian state, focusing particularly on the post–Cold War redefinition of security in the High North. While Norway emphasized *de*securitizing Russian relations immediately after the Cold War, the more recent High North Initiative has heavily securitized the Arctic region within Norwegian national security discourse and policy. I argue that despite many changes in global and European politics, Russia and the extraction of Arctic resources remain the pillars of Norway's official understanding of security in the Arctic in both historical and more recent contexts. To support this claim, I draw on English-language scholarship on Norwegian foreign and security policy, in addition to primary analysis of Norwegian government policy documents and related texts.[1] These sources support the argument that security is the central concept for Norwegian policy in the Arctic and that Norway's Arctic security interests have been constructed around the threat of Russian instability and/or invasion, and the control and extraction of petroleum as necessary for the Norwegian economy and maintenance of its social welfare system.

History and the High North

As with other Arctic countries, Norway's northern region is a contested social and geographic space imbued with a powerful national narrative. The country's northern territory strongly links Norwegians to their national myth as a hardy, peripheral society descended from the Vikings. After the modern Nordic states were consolidated at the end of the eighteenth century, the Scandinavian interior and the Arctic coast became frontiers for exploration and profit-making rather than a theatre of conflict. In the late nineteenth and early twentieth centuries, Norwegian Arctic explorers such as Fridtjof Nansen and Roald Amundsen garnered international acclaim and were treated as international celebrities. Both were prominent supporters of Norway's independence from Sweden, and their Arctic voyages were a source of pride and inspiration for many Norwegians. In many ways, the Arctic remains a source of national pride to this day. Geographically and geopolitically, Norway's long Arctic coast and adjacent seabed are its defining features. Norway is a small country by land area, but if marine territory is included, Norway is the largest country in Europe and the fifteenth-largest country in the world. Its long coastline makes it a key player in political discussions pertaining to circumpolar issues such as maritime boundary delimitation, offshore resource extraction, fisheries, shipping, and search and rescue. During the Cold War, Norway was one of only two NATO allies that shared a land border with the Soviet Union, and its continued proximity makes it a key interlocutor between Russia and the other Arctic states.

Despite Norway's long Arctic history, the term "High North" was first used to refer to Norway's northern territory only in 1973. It entered common usage in the 1980s as the English equivalent of *nordområdene*, or "the northern areas," and was adopted for government use around the turn of the twenty-first century.[2] It has since been used widely, as "the political significance of the High North has risen to heights unheard of since the Cold War."[3] Indeed, the High North is regarded as the single most important aspect of Norwegian foreign policy, and, as discussed below, is routinely identified as a core national interest affecting various other policy domains. But precisely what the High North encompasses is less clear. It was first defined in Norway's 2006 High North Strategy, which specifies that "in geographical terms, it covers the sea and land, including islands and archipelagos, stretching northwards from the southern boundary of Nordland County in Norway and eastwards from the Greenland Sea to the Barents Sea and the Pechora Sea. In political terms, it includes the administrative entities in Norway, Sweden, Finland and Russia that are part of the Barents Co-operation." The High North Strategy goes on to state that "Norway's High North policy overlaps with the Nordic co-operation, our relations with the US and Canada through the Arctic Council, and our relations with the EU."[4]

Though it encompasses a vast geographic and conceptual space, the High North and related foreign policy domains are clearly defined. But this definition shifted in 2009, when the government announced that "its policy does not give a precise definition of what it reads into the expression 'the High North,' nor whether it limits the High North to Norwegian territory. Substantial Norwegian interests are likely to be affected by developments wherever they take place in the circumpolar and Arctic region."[5] As a result of this shift, analysts now observe that "the very precise geographical definition in the 2006 document has disappeared in favour of a vaguer and more open-ended understanding of the High North."[6] Such an understanding allows Norway more flexibility on Arctic issues that it perceives as relevant to its national interests, including many characterized as threatening Norway's national security. By defining the High North as including but not exclusive to Norwegian territory, Norway has also reserved the prerogative to address issues beyond its borders within the framework of its High North Strategy, exemplifying the centrality of the region to Norway's foreign policy goals and national security interests.

Post–Cold War Northern Security

Before the late 1980s, inter-state relations in the European Arctic were shaped by the balance of power between the East and West Blocs. Concerned about their geographic location between the Soviet Union and Western Europe, Norway, Sweden, and Finland pursued interrelated foreign and security policies designed to maintain a "Nordic balance." The objective was to prevent northern Europe from becoming the site of superpower conflict; thus, Norway (along with Denmark and Iceland) joined NATO, Sweden remained neutral, and Finland allied with the Soviet Union.[7] Norway, as the only European NATO member to share a border with the Soviet Union, was thus directly affected by the post–Cold War shift that allowed for greater openness between Russia and its Nordic neighbours. Reduced tensions in the European Arctic catalysed broader rapprochement between East and West and helped facilitate the normalization of European security relations.[8]

The decline in superpower hostilities opened space for a reconfiguration of security politics in northern Europe. The pivotal moment was a speech by Soviet leader Mikhail Gorbachev at Murmansk in October 1987. Framed as part of *perestroika*, the speech contained eight policy initiatives designed to reduce military tensions in the Arctic and foster greater East–West trust and cooperation.[9] While several of his proposals were never enacted, notably denuclearization, the Murmansk speech "is a key discursive point of reference and stands as an epochal event in Norway's understanding of the High North."[10] By helping desecuritize the Arctic as an arena of Cold War competition, the speech opened space for the emergence of a cooperative Arctic regime based on peaceful negotiation of inter-state disputes and the principles of international law.[11] Its proposals for greater scientific and environmental cooperation, and the political inclusion of Indigenous peoples, led to the establishment of the Barents Euro-Arctic Region and the Arctic Environmental Protection Strategy (AEPS), the precursor to the Arctic Council. Gorbachev's call for the Arctic to become a "zone of peace" proved a powerful animating vision for the institutional structures of the post–Cold War Arctic, in which all circumpolar states routinely reiterate their commitment to a rules-governed regional order.

Notwithstanding the improved security conditions brought about by the collapse of the Soviet Union, post–Cold War Norwegian foreign policy remained focused on post-Soviet Russia. Norway had felt threatened by Russian strength throughout the nineteenth and twentieth centuries,[12] but in the immediate post-Soviet period it also perceived its security as threatened by Russian state weakness. Throughout the early 1990s, "the general tendency [was] to emphasize environmental hazards, ethnic conflicts and economic disparities as jeopardizing Norwegian security, while military threats [were] downplayed,"[13] but Norwegian officials also identified new threats associated with disorder on the Russian side of the border. Then–foreign minister Johan Jørgen Holst made clear that "new security policy challenges" had emerged along the eastern edge of Europe, namely a zone of unstable post-Soviet states, including Russia, and that this posed economic, ecological, and political challenges to others on the continent.[14] Citing Holst, Jensen asserts that

> enabling de-securitization by means of de-militarization was, and still is, an explicit discursive component of Norway's security policy. Much-stated reasons why Norway and Russia work together in the Barents region are precisely to offset military tensions, to counter the threats to the environment and to narrow the gap in living standards between the people living on the Norwegian and Russian sides of the region's borders.[15]

The Soviet collapse posed new threats in the Euro-Arctic region, and the government made clear that cessation of superpower hostilities did not entail a commensurate improvement in security threats facing Norway and other European states proximate to the former Soviet Union. In fact, Norwegian policy-makers lamented the lack of stability and predictability associated with the new security threats in the post-Soviet period compared to during the Cold War.

Thus, according to Eriksson, in the early 1990s Norway's three priorities for the Euro-Arctic region were normalization, stabilization, and regionalization.[16] Regionalization pertained to the establishment of more effective Russo-European political institutions, while "'normalization' concerns a qualitative change in relations and perceptions, [and] 'stabilization' is more about dealing with the actual problems that directly or indirectly threaten survival in the area. These threats include environmental pollution, the military factor, the unstable political system and the huge social and economic problems [in Russia]."[17] The Russian military threat to Norway during the Cold War was, at least, fairly predictable, which led Norwegian leaders to perceive the unpredictability of political developments in Russia in the early 1990s as more dangerous. Eriksson concluded that "it is, of course, the internal Russian political development that is to be predicted, or at least in the northern part of the country ... The government considers the growing permeability of state borders and the spill-over potential of environmental, criminal and social problems to be a major challenge to Norwegian security."[18] Deep engagement with Russia was seen as a requirement for re-establishing security in the High North.

Evident in Norway's post–Cold War approach to security is its leading role in embracing a widened conception of in/security in its foreign policy. Just as for many other states, the 1990s were a time of significant transition in Norwegian security and defence policy as the changes in East–West relations precipitated a range of new global challenges. These emergent threats required an "extended security concept" that encompassed new policy and institutional responses in addition to established military instruments. According to then–prime minister Gro Harlem Brundtland, "the new dangers require that we act according to a wider agenda than NATO has offered so far – one that included economic and environmental aspects of stability and cooperation."[19] In 1998, Norway joined with Canada to form the Human Security Network, an intergovernmental group for promoting the human security agenda – that is, the protection of civilians from sudden and chronic threats to their rights, safety, and lives.[20] Norwegian foreign policy embraced a world view whereby the security of Norway and Norwegians was no longer threatened solely by the prospect of military attack by Russia – it was also endangered by various unconventional hazards hitherto omitted from national security policy.

Norway widened its concept of security but also deepened it to focus on protecting objects above and within the sovereign state. Government officials and policy statements from the early 1990s indicate that Norway's national security was increasingly tied to that of the European Union and other groupings of European states, and moreover, that within Norway there existed distinct security interests and threats at the sub-state and community levels, particularly in the High North.[21] According to Foreign Minister Holst, post–Cold War "foreign policy is no longer simply a question of relations between states. It is also a question of interactions between societies. It is also a question about managing common problems. Therefore it is natural that foreign policy becomes more democratically rooted, that it reflects wider commitment and a wider distribution of responsibility."[22] This shift in policy emphasized security at the community level, recognizing the distinctiveness of security concerns in northern Norway owing to its greater proximity to the instability in Russia. In the new regional context, the government noted that "local and regional actors should have operative roles, while the central governments are responsible for the setting-up of general frameworks and allocation of financial resources."[23] For example, county governments administered most of the NOK30 million in emergency aid that the Norwegian government had allocated to northwestern Russia, as they were on the front line of the emerging challenges. But the degree of "security deepening" in Norwegian security policy should not be overstated. The Norwegian government continued to exercise significant control over sub-state actors, and "the central government [was] clearly perceived as the one where ultimate, supreme power is located."[24] Thus, there are contradictory tendencies in the Norwegian approach to post–Cold War security: the state increased the number of actors involved in security, but it also constructed new and diverse issues as security-relevant, which had the reverse effect of bringing more such issues under the ambit of the central government. The expansion of security into new policy areas centralized power over a wider number of issues within the state.

Despite these changes, until the late 1990s Norwegian national security policy remained oriented toward defending against a conventional military attack from the east. A 1998 defence Green Paper maintained that "over the long term the danger of invasion cannot be ruled out … The government therefore seeks to maintain a capacity to repel invasions over a limited time in one region of the country at a time."[25] By the turn of the millennium, however, diminished Russian power, the eastward expansion of NATO, and the emergence of new security issues had largely assuaged this concern. The new security situation was articulated by Defence Minister Eldbjørg Løwer:

> The general direction of security policy today is unpredictable, but it could be just as "dangerous" as the confrontations between superpowers during the Cold War. Russia's constrained economic and social situation has gone, however, hand in hand with other dangers and risk to security in the North. The destruction of the environment, social misery, [and] organized criminality are prevalent on the Russian side of the border; they could destroy the social fabric and destabilize Norway's immediate neighbourhood.[26]

The 9/11 terrorist attacks also disrupted Norwegian national security discourse. The post-9/11 context affected perceptions of threats from non-state violent actors while strengthening the trend away from seeing Russia as the principal threat. Moreover, the attacks occurred at a unique moment in Norwegian politics, parliamentary elections having been held the day before. In 2002, the new defence minister explained the significance:

> The ripple effects of the terrorist attack have spread around the globe. The USA is leading the world in a new war against terrorism, in which Norway is also participating ... We went to the ballot on September 10 to elect a new parliament. A few hours later, the political agenda changed beyond recognition ... September 11 presents us with numerous challenges on how we configure and use our Armed Forces ... In the present security situation today, there is little cause for Norway to see Russia as a likely threat ... Continued stable development in our neighbour and increased readiness to work together [with Russia] after September 11 will benefit Norway's security interests.[27]

Despite the impact of the 9/11 attacks on security discourses around the globe, the immediate policy effects for Norway were limited. Having already widened its understanding of security threats, its response to the emerging Global War on Terror was a renewed centralization of foreign policy decision-making in the central government compared to the diffusion of actors during the 1990s. Jensen suggests that Norwegian participation in the Global War on Terror, particularly its involvement in Afghanistan through Operation Enduring Freedom and NATO's International Security Assistance Force, resulted in a top-down, state-centric conception of in/security concerned with a diversity of possible threats.[28] Put another way, Norway's approach to in/security was wide but not deep, focused on both conventional and unconventional threats but retaining the state and its core interests as the referent object of security policy. These developments "can be read as the beginning of the end of the hegemonic discourse on the threat of invasion in Norwegian security thinking and as the lowly beginnings of the expansion of the security concept in the Norwegian High North debate."[29]

The importance of the High North grew considerably in the early 2000s despite the new focus on global terrorism, culminating in a series of documents outlining a comprehensive set of regional policies collectively called the High North Initiative. In 2003, the government's expert commission to examine High North policy released the White Paper "Mot nord!" (Northwards!), and later a Green Paper, "Muligheter og utfordringer i nord" (Possibilities and Challenges in the North), which further expanded northern foreign policy. When the Conservatives were defeated by the so-called Red–Green coalition led by the Labour Party's Jens Stoltenberg in the autumn of 2005, the centrality of the High North endured. The Soria-Moria Declaration, which laid out the new governing coalition's priorities, further elevated the importance of the High North:

> The Government regards the Northern Areas as Norway's most important strategic target area in the years to come. The Northern Areas have gone from being a security policy department area to being an energy policy power centre and an area that faces great environmental policy challenges ... The handling of Norwegian economic interests, environmental interests and security policy interests in the North are to be given high priority and are to be seen as being closely linked.[30]

In addition to indicating the government's intentions to expand the offshore petroleum sector in the Barents region, combat climate change, and further deepen cooperation with Russia, the Soria-Moria Declaration signalled the creation of a holistic Arctic strategy, which was released in 2006 as the "Regjeringens nordområdestrategi" (Norwegian Government Strategy for the High North), hereafter High North Strategy, and was followed in 2009 by an interim report, "New Building Blocks in the North," which laid out the next steps in Norwegian northern policy. Collectively, this high-level attention indicates that "the European Arctic is at the head of the Norwegian political agenda in a way that has not been since the days of the Cold War."[31]

The High North Strategy identifies the overarching goal of Norway's Arctic policy as "creat[ing] sustainable growth and development in the High North,"[32] similar to how its Arctic objectives were expressed by the previous government three years earlier.[33] The High North Initiative is both diverse and comprehensive in its focus on different policy areas, but despite extensive discursive mobilization the Norwegian government has mostly retained the same priorities that have existed since the early 1990s, if not earlier.[34] What has changed, however, is the routine framing of formerly political issues as security-relevant. While northern Norway is a site of multiple issues not traditionally relevant to national or regional security, these have become increasingly securitized such that "in the public High North discourse since 2005, it has become increasingly difficult to be heard unless the word 'security' is uttered in the course of one's reasoning and argumentation."[35] As a result, northern Norway has become one of the most securitized regions in the Arctic, with security operating as a powerful discourse that elevates Arctic issues within the hierarchy of political importance while legitimizing state intervention in those areas because they are discursively linked to the highest national interest.

The Two Pillars of Norwegian Arctic Security

Based on an assessment of the developments in post–Cold War Norwegian foreign and security policy, two core themes underpin the official understanding of security in the High North: Russia and natural resources. Although recently reiterated as part of the new High North Initiative, both issues have been intimately connected to dominant constructions of the national interest since before Norway achieved independence. In this respect, the central objectives of Norway's Arctic policy have been relatively constant: keeping the Russians out of its northern territory while extracting natural resources from that territory, with both considered vital to the survival and prosperity of the Norwegian state (for further discussion see Østhagen, chapter 7). Somewhat ironically, Norway shares key Arctic policy features with Russia, including "four nodal points that the Norwegian and Russian foreign policy discourses on the European Arctic evolve around[:] … energy, security, the economy and the environment."[36] All four nodes are closely interconnected in High North discourse such that the area is perceived as essential for Norway's national well-being and national security and these areas of public policy have been securitized within broader Norwegian politics.

Undoubtedly, the most persistent security issue in northern Norway is its proximity to Russia. The Russo-Norwegian security relationship remains dynamic and has deteriorated in recent years due to Russia's 2014 annexation of Crimea and support for violent separatist proxies in eastern Ukraine. After that year, Russia, NATO, and the European Union all increased their military activities in northern Europe and all five Nordic states announced unprecedented military cooperation with one another and with the neighbouring Baltic states.[37] Norway's military establishment quickly reinvigorated much of the High North defence apparatus that had fallen moribund after the Cold War due to the improvement in relations with Russia.[38] While Norwegian officials have been quick to dismiss the possibility of a Russian invasion, they stress their concern over Russia's actions and scepticism of its intentions. The situation has been described as a return to the "new old normal" by the general commanding Norway's military headquarters – located in the High North city of Bodø – and Defence Minister Ine Eriksen Soreide had stated that "Russia has created uncertainty about its intentions, so there is, of course, unpredictability."[39] These developments underscore the persistent centrality of Russia to Norwegian conceptions of security. *How* Russia has related to Norway's security interests has varied over time, but it has never ceased being the foremost issue for Norwegian officials.

Indeed, fear of Russian unpredictability is hardly new in Norwegian security discourse. As noted earlier, two core objectives of Norwegian High North policy since the 1990s – stabilization and normalization – have focused on managing security issues associated with the collapse of the Soviet Union and the emergence of a new Russian polity. Stabilization entailed navigating rapid and dramatic instability across the unravelling Soviet empire, while normalization focused on desecuritizing relations between post-Russia and Europe (including NATO members such as Norway) by rebuilding non-conflictual commercial and political interactions across the Russo-Norwegian border. In the early 1990s, "Norway want[ed] to see the 70 years of Euro-Arctic division as a 'historical parenthesis,'"[40] a sentiment echoed a decade later when Foreign Minister Jonas Gahr Støre described the Cold War as an aberration interrupting Norway's "normal" relations with its Russian neighbour: "It used to be the case that security policy and strategic military balance pushed every other approach to the side. But historically we ought perhaps to think of the Cold War as a parenthesis, for the Iron Curtain in the North stands in contrast to commercial and social relations down the centuries."[41] Confronted with changing political contexts globally and within Russia, Norwegian leaders sought to reshape the bilateral relationship in a cooperative fashion, which they suggested reflected the peaceful interactions of an earlier time.

But Norwegian efforts to foster peaceful relations with Russia invoked an idealized history that downplayed the enduring role of Russia as the Other threatening the interests and sovereignty of its neighbours. The Cold War was far from being a "historical parenthesis"; in fact,

Russo-Scandinavian borders have historically been sites of deep tension and mistrust between, on the one hand, Norway and Sweden associated with the liberal European order, and, on the other, Russian polities representing an Orthodox, Asiatic, and autocratic tradition. Through the nineteenth century, depictions of Russia as expansionist and militarily aggressive were ubiquitous in Scandinavian discourse, and "the Russian will to expand westwards was considered a self-evident, almost natural, process."[42] This belief had important political consequences, including that it motivated Norway to submit to the suzerainty of its more powerful Scandinavian neighbours. For instance, Sweden used fear of "the Russian danger" to convince Norwegians to accept the forced union of Sweden and Norway following the latter's brief independence in 1814.[43] Also, Sweden and Norway joined an alliance with Britain and France against Russia during the Crimean War, though they took no part in the hostilities.

Fear of Russia resulted in a significant emphasis on the defensibility of Scandinavia against invasion. Following the union of Sweden and Norway in 1814, Swedish authorities decommissioned and demolished many border fortifications between the two countries that had both defended Norway against Swedish attack and supported Danish–Norwegian assaults on Sweden over the preceding centuries. As a result, after the 1820s the Swedish–Russian border, along with the much shorter Norwegian–Russian border in the High North, effectively formed the boundary separating a new Scandinavian "pluralistic security community" from its common Russian foe.[44] Over the course of the nineteenth century, military infrastructure along the Swedish–Russian border was strengthened. Northern industrial and commercial hubs were felt to be particularly vulnerable. The construction of a railway linking the rich iron mines of northern Sweden with the Norwegian port at Narvik led to a secret Norwegian–Swedish joint defence agreement in the event of Russian attack, notwithstanding the upswell of Norwegian nationalism at the time.[45] Fear of Russian aggression culminated to the construction of an enormous fortification resembling "a Nordic inland Gibraltar" at the village of Boden, 1100 kilometres north of Stockholm.[46] One of the most expensive military undertakings in Scandinavian history, the fortress at Boden indicates the degree of popular and political concern over Russian militarism. It came to serve as an enduring symbol of Scandinavian military capability and political independence. The decision to construct fortifications at Boden had been taken in 1900, while Norway and Sweden were still joined in a political union; thus it was designed to protect both countries from Russian aggression. Although it entered service only in 1907, after Norway had achieved independence, it remained a hub of

Cold War military activity against the Soviet Union, closing only in 1988 as the Cold War was drawing to a close.

The Scandinavians perceived the Russian threat as targeting the natural resources of their northern provinces, and the Boden fortress was explicitly justified in terms of defending Sweden–Norway's control over the north's mineral wealth.[47] Fears that Russia coveted Scandinavian resources reflected deep social and economic disparities on either side of the border. Though Russia was larger and more powerful, northern Scandinavia was far more prosperous. In the late 1800s, Murmansk, the largest Russian town on the Kola Peninsula, had only seven hundred inhabitants, whereas Norway's Finnmark county had four major towns with more than 10,000 residents and supported "trade, magazines, doctors, clergy, mobility, post offices, telegraphs and steam ships," in contrast to the "lawless" Russian north; clearly, "the two sides of the northernmost parts of the Kola peninsula represent[ed] two radically different forms of societies. Sweden–Norway represented civilisation; Finland–Russia manifested the opposite."[48] Thus, for at least two hundred years the defence of northern Norway (and Sweden) against the threat of Russian aggression has been understood as vital not only to territorial integrity and sovereignty but to national prosperity as well.

So it is unsurprising that the second core theme in the official Norwegian understanding of security in the High North is natural resources. Forestry, fisheries, and mineral wealth motivated early Scandinavian competition and settlement in the north before catalysing cooperation to counter potential Russian claims. More recently, Norwegian policy-makers have shifted their focus to a resource perceived as fundamental to the High North and the broader national interest: petroleum. Since its beginnings in the 1970s, the Norwegian energy industry has relied on strong government support for the development of offshore hydrocarbon deposits. The state provided the bulk of funding for the initial development of offshore oil and gas in the North Sea, making it for a time the largest site in the world for oil investment and extraction.[49] Now that North Sea production is declining, Norwegian leaders are looking farther north, and High North energy extraction has become an increasingly attractive option for sustaining Norway's economic prosperity. Given the greater geopolitical relevance of the High North compared to southern Norwegian waters, energy has shifted from being primarily a domestic and economic issue to one deeply embedded in foreign and security policy. "The guidelines on Norwegian oil and gas policy are well established," the High North Strategy states. "At the same time, Norway must be capable of understanding and dealing with the more central position of energy-related questions in the exercise of our foreign and security policy."[50] The challenges for Norway are related not to the regulation or management of the extractive process *per se*, but rather to the context in which petroleum development in the High North is being pursued.

Over the past decade, offshore petroleum reserves in the High North have principally been framed in terms of Norway's energy and economic security, and to a lesser extent that of Europe. "The official Norwegian discourse clearly rides on an energy plot," Jensen and Skedsmo observe, "and on the perceptions of the European Arctic as a future petroleum province of regional and even global significance."[51] This has been driven by overt enthusiasm among Norwegian officials; a major Norwegian financial newspaper reported that "foreign minister Jonas Gahr Støre talks so incessantly about oil and the High North, he wouldn't look amiss in a boiler suit and hard hat."[52] According to Defence Minister Anne-Grete Strøm-Erichsen, "energy supplies and energy security have become security policy, which explains why increasing international interest in the High North as an emerging energy region should come as no surprise."[53] A former minister for petroleum and energy, Ola Borten Moe, was nicknamed "Oil-Ola" due to his support for energy development.[54]

In foreign and defence policy documents of all kinds, securing and developing northern energy reserves is identified as the core objective of the High North Initiative and as integral to Norway's national interest. Reporting to the Storting (Norway's Parliament) in 2007, the Ministry of Defence noted: "In the space of a very short time, energy security has become a leading policy issue. The need to ensure long-term, stable energy supplies is of vital concern to many countries. Norway's position as a major and reliable exporter of power increases the international importance of Norway and contiguous areas. The Government will engage in a long-term policy to ensure internationally stable energy supplies and safe transport routes."[55] The policy document guiding post–Cold War and post-9/11 military restructuring is also explicit that "our strategic position is enhanced by the natural resources we manage. Oil and gas on the Norwegian continental shelf are of major strategic importance to other states."[56] Minister Støre has often discussed the link between energy and security in the High North, including the importance of peaceful cooperation for resource development and its primacy over other policy areas:

> Today, it is the energy question that is pressing all other issues to one side, altering the perspectives – not only those of Norway and our Russian neighbours, but of anyone with an interest in energy production, supply security

and climate and environmental challenges ... Energy is changing how the concept of geopolitics is understood. An industrial country which is unable to secure for itself a steady supply of energy will face considerable problems ... If the development of a predictable framework around energy development fails, this region will lose its main assets, stability, transparency and peaceful progress.[57]

Norwegian officials now see energy extraction as intimately connected to the new security situation, supplanting the earlier focus on defending against Russia. A broader approach to national security is identified as necessary because of both the growing importance of energy resources and possible threats to the energy sector (see Dolata in chapter 8). Such threats include interruption of supply and possible inter-state competition over resource deposits, which is coded reference to Russian challenges in the Barents Sea. Moreover, ensuring energy extraction is identified as the new context in which Norwegian security interests in the High North are to be assessed:

> Norway's security situation is characterized by a broader and more complex risk assessment, in which a comprehensive existential threat has been supplanted by uncertainty and unpredictability about the security challenges we could face. This also applies to potential security challenges in Norway's immediate vicinity, where the strategic importance of the High North and resource management over immense stretches of sea *provided central parameters for Norwegian security and defence policy.*[58]

Among industrialized economies, questions of energy security usually focus on supply and declining global production, but in Norway, as in other petroleum-producing states, energy security is employed as a proxy for the contributions of petroleum extraction to the overall economy. Policy-makers' focus on expanding extraction in the Barents region is driven by concern that "oil production in Norway peaked in 2001 and has since declined by around 30%," with the rate of decline exceeding earlier estimates by the Norwegian Petroleum Directorate and the IEA.[59] The economic challenge of addressing declining petroleum production is stark: as of 2010, there were "about a thousand producing oil and gas wells [in Norwegian waters]. With an anticipated production decrease of about 20%, about 200 new producing wells will have to be drilled each year in order to maintain a relatively stable production level, a target that even the Petroleum Directorate admits is 'not very realistic.'"[60] Expanding drilling in the less developed Barents region is seen as the only viable way to maintain production levels and thereby perpetuate the energy economy, which is particularly important given the unique configuration of energy revenues and society in Norway.

From the outset, there have been strong ties between Norwegian oil production and maintenance of the welfare state. This is enshrined in the "10 Oil Commandments'" passed by the Storting in 1971, which paved the way for the founding of Statoil (now called Equinor) as a state-owned oil company by unanimous parliamentary vote in 1972. The public nature of the Norwegian energy sector has fostered a powerful government- and industry-propagated narrative that "'what is good for the oil industry is good for Norway' … This link has frequently been endorsed by government officials, who have pointed to the importance of oil and revenues in establishing one of the most comprehensive welfare systems in the world."[61] For instance, in 2007 the state's net rents from the petroleum industry comprised around 31 per cent of total government revenues, and they are "seen as an indispensable part of the government's national pension fund."[62] The "Norwegian petroleum fairy tale" has become a popular metaphor for the supposedly virtuous relationship between oil rents, welfare provision, and intergenerational justice.

The extent to which Norway has prioritized petroleum development is evident in the collusion that has developed between government and industry with the goal of maximizing public support for oil and gas extraction. Perhaps the most striking illustration of this is Konkraft, a high-level forum established "with the objective of developing joint strategies between industry and state representatives to make the Norwegian shelf more globally 'competitive.' For the industry that means accessing 'prospective acreage,' primarily the unexplored hydrocarbon deposits in the Barents Sea and the [Lofoten] region in particular."[63] Konkraft facilitates quarterly closed-door meetings between politicians and industry chaired by the Minister of Petroleum and Energy and has served as the channel down which state officials provide information on government policy and upcoming decisions. A 2008 documentary by the Norwegian Broadcasting Corporation revealed that the senior Konkraft bureaucrat at the Ministry of Petroleum and Energy "had secret meetings to advise [industry] on how to run an effective lobby[ing] campaign. For example, he advised them to improve their environmental image and concentrate on influencing mayors in northern Norway and politicians in Parliament."[64] Komkraft illustrates the access enjoyed by industry to the highest levels of the Norwegian state. Given their shared interest in expanding fossil fuel extraction while maintaining a pro-environmental image, "the state is not circumscribed by transnational oil companies but is enrolled as an active participant in efforts to make new hydrocarbon fields accessible."[65] The state has made strong efforts to encourage and sustain public support for the energy sector – in particular, for expanded operations in the High North – even as various actors have challenged the sustainability of the "petroleum fairy tale."

What the Norwegian government and petroleum industry are combating through these efforts is fairly clear. Despite the ongoing narrative power of the petroleum fairy tale, "a series of WWF reports, and other forms of local activism, are rescripting the Norwegian Arctic as an 'ecoregion' that is sustained by a complex network of human and non-human relations and requires new trans-institutional and transnational forms of collaboration."[66] Thus, in addition to geopolitical and military challenges from Russia, political threats to Arctic petroleum development from NGOs, civil society groups, and local communities are being framed as security issues. In particular, direct actions and activist campaigns that threaten production are constructed as dangerous within the framework of energy security. The Ministry of Defence has made it clear that threats to the petroleum sector also threaten the national economy and fall within the purview of security policy: "The sustainability of the petroleum sector is more fragile than ever, and the impact of even minor interruptions will affect not only the economy but security as well."[67]

Thus, security in the Norwegian Arctic is explicitly tied to hydrocarbon extraction. Energy is the cornerstone of all recent Norwegian Arctic policies, such that "the High North has been revitalized by a discourse on the prospects that the Barents Sea could become a new, strategically important petroleum province."[68] This signals an important departure from post–Cold War Norwegian security policy, which emphasized desecuritizing the High North in order to normalize relations with Russia. In his study of High North security discourses, Jensen finds that "data from the 1990s indicate a persistent effort by participants in official discourses to de-securitize and de-politicize energy and petroleum policy, thereby maintaining a clear line of separation between it and security and foreign policy."[69] Driven by global energy demand and increasingly contentious politics over global energy resources and perceived scarcity of supply, this approach was increasingly abandoned post-2000: "As concerns for energy as [a] strategic and scarce resource grew, the High North once again became a subject of high politics. This flew in the face of the stated objectives of Norway's post–Cold War security and foreign policy."[70] The construction of the High North as a key region for Norwegian security has become prevalent in official security discourse and informs all aspects of state policy toward the region. Moreover, the connection between energy and economic security means that the well-being of all Norwegians is implicated in the continued extraction of northern hydrocarbons. Ironically, the emphasis on energy highlights a significant commonality with respect to Arctic security between Norway and Russia. Both countries "regard the European Arctic's most important feature to be its prospects as a resource province, with more or less emphasis on security."[71] Energy is so important to Norway's economy that it warrants securitization and elevation to the apex of policy priorities, and challenges to petroleum extraction also challenge the national interest.

Conclusion

Despite the many political and ecological changes in the circumpolar region, there has been a high degree of continuity in how the Norwegian state has defined its Arctic security interests. This chapter has argued that successive Norwegian governments have understood security in the High North to mean defending against instability emanating from Russia and facilitating the extraction of natural resources, particularly petroleum. Though this conception of the Norwegian national interest in the region is long-standing, predating Norway as an independent state, Norway has undertaken a significant resecuritization of the region under its new High North Initiative since 2006. These policies reflect a shift away from the post–Cold War goal of desecuritizing the Arctic and normalizing relations with Russia. In its place, the Norwegian state has embraced a conception of security that views Russian aggression as threatening and hydrocarbon extraction as vital to Norwegian prosperity. In this light, securitization of the High North has been re-established as the norm for Norwegian politics rather than a Cold War aberration, and the dominant definition of Arctic security continues to be one that privileges the core interests of the sovereign state over the maintenance of a stable natural environment.

NOTES

1 This analysis is particularly indebted to discourse analysis of government documents and Norwegian-language media conducted by Johan Eriksson, "Security in the Barents Region: Interpretations and Implications of the Norwegian Barents Initiative," *Cooperation and Conflict* 30, no. 3 (1995): 259–86; Leif C. Jensen and Pål Wilter Skedsmo, "Approaching the North: Norwegian and Russian Foreign Policy Discourses on the European Arctic," *Polar Research* 29, no. 3 (2010): 439–50; Leif C. Jensen and Geir Hønneland, "Framing the High North: Public Discourses in Norway after 2000," *Acta Borealia* 8, no. 1 (2011): 37–54; Leif C. Jensen, "Seduced and Surrounded by

Security: A Post-Structuralist Take on Norwegian High North Securitizing Discourses," *Cooperation and Conflict* 48, no. 1 (2012): 80–99.

2 Odd Gunnar Skagestad, *The "High North": An Elastic Concept in Norwegian Arctic Policy* (Lysaker: Fridtjof Nansen Institute, 2010).

3 Jensen, "Seduced and Surrounded by Security," 81.

4 Norway, *The Norwegian Government's High North Strategy* (Oslo: Ministry of Foreign Affairs, 2006a), 13.

5 Translated in Jensen and Skedsmo, "Approaching the North," 442.

6 Jensen and Skedsmo, "Approaching the North," 442.

7 Arne Olav Brundtland, "The Nordic Balance: Past and Present," *Cooperation and Conflict* 1, no. 4 (1965): 30–63.

8 Kristian Åtland, "Mikhail Gorbachev, the Murmansk Initiative, and the Desecuritization of Interstate Relations in the Arctic," *Cooperation and Conflict* 43, no. 3 (2008): 289–311.

9 See ibid., 290.

10 Jensen, "Seduced and Surrounded," 88.

11 Åtland, "Mikhail Gorbachev," 2008.

12 Jens Petter Nielsen, "The Russia of the Tsar and North Norway: 'The Russian Danger' Revisited," *Acta Borealia* 19, no. 1 (2002): 75–94.

13 Eriksson, "Security in the Barents Region," 266.

14 Qtd in ibid., 267.

15 Jensen, "Seduced and Surrounded by Security," 81.

16 Eriksson, "Security in the Barents Region," 266.

17 Ibid., 275.

18 Ibid., 276.

19 Quoted in ibid., 267.

20 UNDP, *Human Development Report 1994: New Dimensions of Human Security* (New York, 1994), 23.

21 Eriksson, "Security in the Barents Region," 267.

22 Qtd in ibid., 270.

23 Ibid., 268.

24 Ibid., 268.

25 Ministry of Defence, *Guidelines for the Armed Forces and Development in the Years Ahead 1999–2002* (Oslo, 1998). Qtd in Jensen, "Seduced and Surrounded," 85.

26 Ministry of Defence, "Our Defence in an International Perspective," *Defence Minister's Annual Speech* (Oslo Military Society, 10 January 2000). Qtd in Jensen, "Seduced and Surrounded," 85–6.

27 Ministry of Defence, "The Government's Defence Policy Challenges and Priorities," *Defence Minister's Annual Speech* (Oslo Military Society, 7 January 2002). Qtd in Jensen, "Seduced and Surrounded by Security," 86.

28 Ibid., 87.

29 Ibid., 86.

30 Norway, *The Soria-Moria Declaration on International Policy* (Oslo: Office of the Prime Minister, 2006b), https://www.regjeringen.no/en/dokumenter /the-soria-moria-declaration-on-internati/id438515.

31 Jensen and Skedsmo, "Approaching the North," 439.

32 Norway, *The Norwegian Government's High North Strategy*, 7.

33 Jensen and Skedsmo, "Approaching the North," 442–3.

34 Jensen and Hønneland, "Framing the High North," 44.

35 Jensen, "Seduced and Surrounded by Security," 92.

36 Jensen and Skedsmo, "Approaching the North," 447.

37 Tore Andre Kjetland Fjeldsbø, "The Nordic Countries Extends Military Cooperation," *Nora Region Trends*, 13 April 2014), http://www.noraregiontrends.org /news/news-single/article/ the-nordic-countries-extends-military-cooperation/87.

38 Andrew Higgins, "Norway Reverts to Cold War Mode as Russian Air Patrols Spike," *New York Times*, 1 April 2015, http://www.nytimes.com/2015/04 /02/world/europe/a-newly-assertive-russia-jolts-norways-air-defenses-into -action.html?mwrsm=Email&_r=0.

39 Qtd in Higgins, "Norway Reverts to Cold War Mode."

40 Eriksson, "Security in the Barents Region," 274.

41 Ministry of Foreign Affairs, "An Ocean of Possibilities: A Responsible Policy for the High North," Speech by Foreign Minister Jonas Gahr Støre (Tromsø: University of Tromsø, 2005). Qtd in Jensen, "Seduced and Surrounded," 89.

42 Magnus Rodell, "Fortifications in the Wilderness: The Making of Swedish–Russian Borderlands around 1900," *Journal of Northern Studies* 1 (2009): 72.

43 Nielsen, "The Russia of the Tsar and North Norway," 77.

44 Roald Berg, "The Nineteenth-Century Norwegian–Swedish Border: Imagined Community or Pluralistic Security System?" *Journal of Northern Studies* 1 (2009): 94.

45 Berg, "The Nineteenth Century Norwegian–Swedish Border," 97.

46 Rodell, "Fortifications in the Wilderness," 70.

47 Ibid., 81.

48 Ibid., 76.

49 Berit Kristoffersen and Stephen Young, "Geographies of Security and Statehood in Norway's 'Battle of the North,'" *Geoforum* 41, no. 4 (2010): 579.

50 Norway, *The Norwegian Government's High North Strategy*, 10.

51 Jensen and Skedsmo, "Approaching the North," 448.

52 Qtd in ibid., 443.

53 Anne–Grete Strøm-Erichsen, *Nordlys*, 26 September 2007). Qtd in Jensen, "Seduced and Surrounded," 90.

54 Berit Kristoffersen and Brigt Dale, "Post-Petroleum Security in Lofoten: How Identity Matters," *Arctic Review on Law and Politics* 5, no. 2 (2014): 204.

55 Ministry of Defence, *Proposition to the Storting no. 1 2007–2008* 2007 (Oslo, 2007). Qtd in Jensen, "Seduced and Surrounded," 93.

56 Ministry of Defence, *Restructuring the Armed Forces, 2002–2005* (Oslo, 2001). Qtd in Jensen, "Seduced and Surrounded," 86.

57 Ministry of Foreign Affairs, "An Ocean of Possibilities." Qtd in Jensen, "Seduced and Surrounded," 89.

58 Ministry of Defence, "Continuing the Modernisation of the Armed Forces," *Proposition to the Storting no. 42 2003–2004* (Oslo, 2004). Qtd in Jensen, "Seduced and Surrounded," 87–8; emphasis added.

59 Kristoffersen and Young, "Geographies of Security and Statehood," 580.

60 Ibid., 580.

61 Kristoffersen and Dale, "Post-Petroleum Security," 208.

62 Kristoffersen and Young, "Geographies of Security and Statehood," 580.

63 Ibid., 580.

64 NRK Brennpunkt, "Spillet om oljen [Game about oil]," Documentary (March 22, 2008). Available at www.nrk.no/brennpunkt.

65 Kristoffersen and Young, "Geographies of Security and Statehood," 581.

66 Ibid.,, 583.

67 Ministry of Defence, "A Defence for the Protection of Norway's Security, Interests, and Values," *Proposition to the Storting no. 48 2007–2008* (Oslo: 2008). Qtd in Jensen, "Seduced and Surrounded by Security," 90.

68 Jensen and Skedsmo, "Approaching the North," 443.

69 Jensen, "Seduced and Surrounded by Security," 81.

70 Ibid., 81.

71 Jensen and Skedsmo, "Approaching the North," 448.

6 Russia and Arctic Security: Inward-Looking Realities

ALEXANDER SERGUNIN[1]

The outbreak of the Ukrainian crisis and Moscow's military intervention in the Syrian conflict have spurred new North American and Western European accusations that Russia is behaving like an aggressive and militarist power, not only in Eastern Europe and the Middle East but also in the Arctic.[2] This narrative builds upon Western political, media, and academic concerns that modernization programs and changes in Russia's military capabilities in its Arctic territories may represent a game-changing build-up that increases the risk of state-to-state conflict in the region. According to this line of argument, Moscow first revealed its Arctic ambitions in 2007 when it resumed long-range air and naval patrols in the Arctic and North Atlantic regions and Russian explorer and politician Artur Chilingarov planted a titanium flag on the seabed under the North Pole. Vladimir Putin's Munich speech, delivered in February of that year, had denounced the United States' dominance in global relations and its "almost uncontained hyper use of force in international relations," signalling that Russia would chart its own international political course in the future. Russia–NATO relations became strained, with responses to the Ukraine crisis in 2014 feeding even greater Western scepticism about Russia's true aims for the international order – including in the Arctic region.

According to some Western analysts, because of Russia's economic weakness and technological backwardness, the country tends to resort to military-coercive instruments to protect its national interests in the circumpolar North. By extension, this could lead to a regional arms race, remilitarization of the High North, and military conflict. Accordingly, these analysts expected that Moscow would dramatically increase its military activities and presence in the region, as well as accelerate its military modernization programs, in the wake of the Ukrainian and Syrian crises.[3] These concerns have apparently been misplaced, however. Instead of significantly expanding its military build-up and military activities in the region, the Kremlin has continued to make the socio-economic development of the Arctic Zone of the Russian Federation (AZRF) its central priority. In parallel, Moscow has managed to bracket out Arctic cooperation from its current tensions with the West so that it can maintain relations with other regional players on a cooperative track. Thus, in sharp contrast with the internationally widespread stereotype of Russia as a revisionist power in the Arctic, Moscow's future actions in the region are more likely to be fairly pragmatic.

This chapter explores how Russia's actions can be evaluated in more positive terms, particularly as a country that is interested in circumpolar security and stability and is open to international cooperation in the High North. Moscow insists that its intentions, as articulated in the Arctic doctrines of 2008, 2013, and 2020, are inward-focused and purely defensive, aimed principally at the protection of the country's sovereign rights and legitimate interests.[4] Primary among those interests is the development of the AZRF, already a vital region for the national economy and one with great promise for further development in energy, mining, infrastructure, communications, and other sectors. The Kremlin also maintains that it is not pursuing a revisionist policy, but rather wishes to resolve all disputes in the Arctic by peaceful means, relying on international law and organizations.[5] Military strategists generally insist that the country must be prepared for contemporary and emerging security issues, no aggression implied.

Conceptually, Russia's leadership now realizes that most of the threats and challenges to the AZRF originate from inside rather than outside the country. These problems are rooted in a confluence of factors, including the degradation of Soviet-made economic, transport, and social infrastructure in the region, the current resource-oriented model of the Russian economy, and the lack of funds and managerial skills in Russia to properly develop the AZRF. It follows that Russia's current Arctic strategy is inward- and not outward-looking. It aims to solve existing domestic problems rather than focus on external expansion. Moreover, in developing the AZRF, Moscow is seeking to demonstrate that it is open for international cooperation and to foreign investment and know-how. In short, Moscow's international strategy in the region has been subordinated to its domestic needs. Although Russia's preoccupation with its internal problems does not preclude the Kremlin from a rather assertive international course when it comes to the protection of Russia's national interests, powerful domestic and international incentives are encouraging Russia's political leadership to opt for cooperative behaviour in the Arctic and seek solutions to regional problems via negotiations, compromises, and the strengthening of governance mechanisms.[6]

Threat Perceptions and Security Doctrines

In the decade after the collapse of the Soviet Union, the Kremlin paid little attention to the Arctic. With the end of the Cold War, the region lost its former military-strategic significance for Moscow as a zone of potential confrontation with the United States and NATO. During the Yeltsin era, the economic potential of the region was underestimated. Moreover, in the 1990s, Russia's Arctic regions were perceived by the federal government as a burden or source of various socio-economic problems rather than an economically promising region. Moscow almost abandoned the far northern regions, which had to rely on themselves (or on foreign humanitarian assistance) for sustenance.

The situation started to change slowly in the early 2000s, when the general socio-economic situation in Russia improved and the Putin government came to power with an ambitious agenda of Russia's revival. In 2008, President Dmitry Medvedev approved the first Russian post-Soviet Arctic strategy, titled *Foundations of the State Policy of the Russian Federation in the Arctic Up to and Beyond 2020* (Strategy-2008).[7] The six-page document listed Russia's national interests in the region as follows: to develop the resources of the Arctic; to turn the Northern Sea Route (NSR) into a unified national transportation corridor and line of communication; and to maintain the region as a zone of peace and international cooperation. According to plans, the multifaceted development of the northern territories is expected to culminate in the Arctic becoming Russia's "leading strategic resource base" between 2016 and 2020. The strategic security goal was defined as "maintenance of the necessary combat potential of general-purpose troops (forces)," strengthening the Coast Guard of the Federal Security Service (FSS) and border controls in the AZRF, and establishing technical control over straits and river estuaries along the whole NSR. Thus, the Russian armed forces deployed in the AZRF, which were to be organized under a single command (the Arctic Group of Forces or AGF), were tasked not simply with defending territory but also with protecting Russia's economic interests in the region. In turn, this required increasing the capacity of the Northern Fleet, which was (and is) seen as an important instrument for demonstrating Russia's sovereign rights in the High North as well as protecting its economic interests in the region.

Although the document was designed primarily for domestic needs (particularly, it aimed at setting priorities for development in the AZRF), many foreign analysts tended to interpret the Strategy-2008 as "solid evidence" of Russia's revisionist aspirations in the region.[8] For them, Russian plans to "define the outer border of the AZRF," create the AGF, and build a network of border guard stations along the coastline of the Arctic Ocean were evidence of Moscow's expansionist desires in the Arctic region more broadly. The Kremlin's mantra that these initiatives were of a purely defensive nature was met with great scepticism, particularly amongst "hawkish" Western analysts who wrongly equated any investments in military capabilities with an intent to use these capabilities for offensive purposes.

Strategy-2008 was rather general in nature, so its provisions needed to be articulated in more specific detail and updated regularly by other documents. On 20 February 2013, President Vladimir Putin approved *The Strategy for the Development of the Arctic Zone of the Russian Federation* (Strategy-2013),[9] which was both a follow-up and an update of the Strategy-2008 (although it could not be viewed as Russia's full-fledged Arctic doctrine, for it covered only the AZRF rather than the whole Arctic region). In this sense, the document was comparable with the Canadian (2009) and Norwegian (2006) strategies for the development of their northern territories. Strategy-2013 also contained some international dimensions, including Moscow's intention to legally define Russia's continental shelf in the Arctic Ocean and file a new application to the UN Commission on the Limits of the Continental Shelf (CLCS), as well as the need for international cooperation in areas such as exploration and exploitation of natural resources, environmental protection, preservation of Indigenous peoples' traditional economy, and culture. The main objective of the document, however, was first and foremost to provide a doctrinal/conceptual basis for the sustainable development of the AZRF. In short, it was designed for domestic rather than international consumption.

Russia's new strategy reflected much more openness to international cooperation to solve numerous Arctic problems and ensure the sustainable development of the region as a whole. Much like the 2008 document, Strategy-2013 emphasized Russia's national sovereignty over the AZRF and NSR and called for the protection of the country's national interests in the region. Along with this rather traditional stance, the new strategy articulated an impressive list of priority areas for cooperation with potential international partners. This provided Strategy-2013 with a more positive international image than the previous document. As far as the purely military aspects of Strategy-2013 were concerned, the document laid out the following tasks:

• Ensuring a favourable operational regime for Russian troops deployed in the AZRF to adequately meet military dangers as well as threats to Russia's national security.

- Providing the AGF with military training and combat readiness to protect Russian interests in its exclusive economic zone (EEZ) and to deter threats to and aggression against the country.
- Improving the AGF's structure and composition, providing these forces with modern armaments and infrastructure.
- Improving air and maritime monitoring systems.
- Applying dual-use technologies to ensure both AZRF's military security and sustainable socio-economic development.
- Completing hydrographic work to define more precisely the external boundaries of Russia's territorial waters, EEZ, and continental shelf.[10]

In sum, Strategy-2013 invited further discussions on Russia's Arctic policies rather than offering a sound and comprehensive doctrine. For it to become an efficient national strategy, it would need to be further clarified, specified, and instrumentalized in a series of federal laws, regulations, and task programs. The Russian Arctic strategy would also need to be made more palatable to the international community. Although the Russian Arctic doctrine of 2013 clearly addresses soft security, foreign audiences – by virtue of inertia – have continued to perceive Russian documents of this kind as manifestations of Moscow's expansionist plans in the High North.

The Ukrainian crisis amounted to a total overhaul of Russia's national security doctrine, beginning with Russia's military strategy. On 26 December 2014, President Vladimir Putin approved a new version of Russian military doctrine. Although the Arctic was mentioned only once in that document, it is remarkable that, for the first time, the protection of Russia's national interests there in peacetime was assigned to the Russian armed forces.[11] In general, the new military doctrine remained defensive in character; even so, Russia's neighbours (including those in the High North) remained concerned about Moscow's intentions in the region. In July of the following year, President Putin approved a new version of Russia's maritime doctrine,[12] which identified the Arctic as one of two regions (the other being the North Atlantic) where NATO activities and international competition for natural resources and sea routes continued to grow and required an "adequate response" from Russia. According to the document, naval forces and the nuclear icebreaker fleet were to be modernized by the 2020s. In late December 2015, President Putin also approved a new national security strategy.[13] The Arctic was mentioned three times in that document. First, the region was identified as one where the international competition for natural oceanic resources could increase. Second, the Arctic was described as an important transport/communication corridor crucial to Russia's economic security. Third, the High North was depicted as a region of peace, stability, and international cooperation.

The West's response to the Ukrainian crisis has affected Moscow's threat perceptions in the Arctic to some extent but has not significantly changed the Kremlin's general attitude toward the region, which, according to the Russian leadership, should remain a zone of peace and security. In November 2016, President Putin signed a new version of the *Russian Foreign Policy Concept*,[14] which mentioned the Arctic twice. First, it was described as a region for potential cooperation with Canada. Second, it was mentioned in the special section on the High North. The document underscored the importance of cooperation between the regional players in areas such as sustainable development of natural resources, transportation systems (including the NSR), environment protection, and preservation of peace and stability. The concept also emphasized the need to strengthen regional multilateral institutions, including the Arctic Council and the Barents Euro-Arctic Council (BEAC). The document insisted particularly on the need to insulate the Arctic from current tensions between Russia and the West and to prevent any military confrontation in the region, thus reaffirming that cooperation should remain the dominant paradigm in the circumpolar region.[15]

Hard Security Strategy

As mentioned above, a radical shift in Russia's threat perceptions in the Arctic region has taken place over the last quarter of a century. This shift has engendered a clear tendency toward an increased role for soft rather than hard security-related concerns. These soft security concerns include ensuring Russia's access to and control over the natural resources and transportation routes in the region, climate change mitigation, and the clean-up of environmental "hot spots." At the same time, some Russian strategists believe that various security threats and challenges in the region require the preservation and further development of certain military capabilities and an expanded presence in the North. They note that the ongoing Ukrainian crisis has negatively affected Russia's relations with NATO and its member-states, with NATO suspending several cooperative projects with Russia, including military-to-military contacts and the development of confidence- and security-building measures.

In contrast to some pessimistic expectations, however, there has been no substantial change in Russia's perceptions of the role of military power in the Arctic. Moscow's military strategies remain geared toward three major goals: to demonstrate and ascertain Russia's sovereignty over the AZRF, including the exclusive economic zone and the continental shelf; to protect its economic interests in the High North; and to demonstrate that Russia retains its great power status and has world-class military capabilities.[16] In a sense, Russian military strategies are comparable with those of other coastal states (especially the United States and Canada).

Foreign analysts tend to forget, or completely misunderstand, that the extent of Russian strategic and conventional forces deployed in the Arctic – and the scale of its military modernization programs – is a function of the fact that Russia inherited the Soviet Union's nuclear strategic forces structure. Thus, the naval bases on the Kola Peninsula in northwestern Russia are still home to two thirds of Russia's strategic nuclear submarines. This military potential is strictly for purposes of strategic deterrence on a global scale, not to ensure Moscow's military dominance in the Arctic.[17] The significant degeneration of the Soviet-era military machine in the Arctic in the 1990s and early 2000s left Russia's nuclear and conventional forces badly in need of modernization in order to meet new challenges and threats. The main idea behind the modernization plans is to make the Russian armed forces in the Arctic more compact, better equipped, and better trained – an effort that began with the launch of the third State Rearmament Program (2007–15), which covered both nuclear and conventional components and started well before the Ukrainian crisis.

Russia's modernization program for its strategic forces in the North is limited in scope and aims to replace decommissioned submarines and surface vessels rather than to increase these forces in terms of quantity and offensive potential. In fact, the total number of strategic submarines and large surface ships continues to decrease relative to Soviet days in the 1980s. Russia's current programs include the renewal of its fleet of eight strategic nuclear submarines – a decision that was not influenced by the Ukrainian crisis. At present, only six Delta IV-class submarines are earmarked for modernization. Russia intends to replace its Typhoon- and Delta IV-class submarines with new Borey-class fourth-generation nuclear-powered strategic submarines. The first Borey-class submarine, the *Yuri Dolgoruky*, has been in operation with the Northern Fleet since January 2013. Three other Borey-class submarines – the *Prince Vladimir,* the *Prince Oleg,* and the *Prince Pozharsky* – have been designed for the Northern Fleet and will be operational between 2018 and 2020.[18] These components of the Russian forces in the High North are geared toward strategic deterrence and have little to do with geopolitical rivalry in the Arctic theatre.

Russia's conventional forces *have* been affected by the Ukrainian crisis in terms of their composition and posture. These modernization programs are quite modest, however, and involve upgrading rather than new offensive capabilities or the restoration of Soviet military power.

These projects serve a twofold purpose: to provide the Russian forces with infrastructure that meets modern requirements; and to have this revamped infrastructure serve non-military policy objectives, including allowing Russia to implement international agreements on Arctic search and rescue (2011), and with respect to preparedness for responding to oil spills in the Arctic (2013). The new radar stations, airfields, and search-and-rescue centres along the Arctic coast will be also helpful in terms of further development of the Northern Sea Route and cross-polar flights. Plans have been announced to transform the motorized infantry and marine brigades near Pechenga (Murmansk region) into an Arctic special forces unit. Soldiers in this unit are to be specially trained and equipped with modern personal equipment for Arctic military operations. As mentioned above, all conventional forces in the AZRF are to be organized into the AGF, to be led by a joint Arctic command.[19]

The Ukrainian crisis and NATO's reaction to it have precipitated some adjustments to Russia's military planning. While two Pechenga-based brigades were left in place, the Arctic brigade was created ahead of schedule (in January 2015) and deployed to Alakurtti, near the Finnish–Russian border. Given the "increased NATO military threat" in the North, President Putin decided to accelerate the creation of a new strategic command, "North"; this was accomplished by December 2014 (three years ahead of the schedule). It was also announced that a second Arctic brigade would be formed and stationed in the Yamal-Nenets autonomous district east of the Urals above the Arctic Circle.[20] Also, the Russian defence minister Sergei Shoigu announced that two new Arctic coast defence divisions would be founded by 2018 as part of an effort to strengthen security along the NSR. One of these is now stationed on the Kola Peninsula (in addition the existing military units), the other in the eastern Arctic (Chukotka Peninsula). The new forces are tasked with anti-assault, anti-sabotage, and anti-aircraft defence duties along the NSR.[21] Both units cooperate closely with law enforcement authorities, including the Ministry of Interior, the National Guard, and the Border Guard Service (BGS).

Growing tensions with NATO have compelled Russia to pay more attention to its air defence units in the AZRF, on the Kola Peninsula near Severodvinsk (Arkhangelsk region), at Chukotka, and on several Russian islands in the Arctic: Novaya Zemlya, Franz Josef Land, the New Siberian Islands, and Wrangel Island. Some of these units have "rebooted" old Soviet airfields and military bases. These units, which are equipped with (among other things) RS-26 Rubezh coastal missile systems, S-300 air-defence missiles, and the Pantsyr-S1 anti-aircraft artillery weapon system,[22] were merged into a joint task force in October 2014. Measures to increase Moscow's military power in the region include the creation of a new air force and air defence army, including regiments armed with MiG-31 interceptor aircraft, S-400 air-defence missile systems (to replace the S-300 systems), and radar units.[23] One goal is to restore continuous radar coverage along Russia's entire northern coast – a capacity that had been lost in the 1990s. To that end, thirteen airfields, an air force test range, and ten radar sites and direction centres will be established in the Arctic in the coming years.

According to a statement in 2010 by the head of the FSB's Border Guard Service (BGS), Vladimir Pronichev, the main challenges facing the BGS were the unauthorized presence of foreign ships and research vessels in Russian Arctic waters, illegal migration, drug smuggling, and poaching.[24] Terrorist attacks against oil platforms were also seen as a threat to Arctic security.[25] Russia is also seriously concerned about nuclear terrorism. Possible targets for terrorists include industrial infrastructure and oil platforms, as well as nuclear power plants and nuclear waste storage facilities. There are two nuclear plants – Kola and Bilibin – in the AZRF. Most notably, more than 200 decommissioned nuclear reactors from submarines and icebreakers from the Soviet period are stored on the Kola Peninsula and must be carefully protected against terrorist attacks.[26]

The strengthening of the BGS is a high priority of Russia's national security policy in the High North. The first Arctic border guard unit, tasked with monitoring ship traffic and poaching activities, was created as early as 1994. The unit was reorganized in 2004–5, and new Arctic units were placed at border guard stations in Arkhangelsk and Murmansk in 2009. Since then, two new border guard commands – one in Murmansk for the western AZRF regions, the other in Petropavlovsk-Kamchatsky for the eastern – have been established. Border guards are now addressing more recent soft security threats and challenges, for example, by establishing reliable border control systems, applying new special visa regulations for certain regions, and implementing technological controls over fluvial zones and sites along the NSR, which today are being monitored from the air by border guard aircraft and on land and sea by the North-Eastern Border Guard Agency. The Russian border guards plan to establish a global monitoring network from Murmansk to Wrangel Island. Overall, Moscow plans to build twenty border guard stations along its Arctic coastline.[27]

Another structural change is the ongoing reorganization of the Russian Coast Guard (part of the BGS), which has been vested with wider responsibilities in the Arctic: in addition to its long-standing task of protecting biological resources in the Arctic Ocean, it now oversees oil and gas installations and shipping along the NSR. There are plans to equip the Coast Guard in the AZRF with the brand-new vessels of project 22,100. An Okean-class icegoing patrol ship, the *Polyarnaya Zvezda* (Polar Star), is currently undergoing sea trials in the Baltic Sea. Vessels of this class can break through ice up to a thickness of 31.4 inches. They can stay at sea for 60 straight days and have a range of 12,000 nautical miles at 20 knots. Each is equipped with a Ka-27 helicopter and can be supplied with Gorizont drones.[28] The attention that Russia now pays to the Coast Guard now is in line with that of other coastal states (especially Norway and Denmark). Moreover, Russia was actively involved in creating the Arctic Coast Guard Forum with the other Arctic coastal states in November 2015. This, along with the search-and-rescue agreement and other forms of international cooperation, affirms the perceived benefits of developing common situational awareness and practical interoperability to respond to incidents in the Arctic.[29]

Russia contends that its Arctic build-up is defensive and that the numbers of additional armed forces are small. The Kremlin views these activities as prudent, given the importance of the North to Russia's economic development plans, the increasing permeability of Russia's vast northern borders, and the anticipated increase in commercial shipping along Russia's Arctic coast as the sea ice disappears. Accordingly, Russia's modernized military infrastructure in the Arctic, including the Soviet air and naval bases that have been reopened in recent years, is dual-use in nature (meaning it can be used for military *or* civilian purposes, including search-and-rescue operations). Generally speaking, all of the Arctic nations' armed services and public safety organizations (army, navy, border and coast guards, and agencies dealing with emergency situations) have been charged with implementing the 2011 Arctic Search and Rescue Treaty negotiated under the auspices of the Arctic Council. Because each country is responsible for its own sector of the Arctic, Russia has the largest zone to cover. SAR activities, alongside responsibilities to facilitate safe navigation and respond to human or natural disasters, indicate a shift from armed forces performing purely military functions to also bearing responsibility for soft security missions.[30]

Soft Security Agenda

Russia has vital economic interests in the Arctic region. The industrial base in the AZRF currently accounts for as much as 20 per cent of the entire Russian GDP – even if only about 1.6 per cent of the country's population lives there – as well as nearly one quarter of Russia's export revenues. Fuelling these figures is the fact that the region produces no less than 95 per cent of the country's gas and around 70 per cent of its oil. Russian geologists have discovered some 200 oil and gas deposits, and it is anticipated that more than twenty large shelf deposits in the Barents and Kara Seas will be developed when prices rise. The AZRF's mining industries yield 99 per cent of Russia's diamonds, 98 per cent of its platinum, and most of its other rare metals. Reduced ice coverage as a result of global warming will mean improved access to these natural resources and a correspondingly greater significance for the AZRF. Russia's federal and regional governments, along with the private sector, have articulated plans to further develop the region's industries and infrastructure; this will involve hundreds of billions of dollars in Russian and foreign direct investment in energy, mining, transportation, and communications. Moreover, as the Arctic's sea ice continues to vanish, Russia stands to garner considerable economic benefits from the development of the NSR, which, when navigable, offers the shortest shipping route between European and East Asian ports. Moscow believes that with improvement to NSR infrastructure and safety, the NSR will be attractive not only to Russian shipping companies but also to foreign ones.

Accordingly, the economic dimension of the Russian soft security strategy has the following priorities regarding the AZRF: sustainable economic activity and increasing prosperity for Arctic communities; sustainable use of natural (including living) resources; and the development of transportation infrastructure (including aviation and marine and surface transportation) as well as information technologies and modern telecommunications.[31] These priorities underwent a slight revision in the aftermath of the Ukrainian crisis owing to Western sanctions. First and foremost, Moscow had to adjust its energy policy priorities. Because Western technologies and investments were suddenly lacking, the offshore projects were slowed down or postponed. The emphasis was placed on LNG production, which is seen as a more promising export-oriented project than the oil-related ones (e.g., the Yamal LNG plant in Sabetta). To counter the Western sanctions, Russia has invited China, South Korea, India, and Vietnam – countries that did not introduce sanctions against Russia – to support its Arctic projects through funding, technology, and joint development projects.[32]

The environmental dimension of Russia's AZRF strategy includes the following: monitoring and assessing the Arctic environment; preventing and eliminating pollution in the Arctic; protecting the marine environment, including Arctic biodiversity; assessing the impact of climate change on the Arctic; and preventing and addressing ecological emergencies in the Arctic, including those related to climate change.[33] This reflects Moscow's serious concern about the Arctic environment. As a result of intensive industrial and military activity, many AZRF areas are heavily polluted and pose serious health hazards. Russian scientists have identified twenty-seven impact zones where pollution has degraded the environment and increased morbidity in local populations. The main impact zones are the Murmansk region (10 per cent of total pollutants for the 27 impact zones), the Norilsk urban agglomeration (over 30 per cent), the West Siberian oil and gas fields (over 30 per cent), and the Arkhangelsk region (around 5 per cent).[34] In total, some 15 per cent of the AZRF territory is polluted or contaminated.[35]

In 2011 the Russian government launched a program worth 2.3 billion roubles to begin cleaning up the AZRF, including the Franz Joseph Land and Novaya Zemlya archipelagos. By the end of 2016, some 42,000 tons of waste had been removed from these archipelagos and 349 hectares of insular land had been cleaned.[36] In 2015, another AZRF clean-up program was launched – this time with a 21-billion-rouble funding envelope. By the end of the following year, the clean-up of Wrangel Island – including the removal by the Russian military of 36,477 barrels and 264 tons of scrap metal – was nearly complete.[37] A comprehensive analysis of the environmental situation in another seven major AZRF areas is planned, but the federal government has been unable to find reliable contractors to conduct the requisite studies.[38]

Nuclear safety in the High North is another issue that encourages cooperation between Russia and the other Arctic states. As noted earlier, more than 200 decommissioned nuclear reactors from Soviet-era submarines and icebreakers are stored on the Kola Peninsula – a Soviet "legacy" that is especially problematic for neighbouring countries such as Norway, Finland, and Sweden. Note that the US–Russian Cooperative Threat Reduction Program (Nunn–Lugar) of 1991–2012[39] and the Multilateral Nuclear Environmental Program in the Russian Federation (Framework Agreement on a Multilateral Nuclear Environmental Program in the Russian Federation 2003)[40] played a significant role in nuclear waste treatment. Between 2008 and 2015, the Russian government program for nuclear and radiological safety succeeded in dismantling 195 retired nuclear submarines (97 per cent of them), removing 98.8 per cent of radioisotope thermoelectric generators from service, and dismantling 86 per cent of these generators. Centralized long-term storage facilities for spent nuclear fuel have been constructed. Moreover, fifty-three hazardous nuclear facilities have been decommissioned, 270 hectares of contaminated land have been remediated, and open-water storage of radioactive waste has ended.[41]

Russia is engaged in various international forums where Arctic environmental problems are discussed and solved. At the regional level, these include the Barents Euro-Arctic Council (BEAC) and Arctic Council; both bodies have stimulated collaborative environmental research and assessment, as well as joint initiatives to tackle urgent challenges (such as the forty-two hot spots in Russia's Barents region, where the permafrost is vulnerable to collapse).[42] Russia also has supported and vigorously participated in all UN-related environmental initiatives, including the Intergovernmental Panel on Climate Change report (2014) and the Paris Agreement on Climate Change (2015), and it has worked to co-develop the International Maritime Organization's mandatory Polar Code (2014–15).

The social dimension of Moscow's soft security strategy focuses on health of the people living and working in the Arctic; education and cultural heritage; prosperity and capacity-building for children and youth; gender equality; and enhancing well-being and eradicating poverty among Arctic people.[43] Although good ideas have been articulated, implementation remains problematic – something true of many areas of Russian public policy. The serious social and economic problems faced by the country's Arctic Indigenous communities are a case in point, evidenced by the incompatibility between present economic realities and their traditional ways of life, rising disease rates, high infant mortality, and endemic alcoholism. Unemployment among Russia's Indigenous peoples is somewhere between 30 and 60 per cent, which is three to four times higher than for other AZRF residents. Life expectancy is forty-nine years, compared to seventy-two for the average Russian. Moscow's efforts to remedy these ills have still not come close to their targets and have been harshly criticized by Indigenous peoples and by national and international human rights organizations. The quality of life for the Indigenous communities in regions such as Khanty-Mansi, Nenets, Koryakia, and Chukotka remains unacceptably low. The Yamalo-Nenets area, perhaps exceptionally, has a booming Indigenous economy built around reindeer-herding, with social programs implemented effectively and major conflicts between Indigenous interests and energy companies generally avoided.[44]

The path to modernization and innovation in the AZRF charted by the Russian government must begin to move away from policy declarations toward actual implementation of specific, realistic projects in the region. The Kremlin appears to understand the need for constructive dialogue and deeper political engagement with all of Russia's AZRF regions, municipalities, Indigenous peoples, and non-governmental organizations (e.g., the Russian Association of Indigenous Peoples of the North [RAIPON], as well as environmental and human rights groups). Moscow generally encourages these actors to work with international partners – unless, of course, such engagement assumes a separatist character or involves attempts to challenge Moscow's foreign policy prerogatives. In practice, however, the federal bureaucracy's policies and approaches often confront the projects of subnational actors and civil society groups. Instead of using the resources of these actors in creative ways, Moscow tries to control them. In so doing, the state undermines their initiative, rendering them passive, both domestically and internationally.

Conclusions

The post–Cold War era brought a significant shift in Russia's threat perceptions and security policies in the High North. In contrast to the Cold War era, when the Arctic was a zone of global confrontation between the Soviet Union and the United States and NATO, Moscow now sees this region as a platform for international cooperation. The Kremlin now believes that there are no serious hard security threats to the AZRF and that the soft security agenda is more important.

While some media, politicians, and strategic analysts portray the changes in Russia's military capabilities as a significant military build-up and even a renewed arms race in the region, the real picture is far from this apocalyptical scenario. It is more accurate to characterize the military developments as limited modernization and increases or changes in equipment, force levels, and force structure. Some of these changes – for example, the creation of new Russian Arctic units, the commissioning of more sophisticated and better-armed warships, and the establishment of new command structures in the North – have little or nothing to do with projecting power into potentially disputed areas where the Arctic coastal states' claims overlap, or into the region at large. Instead, they are designed to patrol and protect recognized national territories, which are becoming increasingly accessible, including for illegal activities such as overfishing, poaching, smuggling, and uncontrolled migration. Other changes – such as the modernization of Russian strategic nuclear forces – have more to do with maintaining a deterrent than with developing offensive capabilities. These programs need not provoke an arms race or undermine regional cooperation.

Moscow is mostly concerned with soft security challenges to the AZRF, such as dependence on extractive industries and export of energy products, socio-economic disparities between Russia's northern regions, the degradation of urban infrastructure, debilitating ecological problems, and threats to Indigenous peoples' traditional economies and ways of life. Furthermore, Russia's foreign policy has clearly demonstrated that it prefers soft-power instruments (diplomatic, economic, and cultural) in the

Arctic theatre, as well as activity and discourse via multilateral institutions. Moscow has developed a pragmatic international strategy that aims at using Arctic cooperative programs and regional institutions for solving first and foremost Russia's specific problems rather than addressing abstract challenges. Russia's pragmatism should be taken into account by other regional players and should not be misinterpreted. Currently, there is no Russian "hidden agenda" in the Arctic. Moscow insists that its strategy in the region is predictable and constructive rather than aggressive or improvised. The Kremlin is quite clear about its intentions in the region, insisting that Russia does not want to be a revisionist power or troublemaker in the Arctic. To achieve its national goals in the region, Russia will use peaceful diplomatic, economic, and cultural means and act through international organizations and forums rather than unilaterally.

For the foreseeable future, we should anticipate that Moscow's strategy in the Arctic region will be predictable and pragmatic rather than aggressive or improvised. In contrast to the widespread stereotype of Russia around the world as a revisionist power or troublemaker in the Arctic, Moscow will continue to pursue a dual-track strategy of defending Russia's legitimate economic and political interests while remaining open to cooperation with foreign partners that are willing to contribute to exploiting Arctic natural resources, developing sea routes, and solving socio-economic and environmental problems facing the region.[45] Moscow understands well that the country's success in the Arctic theatre depends on the effectiveness of its socio-economic and environmental policies in the region as well as a favourable international environment. The Arctic doctrines of 2008, 2013, and 2020; the 2014 state programs on the socio-economic development of the AZRF up to 2035; and the 2002 law on environmental protection together suggest a coherent national approach to a sustainable development strategy (SDS) in the AZRF – one supported by the official and academic communities in Russia. Achieving these desired domestic outcomes will require regional peace and stability. To avoid misunderstandings, prevent potential international conflicts, and facilitate regional cooperation, the Arctic states should be clearer about their military policies and doctrines and should include arms control initiatives and confidence- and security-building measures in their bilateral or multilateral relations in the Arctic. The institutional mechanisms to achieve this outcome, however, remain to be developed. In the meantime, regional multilateral forums that facilitate cooperation on soft security issues (including the Arctic Council) remain practical venues for encouraging constructive engagement and promoting a collaborative agenda, thus ensuring that recent tensions between Russia and the West do not unnecessarily preclude action on shared Arctic interests.

NOTES

1 This chapter builds upon the author's chapter "Arctic Security Perspectives from Russia" in *Breaking the Ice Curtain? Russia, Canada, and Arctic Security in a Changing Circumpolar World*, ed. P. Whitney Lackenbauer and Suzanne Lalonde (Calgary: Canadian Global Affairs Institute, 2019), 43–60. He wishes to acknowledge the support of the Donner Canadian Foundation; Research Council of Norway (grant number 287576); and Norwegian Institute of International Affairs GPARC project (grant number 17/2200).

2 Aiswarya Lakshmi, "Is Russia Militarizing the Arctic?," *Marinelink*, 20 August 2015, https://www.marinelink.com/news/militarizing-russia396525.aspx; Andrew Poulin, "5 Ways Russia Is Positioning to Dominate the Arctic," *International Policy Digest*, 24 January 2016, https://intpolicydigest.org/author/andrew-poulin; Shane C. Tayloe, "Projecting Power in the Arctic: The Russian Scramble for Energy, Power, and Prestige in the High North," *Pepperdine Policy Review* 8, no. 4 (Spring 2015): 1–19.

3 Lakshmi, "Is Russia Militarizing the Arctic?"; Tayloe, "Projecting Power in the Arctic"; *Stratfor*, "Russia's Plans for Arctic Supremacy," 16 January 2015, https://www.stratfor.com/analysis/russias-plans-arctic-supremacy.

4 Unsurprisingly, the Kremlin aims "to ensure the sovereign rights of Russia's Arctic and features the smooth implementation of all of its activities, including the exclusive economic zone and the continental shelf of the Russian Federation in the Arctic." *Strategiya Razvitiya Arkticheskoi Zony Rossiyskoi Federatsii Obespecheniya Natsional'noi Bezopasnosti na Period do 2020 Goda* [The Strategy for the Development of the Arctic Zone of the Russian Federation and Ensuring National Security for the Period up to 2020], approved by President Vladimir Putin on 20 February 2013, http://www.ppavitel_ctvo.pf/docs/22846 (in Russian). See also *Ob Osnovakh Gosudarstvennoi Politiki Rossiyskoi Federatsii v Arktike na Period do 2035 Goda* [On the Foundations of State Policy of the Russian Federation in the Arctic for the Period up to 2035], approved by President Vladimir Putin on 5 March 2020, http://static.kremlin.ru/media/events/files/ru/f8ZpjhpAaQ0WB1zjywN04OgKiI1mAvaM.pdf (in Russian).

5 As for existing territorial disputes with other coastal states, the Kremlin has repeatedly underscored that all of these disputes should be solved in a peaceful way and on the basis of international law (e.g., the UN Convention on the Law of the Sea, and also the 2008 Ilulissat Declaration). For example, Moscow has adhered fully to the established international legal process for delineating the outer limits of its extended continental shelf, submitting its data to the UN Commission on the Limits of Continental Shelf and agreeing to negotiate any overlaps with Denmark and Canada over the Lomonosov Ridge.

6 Valery Konyshev, Alexander Sergunin, and Sergei Subbotin, "Russia's Arctic Strategies in the Context of the Ukrainian Crisis," *Polar Journal* 7, no. 1 (2017): 104–24 at 106.

7 Dmitry Medvedev, *Osnovy Gosudarstvennoi Politiki Rossiiskoi Federatsii v Arktike na Period do 2020 Goda i Dal'neishuiu Perspektivu* [Foundations of the State Policy of the Russian Federation in the Arctic Up to and Beyond 2020] (2008), http://www.rg.ru/2009/03/30/arktika-osnovy-dok.html. Moscow was one of the first among the Arctic states to adopt such a document, with only Norway shaping its official doctrine for the North (2006) prior to Russia.

8 Rob Huebert, *The Newly Emerging Arctic Security Environment* (Calgary: Canadian Defence and Foreign Affairs Institute, March 2010).

9 Vladimir Putin, *Strategiya Razvitiya Arkticheskoi Zony Rossiyskoi Federatsii i Obespecheniya Natsional'noi Bezopasnosti na Period do 2020 Goda* [The Strategy for the Development of the Arctic Zone of the Russian Federation and Ensuring National Security for the Period up to 2020] (2013), http://правительство.рф/docs/22846. Approved by President Vladimir Putin on 20 February 2013.

10 Ibid.

11 "The Military Doctrine of the Russian Federation," approved by the President of the Russian Federation, 25 December 2014, English translation released through the Embassy of the Russian Federation to the United Kingdom of Great Britain and Northern Ireland on 29 June 2015, https://rusemb.org.uk/press/2029.

12 Vladimir Putin, *Morskaya Doktrina Rossiyskoy Federatsii* [Maritime Doctrine of the Russian Federation] (July 2015), http://statc.kremlin.ru/media/events/files/ru/uAFi5nvux2twaqjftS5yrIZUVTJan77L.pdf.

13 Vladimir Putin, *O Strategii Natsional'noi Bezopasnosti Rossiiskoi Federatsii* [On the National Security Strategy of the Russian Federation] (31 December 2015), http://www.scrf.gov.ru/documents/1/133.html.

14 Vladimir Putin, *Kontseptsiya Vneshnei Politiki Rossiiskoi Federatsii* [The Foreign Policy Concept of the Russian Federation] (30 November 2016), http://publication.pravo.gov.ru/Document/View/0001201612010045?index=0&rangeSize=1.

15 On 5 March 2020, President Vladimir Putin approved a document titled "On the Foundations of State Policy of the Russian Federation in the Arctic for the Period up to 2035," which defined Moscow's Arctic strategy for the next fifteen years. Similar to the previous documents, the new strategy focuses on the AZRF's sustainable development and calls for international cooperation in such areas as the development of the NSR land and telecommunications infrastructure; modernization of icebreaker, rescue, and

support fleets; increased maritime safety; improved hydrometeorological, cartographic, navigational, and SAR services; early prevention of natural and man-made catastrophes, including oil spills; establishment of marine-protected areas; the combating of illegal, unregulated, and unreported fishing; and improved border controls along the lengthy coastline of the Arctic Ocean (*Ob Osnovakh Gosudarstvennoi Politiki*, 2020).

16 Valery Konyshev and Alexander Sergunin, "Is Russia a Revisionist Military Power in the Arctic?" *Defence and Security Analysis* 30, no. 4 (2004): 323–35.

17 The largest part of the Northern Fleet's surface vessels, including the cruiser *Peter the Great* and the aircraft carrier *Admiral Kuznetsov*, is also designated for the projection of Russia's sea power beyond the Arctic military theatre.

18 Dimmi, "Project 955 – Borey/Dolgorukiy," 19 March 2017, http:// militaryrussia.ru/blog/topic-338.html (in Russian).

19 Alexander Sergunin and Valery Konyshev, *Russia in the Arctic: Hard or Soft Power?* (Stuttgart: Ibidem Press, 2016), 152.

20 Ibid., 152–3.

21 Atle Staalesen, "New Russian Forces to Protect Arctic Coast," *The Independent Barents Observer,* 20 January 2017, https://thebarentsobserver.com/en /security/2017/01/new-russian-forces-protectarctic-coast.

22 Ekaterina Klimenko, *Russia's Arctic Security Policy: Still Quiet in the High North?* (Stockholm, SIPRI Policy Paper no. 45, 2016), 21.

23 *The Military Balance 2016* (London: International Institute for Strategic Studies, 2016), 165–6.

24 "Граница меняет замки," 2 June 2010, http://www.rg.ru/2010/06/02 /pronichev.html.

25 Anton Vasiliev, "Russia's Approaches to International Cooperation in the Arctic," *Arctic Herald* 1 (2012): 12–27 at 14.

26 In 2016, Russia launched a large-scale program for removing nuclear waste from the former Soviet submarine base in Andreev Bay in the Murmansk region. A total of 22,000 containers of spent fuel from nuclear submarines and icebreakers were stored in three storage tanks. There were also approximately 18,000 cubic metres of solid waste and 3400 cubic metres of liquid radioactive waste, which, according to Norwegian sources, are collectively as radioactive as 5,000 Hiroshima bombs. http:// sputniknews.com/environment/20160610/1041126139/russia-norway -arctic-nuclearwaste.html.

27 Klimenko, *Russia's Arctic Security Policy,* 14–15; Andrei Zagorsky, *Arkticheskie Ucheniya Severnogo Flota* [The Arctic Exercises of the Northern Fleet] (2013), http://www.imemo.ru/ru/publ/comments/2013/comm_2013 _053.pdf (in Russian).

28 Staalesen, "New Russian Forces."

29 Andreas Østhagen, "The Arctic Coast Guard Forum: Big Tasks, Small Solutions," *Maritime Security Challenges: Focus High North* (2016): 3–8.

30 Moscow also considers the field of civil protection as a promising venue for Arctic regional cooperation. For example, according to the EU Russia 2005 roadmap to the Common Space on External Security, a strategic objective of Brussels–Moscow cooperation is to strengthen EU–Russia dialogue on promoting common ability to respond to disasters and emergencies, including crisis management situations. This requires implementing existing arrangements between Russia's EMERCOM (Ministry for Emergency Situations) and its foreign counterparts to improve communications and the exchange of information. V. Konyshev and Alexander Sergunin, "The Changing Role of Military Power in the Arctic," in *The Global Arctic Handbook*, ed. Matthias Finger and Lassi Heininen (Cham: Springer, 2019), 190–1.

31 Government of the Russian Federation, *Sotsial'no-Ekonomicheskoe Razvitie Arkticheskoy Zony Rossiyskoi Federatsii na Period do 2020 Goda* [Socio-Economic Development of the Arctic Zone of the Russian Federation for the Period up to 2020] (2014), 11–4, http://government.ru/media/files/AtEYgOHutVc.pdf.

32 The economic sanctions levelled against Russia since 2014 have had the paradoxical effect of creating significant incentives for national innovation in the Arctic (in place, for instance, of imported foreign equipment and technology). On the other hand, Moscow understands that without foreign technologies and investment it will be rather difficult to solve numerous socio-economic and environmental problems in the Russian North. This creates a powerful incentive for the Kremlin to seek cooperative rather than confrontational relations with regional players. Konyshev, Sergunin, and Subbotin, "Russia's Arctic Strategies," 6.

33 Russian Federation, *Sotsial'no-Ekonomicheskoe Razvitie Arkticheskoy Zony Rossiyskoi Federatsii na Period do 2020 Goda*, 9–11.

34 D. Dushkova and A. Evseev, "Analiz Techogennogo Vozdeistviyana Geosistemy Evropeiskogo Severa Rossii" [Analysis of Technogenic Impact on Geosystems of the European Russian North], *Arktika i Sever* [The Arctic and the North], no. 4 (2011): 1–34.

35 Y.V. Kochemasov, B.A. Morogunov, and V.I. Solomatin, *Ekologo-ekonomicheskaya Otsenka Perspectivy Razvitiya Arktiki* [Ecological Assessment of the Prospects for Arctic Development] (2009), http://www.perspektivy.info/rus/ekob/arktika_perspektivy_razvitija_2009-04-24.htm.

36 "*Likvidatsiya Nakoplennogo Ekologicheskogo Usherba v Arktike*" [Elimination of Accumulated Environmental Damage in the Arctic], *RIA Novosti*, 21 November 2016, https://ria.ru/infografika/20161121/1481781022.html.

37 "Usiliyami Rossiyskih Voennyh s Ostrova Vrangelya Bylo Vyvezeno 36,477 Bochek i 264 tons Metalloloma" [The Russian Military Removed 36,477 Barrels and 264 Tons of Scrap Metal from Wrangel Island], *Neftegaz.ru*, 2 November 2016, http://neftegaz.ru/news/view/154946-Usiliyami -rossiyskih-voennyh-s-ostrova-Vrangelya-bylo-vyvezeno-36-477-bochek-i-264 -tmetalloloma.

38 Similarly, the cleaning of the Russian mining villages on Spitsbergen, planned for 2011–13, was never implemented.

39 Mary Beth D. Nitkitin and Amy F. Woolf, *The Evolution of Cooperative Threat Reduction: Issues for Congress* (Washington, D.C.: Congressional Research Service, 2014), https://fas.org/sgp/crs/nuke/R43143.pdf.

40 Government of the Russian Federation, *Framework Agreement on a Multilateral Nuclear Environmental Program in the Russian Federation* (28 October 2003), http://www.pircenter.org/media/content/files/11/13613597850.pdf.

41 Rosatom, *Back-end* (2017), http://www.rosatom.ru/en/rosatom-group /back-end/index.php?sphrase_id=11699.

42 Nordic Environment Finance Corporation (NEFCO), *Environmental Hot Spots in the Barents Region*, 2013, http://www.nefco.org/en/financing /environmental_hot_spots_in_the_barents_region.

43 Russian Federation, *Sotsial'no-Ekonomicheskoe Razvitie Arkticheskoy Zony Rossiyskoi Federatsii na Period do 2020 Goda* (2014), 8–9; Vladimir Putin, *Kontseptsiya Ustoychivogo Razvitiya Korennykh Malochislennykh Narodov Severa, Sibiri i Dal'nego Vostoka Rossiyskoi Federatsii* [The Concept for the Sustainable Development of Small Indigenous Population Groups of the North, Siberia, and the Far East of the Russian Federation] (4 February 2009), http://docs .cntd.ru/document/902142304.

44 Alexander Sergunin, "Is Russia Going Hard or Soft in the Arctic?" *Wilson Quarterly* 41, no. 3 (2017): 5–6.

45 The Russian leadership believes that the Arctic cooperative agenda could include the following areas: climate change mitigation, environmental protection, emergency response, air and maritime safety (including the Polar Code implementation, charting safe maritime routes, and cartography), search and rescue operations, Arctic research, Indigenous peoples, cross- and trans-border cooperative projects, and culture.

7 Toward a Comprehensive Approach to Canadian Security and Safety in the Arctic

P. WHITNEY LACKENBAUER

An extensive literature has unpacked state and media discourses about Arctic sovereignty and security over the past decade, with the Canadian government under Conservative prime minister Stephen Harper (2006–15) drawing particular attention as a key protagonist in the framing of the circumpolar world as a zone of potential conflict.[1] Scholars typically cast Harper and his government as having promoted a "militarized understanding of Arctic security";[2] as a securitizing actor that prioritizes state-based, orthodox understandings of sovereignty and national security over broader definitions;[3] and as an advocate of a robust defence posture rather than diplomacy as a means to differentiate his government from its Liberal predecessors.[4] Because of Harper's perceived emphasis on military capabilities to secure borders and assert control over "contested" sovereign space (lands and waters), academic commentators often hold up the Conservative government's Arctic policy as an example of "an aggressive assertion of Canadian strength,"[5] describing it as a series of moves that have "militarized" the Arctic agenda[6] and contributed to an emerging security dilemma in the Arctic.[7]

Sweeping assessments of the Harper government's political rhetoric on Arctic affairs are usually based upon anecdotal work that either fixates on single events or focuses on early speeches. Rarely do commentators undertake a more systematic analysis of his entire tenure in office. For example, Philippe Genest and Frédéric Lasserre recently offered a discursive analysis of Harper government speeches from 2006 to 2009, observing that these statements played on identity politics to drum up support for investments in military equipment. They do not, however, attempt to critically interrogate the terms "sovereignty" and "security" beyond their broadest political utility, and while noting a shift in sovereignty discourse in 2010 to emphasize resource development rather than foreign threats, they stress that the government always highlighted the idea of the "fragility" of Canada's Arctic sovereignty to justify "une posture très axée sur la rhétorique militaire."[8] As Mathieu Landriault's methodical work on public polling and media coverage affirms (see chapter 3),[9] systematic analysis of the full period from 2006 to 2015 can yield new insights into the Harper government's Arctic strategies, moving beyond the simple normative assumptions about sovereignty and security that dominate much of the literature produced over the past decade (including my own).

This chapter suggests that the government's sovereignty/security rhetoric became more nuanced over time, reflecting an attempt to balance messaging that promised to "defend" Canada's Arctic sovereignty (intended primarily for domestic audiences) with a growing awareness that the most likely challenges were "soft" security- and safety-related issues that required "whole of government" responses.[10] Historian Petra Dolata gestures toward a similar conclusion when she notes that "until 2009, Conservative Arctic policy was characterized by the linkage between security and sovereignty as well as the focus on hard power," a dimension that peaked with the 2008 Canada First Defence Strategy before shifting "away from an exclusive focus on sovereignty to the recognition of the complexity of Arctic policy and the inclusion of stewardship."[11] Testing these ideas in a more systematic way, and discussing how ideas of sovereignty and security were translated into new frameworks after 2008, yields a more nuanced understanding of how the official "discourse space" evolved over time. Furthermore, it suggests that early Harper government messaging set political preferences that did not preclude the military from exercising its agency to discern an appropriate role that did not conform to pithy "use it or lose it" logic.

This chapter re-examines how the Harper government conceptualized and mobilized Arctic sovereignty and security in its political discourse during its decade in office and, in turn, how the Department of National Defence (DND) and the Canadian Armed Forces (CAF) articulated these concepts in Arctic policy and implementation plans during this period. Although "commonsense" logic might assume that the military would seek to amplify defence threats to bolster its claims to power and resources within government, the propensity of defence officials to downplay conventional military threats to the region and to articulate the CAF's roles in a whole-of-government context meant they deliberately avoided the "militarization" of Arctic sovereignty. Instead, they consistently applied broader Northern Strategy frameworks that placed more emphasis on the human dimension of sovereignty than on the need for a conventional military presence to ward off hostile foreign adversaries threatening Canada's territorial integrity. Thus, by analysing sovereignty and security as contested concepts and allowing for change over time, and by avoiding the tendency to conflate high-level political rhetoric (speech acts) with policy outcomes and to treat the Government of Canada as a unified actor, this chapter seeks to examine the logic of how the Harper government (re)presented ideas about Arctic sovereignty vis-à-vis the Canadian military and, in turn, how implementation plans by an individual department can influence the discourse space and the implementation of the political echelon's security program.[12]

Securitization theory, first developed by the "Copenhagen School" in the 1990s, posits that a security issue is produced through *speech acts* after a *securitizing actor* presents it as an existential threat requiring policies that go beyond "normal" political practice and convinces the *audience* that this is the case. Barry Buzan, Ole Weaver, and Jaap de Wilde, who pioneered this approach, identify three units of analysis: the *referent object* (the object of securitization); the *security actors* (who declare a referent object to be existentially threatened); and *functional actors* (who significantly influence decisions in the security sector). Furthermore, *audiences* and *context* are essential units of analysis if we are to understand the practices and methods that produce security as an intersubjective construction.[13] As Adam Cote observes, securitization analysis is consistent with the understanding that security constructions are derived, at least in part, from contextual or "objective" circumstances.[14]

The following analysis discerns more subtle trends than previous scholarly assessments based on a careful reading of the *speech acts* around Arctic sovereignty and security in major speeches and press releases issued by the Harper government that I have compiled with political scientist Ryan Dean. Rather than simply noting the presence of the words "sovereignty" and "security" and the broad contexts in which they are used, I seek to analyse these speeches and press releases as speech acts that contain or imply an existential threat, an emergency (or urgency), and a justification for actions beyond the "normal bounds of political procedure" in order to meet the theoretical threshold of "securitization."[15] In this case, the "action" verbs preceding "sovereignty" often reveal shifting government understandings and articulations of sovereignty and security – more specifically, the quiet transition from an urgent, "crisis" mentality predicated on the need to "defend" against external threats toward a more empowered, proactive, "exercise" and "demonstrate" mentality that after 2008 internalized a sense of Canadian government agency and a return to "normal" politics. Stated in other terms, scholars have failed to observe how the early *securitization* of the Arctic sovereignty agenda under Harper was methodically *desecuritized* in such a way that sovereignty and unconventional security challenges came to be addressed through normal political processes and structures pursued through a whole-of-government approach.

Building on Adam Côté's recent articulation of a social securitization model, I then analyse DND/CAF as an integral, *active* part of the securitization process in terms of how it interpreted sovereignty and security meanings as an *audience* to political rhetoric and how it then articulated and selected security policies as a *functional actor*. Inspired by civil/military relations literature that examines how the political and military echelons interact in discursive space and what outcomes these encounters produce,[16] I undertake a careful reading of Arctic documents produced by DND officials between 2010 and 2014. These suggest that the military did not subscribe to a "sovereignty on thinning ice" thesis, nor did its Arctic implementation plans suggest an adherence to the Harper government's early ideas about an acute need to "defend sovereignty" against foreign military threats emanating from resource or boundary disputes. While political leaders often cited the need for enhanced military capabilities and an increased "presence" under the sovereignty pillar of Canada's Northern Strategy, the military did not accept that the Arctic threat environment required an exceptional mandate (which would have encroached on the responsibilities of other federal departments and agencies). Instead, the Canadian military articulated, promoted, and sought to implement a whole-of-government approach, predicated on inter-agency cooperation, that placed a clear emphasis on unconventional security and safety challenges.[17] Rather than asserting the need to "securitize" the Arctic as an exceptional space requiring an expanded DND mandate, the military formulated strategies and policies that reveal a deliberate, proportionate understanding and articulation of its Arctic roles within a comprehensive whole-of-government approach. This stance, which reflected a continuation of "normal" politics, encouraged the political echelon to adjust its messaging within the expanded discourse space that the military legitimized.

Setting the Context: "Sovereignty on Thinning Ice" and "New" Security Threats

After the Cold War abruptly ended at the start of the 1990s, Canada's official discourse on Arctic affairs shifted away from continental security and narrow sovereignty interests to emphasize circumpolar cooperation and broad definitions of security that prioritized the human and environmental dimensions.[18] Canada was an early and tireless champion of the Arctic Council, established in 1996, and promoted the inclusion at the table of Indigenous Permanent Participants.[19] In 1997, a Canadian parliamentary committee recommended that the country focus on international Arctic cooperation through multilateral governance as a means to promote environmentally sustainable human development; this would serve as "the long-term foundation for assuring circumpolar security, with priority being given to the well-being of Arctic peoples and to safeguarding northern habitants from intrusions which have impinged aggressively on them."[20] The Liberal government under Jean Chrétien (1993–2003) embraced this emphasis on international cooperation with its 2000 policy statement, *The Northern Dimension of Canada's Foreign Policy*, which situated environmental and human security as focal points for circumpolar action predicated on "inclusion and co-operation."[21] The seven main goals articulated in the integrated 2004 Northern Strategy (devised in concert with the premiers of the northern territories) also emphasized human and environmental security; traditional sovereignty and defence priorities were conspicuously absent.[22]

In the mid-2000s, however, the rising tide of scientific evidence about the pace and impact of global warming in the Arctic led some Canadian commentators to push for a more proactive Arctic strategy that anticipated a rising tide of new sovereignty and security challenges. Former Canadian Forces Northern Area commander Pierre Leblanc and political scientist Rob Huebert warned that climate change portended new crises, including renewed challenges to the legal status of the waters of the Northwest Passage owing to an anticipated influx of international shipping exploiting ice-free waters.[23] According to their narrative, heightened international activity in the circumpolar Arctic would amplify the significance of boundary disputes (such as those in the Beaufort Sea and over Hans Island); furthermore, a growing demand for Arctic resources would jeopardize international recognition of Canadian sovereignty. While this suite of issues suggested a widening of security beyond military issues to other sectors (such as economic, environmental, and human), Huebert and his followers seemed to conflate *non-traditional* security risks or threats with a heightened need for more *traditional* security tools (defence and, to a lesser extent, law enforcement). Buoyed by this messaging, other academics and journalists echoed that a continued reliance on international law and friendly relationships with other Arctic states would no longer suffice to meet future sovereignty challenges.[24]

This return to traditional state sovereignty (territorial integrity and status of waters) and national security discussions provoked debate within the academic community, with commentators such as Franklyn Griffiths criticizing the "purveyors of polar peril"[25] for inflating sovereignty and security issues into supposed threats that deflected attention from the well-being of northerners (his human security priority) in an era of climate change.[26] Griffiths's message was overwhelmed in the popular sphere, however, by the alarming imagery offered by the "sovereignty on thinning ice" thesis, coupled with the shocking revelations of the 2004 Arctic Climate Impact Assessment[27] and global talk of "peak oil," all of which made for simple media narratives predicated on uncertainty and fear.[28] Federal political constructions of Arctic sovereignty and security began to reflect these frames. In 2005, prime minister Paul Martin's Liberals released their *International Policy Statement*, which identified the Arctic as a priority area in light of "increased security threats, a changed distribution of global power, challenges to existing international institutions, and transformation of the global economy." It anticipated that the next two decades would bring major challenges requiring creative diplomacy as well as investment in new defence capabilities to meet these challenges.[29] The Liberal government fell before it could implement its vision, but by then it had intertwined sovereignty and security in political rhetoric and strategic documents in ways that had not been seen since the 1980s. It fell to the Conservatives, who came to office in January 2006, to further articulate and implement Canada's Arctic sovereignty and security agenda.

"Defending Sovereignty": Militant Sovereignty and Security Rhetoric, 2005–2007

The Canadian North was a key component of the Conservatives' 2005 election platform, which played on the idea of an Arctic sovereignty "crisis" demanding decisive action. Stephen Harper promised that Canada would acquire the military capabilities necessary to meet the new sovereignty and security threats created by the opening of the Arctic and the potential challenges to Canadian sovereignty and resource rights. "The single most important duty of the federal government is to defend and protect our national sovereignty," Harper asserted. "It's time to act to defend Canadian sovereignty. A Conservative government will make the military investments needed to secure our borders. You don't defend national sovereignty with flags, cheap election rhetoric, and advertising campaigns. You need forces on the ground, ships in the sea, and proper surveillance. And that will be the Conservative approach."[30]

Harper's Arctic agenda was highly political and partisan from the outset. Within days of taking office in January 2006, he rebuked US Ambassador David Wilkins for reiterating America's long-standing rejection of Canada's claims to the Northwest Passage as internal waters. "The United States defends its sovereignty," the new prime minister proclaimed. "The Canadian government will defend our sovereignty ... It is the Canadian people we get our mandate from, not the ambassador of the United States." This made for good political theatre, allowing him at once to show his nationalist resolve and to distance his government from the unpopular Bush administration.[31] It also anticipated a deliberate strategy "to cultivate a legacy as a champion of the North," blending "opportunism and statecraft, shoring up both his party and Canadian unity." As a former senior PMO insider told reporter Steven Chase, the articulation of a strong Arctic agenda helped address the long-standing frustration among Conservative strategists "that the rival Liberal Party owned the flag. In most Western democracies, right-of-centre parties tend to own the patriotic vote, but in Canada 'Liberals had effectively defined being pro-Canadian as being for the social-welfare state [and] for the CBC,' with a dose of anti-Americanism thrown in." Accordingly, Harper's "Canada-first approach" to the Arctic constituted "part of an effort to fashion a conservative nationalism, which also includes the celebration of soldiers as part of a Canadian martial tradition, rather than as peacekeepers, and the heavy promotion of the bicentennial of the War of 1812." The North offered a powerful source of "myths and narratives" conductive to nation-building, and Prime Minister Harper was "a big believer in the idea that nations are built by narratives – stories they tell themselves."[32]

The story the Harper government constructed in official statements during its first mandate defined security in terms of state survival and power (sovereignty) and in external terms of meeting threats from beyond Canada's borders. Arctic sovereignty and security became inextricably linked to direct or indirect military consequences and, therefore, required an immediate investment in new defence capabilities that went beyond "normal" political approaches to managing Arctic risks that preceding governments had adopted. This traditional security message was both reactive and militaristic, suggesting a need to break from established understandings and "rules" to respond to a perceived threat. Contextually, both expert and popular media commentaries pointing to the potential for inter-state or unconventional conflict in the future Arctic or, at the very least, challenges to Canada's legal position in the region (particularly the Northwest Passage, which Canada considers historical internal waters and not an international strait) stoked these fears. Rapid environmental change, instead of highlighting the need for action on global climate change mitigation (environmental security), portended new traditional sovereignty and security threats demanding "urgent" attention and a robust "defence" posture.

Along these lines, in speeches in Nunavut and the Northwest Territories in August 2006, Harper crafted a powerful narrative predicated on patriotism, external sovereignty threats, and the need for a stronger military "presence." He also he introduced his "first principle of Arctic sovereignty: use it or lose it." This strong imagery suggested the possibility that Canada might lose its sovereignty and that the Conservatives were prepared to act – to "use it" – and save a region that was "planted ... deep in the Canadian soul." Emphasizing that "you can't defend Arctic sovereignty with words alone," the prime minister suggested that Canada's capabilities and commitment had atrophied under previous governments:

> Ladies and Gentlemen, for far too long, Canadian Governments have failed in their duty to rigorously enforce our sovereignty in the Arctic.
>
> They have failed to provide enough resources to comprehensively monitor, patrol and protect our northern waters.
>
> As a result, foreign ships may have routinely sailed through our territory without permission.
>
> Any such voyage represents a potential threat to Canadians' safety and security.
>
> We always need to know who is in our waters and why they're there.
>
> We must be certain that everyone who enters our waters respects our laws and regulations, particularly those that protect the fragile Arctic environment.
>
> Our new Government will not settle for anything less.

Harper was depicting an uncertain and increasingly volatile circumpolar world where not all countries respected the Law of the Sea, where climate change could open the Northwest Passage "to year-round shipping within a decade," and where the government needed to bear a tremendous burden "to ensure that development occurs on our own terms" in a region "attracting international attention" that was "poised to take a much bigger role in Canada's economic and social development." Evoking a tone of immediacy – indeed, crisis – he insisted that "it is no exaggeration to say that the need to assert our sovereignty and take action to protect our territorial integrity in the Arctic has never been more urgent."[33] In framing his imperative for emergency political action, Harper crafted Arctic sovereignty rhetoric to evoke "a sense of national pride" and to introduce a "rhetoric of fear,"[34] all the while insisting that "protecting Canadian sovereignty is Ottawa's responsibility."[35]

The Harper government's regular resort to the term "defend Canadian sovereignty" reinforced a logic that linked sovereignty and national defence. The "sovereignty on thinning ice" storyline justified this muscular approach to "standing up for Canada" and the Conservatives' emphasis on defence or "hard security" in general. Defence minister Gordon O'Connor declared in October 2006 that "I want to be able to have the

Navy, Army, and Air Force operate on a regular basis throughout the Arctic," framing this as a sovereignty initiative that would strengthen the capabilities of the Canadian Forces. [36] This resonated with his earlier messaging that Canada's sovereignty "claims must also be backed by strong military capabilities,"[37] as well as Prime Minister Harper's broader political goals. "We believe that Canadians are excited about the government asserting Canada's control and sovereignty in the Arctic," Harper told a *Toronto Sun* reporter in February 2007. "We believe that's one of the big reasons why Canadians are excited and support our plan to rebuild the Canadian Forces. I think it's practically and symbolically hugely important, much more important than the dollars spent. And I'm hoping that years from now, Canada's Arctic sovereignty, military and otherwise, will be, frankly, a major legacy of this government."[38]

The political echelon thus established its preference for framing the Arctic as a strategic challenge requiring a military response. For example, Harper used his July 2007 speech announcing the construction of new Arctic offshore patrol ships – which he referred to as "our first moves to defend *and strengthen* Canada's Arctic sovereignty" – both to establish the need for "emergency" politics and to evoke nation-building. "Just as the new Confederation [in 1867] looked to securing the Western shore," he proclaimed, "Canada must now look north to the next frontier – the vast expanse of the Arctic." Toward that end, the federal government's "highest responsibility is the defence of our nation's sovereignty," and "nothing is as fundamental as protecting Canada's territorial integrity: Our borders; Our airspace; and Our waters." In stressing that "Canada's Arctic is central to our identity as a northern nation," he construed growing international interest (and changes) in the circumpolar world as existential threats validating the need to "provide the Canadian Forces with the tools they need to enforce our claim to sovereignty and our jurisdiction over the Arctic."[39] This speech and subsequent ones suggesting that military investments would not only "defend" but also "significantly strengthen Canada's sovereignty over the Arctic" led to messaging that conflated international legal definitions of "sovereignty," based on an internationally recognized *right* to control activities in a given jurisdiction, with the notion that a military presence as a *tool* to control activities would confirm that right.[40]

The international context in 2007 seemed to validate assumptions that the Arctic security environment was in a state of flux and that external forces threatened to undermine Canadian sovereignty. In early August, a Russian expedition led by Artur Chilingarov planted a titanium flag on the Arctic seabed below the North Pole, demonstrating Russia's unparalleled capabilities in the region at a time when it was "claiming vast swaths of the

Arctic Ocean seabed," pursuant to the UN Convention on the Law of the Sea.[41] Although Canadian foreign affairs minister Peter MacKay dismissed the Russian action as "just a show" with no legal bearing, the NDP MP for the Western Arctic, Dennis Bevington, criticized the government for its lagging efforts "when it comes to asserting our legitimate claim to Arctic sovereignty" and suggested that the Russian mission "demonstrates a troubling reality for Northern communities and all Canadians concerning Arctic sovereignty."[42] Later that month, Russian president Vladimir Putin announced that Russia had, for the first time since 1992, resumed "on a permanent basis" long-range flights by strategic bombers capable of striking targets inside the United States – a change quickly linked in the media to Russia's claims to "a large chunk of the Arctic."[43] That fall, scientists confirmed that the Arctic sea ice during the 2007 melt season had shrunk sharply to its lowest expanse on record, leaving the Northwest Passage "completely opened for the first time in human memory." The US National Snow and Ice Data Center reported that "a standard ocean-going vessel could have sailed smoothly through ... the normally ice-choked route."[44]

This context of uncertainty, coupled with the government's speech acts during its first two years in office situating the Canadian Forces at the forefront of its efforts to "defend" and "strengthen" Canada's Arctic sovereignty, set off vigorous debate about what Canada needed to do to "defend" or assert its Arctic sovereignty. At one end of the spectrum, experts such as Rob Huebert, Michael Byers, and Suzanne Lalonde asserted that the Harper government was not going far or fast enough to defend Canada's Arctic interests.[45] At the other end, some critics questioned the entire sovereignty-on-thinning-ice framework, suggesting that a fomented sovereignty crisis was deflecting attention from substantive issues best dealt with through cooperation. Griffiths, for example, promoted an emancipatory message that sought to engender a norm of "cooperative stewardship" rather than insecurity and military competition.[46] Domestically, the "use it or lose it" rhetoric frustrated and even offended some Northerners, particularly Indigenous people, who had lived in the region since "time immemorial" (and thus resented any intimation that the North was not sufficiently "used") and who continued to express concerns about their lack of substantive involvement in national and international decision-making. Inuit political leaders, for example, suggested that the government agenda was prioritizing military investments at the expense of environmental protection and improved social and economic conditions in the North. They insisted that "sovereignty begins at home" and that the primary challenges were domestic human security issues, which required investments in infrastructure, education, and health care.[47] Other commentators argued for a balance between traditional military and non-traditional security approaches. This included my argument that the Harper government's early Arctic policy statements had overplayed the probability of military conflict in the region, producing only a partial strategy that neglected diplomacy and development.[48]

Toward a Comprehensive Approach: The Emergence of New Narratives, 2008–2015

Notwithstanding that the Harper government clearly associated "defending sovereignty" with more robust military capabilities, the discourse space on Arctic sovereignty and security began to open up in 2007 after other government departments articulated their particular roles and responsibilities in this domain. This, in turn, quietly displaced the military from a leading to a supporting role. "While other government departments and agencies remain responsible for dealing with most security issues in the North," defence minister Gordon O'Connor noted in March 2007, "the Canadian Forces have a significant role to play in supporting them, asserting our sovereignty, and providing assistance to our citizens."[49] This was a relatively innocuous statement framed in an explicit context of the "New Government's" commitment "to defending Canada's Arctic and its jurisdiction over northern lands, waterways, and resources" through military "sovereignty" patrolling, as well as the *Canada First Defence Strategy* goal to "strengthen Canada's independent capacity to defend our national sovereignty and security – including in the Arctic." Even so, it acknowledged that the military was not alone or supreme in dealing with "most security issues."

The 2007 Speech from the Throne suggested that the Harper government's broader vision for the Arctic went beyond traditional sovereignty and security frames. Arguing that "the North needs new attention" and that "new opportunities are emerging across the Arctic," the Conservatives promised to "bring forward an integrated northern strategy focused on strengthening Canada's sovereignty, protecting our environmental heritage, promoting economic and social development, and improving and devolving governance, so that Northerners have greater control over their destinies." This four-pillar strategy would be expanded to "improve living conditions in the North for First Nations and Inuit through better housing," with a new pledge to "build a world-class Arctic research station that will be on the cutting edge of arctic issues, including environmental science and resource development." While the government proceeded with its election promises to bolster Canada's military presence in the Arctic, its sovereignty agenda now included a new civilian

Coast Guard icebreaker and "complete comprehensive mapping of Canada's Arctic seabed."[50] Northern leaders received the throne speech with mixed sentiments, applauding their inclusion in the Harper government's expanded conceptualization of Arctic sovereignty even while lamenting the lack of detail and criticizing what they saw as an excessive emphasis on the military dimensions of sovereignty and foreign policy.[51]

Thus, while the government in its official messaging continued to highlight the military's role in "defending," "protecting," and "asserting" sovereignty through 2008, it also quietly began to reposition the military to take a more practical *supporting* role. The *Canada First Defence Strategy*, released in May 2008, gestured toward "sovereignty on thinning ice" assumptions to justify why "the Canadian Forces must have the capacity to exercise control over and defend Canada's sovereignty in the Arctic." Anticipating "new challenges from other shores" (left unspecified), the defence policy suggested that, "as activity in northern lands and waters accelerates, the military will play an increasingly vital role in demonstrating a visible Canadian presence in this potentially resource-rich region, and in helping other government agencies such as the Coast Guard respond to any threats that may arise."[52] The language of "helping" civilian agencies implied that other federal departments and agencies had the mandate and primary responsibility to address potential "threats," thus pointing toward a "whole of government" approach – the military's preferred path.

The August 2008 iteration of the government's flagship northern "sovereignty exercise" during the Harper era, Operation NANOOK, reflected this emergent dual messaging. Defence minister Peter MacKay's press release repeated the established Conservative narrative. "There is nothing more fundamental than the protection of our nation's security and sovereignty," he asserted. "Our Government knows that we have a choice when it comes to defending our sovereignty over the Arctic. We either use it or lose it. That is why defending our Arctic sovereignty is a key strategic priority." By contrast, the new Chief of the Defence Staff Walter Natynczyk explained more precisely that

> the CF have a significant role to play in supporting government departments that deal with security issues in the north, exercising our sovereignty and providing assistance to our citizens. Multi-agency exercises like Op NANOOK, which involves the Navy, Army, Air Force, and Nunavut territorial and federal government departments, are important because they provide an opportunity to enhance our capacity to operate together effectively in the case of an emergency or security operation.[53]

As MacKay explained in a speech, the operation suggested two purposes: "to exercise Canada's sovereignty in the Arctic through a strong Canadian Forces presence," and "and to strengthen the collaboration between the Canadian Forces and other government departments and agencies in the region." While the former might imply "extraordinary" measures for Canada, the latter certainly implied a more "normal" whole-of-government political framework.

The dominant political message that the circumpolar world was increasingly hostile – that a "polar race" had begun – also seemed to shift, and the prospect of a more optimistic "polar saga" seemed increasingly prevalent. Government statements in 2008 slowly began to expand discussions about strengthening Canada's Arctic sovereignty to include more direct references to the Arctic states' shared adherence to international law and Canada's commitment to "building a stable, rules-based region under which we cooperate with other circumpolar countries on issues of common concern."[54] The May 2008 Ilulissat Declaration by Canada and the four other Arctic coastal states reinforced the view that these states would adhere to the UN Convention on the Law of the Sea (UNCLOS) and peacefully resolve any competing sovereignty claims.[55] In January 2009, foreign affairs minister Lawrence Cannon stated that although new American and European Arctic policy statements outlined some interests contrary to Canada's, these did not place Canadian sovereignty under serious threat.[56] That March, Cannon acknowledged in a speech that geological research and international law (not military clout) would resolve continental shelf and boundary disputes, and he emphasized "strong Canadian leadership in the Arctic ... to facilitate good international governance in the region."[57]

Canada's Northern Strategy: Our North, Our Heritage, Our Future, released in July 2009, echoed these messages. Although this Arctic policy statement trumpeted the government's commitment to "putting more boots on the Arctic tundra, more ships in the icy water and a better eye-in-the-sky," it also emphasized that Canada's disagreements with its Arctic neighbours were "well-managed and pose no sovereignty or defence challenges for Canada." This signalled a rather abrupt change of tone from previous political messaging.[58] Rather than perpetuating a unilateralist "use it or lose it" message (which was last used by the prime minister in August 2008),[59] *Canada's Northern Strategy* stressed opportunities for bilateral and multilateral cooperation in the circumpolar world. "We're not going down a road toward confrontation," Cannon stressed. "Indeed, we're going down a road toward co-operation and collaboration. That is the Canadian way. And that's the way my other colleagues around the table have chosen to go as well."[60]

The Department of Foreign Affairs released its *Statement on Canada's Arctic Foreign Policy* the following August. This document, intended to elaborate on the international dimensions of the Northern Strategy, reiterated the importance of the Arctic to Canada's national identity and Canada's role as an "Arctic power" while outlining a vision of the Arctic as "a stable, rules-based region with clearly defined boundaries, dynamic economic growth and trade, vibrant Northern communities, and healthy and productive ecosystems."[61] The central pillar of Canada's foreign policy remained "the exercise of our sovereignty over the Far North," but the "hard security" message of the 2006–8 period was supplemented (if not supplanted) by louder calls for cooperation with circumpolar neighbours and Northerners. Reaffirming that Canada's Arctic sovereignty is long-standing, well-established, and based on historic title (rooted, in part, on the presence of Canadian Inuit and other Indigenous peoples in the region from time immemorial), the statement projects a stable and secure circumpolar world, but one in which Canada will continue to uphold its rights as a sovereign, coastal state.[62]

An analysis of the verbs used alongside "sovereignty" in official Harper government statements and press releases (see Table 7.1) suggests that the language of "defending" sovereignty was largely superseded by the idea of "exercising" sovereignty from 2009 to 2014. While official discourse consistently emphasized the need to "protect" sovereignty (thus reaffirming that it was threatened, but with a softer connotation than the need to "defend"), the notions of "exercising" and "asserting" implied that Canada already *had* sovereignty. Furthermore, the military's "visible Canadian presence" was trumpeted repeatedly as an important means of "exercising sovereignty and supporting the safety and security of Canadians,"[63] but practical roles typically highlighted assisting with emergency response (from oil spills to plane crashes), patrolling, and improving domain awareness. While the messaging remained unambiguously state-centric, the military's central place in the Harper government's sovereignty strategy was no longer articulated in simplistic "use it or lose it" language that implied a need for hardened defences to ward off enemy forces amassing at Canada's Arctic gates.

The Canadian Military: Downplaying Conventional Defence Threats and Articulating a "Whole of Government" Role

Civil/military relations theory has long grappled with the relationship between the political and military echelons within democracies. Civilian political leadership defines national security interests and goals, and controls or directs the military's actions to ensure their concordance

Table 7.1. Verbs Used alongside Sovereignty in Official Statements, 2005–2015

	Dec. 2005–Sept. 2007	Oct. 2007–Dec. 2008	Jan. 2009–Dec. 2010	Jan. 2011–Apr. 2014	May 2014–July 2015
"defend"	**16**	7	6	7	2
"assert"/"reassert"	**10**	7	4	7	**21**
"protect"	5	**13**	**11**	**10**	5
"strengthen"	5	**8**	5	2	4
"preserve"	2				3
"enforce"	2		1	2	2
"bolster"	2	1			
"enhance"	1	1	1	1	
"establish"	1		1		
"exercise"	1	7	**63**	**29**	**8**
"secure"	1	4			1
"confirm"	1				
"project"	1				
"affirm"/"reaffirm"		1	1		1
"support"		2		2	2
"safeguard"		1		2	
"demonstrate"		1	5	2	4
"advance"			2		
"promote"			1	4	4
"ensure"				2	2
"build on"					1

Note: Numbers in bold represent the two most frequent verbs used alongside sovereignty in each date range.
Source: "Speeches, Statements, and Press Releases" in P. Whitney Lackenbauer and Ryan Dean, eds., *Canada's Northern Strategy under the Harper Conservatives: Key Speeches and Documents on Sovereignty, Security, and Governance, 2006–15* (Calgary: Centre for Military, Security, and Strategic Studies and Arctic Institute of North America, 2016).

with political objectives; the military, for its part, retains the authority to determine appropriate military doctrine to manage its appropriate use of force. How the military chooses to interpret and implement political directives gives it agency, and it can influence decision-making and strategic outcomes accordingly.[64] For example, the information and knowledge provided by the agent (the military) can influence the preferences of the principal (the civil political authority). Unfortunately, these inputs are difficult to discern owing to the "black box problem" of accessing evidence about internal interactions between senior military officials and civilian decision-makers – particularly in the case of a government with a reputation for muzzling civil servants to prevent them from disclosing inside information. By analysing military documents and comparing them to high-level political messaging, however, we can glean insights into how the military interpreted political preferences and translated them into military discourse. In turn, by clarifying the essence of political goals and directives and framing the narrative in particular ways, the military echelon influenced the discursive space around Canadian Arctic sovereignty and security issues.

The Harper government assigned the CAF the overarching tasks of "defending" Canadian sovereignty, exercising control over the Arctic, and protecting the region;[65] however, it was not obvious how these broad objectives were to be achieved. Popular wisdom might suggest that the military would seek to maximize its self-interest by trumpeting conventional military threats to Canadian sovereignty and defence, given that Prime Minister Harper's early "graduated and paternal sovereignty" strategy and policy announcements implied this kind of narrative.[66] Along these lines, much of the academic literature intimates that Canada's sovereignty and hard security mandate under Harper, by fixating on geopolitical threats and territorial integrity, ultimately compromised "a more general comprehensive security, if not soft security practices."[67] A second look at the evidence, however, suggests that the military's interpretation of political directives widened the discursive space surrounding Arctic sovereignty and security and reshaped preferred political goals to downplay the risk of conventional military threats to Canada's territorial integrity or "sovereignty" while amplifying the importance of whole-of-government approaches to frame military support in terms of broader security and safety priorities.

While high-level political rhetoric continued to reiterate the primacy of Arctic sovereignty from 2008 to 2014 (albeit in a less militaristic tone than before), the articulation of how the military itself intended to implement political directives in policy and practice reveals an embracing rather than a sacrificing of "soft" security and safety considerations. Even during Harper's "chest-thumping" northern tours each August, during which he "highlighted the planks of his government's own northern agenda – military muscle, economic development, and environmental stewardship," senior military officials downplayed the risk of foreign military aggression that might threaten Canada's territorial integrity and require a military response. In August 2009, General Walt Natynczyk, Canada's Chief of Defence Staff, admitted to the *Toronto Star* that "despite Russian sabre-rattling over its own Arctic ambitions, there is no conventional military threat to the Arctic." Instead, he highlighted criminal and environmental threats. "There's a huge environmental risk here in the North. A record number of ships. If they go up on the rocks somewhere, you will have a significant environmental spill but also you'll have a search-and-rescue issue."[68] He later quipped that "if someone was foolish enough to attack us in the High North, my first duty would be search and rescue" – an obvious dismissal of threat narratives portending the possibility of conventional offensive military threats to the Canadian Arctic.[69]

Notwithstanding the considerable media and academic ink spilled on unresolved Arctic boundary disputes, uncertainty surrounding the delineation of the outer limits of extended continental shelves, and suggestions of "resource wars" in the Arctic, a detailed examination of key defence documents from 2010 to 2014[70] reveals that the Canadian defence establishment did not succumb to the popular myth that these issues had strong defence components. In short, the CAF saw no risk of armed conflict between Canada and its close allies. Similarly, managing the long-standing disagreement with the United States over the status of the waters of the Northwest Passage had consequences for Canadian defence and security in terms of transit rights and regulatory enforcement, but it was not considered to pose a serious obstacle to continental defence cooperation. Furthermore, despite punchy headlines in Canada and Russia suggesting conflicting interests between the countries over the delimitation of the extended continental shelf and increasing investments in Arctic military capabilities, defence documents from 2008 to 2014 did not treat these dynamics as acute threats. In short, sensational narratives of unbridled competition for rights and Arctic "territory" did not find strong grounding in DND efforts to define the Canadian Armed Forces' role in the Arctic.

In April 2010, Vice-Admiral Dean McFadden, the Commander of the Navy, told a Washington audience: "Let me be clear. Canada does not see a conventional military threat in the Arctic in the foreseeable future. The real challenges in the region are, therefore, related to safety and security."[71] Confirming this assessment, the defence department's implementation plans from 2010 to 2015 consistently operated on the explicit assumption that Canada faced no direct, conventional military threat to its security in the near- to mid-term.[72] While noting enduring responsibilities to defend Canada and North America and deter would-be aggressors, as well as the importance of monitoring military activities across the Arctic region (particularly by Russia) primarily through surveillance missions,[73] these strategic documents emphasized that the security risks and "threats" facing Canada's Arctic were unconventional, with the lead management responsibilities falling primarily to other government departments and agencies (OGDAs).[74] Strategic and operational-level documents guiding the military's northern planning focused on whole-of-government responses to law enforcement challenges (such as upholding Canadian fishing regulations vis-à-vis foreign fishing fleets), environmental threats (such as earthquakes and floods), terrorism, organized crime, foreign (state or non-state) intelligence gathering and counterintelligence operations, attacks on critical infrastructure, and pandemics.[75] Accordingly, rather than focusing on training for Arctic combat, the military embraced what the *Land Force Operating Concept* (2011) describes as a "comprehensive approach" to whole-of-government integration, with the CAF providing assets and personnel to support other government departments and agencies dealing with issues such as disaster relief, pollution response, poaching, fisheries protection, and law enforcement.[76] From a military perspective, this meant *supporting* the many stakeholders responsible for implementing federal, regional, and local government policies in the North.[77]

Defence officials recognized the need to build strong, collaborative relationships with other government departments and agencies, local and regional governments, and other Northern partners in order to fulfil the military's roles in leading or assisting in the response to security incidents. Instead of dismissing or failing to prioritize Indigenous Northerners' concerns and priorities, the military's strategic documents clearly highlighted threats to Indigenous communities posed by climate change, economic development, and increased shipping activity. Furthermore, these documents consistently emphasized that Northern domestic partners must be involved in the planning and enactment of policies and activities in the region, with information shared across government departments and with Arctic stakeholders. Because of the military's training, material assets, and discretional spending powers, and the specialized skill set held by its personnel, defence documents affirmed that the CAF had an essential role to play in government operations in the North – albeit an explicitly supporting one.[78] Otherwise stated, while other departments and agencies were mandated to lead the responses to northern security threats and emergencies, the military would "lead from behind" in the most probable, major security and safety scenarios.[79]

This understanding played out in the annual military-led Nanook operations after 2007. Although academic critiques of these operations tend to analyse them as a form of political theatre or examples of the Harper government's propensity to "militarize" the Arctic agenda,[80] they usually overlook or downplay the whole-of-government scenarios that formed the core of these exercises and that encouraged interdepartmental planning, communication, and interoperability to respond effectively to soft-security and safety-oriented emergencies.[81] These included counter-drug operations, oil spill response, hostage taking, shipboard fire response, criminal activity, disease outbreak, crashed satellite recovery, grounded vessels, a major air disaster, and search and rescue.[82] Rather than being a mere add-on to a military exercise, the whole-of-government aspect could be considered the most substantive, practical component of Nanook operations designed to address security and safety risks during the Harper era.

In summary, a systematic reading of the strategic documents produced by DND from 2010 to 2014 indicates that military planners did not subscribe to a "sovereignty on thinning ice" thesis, nor did military implementation plans build on rhetoric about a foremost need to "defend sovereignty" against foreign military threats arising from resource or boundary disputes. While political leaders often cited the need for enhanced military capabilities under the sovereignty pillar of Canada's Northern Strategy, the military did not interpret this as an urgent need to develop conventional war-fighting capabilities to ward off foreign state aggressors. Instead, the military articulated, promoted, and sought to implement a whole-of-government approach, predicated on interdepartmental cooperation, that clearly emphasized unconventional security and safety challenges. Rather than dismissing human and environmental security considerations, DND/CAF conceptualized these "soft" missions as the most probable situations where it would be called upon to provide security to Canadians. In most scenarios, enhanced military capabilities would help address these challenges in a *supporting* way rather than as the main line of government efforts to "enhance" sovereignty.[83]

Conclusion

Academic analysis commonly misses a salient shift in the Harper government's Arctic sovereignty and security messaging by placing excessive emphasis on selected speeches from the early years when "militaristic," conflict-oriented statements dominated. A more systematic analysis of the government's statements and actions through to 2015 suggests that rhetorical constructs and perceptions of Arctic sovereignty and security changed over time. By 2008, political statements had begun downplaying the danger of state-to-state conflict over Arctic boundaries and resources.

While the original conflict narrative was never totally banished from political rhetoric (and was resurrected after the Russian invasion of Crimea
and eastern Ukraine in 2014[84]), it was complemented and then largely
supplanted by broader whole-of-government frameworks that placed the
Canadian Armed Forces in a supporting role to other government departments to deal with the most probable "soft" security threats.

Since 2008, most (although not all) Arctic policy experts, senior military officers, and scholars have sought to discredit pervasive myths about
the centrality of "sovereignty threats," the so-called "race for resources,"
and the concomitant "militarization of the Arctic."[85] Despite academic
and popular commentary characterizing the Harper government based
on its early, excessively militaristic approach to Arctic sovereignty and
security, this chapter suggests the need for more systematic analysis. The
broadening and softening of Arctic defence and foreign policy from 2009
to 2014 is reflected in an area where one would expect hard-line sovereignty, defence, and security rhetoric to dominate: Arctic defence policy
and planning. While the Harper government never explicitly repudiated
or abandoned its early rhetoric emphasizing the need to "defend" sovereignty and security, the actual practice of Canadian Arctic defence policy
from 2006 to 2015 indicates that this aggressive approach did not serve
as a robust pretext for strategic and operational military planning. The
early focus on sovereignty as something that must be "used" and "defended" was supplemented and eventually supplanted by an expanding
focus on circumpolar cooperation, "soft" safety and security concerns,
and the military's role in "exercising" Canadian sovereignty through support to other departments. In short, the Harper government gradually
came to define sovereignty and security as more complex, multifaceted
concepts. While official discourse continued to substantiate concepts of
security that fell within the purview of state elites (and there remains
ample space for critical security scholars to challenge the state-centric
assumptions and socio-political power relationships that persisted), the
discourse space nevertheless expanded to embrace whole-of-government
considerations that did not simply equate Arctic sovereignty and security
with the need for more military capabilities and presence.

CAF activities and policy development demonstrate this transition
in thinking and also suggest that within the "black box" of government
the military's interpretations of political directives offered and legitimated more nuanced understandings of where the military fit within
broader sovereignty and security efforts. By positioning the Canadian
Armed Forces at the centre of the government's early push to defend
Canada's North, the political echelon held up the military as the guar-
antor of Canadian sovereignty and as the first line of defence against

anticipated security threats. Although publicly cast in a hard security, defensive role in political speeches from 2006 to 2009, senior military strategists and planners recognized the limited conventional threats actually facing Canada and devised policies and doctrine that emphasized "soft" security and safety challenges in the North, which were more probable. Designing capabilities and doctrine to focus on supporting roles in whole-of-government operations, as played out during annual Operation Nanook scenarios, the military prioritized safety and security roles rather than the conventional defence of "sovereignty" (territorial integrity) side of the mission spectrum.

Without directly repudiating the government, the Canadian military's propensity to downplay conventional military threats to the region and articulate its roles in a whole-of-government context deliberately avoided "militarizing" Arctic sovereignty and invoked broader Northern Strategy frameworks thatw emphasized the human dimension of sovereignty as much as the need for a conventional military presence. DND/CAF documents produced during the Harper era reveal an explicit recognition that lasting solutions to complex security challenges require system-wide, multifaceted responses that integrate civilian and military resources. Although academics typically cast the Harper government and the military as proponents of a narrow, militaristic fixation on inter-state conflict and defence of territory in the Arctic, this chapter suggests the need for a modest reinterpretation. "From a Defence perspective, successfully implementing government policy in the North will mean setting the conditions for human safety and security as increasing economic development takes place," the Chief of Force Development's 2010 *Arctic Integrating Concept* explained.[86] Indeed, official documents from 2008 onward incorporate, rather than isolate, military mandates for enhancing security and asserting sovereignty within broader strategic and policy frameworks designed to address the most pressing human and environmental challenges now facing the North and its resident populations.

Although a more cooperative approach has dominated Canadian defence and foreign policy over the past decade, assumptions underlying the "sovereignty on thinning ice" framework continue to echo in the popular media. Russian aggression in Ukraine since 2014 has led to the resurgence of "new Cold War" frameworks, predicated on escalating great power rivalry and potential impacts on Arctic peace and stability.[87] These narratives threaten to overshadow the calm, considered, and cooperative framework that underlay Canadian Arctic foreign and defence policy from the 1990s to the mid-2000s and that returned to the fore beginning in 2009. Exploring how understandings and articulations of sovereignty and security may have changed during Prime Minister Harper's decade in power, and more carefully examining how political direction was interpreted and enacted by federal departments and agencies, may lead scholars to revisit some basic assumptions. Rather than suggesting the need for a fundamental shift in Arctic policy by the Liberal government under Justin Trudeau, based on a simple caricature of the Harper government as excessively militaristic, unilateralist, "parochial and sovereignty-obsessed,"[88] the case might be made that the Conservatives ultimately articulated a whole-of-government approach to Arctic security that situated the military in an appropriate, supporting role that legitimized the primacy of "soft" security and safety threats over conventional military ones.

NOTES

1   See, for example, Klaus Dodds, "Flag Planting and Finger Pointing: The Law of the Sea, the Arctic, and the Political Geographies of the Outer Continental Shelf," *Political Geography* 29, no. 2 (2010): 63–73; Michael Byers, *Who Owns the Arctic: Understanding Sovereignty Disputes in the North* (Vancouver: Douglas and McIntyre, 2010); Elena Wilson Rowe, "A Dangerous Place? Unpacking State and Media Discourses on the Arctic," *Polar Geography* 36, no. 3 (2013): 232–44; and Scott Stephenson, "Collaborative Infrastructures: A Roadmap for International Cooperation in the Arctic," *Arctic Yearbook 2012* (Akureyri: Northern Research Forum, 2012), 311–33.

2   Wilfrid Greaves, "Canada, Circumpolar Security, and the Arctic Council," *Northern Public Affairs* (September 2013): 58.

3   Petra Dolata, "How 'Green' Is Canada's Arctic Policy?" *Zeitschrift für Kanada-Studien* 32, no. 2 (2012): 65–83 at 65.

4   P. Whitney Lackenbauer, *From Polar Race to Polar Saga: An Integrated Strategy for Canada and the Circumpolar World*, Foreign Policy for Canada's Tomorrow no. 3 (Toronto: Canadian International Council, July 2009), 35–6.

5   Adam Chapnick, "A Diplomatic Counter-Revolution: Conservative Foreign Policy 2006–2011," *International Journal* 67, no. 1 (2011–12): 153.

6   See, for example, Byers, *Who Owns The Arctic?*, 4; Heather A. Smith, "Choosing Not to See: Canada, Climate Change, and the Arctic," *International Journal* 65, no. 4 (2010): 931–42; Lee-Anne Broadhead, "Canadian Sovereignty versus Northern Security: The Case for Updating Our Mental Map of the Arctic," *International Journal* 65, no. 4 (2010): 913–30; Wilfrid Greaves, "For Whom, from What? Canada's Arctic Policy and the Narrowing of Human Security," *International Journal* 67, no. 1 (2011): 219–40; Klaus Dodds, "We Are a Northern Country: Stephen Harper and the Canadian Arctic," *Polar Record* 47, no. 4 (2011): 371–4; Scott Stephenson, "Collaborative

Infrastructures: A Roadmap for International Cooperation in the Arctic," *Arctic Yearbook 2012* 1 (2012): 316; and Ciara Sebastian, "New Power, New Priorities: The Effects of UNCLOS on Canadian Arctic Foreign Policy," *Polar Journal* 3, no. 1 (2013): 136–48.

7   See, for example, Kristian Åtland, "Interstate Relations in the Arctic: An Emerging Security Dilemma?," *Comparative Strategy* 33, no. 2 (2014): 145–66.

8   Philippe Genest and Frederic Lasserre, "Souveraineté, sécurité, identité: éléments-clés du discours du gouvernement canadien sur l'Arctique," *Canadian Foreign Policy Journal* 21, no.1 (2015): 74. For a contrasting interpretation of Harper and identity politics vis-à-vis the Arctic, see Petra Dolata, "A New Canada in the Arctic? Arctic Policies under Harper," *Études canadiennes/Canadian Studies : Revue interdisciplinaire des études canadiennes en France* 78 (2015): 149.

9   Mathieu Landriault, "La sécurité arctique 2000–2010: une décennie turbulente?" (unpublished PhD diss., University of Ottawa, 2013); Mathieu Landriault and Paul Minard, "Does Standing Up for Sovereignty Pay Off Politically? Arctic Military Announcements and Governing Party Support in Canada from 2006 to 2014," *International Journal* 71, no. 1 (2015): 41–61; Landriault, "Public Opinion on Canadian Arctic Sovereignty and Security," *Arctic* 69, no. 2 (2016): 160–8.

10   See, for example, P. Whitney Lackenbauer: "Mirror Images? Canada, Russia, and the Circumpolar World," *International Journal* (Autumn 2010): 879–97; "'Use It or Lose It,' History, and the Fourth Surge," in *Canada and Arctic Sovereignty and Security: Historical Perspectives*, ed. Lackenbauer (Calgary: Centre for Military and Strategic Studies, 2011), 423–36; "Afterword," in *Canada and the Changing Arctic: Sovereignty, Security, and Stewardship*, ed. Franklyn Griffiths, Rob Huebert, and Lackenbauer, 227–32 (Waterloo: Wilfrid Laurier University Press, 2011).

11   Dolata, "A 'New' Canada in the Arctic," 143–4.

12   Because my analysis focuses on federal politicians and government officials, it is inherently state-oriented, thus privileging particular understandings of sovereignty and security threats. While critical security scholars might adopt a different approach, my intention to analyse how government officials seek to frame and legitimize their understandings and policy preferences warrant this particular methodology, even if it does not speak to the full spectrum of sovereignty and security frameworks introduced by the authors in this book. Indeed, what is left out of government understandings can be just as interesting as what is included.

13   Barry Buzan, Ole Weaver, and Jaap de Wilde, *Security: A New Framework for Analysis* (New York: Lynne Reinner, 1998); Thierry Balzacq, "The Three Faces of Securitization: Political Agency, Audience, and Context," *European Journal of International Relations* 11, no. 2 (2005): 171–201; Thierry Balzacq, ed., *Securitization Theory: How Security Problems Emerge and Dissolve* (London: Routledge, 2010).

14 Adam Côté, "Social Securitization Theory" (unpublished PhD diss., University of Calgary, 2015), 26.

15 Buzan, Waever, and de Wilde, *Security*, 23–4.

16 See, for example, Kobi (Jacob) Michael, "The Dilemma behind the Classical Dilemma of Civil–Military Relations," *Armed Forces and Society* 33, no. 4 (July 2007): 518–46; D. Peter Feaver, *Armed Servant: Agency, Oversight, and Civil-Military Relations* (Cambridge, MA: Harvard University Press, 2003); C. Michael Desch, *Civilian Control of the Military – the Changing Security Environment* (Baltimore: Johns Hopkins University Press, 1999).

17 How well this WoG concept of operations was actually implemented is a separate issue. See, for example, Whitney Lackenbauer and Adam Lajeunesse, "The Emerging Arctic Security Environment: Putting the Military in Its (Whole of Government) Place," in *Whole of Government through an Arctic Lens*, ed. Heather Nicol and Lackenbauer (Antigonish: Mulroney Institute of Government, 2017), 1–36.

18 For general background, see Rob Huebert, "New Directions in Circumpolar Cooperation: Canada, the Arctic Environmental Protection Strategy, and the Arctic Council," *Canadian Foreign Policy* 5, no. 2 (Winter 1998): 37–58; Huebert, "Canadian Arctic Security Issues: Transformation in the Post-Cold War Era," *International Journal* 54, no. 2 (Spring 1999): 203–29; and Ken Coates, P. Whitney Lackenbauer, William Morrison, and Greg Poelzer, *Arctic Front: Defending Canada in the Far North* (Toronto: Thomas Allen, 2008).

19 John English, *Ice and Water: Politics, Peoples, and the Arctic Council* (Toronto: Allen Lane, 2013).

20 House of Commons Standing Committee on Foreign Affairs and International Trade, *Canada and the Circumpolar World: Meeting the Challenges of Cooperation into the Twenty-First Century* (1997), ix, 100.

21 *The Northern Dimension of Canada's Foreign Policy* (2000), excerpted in Ryan Dean, P. Whitney Lackenbauer, and Adam Lajeunesse, *Canadian Arctic Defence and Security Policy: An Overview of Key Documents, 1970–2012* (Calgary and Waterloo: Centre for Military and Strategic Studies / Centre on Foreign Policy and Federalism, 2014), 36, 38.

22 See Canadian Arctic Resources Committee, "Renewing the Northern Strategy," *Northern Perspectives* 30, no. 1 (2006): 2.

23 See, for example, Canadian Forces Northern Area, *Arctic Capabilities Study* (Yellowknife, 2000); Rob Huebert, "Climate Change and Canadian Sovereignty in the Northwest Passage," *Isuma* 2, no. 4 (Winter 2001): 86–94; and Huebert, "The Shipping News Part II: How Canada's Arctic Sovereignty Is on Thinning Ice," *International Journal* 58, no. 3 (Summer 2003): 295–308.

24 See, for example, Michael Byers and Suzanne Lalonde, "Our Arctic Sovereignty Is on Thin Ice," *Globe and Mail*, 1 August 2005.

25 Griffiths used this phrase in reference to Huebert, Byers, and Lalonde. Early appearances of this phrase in print include Bruce Valpy, "Canada's Control of Arctic Waters Questioned," *Northern News Services* (April 28, 2008); and Chris Windeyer, "Canadian Visit Welcomed, but Northern Issues Low on Agenda," *Nunatsiaq News* (January 22, 2009).

26 See Franklyn Griffiths, "The Shipping News: Canada's Arctic Sovereignty Is Not on Thinning Ice," *International Journal* 58, no. 2 (2003): 257–82.

27 ACIA, *Arctic Climate Impact Assessment* (Cambridge: Cambridge University Press, 2005).

28 On this context, see Lackenbauer, *From Polar Race to Polar Saga*.

29 See Canada, *Canada's International Policy Statement,* Overview (2005), excerpted in Dean, Lackenbauer, and Lajeunesse, *Canadian Arctic Defence,* 39–40.

30 Stephen Harper, "Harper Stands Up for Arctic Sovereignty," address in Ottawa, 22 December 2005, *Canada's Northern Strategy under the Harper Conservatives: Key Speeches and Documents on Sovereignty, Security, and Governance, 2006–15,* ed. P. Whitney Lackenbauer and Ryan Dean (Calgary: Centre for Military, Security, and Strategic Studies and Arctic Institute of North America, 2016), 1.

31 As Wilkins told reporters, however, the US position was "old news" and there was "no reason to create a problem that doesn't exist." CBC News, "Wilkins Says Arctic Comment Old News," 27 January 2006. For US Ambassador David Jacobson's views on these events two years later, see CTV News, "U.S. Pokes Fun at Harper's Arctic Pledges: WikiLeaks," 12 May 2011, http://www.ctvnews.ca/u-s-pokes-fun-at-harper-s-arctic-pledges-wikileaks-1.643259.

32 Steven Chase, "The North: Myth versus Reality in Stephen Harper's Northern Strategy," *Globe and Mail,* 27 January 2014. On Harper and the importance of stories, see also Roland Paris, "Are Canadians Still Liberal Internationalists? Foreign Policy and Public Opinion in the Harper Era," *International Journal* 69, no. 3 (2014): 283.

33 Stephen Harper, "Securing Canadian Sovereignty in the Arctic," 12 August 2006, reprinted in Lackenbauer and Dean, eds., *Canada's Northern Strategy,* 8–11.

34 Chapnick, "A Diplomatic Counter-Revolution," 143. Chapnick suggests that Harper played on fear and not on national pride, but this seems to overlook the unabashed chest-thumping rhetoric celebrating Canada's historical achievements in the North in key prime ministerial speeches such as "The Call of North," delivered on 17 August 2006, reprinted in Lackenbauer and Dean, eds., *Canada's Northern Strategy,* 12–18.

35 Harper, "The Call of the North," 14.

36 Bea Vongdouangchanh, "Cabinet Waiting for Defence Department's 10-Year Arctic Military Plan: O'Connor," *The Hill Times,* 16 October 2006.

37 Speaking notes for the Honourable Gordon J. O'Connor, at the Conference of Defence Associations Institute Annual General Meeting, 23 February

2006, in Lackenbauer and Dean, *Canada's Northern Strategy*, 2–4. Explicit "sovereignty" measures included expanding the Canadian Rangers, ordering new Arctic/Offshore Patrol (AOPS) vessels, building a deepwater Arctic docking and refuelling facility in Nanisivik, launching RadarSat-2 to provide enhanced surveillance and data-gathering capabilities, holding military exercises, building a Canadian Forces Arctic Training Centre in Resolute, and establishing a new reserve unit in Yellowknife. On these promises, see Griffiths et al., *Canada and the Changing Arctic*; and P. Whitney Lackenbauer and Adam Lajeunesse, "The Canadian Armed Forces in the Arctic: Building Appropriate Capabilities," *Journal of Military and Strategic Studies* 16, no. 4 (2016): 7–66.

38 Kathleen Harris, "Laying Claim to Canada's Internal Waters," *Toronto Sun*, 22 February 2007. The October 2007 Speech from the Throne reiterated that "Ensuring our capacity to defend Canada's sovereignty is at the heart of the Government's efforts to rebuild the Canadian Forces." Lackenbauer and Dean, *Canada's Northern Strategy*, 35.

39 "Prime Minister Stephen Harper Announces New Arctic Offshore Patrol Ships" [Speech], 9 July 2007, in Lackenbauer and Dean, *Canada's Northern Strategy*, 27. For another prime example combining nation-building and security, see Harper's reply to the Speech from the Throne, 17 October 2007, in ibid., 36–8.

40 On this theme, see Lackenbauer, *From Polar Race to Polar Saga*; and Lackenbauer and Peter Kikkert, eds., *The Canadian Forces and Arctic Sovereignty: Debating Roles, Interests, and Requirements, 1968–1974* (Waterloo: Laurier Centre for Military Strategic and Disarmament Studies, 2010). Legal advisers in the Department of Foreign Affairs stressed the importance of not conflating the two concepts in public presentations and testimonies before parliamentary committees.

41 Douglas Birch, "Russia Presses Claim on Arctic," *Boston Globe*, 2 August 2007.

42 Unnati Gandhi and Alan Freeman, "Russian Mini-subs Plant Flag at North Pole Sea Bed," *Globe and Mail*, 2 August 2007.

43 Putin explained that Russia had "stopped this practice in 1992. Unfortunately not everybody followed suit. This creates a strategic risk for Russia … we hope our partners show understanding towards the resumption of Russian air patrols." Luke Harding and Ewen MacAskill, "Putin Revives Long-Range Bomber Patrols," *The Guardian* (UK), 18 August 2007.

44 See, for example, National Snow and Ice Data Center Newsroom, "Arctic Sea Ice Shatters All Previous Record Lows," 1 October 2007, https://nsidc.org/news/newsroom/2007_seaiceminimum/20071001_pressrelease.html.

45 Rob Huebert, "Canadian Arctic Sovereignty and Security in a Transforming Circumpolar World," *Foreign Policy for Canada's Tomorrow*, no. 4 (2009); Michael Byers and Suzanne Lalonde, "Who Controls the Northwest Passage?," *Vanderbilt Journal of Transnational Law* 42, no. 4 (2009): 1191–9.

46 Franklyn Griffiths, "Canadian Arctic Sovereignty: Time to Take Yes for an Answer on the Northwest Passage," in *Northern Exposure: Peoples, Powers, and Prospects for Canada's North,* ed. Frances Abele et al., 1–30 (Ottawa: Institute for Research on Public Policy, 2008); Franklyn Griffiths, *Towards a Canadian Arctic Strategy,* Foreign Policy for Canada's Tomorrow No. 1 (Toronto: Canadian International Council, June 2009), 20.

47 See, for example, Paul Kaludjak, "The Inuit Are Here, Use Us," *Ottawa Citizen,* 18 July 2007; Mary Simon, "Does Ottawa's Northern Focus Look Backwards?" *Nunatsiaq News,* 11 April 2008; and the perspectives in Scot Nickels, ed. *Nilliajut: Inuit Perspectives on Security, Patriotism, and Sovereignty* (Ottawa: Inuit Tapiriit Kanatami, 2013). Furthermore, the Inuit Circumpolar Council's transnational Circumpolar Inuit Declaration on Sovereignty in the Arctic (2009) emphasized that "the inextricable linkages between issues of sovereignty and sovereign rights in the Arctic and Inuit self-determination and other rights require states to accept the presence and role of Inuit as partners in the conduct of international relations in the Arctic." The declaration envisages the Inuit playing an active role in all deliberations on environmental security, sustainable development, militarization, shipping, and social and economic development. Inuit Circumpolar Council (ICC), *A Circumpolar Declaration on Sovereignty in the Arctic* (2009), https://www.itk.ca/publication/circumpolar-declaration-sovereignty-arctic.

48 P. Whitney Lackenbauer, "Striking an Arctic Balance," *Globe and Mail,* 7 August 2008; Lackenbauer, *From Polar Race to Polar Saga.*

49 "Canada's New Government Praises Canadian Forces Arctic Sovereignty Patrol" [News release], 22 March 2007, in Lackenbauer and Dean, *Canada's Northern Strategy,* 21.

50 Speech from the Throne to Open the Second Session of the 39th Parliament of Canada, 16 October 2007, in Lackenbauer and Dean, eds., *Canada's Northern Strategy under the Harper Conservatives,* 35–6. The following year, Prime Minister Harper reiterated his government's commitment to the "New North" during his fifth northern tour, insisting that the four pillars constituted "a comprehensive vision for a new North, a Northern Strategy that will turn potential into prosperity for the benefit of all Northerners and all Canadians." News Release: "Prime Minister Harper Delivers on Commitment to the 'New North'" [News release], 10 March 2008.

51 Mary Simon, then president of Inuit Tapiriit Kanatami (the national Inuit political organization), asserted that the Northern Strategy should have a strong domestic focus aimed at improving the lives of Northerners, particularly Inuit, whose "use and occupation of Arctic lands and waters by Inuit for thousands of years" constituted "the bedrock of Canada's status as an Arctic nation." Bob Weber, "Northern Leaders Like that Harper Has Expanded View of Arctic Sovereignty," Canadian Press, 16 October 2007;

Mary Simon, "Inuit: The Bedrock of Canadian Sovereignty," *Globe and Mail,* 26 July 2007. See also Michael Byers and Jack Layton, "How to Strengthen Our Arctic Security: Keep Our Promises to the Inuit," *The Tyee,* 6 September 2007; and Mary Simon, "Inuit and the Canadian Arctic: Sovereignty Begins at Home," *Journal of Canadian Studies* 43, no. 2 (2009): 251.

52 DND, *Canada First Defence Strategy* (2008), http://www.forces.gc.ca/en /about/canada-first-defence-strategy-summary.page.

53 "Minister of National Defence and Chief of the Defence Staff Travel to Arctic" [News release], 15 August 2008, in Lackenbauer and Dean, *Canada's Northern Strategy,* 61–2.

54 "Canada Commemorates 25th Anniversary of UN Convention on the Law of the Sea" [News release], December 2007, in Lackenbauer and Dean, *Canada's Northern Strategy,* 44.

55 Ilulissat Declaration, Arctic Ocean Conference, Ilulissat, Greenland, 27–9 May 2008, http://www.oceanlaw.org/downloads/arctic/Ilulissat _Declaration.pdf.

56 Minister Cannon also responded that "Canada already has its own Arctic northern strategy defined in the 2007 throne speech." Bob Weber, "Arctic Sovereignty Not under Threat Despite U.S., European Policies: Cannon," Canadian Press, 13 January 2009.

57 Speaking notes for the Hon. Lawrence Cannon, Minister of Foreign Affairs, "Canada's Arctic Foreign Policy: The International Dimension of Canada's Northern Strategy," Whitehorse, Yukon, 11 March 2009, reproduced in Lackenbauer and Dean, *Canada's Northern Strategy under the Harper Conservatives,* 80–6.

58 Canada, *Canada's Northern Strategy: Our North, Our Heritage, Our Future* (Ottawa: Department of Indian Affairs and Northern Development, 2009), http://www.northernstrategy.gc.ca/cns/cns-eng.asp.

59 See Lackenbauer and Dean, *Canada's Northern Strategy,* 66. Minister of Foreign Affairs Lawrence Cannon quoted it in a speech on 9 April 2010. See ibid., 142.

60 Quoted in CBC News, "Canada Unveils Arctic Strategy," 26 July 2009, http://www.cbc.ca/news/canada/canada-unveils-arctic-strategy-1.820074.

61 See Canada, *Statement on Canada's Arctic Foreign Policy* (Ottawa: DFAIT, 2010), 2.

62 Leading Canadian academic experts seemed to have reached a similar consensus around 2009, with the most strident proponents of the "sovereignty on thinning ice" school largely abandoning their earlier arguments that Canadian sovereignty will be a casualty of climate change and concomitant foreign challenges. Instead, academic narratives anticipating potential conflict have tended to emphasize how other international events (such as Russian aggression in the Ukraine) could "spill over" into the Arctic or how

new non-Arctic state and non-state actors might challenge or undermine Canadian sovereignty and security. See for example, Rob Huebert, "Why Canada, US Must Resolve Their Arctic Border Disputes," *Globe and Mail*, 21 October 2014; Derek Burney and Fen Osler Hampson, "Arctic Alert: Russia Is Taking Aim at the North," *Globe and Mail*, 9 March 2015; Michael Byers, "The Northwest Passage Dispute Invites Russian Mischief," *National Post*, 28 April 2015; and Scott Borgerson and Michael Byers, "The Arctic Front in the Battle to Contain Russia," *Wall Street Journal*, 8 March 2016. For a less alarmist view of Russia, see Adam Lajeunesse and Whitney Lackenbauer, "Canadian Arctic Security: Russia's Not Coming," *Arctic Deeply*, 14 April 2016); and Lackenbauer, "Canada and Russia: Toward an Arctic Agenda," *Global Brief* (Summer–Fall 2016): 21–5.

63 "Operation NANOOK 14" [News release], 20 August 2014, in Lackenbauer and Dean, *Canada's Northern Strategy*, 332.
64 Michael, "The Dilemma," 520.
65 The military's overriding purpose and occupation in the Canadian Arctic was laid out in various core government and National Defence policy documents. In 2008 the Canada First Defence Strategy characterized the military's role in the North as ensuring "the security of our citizens and help[ing] exercise Canada's sovereignty." Achieving this objective meant exercising "control" and "demonstrating a visible Canadian presence" in the Arctic. Department of National Defence, *Canada First Defence Strategy* (Ottawa, 2008), 7–8. Two years later, the Northern Strategy (2010) emphasized the need to "patrol and protect our territory through enhanced presence on the land, in the sea and over the skies of the Arctic" and, in so doing, "[exercise] our Arctic sovereignty." Aboriginal Affairs and Northern Development Canada, *Canada's Northern Strategy: Our North, Our Heritage, Our Future* (Ottawa, 2009). Similar messaging is found in the Statement on Canada's Arctic Foreign Policy (2010), which cites as its first and foremost pillar "the exercise of our sovereignty over the Far North. DFAIT, *Statement on Canada's Arctic Foreign Policy* (Ottawa, 2010), 4.
66 Klaus Dodds, "Graduated and Paternal Sovereignty: Stephen Harper, Operation Nanook 10, and the Canadian Arctic," *Environment and Planning D: Society and Space* 30, no. 6 (2012): 989–1010.
67 Heather N. Nicol, "Ripple Effects: Devolution, Development, and State Sovereignty in the Canadian North," in *Future Security of the Global Arctic: State Policy, Economic Security and Climate*, ed. Lassi Heininen (London: Palgrave Macmillan, 2016), 99.
68 Bruce Campion-Smith, "PM's Tour Fuels Debate on Arctic," *The Star* [Toronto], 22 August 2009. On the success of these visits in generating support for the PM, see Landriault and Minard, "Does Standing Up for Sovereignty Pay Off Politically?"

69   Natynczyk quoted in James Stavridis, "High North or High Tension? How to Head Off War in the Last Frontier on Earth," *Foreign Policy*, 21 October 2013), http://foreignpolicy.com/2013/10/21/high-north-or-high-tension.

70   My analysis here focuses on Chief of Force Development, *Arctic Integrating Concept* (2010); *Chief of the Defence Staff (CDS)/Deputy Minister (DM) Directive for DND/CF in the North*, 12 April 2011; *Canadian Forces Northern Employment and Support Plan* (*CFNESP*) (November 2012); and Canadian Joint Operations Command (CJOC), *CJOC Plan for the North*, 28 January 2014.

71   Vice-Admiral Dean McFadden, speaking notes, "The Evolution of Arctic Security and Defense Policies: Cooperative or Confrontational?," Center for Strategic and International Studies conference, Washington, D.C., 28 April 2010.

72   See, for example, *Arctic Integrating Concept*, 4; *CDS/DM Directive*, 9; *NESP*, 7.

73   *Arctic Integrating Concept*, 4, 25–6; *CDS/DM Directive*, 8, 11.

74   Arctic Integrating Concept, 5, 6; *CDS/DM Directive*, 9.

75   *Arctic Integrating Concept*, 23–4; *CDS/DM Directive*, appendix A: 1–2.

76   J.T. Sheahan and P.J. Gizewski, "Land Force Operating Concept 2021" (January 2011), 1. The first mention of whole-of-government integration appeared in the *Canada First Defence Strategy* (2008), pages 4, 9, and 14, with the 2010 *Arctic Foreign Policy* explicitly situating the CAF within a broader whole-of-government Arctic effort designed to exercise Canada's sovereign rights and responsibilities (6). That same year, the Chief of Force Development's *Arctic Integrating Concept* anticipated that "the types of defence or security challenges that Canada will face over the next 10 years (to 2020) will not appreciably change from those facing the country today." The document clearly defined a whole-of-government approach, conceptualizing Arctic "security" in a broad, integrated manner. Within this framework, "defence" involves more than merely maintaining a presence in the region but results from "working closely with all partners" to achieve the government's broader Arctic objectives. *Arctic Integrating Concept*, ix, 10, 23. On the comprehensive approach, see also Bill Bentley and Grazia Scoppio, *Leading in Comprehensive Operations*, Monograph 2012-02 (Kingston: Canadian Forces Leadership Institute, 2012), 2–4.

77   *Arctic Integrating Concept*, 10.

78   See, for example, *Arctic Integrating Concept*, ix, 10, 23, 49.

79   The exception is search and rescue, where DND has the lead for coordinating air and maritime SAR and providing aeronautical SAR.

80   See, for example, Rob Huebert, "Welcome to a New Era of Arctic Security," *Globe and Mail*, 24 August 2010; Dodds, "Graduated and Paternal Sovereignty," 989–1010; Helga Haftendorn, "NATO and the Arctic: Is the Atlantic Alliance a Cold War Relic in a Peaceful Region Now Faced with Non-military Challenges?," *European Security* 20, no. 3 (2011): 337–61; Landriault

and Minard, "Does Standing Up for Sovereignty Pay Off Politically?"; and Nicol, "Ripple Effects," 99–120.

81 CJOC Plan for the North, Appendix A1, 1–2, notes that Nanook exercises are "designed to build relationships, establish conditions for partnership, and/or build capacity with partners or regions of choice."

82 Operation Nanook principal training scenarios (2007–15), Department of National Defence, "Operation Nanook," http://www.forces.gc.ca/en /operations-canada-north-america-recurring/op-nanook.page.

83 How well this WoG concept of operations was actually implemented warrants additional analysis. See, for example, Lackenbauer and Lajeunesse, "Emerging Arctic Security Environment."

84 Ilulissat Declaration, adopted at the Arctic Ocean Conference hosted by the Government of Denmark and attended by the representatives of the five costal states bordering on the Arctic Ocean (Canada, Denmark, Norway, the Russian Federation, and the United States), held at Ilulissat, Greenland, 27–9 May 2008. The declaration stated that all states will adhere to the existing legal framework to settle overlapping claims. For access to the national Arctic strategies and statements from the Arctic states, see Arctic Council Document Archive, "Arctic Strategies," http://www.arctic -council.org/index.php/en/document-archive/category/12-arctic -strategies.

85 See, for example: Lackenbauer, *From Polar Race to Polar Saga*; and Frédéric Lasserre, Jérôme Le Roy, and Richard Garon, "Is There an Arms Race in the Arctic?" *Journal of Military and Strategic Studies* 14, nos. 3–4 (2012): 1–56.

86 Chief of Force Development, *Arctic Integrating Concept* (Ottawa: DND, 2010), 1.

87 See, for example, Rob Huebert, "How Russia's Move into Crimea Upended Canada's Arctic Strategy," *Globe and Mail*, 2 April 2014; and "Baird Visits Norway, Reaffirms Canada's Position on Ukraine and the Arctic" [News release], 22 August 2014, in Dean and Lackenbauer, *Canada's Northern Strategy*, 335.

88 See, for example, Joel Plouffe and Heather Exner-Pirot, "Polar Opposites: Time for a 180 Turn in Canada's Arctic Policy," *iPolitics*, 16 December 2015.

8 One Arctic? Northern Security in Canada and Norway

ANDREAS ØSTHAGEN

As rhetoric and statements concerning Arctic security threats have intensified over the last decade, there has been a tendency to describe security challenges as coherent across the region. Scholars and media alike often describe the Arctic as *one* region, where states' various security interests are inherently intertwined.[1] But how well does this hold up when examining the national interests and policies of the specific Arctic countries?

Norway and Canada have both placed considerable emphasis on the North in foreign policy as well as domestic debates, yet they actually hold dissimilar interests concerning security in the Arctic. When Russia reasserted itself after 2005–6, Norway called for NATO to engage more strenuously in the Arctic and develop an Arctic policy.[2] Canada, by contrast, has rejected the notion that NATO needs an Arctic policy.[3] Norway and Canada thus have differing positions with regard to NATO's role in the North. Consequently, this chapter asks: why do Norwegian and Canadian interests differ in the Arctic? And what does this entail for the Arctic as a so-called "security region"? Can we even attempt to describe the Arctic as *one* coherent region in terms of security?

This chapter questions some of the theoretical assumptions that underpin much of the contemporary debate on Arctic security. Recognizing that theoretical constructs are inherently simplifications that cannot capture all empirical nuances, I wish to shed light on how the concept of a "security region" can hold relevance for a specific part of the world that has received considerable attention in recent years. The concept itself can prove useful in highlighting certain aspects of the Arctic related to Norway and Canada. While recognizing the whole range of security studies and the linkages among different types of security and safety, this article emphasizes what is often referred to as "military" – more accurately, "state" – security.[4] This definition takes on a state-centric point of view, primarily concerned with the survival of the state structure itself.[5]

After briefly examining the theoretical foundations of a "security region," this chapter looks at Arctic security as a whole and how the North figures into Norwegian and Canadian security considerations. From this foundation, I compare and contrast the two countries' approaches to draw conclusions about the larger Arctic security environment. I conclude that, notwithstanding the growing tendency to describe the Arctic as a single coherent security region, the lack of security commonalities between Canada and Norway renders such depictions inaccurate.

Security Regions

Examining the role of regions (subsystems) in international relations (IR) is a modern endeavour. Since the 1970s, scholars classified along the various strands of neorealism and neoliberalism have occupied themselves with system-level interactions between states, while paying scant attention to regions in traditional security deliberations.[6] Kelly argues this is because of the limited role that subsystems played in systemic security concerns throughout the Cold War (bipolarity) and the post–Cold War years (American hegemony).[7] Also, regional-level analysis can quickly become too complex, as well as limited in its theoretical value.

Yet since the mid-1990s, scholars have embarked on downscaling IR methods to explain the variations and nuances found across the world's various (security) regions.[8] In particular, Barry Buzan's theory of regional security complexes has become the hallmark of regional security studies.[9] He argues that with the end of bipolarity after the Cold War, local and regional powers have more room to manoeuvre. This only extends to their specific geographic region, however, given that small and medium-sized countries have limited capability to assert power. It is patterns of enmity and amity, in turn defined by the capacities of the states themselves and their adjacency to other states, that determine how the security region "plays out."[10]

By contrast, David Lake argues that it is not geographic distance or proximity that determines regional security. Rather, states are bound together by shared security "externalities," even when the states themselves are geographically far apart.[11] Raimo Väyrynen, as a "critical" or "new" regionalist, offers a third approach that encourages a search for "imagined or cognitive regions."[12] Instead of being defined by clear power structures or common externalities, these regions are what states make of them; thus, associative security regions are constructed through interaction and cooperation.

In sum, studies of security regions are diverse and by no means conclusive. Taking a state-centric approach, regions can be defined geographically, functionally, and cognitively.[13] These divisions are not definite, but they do provide a starting point for analysis when we try to conceptualize the Arctic. This chapter largely adopts the first of these three conceptualizations of a security region, given that Buzan and Wæver's theory of regional security complexes has gained the strongest foothold in studies of regional security. The other approaches, however, add nuance to and new perspectives on the Arctic as a security region.

Arctic Security

Arctic states are not exempt from conflict and instability. Although there is no immediate need to fear an armed struggle over the Arctic itself, the regional relationships between Russia and other Arctic states cannot be separated from the more general deterioration of the relationship between Russia and the West.[14] Military activity in the Arctic is today at its highest point since the end of the Cold War. Russian bombers continue to fly in large numbers along the coast of northern Norway and over the North Pole from the Kola Peninsula.[15] Moreover, while Russian investment in military infrastructure in its northern regions predominantly reflects the region's strategic importance for Russia, other countries in the Arctic region perceive this as a source of concern for their own security.[16]

NATO has always been implicitly present in the Arctic through five of its member-states (Canada, the United States, Norway, Iceland, and Denmark). Yet it has never had an explicit policy for the region. As Russian activity in the North started to increase at the beginning of the new millennium, fears arose that active NATO engagement in the Arctic would damage relations with Russia and raise tensions unnecessarily.[17] Yet after 2008, both Norway and Iceland argued for a more active NATO role in the North. Arguments concerning "new Arctic challenges," such as search and rescue, environmental protection, and general domain awareness, underlay calls for greater NATO engagement in the North. At the same time, Russia's increased military assertiveness after 2006 led to calls to improve the alliance's conventional military capabilities in the North, so as to retain its credibility as a security provider for countries like Iceland and Norway.[18] But in 2009, Canada firmly rebuffed calls for a more explicit mention of the Arctic in NATO's future policy guidelines, arguing that it did not see a role for NATO in addressing the "softer" security challenges in the Arctic.[19] Since then, NATO policy explicitly dealing with the Arctic has been put on hold.

In 2014, tensions between Russia and the West reached new heights when Russia annexed Crimea and invaded eastern Ukraine. The United States, the European Union, Canada, Norway, and other countries imposed sanctions on the Russian Federation. Military exercises in the North *with* Russia were cancelled or postponed, while larger exercises in both the Russian Arctic and between NATO allies in the North were conducted to showcase the two sides' military capacities [20] Calls arose for Sweden and Finland – both of them Arctic countries – to join NATO,[21] and NATO's northern role has returned to the agenda (see also Huebert, chapter 4, and Greaves, chapter 5, in this volume).[22] These trends are not coherent across the Arctic, however: Canada has been reticent to discuss Arctic security in a NATO context. What explains these differences between Norway and Canada when it comes to NATO in the Arctic?

Norway's High North

In Norway, the "Arctic" refers to everything north of the Arctic Circle (66°34N). Yet there is little difference between the areas north and south of that latitude in terms of climate and level of development. In its foreign policy, Norway distinguishes between the extreme Arctic (referring to the North Pole and the uninhabited parts of the "High Arctic") and the more hospitable and populated parts of northern Norway and Svalbard, deemed the "High North."[23] Though sparsely populated by European standards, that region's population of almost 500,000 is high relative to that of the North American Arctic. Norway is a small Nordic state with one third of its territory and 80 per cent of its maritime zones in the Arctic; for Norwegians, the Arctic is not remote, nor can it be separated from national security and defence policies. Indeed, Norwegians view the North as integral to their security. This is not because of the melting sea ice or the Arctic's resource potential, but because Norway shares land and maritime borders with Russia.

Ever since the Soviet Union liberated northern Norway from the Nazi occupiers in the winter of 1944 and spring of 1945, Norwegian security policy has focused on managing the "Russian Bear" to the east. Norway is well aware that it is weaker militarily than Russia.[24] It manages this imbalance through its transatlantic relationship with NATO (Norway is a founding member) and its bilateral relationship with the United States. Norway thus guarantees its security by keeping the United States and other NATO allies engaged in the Norwegian security environment. Norway is also a strong supporter of multilateralism and cooperative solutions in its foreign policy.[25] It therefore seeks the active engagement of the United States and its European allies in its security concerns, which are dominated by the presence of Russia. At the same time, Norway pursues multilateral work with Russia in global organizations such as the UN, and regionally in the Nordic Council, the Arctic Council, and the

Barents Euro-Arctic Council, to foster an international system governed by law and stability.

The "new" interest in Arctic affairs in Norway can be traced back to then foreign minister Jonas Gahr Støre's decision to focus on the High North (in a Norwegian context) and the Arctic (internationally) once he took office in the autumn of 2005 (see Greaves, chapter 5).[26] This was paralleled by two specific events, both related to Russia. The elevation of the Arctic to Norway's number one strategic foreign policy priority in 2005 coincided with the failed arrest of the Russian trawler *Elektron*, which turned the focus toward maritime cooperation with Russia in the Barents Sea. Worldwide attention turned toward the region when Russia planted a flag on the North Pole seabed in 2007; Støre made use of that event to emphasize Arctic multilateral cooperation.[27]

In Norway, the Arctic is not necessarily framed in a security context. The Arctic has connotations of a frozen wilderness, yet the Norwegian Arctic (*nordområdene*) – at least the part on the Norwegian mainland – is rather heavily populated and has always been ice-free. This ties into a general Norwegian perspective that circumpolar cooperation is required on softer issues such as environmental challenges and human security affairs, in addition to economic opportunities.[28] As Wilfrid Greaves discussed in chapter 5, this contrasts with Norwegian security policy, which focuses on the relationship with Russia in the Arctic but is not framed as an Arctic endeavour as such. Even issues concerning the Svalbard Archipelago generally march under the "High North" banner. Norway was granted sovereignty over Svalbard with the Svalbard Treaty, signed in 1920 in Paris, which came into effect in 1925. The treaty gives all signatories the right to live and work on the islands, while placing some limitations on Norway's ability to impose taxes on Svalbard and to use Svalbard for military purposes. Norway claims that the 200-mile zone around Svalbard is part of the Norwegian EEZ, as this innovation in maritime law did not exist when the treaty was formalized in 1920. To avoid an outright challenge to the Norwegian claim and to protect and manage what is the main spawning ground for northeastern Arctic cod, the Norwegian government established a Fisheries Protection Zone (FPZ), allowing only limited fishing in the area.[29] Although the other treaty signatories have so far accepted this, Russia and Iceland in particular have been outspokenly critical of what they perceive to be discrimination against foreign fishing vessels in the area by the Norwegian Coast Guard.[30]

Svalbard presents a potential source of conflict with Russia, but it has also been a long-standing pillar of bilateral cooperation and mutual exchange of information and services since the 1970s.[31] Norway and Russia signed a maritime boundary treaty for the Barents Sea and the Arctic

Ocean in September 2010, which gives both states the right to freely develop their parts of the Arctic shelf, and a new border agreement in September 2018, which is based on earlier agreements forged between 1826 and 1949. These reflect a realization that the relationship with Russia needs to be built on pragmatism, for the two states need to manage everything from joint fish stocks to border crossings and trade needs.[32] Norway is proud of this bilateral relationship, which focuses on environmental management (particularly fisheries) and people-to-people cooperation at the local and regional levels.[33] This does not diminish the overarching security concerns related to a resurgent Russia under Vladimir Putin – Russia has been strutting its military along the Norwegian border with naval and aerial activities.[34]

In sum, Norway's quest for an active NATO in the Arctic builds on its desire to uphold its own defence guarantee now that Russia is resurgent in the North. Norway is seeking to turn NATO northwards, and this is drawing the attention of the United States and of the alliance writ large. Deteriorating relations with Russia since 2014 have amplified Norway's calls for a stronger focus on the Arctic. While safeguarding local and low-level cooperation with Russia, Norway has reaffirmed its commitment to NATO as "inextricably linked," while upholding its role as the northern flank of the alliance.[35]

Northern Canada

In Canada, the Arctic is generally defined as the three federal territories above the 60th Parallel.[36] The Arctic can also be defined as the region above the treeline, or as "Inuit Nunangat" (the homeland of the Inuit), which includes parts of Quebec and Labrador as well as the three northern territories.[37] This region resonates strongly with Canada's conception of security and sovereignty, and the idea of "the North" plays a significant part in Canada's national self-concept.[38] Yet the distance between Canada's urban centres – most of which hug the US border – and the Canadian Arctic is considerable. Norway is relatively well integrated and unified across its Arctic and non-Arctic territories; Canada's sheer vastness has imposed a different reality. Also, climatic differences have affected population patterns: only around 110,000 people live in the three northern territories that account for 40 per cent of Canada's land mass.

Canada's only land neighbour to the south and west (Alaska) is the United States, but only 25 kilometres separate Nunavut and Greenland at the closest point to the east, making Greenland (and thus the Kingdom of Denmark) another immediate neighbour. Notwithstanding Canada's ongoing dispute with Greenland/Denmark over the relatively insignificant Hans Island/Hans Ø,[39] Denmark is a close ally, and the two countries enjoy amicable relations. Similarly, despite well-publicized historical disputes over sovereignty and the status of waters in Canada's Arctic, bilateral relations with the United States are amicable and cooperative.[40] The two countries disagree over the status of the Northwest Passage, which Canada claims as historic internal waters but which the United States views as an international strait. This ongoing issue feeds Canadian anxiety about its ability to control its sovereign waters and, by extension, Arctic sovereignty writ large.

Framed within the broader relationship between the two allies and primary trading partners, the Northwest Passage dispute is a minor issue. The two countries have "agreed to disagree," cooperating behind closed doors while upholding so-called national interests publicly.[41] The North American Aerospace Defense Command (NORAD), established in 1957–8 as a commitment to jointly provide surveillance of potential air space threats in North America, has become the foundation of defence collaboration between the United States and Canada.[42] At the same time, Canada's own relationship with its North has been characterized by what Canadian scholars term "sovereignty anxiety": the idea that Canada must struggle to uphold its sovereignty in the Arctic and is prone to security threats in the region.[43] Here the dispute with the United States over the Northwest Passage comes into play. "The core issue of Canadian Arctic sovereignty is control," Rob Huebert suggests. "The core issue of Canadian Arctic security is about responding to threats. The threats to Canadian Arctic security are nebulous, multi-dimensional, and evolving."[44]

These words resonate with Canada's approach to the Arctic under a Conservative government between 2006 and 2015 (see Lackenbauer in chapter 6). Under prime minister Stephen Harper, the Arctic was elevated on the national agenda, with the emphasis on security challenges and on preparing for a "new" North. In particular, Russian bombers and fighter aircraft were cited as an example of an imminent threat to Canadian sovereignty in the North,[45] and promises were made to enhance Canada's Arctic presence.[46] The lack of security threats beyond occasional Russian aircraft, however, led some commentators to argue that social and economic development in Canada's northern communities (often neglected in national policy planning and economic redistribution) were a more pressing concern in the North.[47] "Anxiety about 'using or losing' our Arctic inheritance is more revealing of the Canadian psyche – particularly our chronic lack of confidence – than of objective realities," Whitney Lackenbauer suggested. "This anxiety encourages a disproportionate emphasis on national defence at the expense of a broader suite of social, economic, and diplomatic initiatives."[48]

Two Arctics

In sum, Norway and Canada relate to their northern areas in different ways. For each country, the Arctic embodies different conceptions of security. So does it even make sense to talk about the Arctic as *one* security region? Or are we, when examining Norway and Canada, discussing two completely different regions?

Buzan and Ole Wæver's theoretical approach builds on *geographic proximity* as a core assumption.[49] A state is more concerned with its neighbours than with geographically distant countries. For both Norway and Canada, Russia is a key factor in Arctic security considerations. The argument often set out in the media and by scholars is that melting Arctic sea ice is opening the region. The Arctic's geography is changing, and previous security concerns that were literally frozen are becoming increasingly relevant.[50] This, however, simplifies the Arctic and the fundamental role of geography in the North. As Norway and Canada showcase, geographic proximity still matters. For the other Arctic countries, security concerns relate not to the melting sea ice but to Russia's resurgence.[51] Russia does not play the same role in every Arctic country's security policy. Geography comes into play, and proximity is the defining feature.

The shared land and maritime border with Russia has dominated, and will continue to dominate, the security concerns of Norway. Maintaining a balancing act between friendly relations and posing a credible defence of its own territory is the main task at hand. Norway's security concerns and "neighbourly relations," however, do not reach across the Atlantic or the Arctic to Canada. Canada does not have the global reach of a superpower, nor is it heavily invested even in its *own* Arctic areas, where few Canadians live. Russia does not pose the same security concerns for Canada as for Norway. The Russian Northern Fleet – Russia's core military asset in the Arctic – is considerably farther from Canada than from Norway. Although Russian military aircraft have been flying near Canadian airspace, this threat is arguably limited and contained well enough by Canada's NORAD alliance with the United States. Any threatening force would have to cross multiple geographical barriers just to reach the Canadian Arctic's shores, which arguably hold little strategic benefit. As Canadian Chief of Defence General Walter Natyncyk stated in 2009: "If someone were to invade the Canadian Arctic, my first task would be to rescue them."[52] This is in stark contrast to Norwegian security concerns, exemplified by the Expert Commission on Norwegian Security and Defence Policy statement that "the High North constitutes Norway's most important strategic area of responsibility."[53]

The basic principle that geographic proximity spurs mutual threat conceptions, or "interlinkage" (as Buzan and Wæver call it), does not seem to hold between Norway and Canada. This reflects the simple but relevant fact that the distance between Norway and Canada is far too great. The two countries are on different continents, and even a transpolar route from Svalbard to Nunavut would entail a considerable voyage (in addition to geophysical barriers). In this sense, Buzan and Wæver are correct in not considering the Arctic a separate region. Instead, they indirectly describe the Arctic as a buffer between various regional complexes, with only the European security region making use of the Arctic.[54] So the Arctic as a whole cannot really be described as a single security region.

Lake, by contrast, argues that shared *security externalities*, not geographic proximity, are what define security regions.[55] Both Norway and Canada strongly support human rights and multilateral solutions in international affairs. Since the events in Ukraine in 2014, both have highlighted Russia as a threat to the extent that they have contributed armed forces to reassurance operations in Eastern Europe. Yet this threat perception has arguably not spilled over into the Arctic to the degree that a "security region" has materialized across the North Atlantic. Although both countries are NATO members (which could spur common threat perceptions), the fact that NATO does not have an Arctic policy points to an absence of mutual security considerations concerning the Arctic.

In Canada's view, the NATO alliance is concerned with European security and international operations.[56] By this logic, the alliance has no clear role to play in the Arctic, a region that Canada considers a domestic or North American continental security concern. Accordingly, the two countries perceive threats differently. At most, the wider security context of Canada can be said to include the northeast Atlantic, meaning Iceland and Greenland. For Norway, NATO is pivotal to national security and defence in its relationship with Russia, particularly in the High North. Consequently, NATO serves different functions for the two countries in question. Canada does not need NATO in the Arctic to manage Russia, whereas Norway does. Where Norway sees NATO as its formalized defence guarantee, Canada has its own bilateral defence guarantee through NORAD and its close connection with USNORTHCOM.[57]

Lake's conception of *externalities* ties into Väyrynen's *construction* of security regions through interaction, regional organizations, and cooperation. Here again, Norway and Canada are talking about different Arctics. As one senior Norwegian diplomat stated it: "The Arctic Council is founded on a misconception; namely that Canadian and Norwegian interests in the Arctic are concerned with the same thing."[58] This statement also applies to NATO. Although Norway has tried to frame the new challenges in the Arctic since 2007 under the banner of "new" or "soft" security challenges, the real security concern from a Norwegian perspective has always been Russia.[59] That year, Foreign Minister Støre outlined challenges arising from increased activity and presence in the Arctic, partly to avoid securitizing the Arctic by characterizing Russia as a growing concern in Norwegian security and defence policy.[60]

Concurrently, Norway launched its "Core Area Initiative" aimed at getting NATO back to basics by re-emphasizing close-to-home security concerns in areas such as the Arctic, the Baltic, and the Mediterranean.[61] This confused Norway's allies: Norway was arguing for a heightened NATO role in the North because of growing non-traditional security challenges, while also emphasizing traditional concerns related to Russia's resurgence.[62] On the one hand, NATO, as a defensive alliance, is not tailored for "soft" tasks, and there is no consensus that it should assume these in the future; on the other, Canada – under Harper – did not see the need for the defence alliance to get involved in what it deemed domestic affairs.

Both issues led to disinterest on Canada's part, which led to a freezing of any further initiatives in 2009 as well as a halt to the development of NATO policy for the Arctic. The emphasis (or misunderstanding) about NATO's need to perform civilian tasks in the Arctic did not correlate with Canadian interests regarding the alliance. Prime Minister Harper's unwillingness to support NATO involvement indicates a lack of credibility regarding concerns that Russian might aggress against Canada in the Arctic. If anything, Canada needed to invest in its own Arctic capabilities to uphold its domestic interests and sovereignty in anticipation of a more active region.[63] For Norway, the situation was quite different. With a more assertive Russian neighbour, military concerns were precisely why Norway emphasized the Arctic in NATO.

This clear divergence concerning NATO indicates that the two countries had not sufficiently constructed a security region between them. The two countries' reactions to Russian actions in Ukraine in 2014 confirmed this reality. Norway, preferring a balanced approach, called for continued cooperation in Arctic-specific forums, while also increasing military efforts in the North.[64] The Canadian government, however, openly criticized Russian efforts in the Arctic and elsewhere. The Arctic was not kept separate, and it became yet another arena to punish Russia for its actions.[65] This example highlights how these two countries conceive their Arctic(s) in very different terms. For Norway, the Arctic is first and foremost the "High North," which entails a balance between cooperation with, and power projection toward, Russia. For Canada, the Arctic is inherently a domestic domain, where the core issues – from a security perspective – are the lack of situational awareness and the need to uphold sovereignty.

In sum, the NATO example highlights the variation in interests between Norway and Canada. Apart from desiring cooperation in the Arctic, core security concerns and challenges vary too greatly for these two countries to take part in the same "security region." Based on the lack of geographical proximity and of a clear common threat conception, it is a stretch to argue that the Arctic is a security region on its own. There undoubtedly exist regional security concerns in the Arctic that span the various Arctic states, while Russia constitutes the core security variable for all Arctic littoral states. But the role of Russia in security considerations – as exemplified here by the divergence between Norway and Canada – is not constant across the region. To claim that all Arctic states are intrinsically linked in the same security sphere does not hold.

Canada's security region is still grounded in North America and, by extension, the northwest Atlantic and northeast Pacific. The same argument can be extended to include Greenland (Kingdom of Denmark). By contrast, Norway's security concerns resemble those of its Nordic neighbours Sweden and Finland, and even the Baltic States, to a greater extent than those of Canada. When the Arctic is depicted as *one* security region, the notion of geography itself seems to be neglected.[66] Regardless of globalization and the notion of "the end of boundaries,"[67] geography and vast physical space still come into play, at least with regard to traditional security concerns.

Conclusion

I have argued that despite a growing tendency to depict the Arctic as a single security environment, Norwegian and Canadian security domains are only marginally aligned. For Norway, the Arctic includes an extensive border with Russia, with which it has asymmetrical relations. Norway's arguments for a more active northern security role for NATO have thus rested on a combination of military concerns over a resurgent Russia and what then Norwegian Foreign Minister Støre termed "new challenges," such as search and rescue and environmental protection. Neither of these two points resonates with the core security interests of Canada.

NATO's lack of a coherent Arctic policy exemplifies this crucial – but often overlooked – point in contemporary Arctic studies, namely the distinctions among the various security interests in the North. Norway and Canada have diverging views on security in the Arctic, for they see the topic through different lenses. NATO is integral to Arctic security for Norway, but barely at all for Canada. Canada's security concerns in its North are less state-centric than those of its Norwegian counterpart, given the lack of credible state threats in the region. The Norwegian emphasis on unconventional security threats thus resonates, but Canada does not see a role for NATO in handling such challenges. At the same time, Canada's domestic defence is less concerned with NATO, unlike the Norwegian case, and more concerned with its bilateral relationship with the United States under NORAD. In effect, this has divided the Arctic into sub-regions, with the predominant security variable (from a state perspective) being a resurgent Russia, not the melting sea ice.

This distorts any arguments that the Arctic be considered a traditional security region, for it is too vast and inaccessible to fit the most common definitions. This does not discount the concept completely, however, and we can conceptualize contemporary Arctic security debates as constructed beyond the interests of the Arctic states themselves. As Heather Exner-Pirot highlights, non-traditional security concerns are becoming more relevant across the circumpolar region.[68] Nevertheless, as this chapter suggests, the desire to see the Arctic a coherent region in "hard" security terms does not correlate with the diverging interests that exist across different Arctic states.

NOTES

1 For a range of approaches to this issue, see Scott Borgerson, "Arctic Meltdown: The Economic and Security Implications of Global Warming," *Foreign Affairs* 87, no. 2 (2008): 63–77; Oran R. Young, "Whither the Arctic? Conflict or Cooperation in the Circumpolar North," *Polar Record* 45, no. 1 (2009): 73–82; Heather Exner-Pirot, "What Is the Arctic a Case Of? The Arctic as a Regional Environmental Security Complex and the Implications for Policy," *Polar Journal* 3, no. 1 (2013): 37–41; David A. Welch, "The Arctic and Geopolitics," *East Asia–Arctic Relations: Boundary, Security and International Politics* 6 (2013): 1–14; Wilfrid Greaves and P. Whitney Lackenbauer, "Arctic Sovereignty and Security: Updating Our Ideas," *ArcticDeeply.org* (2016), http://www.arcticdeeply.org/op-eds/2016/03/8825/arctic -sovereignty-security-updating-ideas.

2 Rolf Tamnes, "Arctic Security and Norway," in *Arctic Security in an Age of Climate Change*, ed. J. Kraska (New York: Cambridge University Press, 2011), 47–64; Geir Flikke, "Norway and the Arctic: Between Multilateral Governance and Geopolitics," in *Arctic Security in an Age of Climate Change*, ed. J. Kraska (New York: Cambridge University Press, 2011), 64–85.

3 Paal Sigurd Hilde, "Armed Forces and Security Challenges in the Arctic," in *Geopolitics and Security in the Arctic: Regional Dynamics in a Global World*, ed. R. Tamnes and K. Offerdal (London: Routledge, 2014), 159.

4 Gunhild Hoogensen Gjørv and Maria Goloviznina, "Introduction: Can We Broaden Our Understanding of Security in the Arctic?," in *Environmental and Human Security in the Arctic*, ed. G. Hoogensen Gjørv et al. (Abingdon: Routledge, 2014), 2–4.

5   As laid out by Kenneth N. Waltz, *Theory of International Politics* (Boston: McGraw Hill, 1979), 126; and excellently explained in Emily Tripp, "Realism: The Domination of Security Studies," *E-International Relations*, 14 June 2013, http://www.e-ir.info/2013/06/14/realism -the-domination-of-security-studies.

6   Fakhreddin Soltani, "Levels of Analysis in International Relations and Regional Security Complex Theory," *Journal of Public Administration and Governance* 4, no. 4 (2014): 168.

7   Robert E. Kelly, "Security Theory in the 'New Regionalism,'" *International Studies Review* 9, no. 2 (2007): 197–229.

8   Raimo Väyrynen, "Regionalism: Old and New," *International Studies Review* 5, no. 1 (2003): 25–51; David A. Lake, "Security Complexes: A Systems Approach," in *Regional Orders: Building Security in a New World*, ed. D. Lake and P. Morgan (University Park: Pennsylvania State University Press, 1997); Barry Buzan and Ole Wæver, "Regions and Powers – the Structure of International Security," *International Studies* 7, no. 6 (2003b): 564.

9   See, for example, Barry Buzan, "Regional Security," in *People, States, and Fear: An Agenda for International Security Studies in the Post-Cold War Era* (Boulder: Lynne Rienner, 1991), 186–229; Buzan, "From International System to International Society – Structural Realism and Regime Theory Meet the English School," *International Organization* 47, no. 3 (1993): 327–52.

10 Soltani, "Levels of Analysis," 169; Buzan and Wæver, "Regions and Powers," 47–50.

11 Lake, "Security Complexes," 48–9.

12 Väyrynen, "Regionalism," 25–51; Kelly, "Security Theory," 197–229.

13 Ibid., 197–229.

14 Rolf Tamnes and Kristine Offerdal, eds., *Geopolitics and Security in the Arctic: Regional Dynamics in a Global World* (London: Routledge, 2014).

15 Expert Commission, *Unified Effort* (Oslo: Norwegian Ministry of Defence, 2015), 17–20.

16 Katarzyna Zysk, "Military Aspects of Russia's Arctic Policy: Hard Power and Natural Resources," in *Arctic Security in an Age of Climate Change*, ed. J. Kraska (New York: Cambridge University Press, 2011), 85–106.

17 Kristian Åtland, "Security Implications of Climate Change in the Arctic Ocean," in *Environmental Security in the Arctic Ocean*, ed. P.A. Berkman and A.N. Vylegzhanin, 205–16. NATO Science for Peace and Security Series C: Environmental Security (New York: Springer, 2013).

18 Paal Sigurd Hilde, "The 'New' Arctic – the Military Dimension," *Journal of Military and Strategic Studies* 15, no. 2 (2013): 130–53.

19 Hilde, " The'New' Arctic," 159; Michael Byers, *International Law and the Arctic* (New York: Cambridge University Press, 2013), 248.

20 Julian E. Barnes, "U.S. Navy Begins Arctic Exercise Amid Stepped-Up Criticism of Russia," *Wall Street Journal,* 23 March 2016, https://blogs.wsj.com /brussels/2016/03/02/u-s-navy-begins-arctic-exercise-amid-stepped-up -criticism-of-russia.

21 Aurélie Domisse, *Enlargement to the North? Sweden, Finland and NATO.* Facts and Findings no. 202 (Berlin: Konrad Adenauer Stiftung, 2016).

22 Expert Commission, *Unified Effort,* 62–72.

23 Jonas Gahr Støre, "The High North and the Arctic: The Norwegian Perspective," *Arctic Herald,* 2 June 2012, 8–15, https://www.regjeringen.no/no /aktuelt/nord_arktis/id685072; Odd Gunnar Skagestad, "The High North – an Elastic Concept in Norwegian Arctic Policy?" (Lysaker: Fridtjof Nansen Institute, 2010), https://www.fni.no/publications/the-high-north-an-elastic -concept-in-norwegian-arctic-policy-article821-290.html.

24 Tamnes, "Arctic Security and Norway," 47–64.

25 Iver B. Neumann et al., *Norge og alliansene: gamle tradisjoner, nytt spillerom* (Oslo: Norwegian Institute of International Affairs, 2008).

26 Leif C. Jensen and Geir Hønneland, "Framing the High North: Public Discourses in Norway after 2000," *Acta Borealia* 28, no. 1 (2011): 37–54.

27 Astrid Grindheim, *The Scramble for the Arctic? A Discourse Analysis of Norway and the EU's Strategies towards the European Arctic* (Oslo: Fridtjof Nansen Institute, 2009), 6–10.

28 Ibid., 5–17.

29 Geir Hønneland, *Hvordan skal Putin ta Barentshavet tilbake?* (Bergen: Fagbokforlaget, 2013), 31.

30 Rune T. Ege, "Norge sier nei til russisk kystvakt-samarbeid," *VG* (2012), http://www.vg.no/nyheter/innenriks/forsvaret/norge-sier-nei-til-russisk-kystvakt-samarbeid/a/10059093; Svein Kosmo, *Kystvaktsamarbeidet Norge-Russland. En fortsettelse av politikken med andre midler?* Thesis (Oslo: Norwegian Joint Staff College, 2010), 30–2.

31 Torbjørn Pedersen and Tore Henriksen, "Svalbard's Maritime Zones: The End of Legal Uncertainty?" *International Journal of Marine and Coastal Law* 24, no. 1 (2009): 141–61; Norwegian Ministry of Justice, *Meld. St. 32 (2015–2016): Svalbard* (Oslo, 2016), 17–23.

32 Jensen and Hønneland, "Framing the High North," 37–54.

33 Geir Hønneland, "Norsk-russisk miljø- og ressursforvaltning i nordområdene," *Nordlit* (2012), 29, http://septentrio.uit.no/index.php/nordlit /article/view/2303/2134.

34 Tamnes, "Arctic Security and Norway," 47–64; Expert Commission, *Unified Effort,* 15–21.

35 Ibid., 62, 65.

36 Government of Canada, *Canada's Northern Strategy: Our North, Our Heritage, Our Future* (Ottawa, 2009), 7.

37 Government of Quebec, *The Plan Nord: Toward 2035* (Quebec City, 2015), https://plannord.gouv.qc.ca/wp-content/uploads/2015/04/Synthese_PN_EN_IMP.pdf.

38 P. Whitney Lackenbauer, "From Polar Race to Polar Saga: An Integrated Strategy for Canada and the Circumpolar World," in *Canada and the Changing Arctic: Sovereignty, Security, and Stewardship*, ed. F. Griffiths, R. Huebert, and P.W. Lackenbauer (Waterloo: Wilfrid Laurier University Press, 2011), 69–72.

39 Byers, *International Law and the Arctic*, 10–13.

40 P. Whitney Lackenbauer and Rob Huebert, "Premier Partners: Canada, the United States, and Arctic Security," *Canadian Foreign Policy Journal* 20, no. 3 (2014): 320–33.

41 Franklyn Griffiths, "Arctic Security: The Indirect Approach," in *Arctic Security in an Age of Climate Change*, ed. J. Kraska, 10–11 (New York: Cambridge University Press, 2011); Griffiths, "Towards a Canadian Arctic Strategy," in *Canada and the Changing Arctic: Sovereignty, Security, and Stewardship*, ed. F. Griffiths, R. Huebert, and P.W. Lackenbauer (Waterloo: Wilfrid Laurier University Press, 2011), 181–5.

42 Joseph T. Jockel and Joel J. Sokolsky, "Continental Defence: 'Like Farmers Whose Lands Have a Common Concession Line,'" in *Canada's National Security in the Post-9/11 World*, ed. D. McDonough (Toronto: University of Toronto Press, 2012), 114–36. These arrangements are what Jockel and Sokolsky deem "remarkably informal," framed in the broader context of North Atlantic security. Joseph T. Jockel and Joel J. Sokolsky, "Canada and NATO: Keeping Ottawa In, Expenses Down, Criticism Out ... and the Country Secure," *International Journal* 64, no. 2 (2009): 316–18.

43 Lackenbauer, "From Polar Race to Polar Saga," 219.

44 Rob Huebert, "Canadian Arctic Sovereignty and Security in a Transforming Circumpolar World," in *Canada and the Changing Arctic: Sovereignty, Security, and Stewardship*, ed. F. Griffiths, R. Huebert, and P.W. Lackenbauer (Waterloo: Wilfrid Laurier University Press, 2011), 19–20.

45 CBC News, "Canadian Fighter Jets Intercept Russian Bombers in Arctic," 3 February 2014, http://www.cbc.ca/news/canada/canadian-fighter-jets-intercept-russian-bombers-in-arctic-1.2772440; P. Whitney Lackenbauer, "Mirror Images? Canada, Russia, and the Circumpolar World," *International Journal* 65, no. 4 (2010): 879–97; Pamela Wallin and Romeo Dallaire, *Sovereignty and Security in Canada's Arctic* (Ottawa: Senate of Canada, 2011).

46 P. Whitney Lackenbauer, "Harper's Arctic Evolution," *Globe and Mail*, 20 August 2013, http://www.theglobeandmail.com/globe-debate/harpers

-arctic-evolution/article13852195; Wallin and Dallaire, *Sovereignty and Security;* Michael Byers and Stewart Webb, *Titanic Blunder: Arctic Offshore Patrol Ships on Course for Disaster* (Ottawa: Canadian Centre for Policy Alternatives, 2013).

47 François Perreault, "The Arctic Linked to the Emerging Dominant Ideas in Canada's Foreign and Defence Policy," *Northern Review* 33 (Spring 2011): 47–67; Michael Byers, "You Can't Replace Real Icebreakers," *The Globe and Mail,* 27 March 2012, http://www.theglobeandmail.com/globe-debate /you-cant-replace-real-icebreakers/article534351.

48 Lackenbauer, "From Polar Race to Polar Saga," 73.

49 Barry Buzan and Ole Wæver, *Regions and Powers: The Structure of International Security* (Cambridge: Cambridge University Press, 2003), 45–6.

50 Isabelle Mandraud, "Russia Prepares for Ice-Cold War with Show of Military Force in the Arctic." *The Guardian,* 21 October 2014, http://www .theguardian.com/world/2014/oct/21/russia-arctic-military-oil-gas-putin; Julian E. Barnes, "Cold War Echoes under the Arctic Ice," *Wall Street Journal,* 24 March 2014), http://www.wsj.com/articles/SB100014240527023046794 04579461630946609454; Borgerson, "Arctic Meltdown."

51 Hilde, "Armed Forces and Security Challenges in the Arctic," 155–6.

52 Hilde, "The 'New' Arctic," 136.

53 Expert Commission, *Unified Effort,* 14, 20–2.

54 Buzan and Wæver, *Regions and Powers,* 343–51.

55 Lake, "Regional Security Complexes," 50–6.

56 Alexander Moens, "NATO and the EU: Canada's Security Interests in Europe and Beyond," in *Canada's National Security in the Post-9/11 World,* ed. David McDonough, 141–59 (Toronto: University of Toronto Press, 2012).

57 The American commander of USNORTHCOM also commands NORAD.

58 Interview with Norwegian diplomat, 2015.

59 Tamnes, "Arctic Security and Norway," 47–64.

60 Marie Haraldstad, "Embetsverkets rolle i utformingen av norsk sikkerhet-spolitikk: Nærområdeinitiativet." *Internasjonal Politikk* 72, no. 4 (2014): 431–51.

61 Paal Sigurd Hilde and H.F. Widerberg, "NATOs nye strategiske konsept og Norge," *Norsk Militært Tidsskrift* 4 (2010): 10–20.

62 Haraldstad, "Embetsverkets rolle," 442.

63 Huebert, "Canadian Arctic Sovereignty."

64 K. Karlsen,"Venter ikke angrep fra Russland. Men vi ligger der vi ligger (Do not expect attack from Russia. But we are where we are)," *Dagbladet* (2016).

65   Steve Rennie, "Stephen Harper Raises Spectre of Russian Threat in Arctic
     Speech to Troops," *CBC News*, 26 August 2014, https://www.cbc.ca/news
     /politics/stephen-harper-raises-spectre-of-russian-threat-in-arctic-speech
     -to-troops-1.2747703; Andreas Østhagen, "Ukraine Crisis and the Arctic
     : Penalties or Reconciliation?" *The Arctic Institute* (2014), http://www
     .thearcticinstitute.org/2014/04/impact-of-ukraine-crisis-on-Arctic.html.
66   Klaus Dodds and Mark Nuttall, *The Scramble for the Poles: The Geopolitics of the
     Arctic and Antarctic* (Cambridge: Polity Press, 2016).
67   Mathias Albert, "On Boundaries, Territory, and Postmodernity: An Interna-
     tional Relations Perspective," *Geopolitics* 3, no. 1 (1998): 53–68.
68   Exner-Pirot, "What Is the Arctic a Case Of?"

9 Understanding the Recent History of Energy Security in the Arctic

PETRA DOLATA

When the Arctic began to make international headlines after the mid-2000s, energy security was often part of that story. Resorting to geopolitical language, commentators warned of a looming cold front,[1] an impending scramble for the Arctic,[2] and a game of Arctic monopoly,[3] to name but a few of the themes employed. These narratives all assumed a link between conflict and resources. Due to climate change and melting ice, so the argument went, the Arctic would become more accessible both for exploration of oil and gas and for transporting it to markets. Since global forecasts were for dwindling energy resources even while growing economies like India and China demanded ever more oil, states would compete to control these resources. Hence, questions of sovereignty and security in the Arctic were explicitly intertwined with potential resource extraction. These popular commentaries could fall back on common threads in academic discourse. Literature on the resource curse[4] and on resource wars[5] had already established a link between energy and conflict. In addition, some littoral states' Arctic policies were using the very same arguments to justify military build-ups in and financial commitments to the region. As one Norwegian defence official observed in 2008, "access to energy, energy trade, security of supply and security of demand has entered not only global and European security thinking but is also a key feature in our own immediate surroundings."[6]

Accordingly, securing (access to) energy has become a common theme when discussing the trajectory of Arctic politics and recent history. The question remains whether "energy security" is a valuable concept to use when discussing developments in the region. Can we really best understand what is happening there through the lens of energy security? This chapter argues that we have to be careful when employing that concept in our discussions of Arctic events. Since the 1970s, politicians have frequently invoked it to justify certain policies, and the public has accepted it as an important goal of public policy. Thus, much of the debate on energy security is driven by political practice. Consequently, the currency of the term fluctuates alongside trends in oil prices; it is in times of high prices and assumed oil scarcity that debates on energy security are most vocal.

Recognizing this historical link is important for understanding why energy security became such a popular theme in debates on the Arctic in the second half of the 2000s. Generally, this was a time when energy security peaked as an issue. Because heightened interest in the Arctic coincided and in part was necessitated by global discussions of energy security after 2005, energy security became such a prominent trope in talking about the Arctic that it was used to justify Arctic strategies. This energy security narrative, however, was inscribed from the outside due to specific circumstances at the time. Owing to its historical contingency, the concept is not useful for a systematic understanding of energy's role in today's Arctic. It highlights conflict and security threats at the expense of existing cooperation and the influence of non-state actors. It is a very specific discourse focusing on oil and security of supply and is not a suitable analytical tool for facilitating understanding of the complex (energy) challenges in the Arctic, which include local energy insecurities arising from limited access to energy and exposure to exploration activities and oil spills.

What Kind of Energy Security?

To understand the specific circumstances that have catapulted energy security to the forefront of Arctic discussions since 2005, we need to acknowledge the historical origin and genealogy of the concept and situate it in its historical context. Energy security is a fairly recent concept in international politics, which, despite the strategic value of energy for waging wars in the twentieth century, only entered national security discourse in the 1970s. While it addresses the survival of the state and is closely related to economic security more generally, it also goes beyond classic conceptualizations of security in that it includes non-state corporate actors and propagates security for individuals who might be facing energy insecurity or energy poverty. Thus, what is secured can be both the state and the individual.[7]

As an academic concept, energy security remains profoundly undertheorized. Despite increasing scholarly and popular output, there is no robust theory of energy security.[8] Any coherent conceptualization is impeded by the "contested and politicized notion of energy itself,"[9] since actors define energy differently. Some see it as a common or public good, others as a strategic or commercial good. If energy is defined as a common or public good, it links to discussions about human security as it affects individual well-being. According to the "freedom from want" dictum espoused by the United Nations in 1948, energy is crucial for human survival and should thus be considered a basic need that governments and the international community have to secure. Energy supports essential human activities by providing light and heat and facilitating mobility; it also provides jobs and financial prosperity. In this sense, oil and gas developments become strategies for facilitating economic security. At the same time, energy production can adversely affect local populations because of its environmental and social impacts. Here, energy is closely connected to environmental security. Because of its multilayered and all-encompassing meaning, more critical discussions contest the analytical merit of the concept altogether or argue that rather than constituting a specific theoretical approach, energy security may best be conceptualized as a security challenge.[10]

Equally, there exists no accepted methodology for assessing energy security. International organizations such as the International Energy Agency (IEA) measure the threat of energy insecurity using quantitative approaches. Using macro and econometric models, they assess the degree of energy dependence by integrating various levels of robustness, national sovereignty, and resilience. With the use of algorithms, indices are created that look at supply and demand ratios, physical availability, supply market concentration, and oil vulnerability.[11] Some scholars synthesize these multiple indicators to arrive at a more comprehensive understanding of energy security.[12] More interpretive approaches include aspects of "availability, affordability, efficiency, and environmental stewardship,"[13] or they propose the so-called four A's of energy security: "availability, accessibility, affordability and acceptability."[14] One can find variations of these in the policy documents of states and institutions such as the European Union (EU) and the IEA.

Another way to conceptualize energy security is by employing a historical perspective. Conceiving of energy security as a political objective, as has been done in the past, exposes its specific origins and US-centric definition. In the wake of the 1970s energy crises, energy narratives and imaginaries revolving around the themes of scarcity, dependence, and vulnerability have emerged, and they still inform decision-making. The energy security paradigm[15] began as a US concept and was very clearly situated within discussions on national security, which culminated in the 1980 Carter Doctrine, in which President Jimmy Carter proclaimed that US (oil) interests in the Persian Gulf would be defended by military force if necessary. Because of its emergence in the US context, this energy security discourse has been heavily biased toward oil and supply security. With the United States playing a powerful role in global affairs, it developed into a narrative employed in discussions of international politics and as such often meant global (or more precisely Western) energy supply security.

Thus, when energy security became a popular trope in international debates on the Arctic in the first decade of the twenty-first century, it characterized an outside discussion imported to the circumpolar region, which was attracting more and more attention as a potential geopolitical hotspot. This was how the world viewed the Arctic and not necessarily how the Arctic saw itself. It explains why academic journals focusing on the Arctic did not feature many articles on energy security during the first decade of the twenty-first century. Nor did energy publications, which contained an increasing number of contributions on energy security, focus on the Arctic. When energy scholars discussed energy security, they rarely focused on the region and instead examined threats to the energy security of China, the EU, or the United States. As I detail below, even though Russia, as an Arctic state, was named as one of the sources of these threats, no direct Arctic link was made to that country in those academic discussions, which were based largely on Russia's pipeline politics writ large. Thus, energy security only entered the academic discourse on the Arctic as a secondary concept. Because it was inscribed from the outside and driven by a re-emergence of geopolitics in international affairs, the energy security debate did not focus on the needs of Arctic states, nor did it highlight threats to the security of the people who live in the Arctic. Understanding the historical contingency of the popularity of the term "energy security" in the 2000s reveals that term's disconnect with current energy challenges in the region.

The Importance of Historical Contingency

One of the most repeated storylines with respect to energy and the Arctic maintains that "the Arctic is rich in energy resources, and will play an important role in global energy supply in the foreseeable future."[16] This storyline fails to acknowledge several important factors. First, in energy terms there is not really one Arctic – there are many; hence generalized assumptions about the role of energy in the Arctic are not useful in discussing and understanding developments in energy exploration, regulation, and consumption in this region. For example, the geological zones of the Arctic differ immensely in terms of the energy deposits they hold, and so does ease of access to those deposits.[17] This explains why offshore oil and gas production is much more advanced in the Barents Sea region than in the North American Arctic. Second, domestic governance structures, with regard to both environmental issues and Indigenous communities, influence the energy activities of national and international companies. In addition, at the state level, the various economic regimes leave energy activities either to the market or to national governments. Norway and Russia are home to national oil companies, while Canada and the United States are fairly open to corporate energy investors. This is important, because public policy goals can differ from those of market-driven, profit-making economic actors. Energy is where politics and markets intersect, but the *way* they intersect differs from Arctic country to Arctic country. Third, much of this optimistic outlook depends on oil prices. As the current glut shows, low oil prices will always adversely impact capital-intensive oil and gas exploration in the Arctic. By contrast, high energy prices in the mid-2000s propelled the search for new resources in order to ensure global energy security.

Between early 2004 and July 2008, average world oil prices rose from US$30 to US$148.[18] Together with the increasing energy demands from large economies such as the United States, which was only just on the verge of its shale revolution, as well as India and China, this fed worries that global supplies were being depleted. Discussions of peak oil resurfaced, and international and regional institutions such as the G8, NATO, and the EU put energy security on their meeting agendas. Paradoxically, Russia decided to use its 2006 G8 chairmanship to introduce "energy security" as a key theme for this exclusive club of major advanced economies. "Chosen as a major topic that would provide for emphasising Russia's strength," this strategy backfired when Russia was singled out as creating energy insecurity for Western countries in the first place.[19] The US–Russia energy dialogue of the early 2000s had already been "derailed by the Kremlin attack on the oil company Yukos in 2003–2004," and the EU was facing challenging questions with respect to its energy strategy as Russia's pipeline disputes with Ukraine and Belarus in 2006 and 2007 led to supply disruptions in Western Europe.[20]

Germany, which jointly held the G8 and EU chairmanship in 2007, was particularly affected by the supply disruptions, for it relied much more on Russian oil and gas deliveries than any other West European country except Austria. As a result, and in opposition to the long-held trust in markets to deal with energy problems, Berlin adopted a geopolitical response and became "one of the agenda setters on the EU level" by choosing energy security as a central theme both for the G8 summit in Heiligendamm and for its EU presidency.[21] Chancellor Angela Merkel placed reliable energy trade relations with Russia at the core of Germany's agenda. By early 2006, at the Munich Security Conference, the German foreign minister was referring to energy security as one of the "most pressing global security issues [that] affect the future relations between Europe, Russia and the US."[22] Discussions at the Munich Security Conference also informed NATO deliberations on energy security.

The summit declaration from the 2006 NATO meeting at Riga highlighted the alliance's anxieties about the increased dependence of its members on imported energy and their resulting vulnerability to supply disruptions. It tasked "the Council in Permanent Session to consult on the most immediate risks in the field of energy security, in order to define those areas where NATO may add value to safeguard the security interests of the Allies and, upon request, assist national and international efforts."[23] Framing energy dependence as a security issue, even though it did not constitute a clear military challenge, legitimized NATO involvement in matters of energy security. This was an unprecedented shift in alliance discourse.[24] Not even during the energy crises of the 1970s did NATO members accept US attempts to include energy security in the alliance's remit.

In the mid-2000s, the inclusion of energy security was pushed by new NATO members in Central and Eastern Europe, whose heavy dependence on Russian energy supplies made them more sensitive to their energy vulnerabilities and more willing to define them as a matter of national security. These demands, which included an energy solidarity clause, were supported by the United States,[25] which was familiar with the strategic aspects of the energy security argument through its historical experience and the 2001 Report of the National Energy Policy Development Group, which under the chairmanship of Vice President Dick Cheney addressed US dependence on foreign oil supplies, and was now being reminded of those aspects.[26] NATO's International Secretariat, which was focused on determining the changed nature of the global security environment, was equally sympathetic.[27] NATO officials such as Michael Rühle, Head of the Energy Security Section of NATO's Emerging Security Challenges Division, cautioned that any such role could "only be a complementary one – adding value rather than leading the process,"[28] even while the summit declarations at Riga (2006), Bucharest (2008), and Strasbourg-Kehl (2009) underscored the high currency of the issue in the second half of the decade. Because energy security was now being discussed outside the usual institutional frameworks such as the OECD and the IEA, it became more than a routine issue and indeed emerged as a focal point of highly politicized international debates.

By the end of the decade, however, the enthusiasm about NATO assuming a stronger energy security focus had begun to subside. Some NATO member-states continued to oppose the inclusion of energy security on the new strategic agenda, worrying that its embrace by a collective security organization such as NATO could lead to a militarization of the issue.[29] Others cautioned that NATO would antagonize Moscow if it embraced the concept too enthusiastically, since energy insecurity was often directly linked to Russia. Thus, the 2010 NATO Strategic Concept redefined what kind of energy security would be included in NATO's remit, narrowly identifying it as energy infrastructure security.[30] According to Rühle, this was "where NATO can add value."[31]

The EU has gone through a similar development. After decades of indifference, it embraced the concept of energy security in the Lisbon Treaty in December 2007.[32] Earlier publications such as the 2003 European Security Strategy had treated energy security as a minor security threat; the Lisbon Treaty devoted an entire chapter to energy policy. Much as had transpired with NATO, the two EU enlargements of 2004 and 2007 (which brought in the Baltic states and East European countries including Poland) prompted increased attention to energy dependencies, which increased for the EU from 46.7 per cent in 2000 to 52.7 per cent in 2010. In response to the January 2006 supply disruptions, the EU Commission made the case for a supranational approach to addressing energy vulnerabilities. This time, the United Kingdom and Germany did not oppose the inclusion of energy in the treaty. The UK had become a net importer of oil and gas in 2004 and 2005 as the North Sea fields matured, while Germany, as outlined above, was concerned about pipeline closures.[33]

To resolve the previous lack of a legal basis for the EU to intervene in energy policy, the Lisbon Treaty included Article 194 to "ensure" (among other things) "security of energy supply." However, the emergence of a coherent and common approach to promote energy security was immediately limited by a subsequent paragraph stipulating that "such measures shall not affect a Member State's right to determine the conditions for exploiting its energy resources, its choice between different energy sources and the general structure of its energy supply."[34] This "policy window," however, did not stay open long. As Tomas Maltby argued, while the EU Commission continued to prioritize energy security, publishing its Second Strategic Energy Review in 2008 titled "An Energy Security and Solidarity Plan," no binding legislation was introduced that would override individual member-states' external energy security policies.[35] Toward the end of the decade, the EU – like NATO – lost interest in energy insecurity, until the 2014 Ukrainian crisis rekindled a sense of urgency.

When we compare the cases of the G8, EU, and NATO, the years 2006 to 2009 stand out as times when energy security was addressed as a geopolitical priority. These discussions were often closely connected to the issue of climate change. Institutional changes in the United States and Britain reflected this linkage, with President Barack Obama establishing the position of Deputy Assistant to the President for Energy and Climate

Change in 2009 and Britain merging its energy and climate change port-folios in 2008 to form a new Department of Energy and Climate Change. By this time, "a unified conception of climate and energy policy" had developed in the EU.[36] In 2008, EU High Representative Javier Solana reminded Europeans of the "link between global warming and competi-tion for natural resources,"[37] and a year later EU Energy Commissioner Andris Piebalgs explained that "climate change and energy security are two sides of the same coin."[38] Through this linkage of energy security and climate change, the Arctic was included in security deliberations as the region became "the locus of people's projections of the direct effects of climate change"[39] but also the location of "new strategic [resource] interests."[40] Politicians such as David Cameron and Angela Merkel trav-elled to the Arctic and posed for photographs in front of melting gla-ciers, and the media became preoccupied with the region – in particular with its iconic animal inhabitants: polar bears. In 2007, a polar bear cub named Knut, born into captivity in a German zoo, made it onto the cover of the lifestyle magazine *Vanity Fair*.[41]

All of these developments in the second half of the 2000s established the popularity of the energy security narrative, which, when linked to Arctic resources, contributed to stories that likened coming events in the Arctic to the race for resources in Africa in the nineteenth and twentieth centu-ries. The US Geological Survey's first comprehensive report in 2008, which published promising numbers with regard to the Arctic's resource poten-tial, encouraged these views. The report estimated that 13 per cent of the world's undiscovered, technically recoverable oil, 30 per cent of its natural gas, and 20 per cent of its natural gas liquids could be found in the Arctic. The overall estimate of 22 per cent of the world's undiscovered hydrocar-bon resources, however, was an evaluation of *potential* sources based on geological models and not actual exploratory drilling.[42] Nevertheless, this solidified the link between energy security and the Arctic, at least for Eu-ropean actors. In March 2008, the EU High Representative Javier Solana warned that "one of the most significant potential conflicts over resources arises from intensified competition over access to, and control over, energy resources." Elaborating how this affected global and EU security, he dis-cussed several regional case studies, including the Arctic:

> The rapid melting of the polar ice caps, in particular, the Arctic, is opening up new waterways and international trade routes. In addition, the increased accessibility of the enormous hydrocarbon resources in the Arctic region is changing the geo-strategic dynamics of the region with potential con-sequences for international stability and European security interests. The resulting new strategic interests are illustrated by the recent planting of the

Russian flag under the North Pole. There is an increasing need to address the growing debate over territorial claims and access to new trade routes by different countries which challenge Europe's ability to effectively secure its trade and resource interests in the region and may put pressure on its relations with key partners.[43]

Energy Security and the Arctic

The above discussion shows how energy security became integral to geopolitical narratives in the second half of the 2000s, driven by US and non-Arctic European interests that focused on insecurities arising from supply dependence and import vulnerabilities. Since it coincided with the decreasing polar ice cover and reports on potential oil and gas resources in the Arctic, two separate debates linked it to the region: climate change and potential resource conflicts. The latter had been fuelled by the planting of a Russian flag (made of titanium) on the seabed of the North Pole by Duma member Artur Chilingarov in the summer of 2007. Activities by Arctic littoral states such as Canada, Denmark, and Russia to prepare submissions to the International Seabed Authority to extend their two-hundred-mile EEZs to include large parts of the Arctic Ocean seemed to indicate that a race for resources was already in full swing.[44] To repudiate this, the five Arctic coastal states met in Ilulissat in 2008 and declared that they would deal with these issues through existing international frameworks. More importantly, while some of the interest in extending the EEZ may be driven by resource anxieties, these are not based on any conclusive evidence. The aforementioned report by the US Geological Survey revealed that only a very small portion of potential resources lay outside the EEZs. Within their EEZs, Arctic littoral states already have exclusive rights to exploitation. Thus, it was not really energy security that drove those countries' aspirations.

Since four of the five Arctic littoral states – Russia, Norway, the United States, and Canada – were major oil producers in the 2000s, energy security in these countries (with the exception of the United States, which was a net importer until the end of the decade) meant securing energy *demand*, not supply. Because they were net exporters and the global oil market is so interdependent, these three producer-states engaged in international discussions on securing energy supply, but they did so in order to attract new customers and not because energy security was at stake in the Arctic. Since both the United States and the European Union engaged in this narrative, it was no surprise that both Norway (which relied on the EU as its energy export market) and Canada (which relied on the United States as its primary energy market) used the energy security narrative to communicate with their most important trading partners.

This did not mean, however, that they based their own policies on the "energy security paradigm."[45]

As Kristine Offerdal showed in the case of Norway, Arctic states were using energy security as a discourse that could be tapped into in order to "draw political attention." Revealing how Norway sought strategies to maintain US and EU interest in the region after the end of the Cold War, she traced how oil finds in the Norwegian Arctic were instrumentalized to raise "awareness" among EU officials of "the region as important for future EU energy security." Hence, the "Barents Sea was to be presented as a new oil and gas province that could contribute significantly to EU energy security."[46] The 2006 EU Green Paper on energy insisted that "attention should be given to facilitating Norway's efforts to develop resources in the high north of Europe."[47] Canada's case was slightly different. Reflecting the European and transatlantic discussions on energy security, the concluding joint statement of the 2007 Canada–EU summit specifically mentioned "energy and climate security" as one of three critical areas for future cooperation.[48] In addition, Canada portrayed itself not only as an "energy superpower" but also as "a bastion of world energy security."[49] None of this rhetoric was based on Canadian oil and gas production in the Arctic, however; that country's "energy superpower" status derived almost exclusively from production in the Athabascan oil sands.

Canadian and Norwegian motivations to employ the energy security trope for political and trade reasons may explain why their Arctic strategies refer to energy but neither propose nor fully engage with actions that would guarantee energy security. Norway's "Strategy for the High North,"[50] published as one of the first national Arctic strategies in 2006, explicitly introduced energy security as a concept that originated in "international relations," thus conferring a "foreign policy dimension" on energy issues as a result of which "in many countries, energy is becoming more clearly defined as a part of security policy." This does not seem to include Norway, however, which strives to engage in "relations with other countries [to] better reflect the prominent role energy has acquired."[51] Thus, Norway used the concept because it had gained prominence in other countries and in international relations, not because it related to energy insecurities in the Norwegian Arctic. Ottawa's 2010 "Statement on Canada's Arctic Foreign Policy"[52] did not use the term energy security, referring instead to the country's resource wealth in the Arctic to present itself as an "Arctic power." It also declared Canada's interest in supporting "responsible and sustainable development of oil and gas in the North" as an "emerging clean energy superpower." As these two examples show, Arctic states themselves do not frame their Arctic policies as dominated by energy issues. They may engage in energy security discussions in their dealings with NATO allies or trading partners, but this is mainly in response to outside stimuli.

Conclusion

The above discussion has highlighted the importance of understanding the historical contingency of the energy security trope in the Arctic. Timing was influenced by events outside the Arctic and outside energy-producing circumpolar states. Driven by anxieties about supply shortages and energy dependence levels in Europe and to a lesser extent in the United States, this outside perspective established the Arctic as an "energy frontier" and facilitated geopolitical readings of events in the region between 2004 and 2009. At the same time, this discussion was viewed through a specific lens wherein climate change was explicitly linked to energy security. Thus, the emphasis on energy security cannot be fully understood from within the Arctic region and is clearly related to international discussions of global insecurities at a specific time.

This chapter suggests that we need to stop employing the wrong concepts when analysing issues in the Arctic. Energy is important in the Arctic. There are various challenges that create insecurities, such as seismic testing off the coast of Baffin Island and the Davis Strait, community dependence on diesel shipments, oil spills, offshore exploration by multinational oil companies, and a lack of Indigenous participation in energy-related activities. None of these link well to geopolitical understandings of energy security. If they have to be considered as security issues at all, then these have to do much more with the environmental, economic, and human security of those living in the Arctic than with energy security.

NOTES

1 David Fairhall, *Cold Front: Conflict Ahead in Arctic Waters* (London: I.B. Tauris, 2010).

2 Richard Sale and Eugene Potapov, *The Scramble for the Arctic: Ownership, Exploitation and Conflict in the Far North* (London: Francis Lincoln, 2010).

3 Christoph Seidler, *Arktisches Monopoly: Der Kampf um die Rohstoffe der Polarregion* (München: Deutsche Verlags-Anstalt, 2009).

4 Terry Lynn Karl, *The Paradox of Plenty: Oil Booms and Petro-States* (Berkeley: University of California Press, 1997); Michael L. Ross, *Oil Curse: How Petroleum Wealth Shapes the Development of Nations* (Princeton: Princeton University Press, 2012).

5 Michael T. Klare, *Blood and Oil: The Dangers and Consequences of America's Growing Petroleum Dependency* (New York: Metropolitan Books, 2004);

Philippe Le Billon, ed., *The Geopolitics of Resource Wars: Resource Dependence, Governance and Violence* (London: Frank Cass, 2004).

6   Espen Barth Eide, "The Return of Geopolitics and Energy Security," in *High North, High Stakes: Security, Energy, Transport, Environment*, ed. Rose Gotten-moeller and Rolf Tamnes, 42 (Bergen: Fagbokforlaget, 2008).

7   Petra Dolata, "Energy Security," in *The Palgrave Handbook of Security, Risk and Intelligence*, ed. Robert Dover, Huw Dylan and Michael Goodman, 48–52 (Basingstoke: Palgrave Macmillan, 2017).

8   Lynne Chester, "Conceptualising Energy Security and Making Explicit Its Polysemic Nature," *Energy Policy* 38, no. 2 (2010); Benjamin K. Sovacool, ed., *The Routledge Handbook of Energy Security* (London: Routledge, 2010).

9   Ibid., 8.

10   Felix Ciuta, "Conceptual Notes on Energy Security: Total or Banal Security?," *Security Dialogue* 41, no. 2 (2010); Robert W. Orttung and Jeronim Perovic, "Energy Security," in *The Routledge Handbook of Security Studies*, ed. Myriam Dunn Cavelty and Victor Mauer, 211–20 (Abingdon: Routledge, 2010).

11   M.J.J. Scheepers et al., *EU Standards for Energy Security of Supply* (The Hague: ECN/CIEP, 2006), https://publicaties.ecn.nl/PdfFetch.aspx?nr =ECN-C–06-039; Eshita Gupta, "Oil Vulnerability Index of Oil-Importing Countries," *Energy Policy* 36, no. 3 (2008): 1195–211.

12   Aleh Cherp and Jessica Jewell, "The Three Perspectives on Energy Security: Intellectual History, Disciplinary Roots, and the Potential for Integration," *Current Opinion in Environmental Sustainability* 3, no. 4 (2011): 202–12; Jaap C. Jansen and Ad J. Seebregts, "Long-Term Energy Services Security: What Is It and How Can It Be Measured and Valued?," *Energy Policy* 38, no. 4 (2010): 1654–64; Bert Kruyt et al., "Indicators for Energy Security," *Energy Policy* 37, no. 6 (2009): 2166–81.

13   Benjamin Sovacool and Marilyn A. Brown, "Competing Dimensions of Energy Security: An International Perspective," *Annual Review of Environment and Resources* 35, no. 1 (2010): 77.

14   Kruyt et al., "Indicators for Energy Security."

15   Daniel Yergin, "Ensuring Energy Security," *Foreign Affairs* 85, no. 2 (2006): 69–82.

16   Arctic Frontiers, https://www.arcticfrontiers.com/wp-content/uploads /downloads/2015/Science/2015_Book_of_Abstracts.pdf.

17   Kristine Offerdal, "High North Energy: Myths and Realities," in *Security Prospects in the High North: Geostrategic Thaw or Freeze?* ed. Sven G. Holtsmark and Brooke A. Smith-Windsor, 151–78 (Rome: NATO Defense College, 2009).

18   Bassam Fattouh, *Oil Market Dynamics through the Lens of the 2002–2009 Price Cycle* (Oxford: Oxford Institute for Energy Studies, 2010).

19   Pavel K. Baev, "Russia Aspires to the Status of 'Energy Superpower,'" *Strategic Analysis* 31, no. 3 (2007): 448–50, 459.

20 Ibid., 450, 459.
21 Petra Dolata-Kreutzkamp, "Canada–Germany–EU: Energy Security and Climate Change," *International Journal* 63 (2008): 666–70.
22 Qtd in ibid., 668. For a German version of the speech, see http://www .auswaertiges-amt.de/DE/Infoservice/Presse/Reden/2006/060205 -MuenchenKonferenz.html.
23 NATO, "Riga Summit Declaration," 29 November 2007, http://www.nato .int/docu/pr/2006/p06-150e.htm.
24 Thierry Legendre, "The North Atlantic Treaty Organization's Future Role in Energy Security," *Whitehead Journal of Diplomacy and International Relations* 8, no. 2 (2007) 29, 31.
25 Ibid., 31.
26 US National Energy Policy Development Group, "National Energy Policy: Reliable, Affordable, and Environmentally Sound Energy for America's Future" (2001), http://www.wtrg.com/EnergyReport/National-Energy-Policy.pdf.
27 Michael Rühle, "NATO and Energy Security: From Philosophy to Implementation," *Journal of Transatlantic Studies* 10, no. 4 (2012): 388–90.
28 Idem, "NATO and Energy Security," *NATO Review Magazine*, 15 February 2011, http://www.nato.int/docu/review/2011/climate-action/energy _security/EN/index.htm.
29 Robert G. Bell, "NATO's Grapple with Energy Security," in *Energy Security Challenges for the 21st Century: A Reference Handbook*, ed. Gal Lift and Anne Korin, 262–3 (Santa Barbara: ABC-Clio, 2009).
30 NATO, "Active Engagement, Modern Defence: Strategic Concept for the Defence and Security of the Members of the North Atlantic Treaty Organization, Adopted by Heads of State and Government in Lisbon," http:// www.nato.int/nato_static_fl2014/assets/pdf/pdf_publications/20120214 _strategic-concept-2010-eng.pdf, 12, 17. See also Legendre, "The North Atlantic Treaty Organization's Future Role," 32.
31 Rühle, "NATO and Energy Security," 393.
32 Then, toward the end of the decade, it lost interest – until the 2014 Ukrainian crisis rekindled a sense of urgency to address energy insecurities.
33 Tomas Maltby, "European Union Energy Policy Integration: A Case of European Commission Policy Entrepreneurship and Increasing Supranationalism," *Energy Policy* 55 (2013): 438–40.
34 EU, "Consolidated Versions of the Treaty on European Union and the Treaty on the Functioning of the European Union," Doc 2010/C 83/01, 30 March 2010, Title XXI, Article 194, http://eur-lex.europa.eu /legal-content/EN/TXT/PDF/?uri=OJ:C:2010:083:FULL&from=SK.
35 Maltby, "European Union Energy Policy Integration," 440.
36 John Vogler, "Changing Conceptions of Climate and Energy Security in Europe," *Environmental Politics* 22, no. 4 (2013): 636.

37 EU High Representative, "Climate Change and International Security: Paper from the High Representative and the European Commission to the European Council," 14 March 2008, Doc S113/08, http://www.consilium.europa.eu/uedocs/cms_data/docs/pressdata/en/reports/99387.pdf.

38 Andris Piebalgs, "EU Energy and Climate Policy: Speech at the 7th Doha Natural Gas Conference," 11 March 2009, http://europa.eu/rapid/press-release_SPEECH-09-102_de.htm?locale=EN.

39 Dolata-Kreutzkamp, "Canada–Germany–EU," 675.

40 EU High Representative, "Climate Change and International Security."

41 Photographed by renowned artist Annie Leibovitz and paired with actor Leonardo DiCaprio for the US issue (the German version only had Knut on the cover), it brought the Arctic to the fore of public attention. Dolata-Kreutzkamp, "Canada–Germany–EU," 675.

42 USGS, "Circum-Arctic Resource Appraisal: Estimates of Undiscovered Oil and Gas North of the Arctic Circle," Fact Sheet 2008–3049, http://pubs.usgs.gov/fs/2008/3049.

43 EU High Representative, "Climate Change and International Security."

44 Scott G. Borgerson, "Arctic Meltdown: The Economic and Security Implications of Global Warming," *Foreign Affairs* 87, no. 2 (2009): 63–77.

45 Yergin, "Ensuring Energy Security."

46 Kristine Offerdal, "Arctic Energy in EU Policy: Arbitrary Interest in the Norwegian High North," *Arctic* 63, no. 1 (2010): 31, 36.

47 Commission of the European Communities, "Green Paper: A European Strategy for Sustainable, Competitive and Secure Energy," 16 (8 March 2006), http://europa.eu/documents/comm/green_papers/pdf/com2006_105_en.pdf.

48 European Commission, "2007 EU-Canada Summit Statement Berlin, 4 June 2007," https://ec.europa.eu/commission/presscorner/detail/en/PRES_07_131.

49 Government of Canada, "Prime Minister Stephen Harper Calls for International Consensus on Climate Change," Berlin, 4 June 2007, https://www.canada.ca/en/news/archive/2007/06/prime-minister-stephen-harper-calls-international-consensus-climate-change.html.

50 Norwegian Ministry of Foreign Affairs, "The Norwegian Government's High North Strategy" (2006), https://www.regjeringen.no/globalassets/upload/ud/vedlegg/strategien.pdf.

51 Ibid., 14.

52 Government of Canada, "Statement on Canada's Arctic Foreign Policy: Exercising Sovereignty and Promoting Canada's Northern Strategy Abroad," 20 August 2010, http://publications.gc.ca/collections/collection_2017/amc-gac/FR5-111-2010-eng.pdf.

10 Human Insecurities of Marginalized Peoples in the Arctic: The Cost of Arctic and Nordic Exceptionalism

GUNHILD HOOGENSEN GJØRV

The Arctic has long been romanticized as a barren, beautiful, desolate hinterland that was conquered by rugged, courageous, and exceptional explorers.[1] Few encapsulate this image better than Fridtjof Nansen (1861–1930), who was not only a renowned Arctic explorer but also a scientist and Norwegian diplomat, as well as a prominent humanitarian. He is arguably best-known for his attempt to reach the North Pole in the mid-1890s. Thirty years later, however, he was devoting his life to the protection of refugees as the High Commissioner for Refugees for the League of Nations in 1921. In 1922 he would win the Nobel Peace Prize for his work supporting refugees in Russia, Syria, Turkey, and Greece during the First World War. Nansen was thus a proponent of "human security" before the notion of individual security became popularized in the 1990s.[2]

Research in peace and security studies since the 1990s has demonstrated that understanding the mechanisms behind peace and conflict requires a multilevel, multi-actor approach, whereby peace and security are as much about the relations between states and peoples, and between peoples and peoples, as they are about relations between states themselves (see the discussion by Greaves and Lackenbauer in the introduction to this volume).[3] The literature on human security as well as gender and feminist security examines processes of peace and conflict, security and insecurity, from bottom-up perspectives, arguing that peace and security cannot be achieved if individuals and their communities are experiencing insecurity. Definitions of both peace and security are contested; however, the two concepts are intricately linked, and security is integral to achieving peace, whether that peace is negative or positive.[4] Indeed, as discussed below, a fundamental reason for the renewed focus on individual or human security by both scholars and policy-makers during the 1990s was precisely to address situations where the security of states was not being threatened, but multiplicities of human insecurities abounded. We encounter that situation in the Arctic: state security remains largely stable while human insecurities experienced by many Indigenous groups, as well as refugee and migrant populations, continue. The complex relationships between Arctic states and their peoples have been marginalized within, and by, the glow of "exceptional" perspectives, notably "Arctic exceptionalism" and "Nordic exceptionalism." I argue in this chapter that these exceptionalisms, because they continue a state-centric security analysis and identity construction, erase the practical and analytical space that is necessary if we are to include human insecurities within and related to Arctic states and their policies.

States in the Arctic are not perceived as threatening one another, but does this sense of state security transfer to non-state actors – to people? All eight Arctic states are ranked high by the UNDP Human Development Index, ranging from the top of the "very high human development" category (Norway at #1) to the bottom of the same category (Russia at #49).[5] In general UNDP terms, all eight Arctic states are considered "on top of the world." The numbers start to change, however, when accounting for gender inequality: the Nordic states remain in the top 10, but Canada drops its rank almost by double (going from #10 to #18) and the United States plummets to #43 (from an overall HDI ranking of 11), keeping closer company with Russia (which drops to #52 when gender equality is accounted for) than with its northern neighbour or the Nordics. The 2016 Human Development Report *Human Development Is for Everyone* notes that development measures indicate progress in development around the globe, but that certain groups are being left out of this progress – in particular, Indigenous peoples, refugees and migrants, and ethnic minorities are left furthest behind.[6] The same concerns were raised a couple of years earlier in the *Arctic Human Development Report,* which notes that there are significant gaps in knowledge pertaining to the interactions and experiences of "new newcomers" to the Arctic, in addition to the continuous challenges faced by first peoples across the region.[7]

Is there an Arctic exceptional "bubble" that is immune to, or untouched by, inequalities and insecurities? Human security perspectives contest "trickle-down" notions of security from the state to individuals and communities, whereby it is assumed that a secure state means secure people.[8] It is vital to ensure that gaps in security – between different peoples, or between people and their states – are identified, recognized, and examined for ways in which gaps can be reduced. Insecurities continue to be experienced by certain segments of Arctic populations. This includes the marginalization of peoples who have lived in the Arctic for millennia, as well as the treatment of people new to Arctic shores. This means analysing issues of security across levels of analysis, with a focus on security as it relates to the daily lives of people living in Arctic states.

This chapter has two goals. The first is to present what we mean by human security, how the concept developed, and how it can relate to Arctic contexts. The second is to use this understanding of human security, particularly informed by gender and intersectional analytical perspectives, to examine human insecurities in the Arctic, thereby shedding critical light on the claims of exceptionalism in the Arctic and Nordic contexts. This chapter briefly introduces some of the dominant security discourses in the Arctic and then explains the relevance and importance of intersectional human security approaches that might encourage researchers to re-evaluate the meaning of Arctic and Nordic exceptionalism, focusing primarily on the experiences of migrants coming north.

Security Discourses in the Arctic

At its core, security is about power. Arctic security scholarship and policy has been dominated by a largely realist-based understanding of security, rooted in state security and the protection of state borders, economies, and political power through the use of militaries, as encapsulated in classical geopolitics.[9] Through such a lens, perceptions of security in the Arctic find their roots in frameworks of fear and the perceived militarization of this vast region.[10] At the same time, however, the Arctic has been increasingly presented as a region of exception – Arctic or Nordic exceptionalism – embodying unique relations that foster non-violent forms of conflict, if not outright peace.[11] But this argument too relies on a narrow, state-based security perspective rooted in liberal assumptions, claiming a dominance of cooperation and peaceful behaviour replacing the war-like behaviour rooted in realist claims. This perspective is nevertheless restricted to states. It disguises and/or minimizes different levels of security, where the focus on cooperation *between* states might indicate exceptional stability, but examining perceptions of security *within* these Arctic states among people or groups of people might reveal profound and complex insecurities. The Nordic countries also adopt exceptionalism, in this case revolving around "the notion of the Nordic countries as global 'good citizens,' peace-loving, conflict-resolution-oriented, and rational."[12] With the combination of Nordic and Arctic exceptionalism, Arctic peace and security is portrayed as a relatively successful peace project. An examination of current human security issues, including continual challenges for Indigenous peoples in different parts of the Arctic, and more recently those of refugees and the "migration crisis" in northern European states, indicates that the security project can and should be questioned. While security among states may be characterized by lack of violent conflict, current immigration policies in today's Nordic countries are creating various harms among vulnerable populations fleeing conflict – harms that are racialized and gendered. Fridjof Nansen must be rolling in his grave.

Whose Exceptionalism?

The concept of "exceptionalism" has played, and continues to play, a significant role in perceptions of peace and security in the Arctic. This section briefly outlines two types of exceptionalism: Arctic exceptionalism and Nordic exceptionalism. Part of "Arctic exceptionalism" claims relates to the extent of cooperation among Arctic states.[13] Relationships between states, and perceptions of threat versus interest in cooperation, are a distinctive feature of this phenomenon. It is not, however, inclusive only of states. As Michael Byers has noted, the processes of Arctic cooperation involve both state and non-state actors, particularly in the arena of economic interests, but also with regard to marine science and law, as well as the representation of Indigenous peoples.[14] Shipping, oil and gas, mining, fisheries, aviation – all involve industries, states, NGOs, scientists, and, to a degree, local or Indigenous communities. Recent scholarship on Arctic exceptionalism has acknowledged that conflict that happens outside of Arctic "perimeters" (such as in Afghanistan, Iraq, Syria, Libya, and particularly Crimea and Ukraine) presents a challenge to the special Arctic relationship but has not significantly disrupted efforts by states and Arctic regimes to maintain peace among Arctic states. Little discussion ensues regarding the fact that all eight Arctic states have, in various ways, participated in these same non-Arctic conflicts. Peace-loving Arctic states are less peace-loving outside of the Arctic. Russia's advances into Crimea present something of an anomaly as a focal point of tensions between Arctic states, highlighting the potential for Russia to aggress closer to the Arctic home. Russia's activities in Europe, however, have not been perceived as corroding the strength of cooperative arrangements and agreements that exist, or the incentives that states have to maintain this cooperation.

Arctic states are not just "Arctic" states; they also act within a broader, global system. The actions taken by Arctic states outside of the Arctic impact Arctic peace and security and generate cracks in both exceptionalisms. From a human security perspective, the migration of people from the war-torn countries, where all Arctic states have participated in military efforts, challenges notions of peace and security when seen from individual/community perspectives. Nordic exceptionalism picks up where Arctic exceptionalism leaves off, where a relationship between Nordic states and the "other" is created though benevolent Nordic values of humanitarianism and caring for those who are vulnerable. In many ways, Nordic exceptionalism reflects the norms embodied in the "heroic" figure of Nansen. Kristín Loftsdóttir and Lars Jensen have addressed the dynamics of Nordic exceptionalism, a concept that focuses on cooperation between Nordic (Arctic) states and extends into the actual self-image or "nation branding" of Nordic states as conflict-solving, peace-loving, anti-racist, and anti-colonial "without questioning their own involvement in colonial and racist activities."[15] The "goodness" of Nordic exceptionalism is interwoven with notions of whiteness, thus embedding nation-branding with processes of othering through different markers of superiority and inferiority (Nordic and European vs non-Nordic and non-European). Peace and security can be defined as such within these exceptional contexts as long as one does not examine the racialized and gendered foundations on which these exceptional assumptions have been built. Critical approaches in human security, informed by intersectional analyses, can provide a more complex and dynamic picture of how peace and security is understood and maintained.

Thus, we require greater awareness of competing visions of security in the Arctic. The Arctic exceptionalism argument is complicated. On the one hand, it rejects a traditionalist realist perspective where competition and conflict are the focus, relying instead on a liberal focus on cooperation, highlighting a multiplicity of regimes and international bodies that regulate and guide relations between states in the Arctic, where potential conflict is non-violent and well managed.[16] At the same time, however, Arctic exceptionalism also relies on a rejection of broader security perspectives insofar as it insists on focusing on the relations among states, rather than on the multilevel relations among states, societies, communities, and individuals. This approach to security, under which peace implies merely the absence of war, is exclusive and exclusionary and severely minimalizes who decides what security is and how it will be established and maintained. The broader and wider view of security is necessarily more complex and, as such, more difficult to understand and manage. In the latter case, security is not reduced to potential military confrontations and the protection of state borders to protect a universally and monolithically defined, abstract concept (the state). Instead it recognizes the threats of environmental degradation, pollution, and climate change, not only against state structures but also against people. It recognizes the fragility and vulnerability of communities and identities, revealing insecurities experienced on the ground in different Arctic contexts. In this context, this chapter discusses two issues: the role of power in determining how security is defined in the Arctic, including through exceptionalism, and the ways in which an intersectional approach, stemming from gender and feminist research, contributes to increasing our understanding of how security is operationalized at multiple levels. This analysis thus draws on recent examples of research that argue for intersectionality or for feminist approaches in Arctic research. The Arctic, insofar as eight states and all the communities within them can be united as one region, demonstrates that a broader and wider security perspective is imperative.

A narrow approach to security – what is often referred to as "classical," "traditional," or more specifically "national" security – reflects one avenue along which the concept of security has developed.[17] The history of the term "security" is extensive. Cicero, for example, in the first century BCE, referred to "securitas," meaning freedom from worry, fear, anger, and anxiety, which largely focused on individual or community experiences of security.[18] Western political philosophers such as Thomas Hobbes, Jeremy Bentham, and Adam Smith reflected this focus on the individual, problematizing the interactions between evolving states and the individuals who took part in creating and maintaining security.[19] However, the concept became increasingly associated with the state after the Napoleonic Wars, at the cost of individuals.[20] All the while, positivist science played an influential role in how security should be understood. The concept in this way became neutral, measurable, value-free, and "scientific," based on observable "facts."[21]

War being arguably the greatest observable threat to the state, it became the central phenomenon shaping narrowly defined conceptualizations of security. Thus, it was assumed that states were monolithic and generalizable and that they exhibited similar and comparable characteristics, particularly when confronted with external/foreign threats. Narrow definitions of security have not been particularly coherent and consistent, however, and are more dependent on the actors at hand than on a significantly scientific approach to security. Those arguing for a more complex understanding of security (referred to as "wideners") face resistance both from those wishing to preserve the elite stronghold of neorealist security studies, where the narrow definition finds its strongest support,[22] and from those who insist that the term security is inappropriate for broader issues due to its associations with violence and militarization.[23] Those who want to make other issues relevant to security – from violence against women, to homelessness and poverty, to climate change – find themselves competing against the objective weight and authority of war. In this view, in other words, while the non-military aspects of security such as "poverty, AIDS, environmental hazards, drug abuse, and the like" are important, they should not be addressed as aspects of "security" *per se*.[24] Their inclusion, it is argued, not only makes the concept of security unmanageable and meaningless but also detracts from what is meant to be the focus of security, which is "the phenomenon of war."[25]

Human Security

The term "human security" was popularized in the 1994 UN *Human Development Report*, which expanded the notion of security to include food, health, community, environmental, economic, personal, and political security, partly with the intention to address some of the glaring weaknesses of traditional security theory and practice. Human security focuses on the individual. In the UNDP report, human security has two core components, "freedom from fear [and] freedom from want," and as well as four essential characteristics: universal, interdependent, easier to ensure through early prevention, and people-centred.[26]

The current literature on human security, however, is ambivalent about definitions. Human security does not mean the same thing to all people, for values, beliefs, and world views are important and contexts and settings are complex and diverse. Generally speaking, the notion of "security" carries implicit and or explicit assumptions about what security does and/or should mean, and these are highly culturally defined, gendered, and contextual. Put simply, contemporary *securitas* is a politically loaded term.[27] Accordingly, it needs to be recognized that the notion of human security carries with it the weight of many of the assumptions long held about security within the field of security studies.

The 1994 UNDP report was intended to generate "another profound transition in thinking – from nuclear security to human security,"[28] contrasting with the narrow definition that dominated IR during the Cold War. Indeed, the notion of human security has contributed to the "deepening" (from the state down to the individual) and "widening" (from state and military security to economic, environmental, etc.) of the concept of security relative to the Cold War focus on the military defence of the state.[29] The UNDP report argued that the daily security of people around the world usually revolved around fears of unemployment, disease, localized discrimination and violence, and crime. Human insecurity is equally severe under conditions of food insecurity, job or income insecurity, human rights violations and inequality (political insecurity), and gross environmental degradation.

Thus, at its core, human security is concerned about how people *themselves* experience security and insecurity. The definition of human security as "freedom from fear and freedom from want,"[30] incorporates terms that President Franklin Delano Roosevelt had used in his 1941 State of the Union Address[31] and that the UNDP report reinvigorated as the "two major components of human security."[32] This characterization has been criticized for being too vague and all-encompassing – for making *everything* in life a potential human security issue – and for amounting to a "shopping list" of multiple and otherwise disconnected issues.[33] The 1994 UNDP report further defined seven main categories of threats against human security: political, personal, food, health, environment, economic, and community. Newman argues that it is imperative that diverse critical human security perspectives develop simultaneously, informing and pushing institutional approaches toward changing harmful state and global structures that contribute to human insecurity.[34]

Critical human security perspectives are drawing increasingly upon intersectional approaches. Different processes of inquiry result in different constructions and productions of knowledge. Feminists have long critiqued dominant, gendered and masculinist biases in scholarship, not least exemplified by the emphasis on rationality, objectivity, and public domains, often embodied by research in the natural sciences (which dominate in the Arctic) and visibly expressed in unreflexive, silent authorship reinforcing "an unreflective orientation toward objectivist traditions and norms."[35] A core feature of feminist and intersectional methodological approaches therefore includes the practice of "reflexivity," whereby the researcher is "'responsible' and 'responsive' to her work and her 'subjects' of study because it makes explicit the deliberative movement of her scholarship."[36] Reflexivity allows for insight into phenomena while also illuminating how such insights were derived. Arctic research is strengthened when it is provided with complex insights into the broader social and political contexts in which all Arctic research takes place, particularly when the focus is on how dominant perceptions of security in the Arctic rely on marginalizing or ignoring gendered, racialized, ageist, class-based inequalities and insecurities. Is the Arctic secure when some segments of Arctic societies remain insecure?

Human security policies – including those of northern states like Canada and Norway – have been criticized for perpetuating ahistorical claims that assume that "strong states provide better security."[37] The assumption has been that the global North is composed of "strong" states that have succeeded in addressing their own human security issues and that could assist the supposedly insecure global South; but this logic assumes that "securing" the global South will in turn support state security in the North.[38] The co-optation of human security for state security purposes is a type of "virtuous imperialism," whereby the states of the global North engage in humanitarian interventions or other human security measures to ensure that unrest in the global South does not seep north through migration or terrorism.[39]

Contrary to what was first envisioned in the UNDP and CHS reports, the state security orientation and implementation of human security has increasingly rendered non-state actors passive; it also renders invisible any human insecurities and vulnerabilities that states have not identified or that exist below the level of the state. It assumes that community and individual voices are being represented, and attended to, by a state actor, and it prevents peoples across communities and regions (indeed, across states) from sharing human security concerns and experiences. The result is an imbalance in perceptions and explanations regarding what happens within and across regions and around the globe, a tendency that also masks the contributions and competencies of various actors in providing security at different levels.[40]

Feminist and Intersectional Approaches to Security

One important ally when addressing these blind spots in human security research is feminist and gender security studies, a field that has developed in tandem with human security perspectives.[41] Indeed, feminist and gender security studies assume that individuals and their communities are, and have always been, security actors, functioning alongside "traditional" tools of security such as states and their militaries or, more often, functioning in their absence. Narrow or state-based "security narratives," these approaches claim, "limit how we can think about security, whose security matters, and how it might be achieved."[42] In contrast, feminist scholarship has been groundbreaking for security perspectives that adopt a people-centred approach, and these have been developing in parallel with human security theorizing. Gender and feminist analyses work from the bottom up, much like critical human security approaches. However, these analyses exhibit an increased awareness of the impacts of gender on personal relations and how these shape understandings of security. Gender and feminist analyses question the terms used, including the notion of "human" itself – that is, who is included in this category (or not) and why.[43] In acknowledging that the personal is political, these analyses reach down to the individual's experience, claiming that personal experience is relevant to the security of the individual and the community as well as to the security of the state and the global order. In this way, the security needs of those who are least secure or marginalized are identified, which serves to reorient security away from elite or state interests.[44] Significant empirical research has been conducted, particularly in the area of gender and feminist security studies, regarding the efforts of "average" or everyday people to identify their own insecurity and express their vulnerabilities and sources of fear. This research has also focused on capabilities and on enabling people, societies, and groups to ensure their security by a variety of means.[45]

In other words, regardless of how traditional approaches to security position the state as the exclusive security actor, in practice states have never been the only "security" actors, particularly where human security is concerned.[46] Government officials, politicians, and military leaders are not always the leading actors in providing security or identifying threats, nor do they need to intervene at all levels of human insecurity. They can, however, act as important conduits for knowledge between communities and actors, and they can respond to human insecurities when communities can no longer effectively respond to threats.[47]

A critical move contributing to this shift in feminist and gender security scholarship was the incorporation of the concept and practice of "intersectionality," which recognizes that universalizing, homogenous methods and practices were often both inaccurate as well as harmful to research as well as to the societies that were central to such research. Indeed, intersectionality holds that earlier definitions of gender equality, as well as understandings of gender constructions, were grossly inadequate because of their tendency to universalize, even though they had moved beyond realism to incorporate a liberal perspective on peace and human security. Intersectional analysis posits that the three waves of feminism were largely dominated by the experiences by white, middle-class, European/Western women, and that these experiences did not speak to the gendered norms, practices, or experiences of people of colour, Indigenous people, non-white-centric ethnicities and cultures, or to those whose experiences were different as a result of age, class, sexuality, and ability.[48] Coined by Kimberlé Crenshaw in the late 1980s,[49] the term intersectionality was intended to critically assess the intersection between race and gender. At its core it offers a "non-positivistic, non-essentialist understanding of differences among people as produced in on-going, context-specific social processes."[50]

Human Insecurity in the Arctic – from Indigenous to Afghan Insecurities

Mens Vestens intervensjoner har gjort oss tryggere, har den gjort befolkningen i disse landene betydelig mer utrygg. Vi slipper kanskje fiendtlige regimer i sør, men må nå forholde oss til den avledede effekten at innbyggere som skulle befris lokalt, etter hvert ser få andre utveier til trygghet, frihet og en fremtid enn å søke tilflukt hos oss i Europa.

While the West's interventions have made us safer, they have made the populations in these countries considerably less safe. We perhaps avoid hostile regimes in the [global] south, but must now address the resulting effect that the people that would have been liberated locally [where they live], eventually do not see many other options to obtain security, freedom and a future than to seek asylum with us in Europe.[51]

This brings us to a discussion of the status of Arctic security studies in the context of these analytical critiques, and insights within security studies in general. Gunn-Britt Retter has often noted that Arctic discourses reflect a masculine Arctic agenda,[52] while Kristín Loftsdóttir and Lars Jensen make the all too neglected but important point that Arctic discourses also include racist/white supremacist dimensions.[53] All of these dimensions have clear relevance to understanding human insecurities evolving within migration patterns into Arctic states. However, even though integrating "gender awareness" or gender perspectives into the context of Arctic communities and research has been increasingly in focus since the early 2000s,[54] gender and intersectional perspectives are still poorly understood as both a category and a research method, and thus they remain largely marginalized in Arctic research.[55] Even less has Arctic research significantly examined the racialized dimension of Arctic politics.

A critical human security perspective in the Arctic demands that a security analysis include bottom-up, lived experiences of insecurity that have been missed or ignored by state-centred perspectives, on which Arctic and Nordic exceptionalisms have so far been based. When human security perspectives *are* included, they are often subsumed within insecurities about climate change and its impacts on Arctic communities. The role of the Arctic Council is instrumental here, in that its emphasis on environmental issues allows for the inclusion of Indigenous knowledge and perspectives.[56] The inclusion of these does not threaten the socio-economic and political systems on which Arctic states are based; indeed, they are applied in order to *support* those systems. But this ignores the connections between global climate change and the current insecurities of people in the Arctic, as well as between the Arctic and conflicts in non-Arctic parts of the world, from where newcomers to the Arctic are arriving. Pankaj Mishra notes that:

[t]oday, global warming manifests itself in not just a rise in ocean levels, the increasing frequency of extreme weather events, the emptying of rivers and seas of their fish stocks, or the desertification of entire regions on the planet. It can also be seen at work in the violent conflicts in Egypt, Libya, Mali, Syria, and many other places exposed to food price rises, drought and declining water sources. The large-scale flight of refugees and migrants

from damaged areas, which has already caused wars in Asia and Africa, is now creating political turmoil in the heart of Europe.[57]

This latter changing climate is not what dominates Arctic-focused discourses. In the Arctic, clear distinctions are made above and below the artificial dividing line referred to as the Arctic Circle. However, linkages in terms of how marginalized peoples are treated cross this imaginary line, particularly when Arctic states engage in conflicts beyond the Arctic. Afghanistan provides just one example of how the drive to preserve the "exceptional" condition of Arctic security comes into conflict with the demands of human insecurities.

Indigenous peoples continue to fight for recognition as legitimate voices in state-centric systems – to fight for livelihoods that are integral to their identities and survival. Their human security has been and continues to be at stake. The experience of Indigenous peoples can also be shared with new Arctic residents, who are targeted on the basis of perceptions about their own ways of life, and who need to assimilate or leave. These decisions are often made on the basis of racialized and gender identities (e.g. "brown men are threats," "brown women need to be saved"). In a sense, this racialized and gendered narrative has not changed; rather, it has changed targets. Settler or dominant populations sought to eradicate Indigenous populations through war, ethnic cleansing, residential schools, and the destruction of language and livelihoods.[58] These violences committed against the perceived threat posed by Indigenous peoples have not been fully rectified and continue to be a significant issue for reconciliation and self-governance.[59] At the same time, colonial practices continue, both toward Indigenous peoples and toward new groups that have been "othered." How, then, do are Arctic states to maintain an overall image of security, of "exceptionalism," in light of the struggles of long-standing human insecurities as well as those of newcomers?

Illuminating the struggles for human security is crucial to engaging in a critical examination of what security is and who decides. Exceptionalism demands compliance and, quite possibly, the repression/oppression of difference. Marjo Lindroth and Heidi Sinevaara-Niskanen argue that the struggles of Indigenous peoples have been co-opted by institutions that claim to give them voice and have embedded indigeneity in an ongoing neoliberal system. Indigeneity is no longer a threat to the state system and therefore does not need to be suppressed through direct assimilation/integration practices. Instead, indigeneity has been defined in such a way that the qualities of Indigenous peoples are not only non-threatening, but a positive benefit to the state system: "Indigenous peoples are assumed to embody resilience, adaptability and care for the environment and community. It is these very features that are politically celebrated and cared for as the allegedly innate qualities of indigeneity."[60] The same is being demanded of new people, who from the moment they arrive on Arctic shores are suspect until they sufficiently integrate, if they are allowed into northern states in the first place.

In Fridtjof Nansen's Norway, Afghan refugees have been trying to obtain asylum, fleeing a conflict that Norway and other Arctic states have actively participated in under the banner of international security, and to a small degree for Afghan security, but even more to please their NATO allies and the United States.[61] Norwegian armed forces were deployed in Afghanistan from 2001 to 2014 through Operation Enduring Freedom (OEF) and, subsequently, the International Security Assistance Force (ISAF) (with up to 500 troops per contingent), with a more modest contribution to the Resolute Support mission launched in 2015. The military and aid deployments necessitated cooperation with Afghan civilians, who served as translators, information sources, and military base workers (from cooks to carpenters and bus drivers) as well as at access/entry points. Many of the Afghan people who worked with NATO troops, including Norwegians, sought asylum when the ISAF mission was completed in 2014, fearing that stability and security would only worsen with the reduction in international forces. Their fears were warranted, for Taliban attacks have increased, and Daesh (i.e., the Islamic State [IS]) has increased its efforts to gain a foothold in the region.[62] Civilians and their families who worked for the Norwegian and other ISAF troops are potential targets for Taliban or other insurgents fighting the international forces.

Yet Norway has had one of the highest rejection rates for asylum seekers from Afghanistan among the European states, having refused 99 per cent of male Afghan applications by 2016 (the EU average of rejection of male Afghan applications was 47 per cent). Among women the rejection rate has been 86 per cent.[63] The rejection of minors (aged fourteen to seventeen) has also been on the rise. Norway was highlighted in a recent Amnesty International report on the trend in returnee policies; it has one of the highest rates of returning people, including Afghans, back to war-torn countries, based on an assumption that it is safe enough for civilians to go back.[64] As Cecilie Hellestveit notes in the quote that opened this section, Western (including Arctic) security has been bought on the backs of the civilians who live in the countries in which Arctic states have militarily and politically intervened.

Norway's treatment of Afghan refugees is but one example of the approaches to migration being taken by Arctic states. All eight Arctic states have engaged in conflicts beyond the Arctic, and this has contributed to the rise of people fleeing and migrating from these same war zones. Unlike Fridtjof Nansen, who sought ways to support those fleeing from war, the Norwegian government (among other Arctic states) has engaged in practices that continue gendered and racialized policies against the non-settler, non-dominant ethnic "other." As long as that other is framed as a threat, as are certain refugees and migrants today, the acceptance of racist discourses will remain high. Taking the Nordic countries again as an example, the continued rise of far-right, white supremacist groups and actors, including the "Nordic Resistance Movement," and previously "Sons of Odin," and not least the ways in which the terrorist action by Anders B. Brevik has been framed, demonstrate that human insecurities remain muted for the cause of national and Arctic "exceptional" security.

NOTES

1 Gail Osherenko and Oran R. Young, *The Age of the Arctic: Hot Conflicts and Cold Realities* (Cambridge: Cambridge University Press, 1989).

2 He designed identity papers for undocumented individuals fleeing conflict and fear, which were later referred to as "Nansen" passports. Gunhild Hoogensen Gjørv, "Human Security," in *Security Studies: An Introduction*, 3rd ed., ed. Paul D. Williams and Matt McDonald (New York and London: Routledge, 2018).

3 Annick Wibben, *Feminist Security Studies: A Narrative Approach* (London and New York: Routledge, 2011); Swati Parashar, *Women and Militant Wars: The Politics of Injury* (London and New York: Routledge, 2014); Gunhild Hoogensen Gjørv, Dawn R. Bazely, Maria Goloviznina, and Andrew J. Tanentzap, eds. *Environmental and Human Security in the Arctic* (New York: Routledge, 2014).

4 Johan Galtung, "Violence, Peace, and Peace Research," *Journal of Peace Research* 6, no. 3 (1967): 167–91.

5 See UNDP Human Development Index, http://hdr.undp.org/en/content/human-development-index-hdi.

6 UNDP, *Human Development Report 2016 – Human Development Is for Everyone* (New York, 2016).

7 Joan Nymand Larsen and Gail Fondahl, eds., *Arctic Human Development Report: Regional Processes and Global Linkages* (Akureyri: Steffanson Arctic Institute, 2014).

8 Gunhild Hoogensen and Svein Vigeland Rottem, "Gender Identity and the Subject of Security," *Security Dialogue* 25, no. 2 (2004): 155–71.

9 Rolf Tamnes and Kristine Offerdal, eds., *Geopolitics and Security in the Arctic: Regional Dynamics in a Global World* (New York and London: Routledge,

2014); Kristian Åtland, "Interstate Relations in the Arctic: An Emerging Security Dilemma?" *Comparative Strategy* 33, no. 2 (2014): 145–66.

10   Rob Huebert, "Cooperation or Conflict in the New Arctic – Too Simple of a Dichotomy," in *Environmental Security in the Arctic Ocean*, ed. Paul Arthur Berkman and Alexander N. Vylegzhanin, 195–204. NATO Science for Peace and Security Series C: Environmental Security (New York: Springer, 2013).

11   Lassi Heininen, ed., *Future Security of the Global Arctic: State Policy, Economic Security, and Climate* (London: Palgrave, 2016); Michael Byers, "Crises and International Cooperation: An Arctic Case Study," *International Relations* 31, no. 4 (2017): 375–402; Heather Exner-Pirot and Robert W. Murray, "Regional Order in the Arctic: Negotiated Exceptionalism," *Politik* 20, no. 3 (2017): 47–64.

12   Kristín Loftsdottir and Lars Jensen, eds., *Whiteness and Postcolonialism in the Nordic Region: Exceptionalism, Migrant Others, and National Identities* (London: Routledge, 2016), 2.

13   Heininen, *Future Security of the Global Arctic*; Byers, "Crises and International Cooperation"; Exner-Pirot and Murray, "Regional Order in the Arctic."

14   Byers, "Crises and International Cooperation."

15   Loftsdottir and Lars Jensen, *Whiteness and Postcolonialism*, 2.

16   Exner-Pirot and Murray, "Regional Order in the Arctic."

17   Peter Hough, *Understanding Global Security*, 2nd ed. (Abingdon: Routledge, 2008).

18   P.H. Liotta and Taylor Owen, "Why Human Security?," *Whitehead Journal of Diplomacy and International Relations* 7, no. 1 (2006): 1–18; John T. Hamilton, *Security: Politics, Humanity, and the Philology of Care* (Princeton: Princeton University Press, 2013).

19   Emma Rothschild, "What Is Security?," *Daedalus* 124, no. 3 (1995): 53–98; Gunhild Hoogensen, *International Relations, Security, and Jeremy Bentham* (London: Routledge, 2005).

20   Rothschild, "What Is Security?"

21   Stephen M. Walt, "The Renaissance of Security Studies," *International Studies Quarterly* 35, no. 2 (1991): 211–39; Keith Krause and Michael Williams, eds., *Critical Security Studies* (London: UCL Press, 1997).

22   Ibid.; Karin M. Fierke, *Critical Approaches to International Security* (Cambridge: Cambridge University Press, 2007).

23   Barry Buzan, Ole Wæver, and Jaap de Wilde, *Security: A New Framework for Analysis* (Boulder: Lynne Rienner, 1998); Claudia Aradau, "Security and the Democratic Scene: Desecuritization and Emancipation," *Journal of International Relations and Development* 7, no. 4 (2004): 388–413.

24   Walt, "The Renaissance of Security Studies," 213.

25   Ibid., 212.

26   UNDP, *Human Development Report 1994: New Dimensions of Human Security* (New York: United Nations Development Program, 1994).

27 Fierke, *Critical Approaches to International Security.*

28 UNDP, *Human Development Report 1994*, 22.

29 Barry Buzan and Lene Hansen, *The Evolution of International Security Studies* (Cambridge: Cambridge University Press, 2009).

30 Donna Winslow and Thomas Hylland Eriksen, "A Broad Concept that Encourages Interdisciplinary Thinking," *Security Dialogue* 35, no. 3 (2004): 361–2; Francesca Vietti and Todd Scribner, "Human Insecurity: Understanding International Migration from a Human Security Perspective," *Journal on Migration and Human Security* 1, no. 1 (2013): 17–31.

31 Franklin D. Roosevelt, "Annual Message to Congress on the State of the Union" (1941), http://www.presidency.ucsb.edu/ws/?pid=16092.

32 UNDP, *Human Development Report 1994*, 24.

33 Keith Krause, "The Key to a Powerful Agenda, If Properly Delimited," *Security Dialogue* 35, no. 3 (2004): 367–8.

34 Edward Newman, "Human Security: Reconciling Critical Aspirations with Political 'Realities,'" *British Journal of Criminology* 56, no. 6 (2016): 1165–83.

35 Gary Gray, "Academic Voice in Scholarly Writing," *Qualitative Report* 22, no. 1 (2017): 180.

36 Brooke A. Ackerly, Maria Stern, and Jacqui True, *Feminist Methodologies for International Relations* (Cambridge: Cambridge University Press, 2006), 258.

37 Wibben, *Feminist Security Studies*, 70. See also Gunhild Hoogensen Gjørv, "Virtuous Imperialism or a Shared Global Objective? The Relevance of Human Security in the Global North," in *Environmental and Human Security in the Arctic*, eds. Gunhild Hoogensen Gjørv, Dawn R. Bazely, Maria Goloviznina, and Andrew J. Tanentzap, 58–79 (New York: Routledge, 2014); and Shahrbanou Tadjbakhsh and Anuradha Chenoy, *Human Security: Concepts and Implications* (New York: Routledge, 2007).

38 Rob McRae and Don Hubert, *Human Security and the New Diplomacy: Protecting People, Promoting Peace* (Montreal and Kingston: McGill–Queen's University Press, 2001).

39 Hoogensen Gjørv, "Virtuous Imperialism."

40 ICISS, *The Responsibility to Protect: Report of the International Commission on Intervention and State Sovereignty* (ICISS, 2001); Alex J. Bellamy, "Realizing the Responsibility to Protect," *International Studies Perspectives* 10, no. 2 (2009): 111–28; Francis Kofi Abiew, "Humanitarian Action under Fire: Reflections on the Role of NGOs in Conflict and Post-Conflict Situations," *International Peacekeeping* 19, no. 2 (2012): 203–16.

41 Eric M. Blanchard, "Gender, International Relations, and the Development of Feminist Security Theory," *Signs* 28, no. 4 (2003): 1289–312; Gunhild Hoogensen and Kirsti Stuvøy, "Gender, Resistance, and Human Security," *Security Dialogue* 37, no. (2006): 207–28.

42 Wibben, *Feminist Security Studies*, 65.

43   Heidi Hudson, "'Doing' Security as Though Humans Matter: A Feminist Perspective on Gender and the Politics of Human Security," *Security Dialogue* 36, no. 2 (2005): 155–74.

44   Dorothea Hilhorst, *The Real World of NCOs: Discourses, Diversity, and Development* (London: Zed Books, 2003).

45   Hoogensen and Stuvøy, "Gender, Resistance, and Human Security"; Maria Stern, "'We' the Subject: The Power and Failure of (In)Security," *Security Dialogue* 37, no. 2 (2006): 187–205; Kristin Scharffscher, "Disempowerment through Disconnection: Local Women's Disaster Response and International Relief in Post-Tsunami Batticaloa," *Disaster Prevention and Management* 20, no. 1 (2011): 63–81.

46   Mary Kaldor, *New and Old Wars: Organized Violence in a Global Era*, 2nd ed. (Stanford: Stanford University Press, 2007).

47   W.C. Soderlund, E.D. Briggs, K. Hildebrant, and A.S. Sidahmed, *Humanitarian Crises and Intervention: Reassessing the Impact of Mass Media* (Sterling: Kumarian Press, 2008).

48   Mikkel Mouritz Marfelt, "Grounded Intersectionality: Key Tensions, a Methodological Framework, and Implications for Diversity Research," *Equality, Diversity, and Inclusion: An International Journal* 35, no. 1 (2016): 31–47.

49   Kimberlé Crenshaw, "Mapping the Margins: Intersectionality, Identity Politics, and Violence against Women of Colour," *Stanford Law Review* 43, no. 6 (1991): 1241–99.

50   Marfelt, "Grounded Intersectionality," 32.

51   Translation by the author. Cecile Hellestveit, *Syria: En stor krig i en liten verden* (Syria: A Big War in a Small World) (Oslo: Pax, 2017), 10.

52   Gunn-Britt Retter, "Sustainability and Development in the Arctic," in *Gender Equality in the Arctic: Current Realities*, ed. E. Oddsdóttir, A.M. Sigurdsson, and S. Svandal (Reykjavik: Ministry of Foreign Affairs, 2015).

53   Loftsdottir and Jensen, *Whiteness and Postcolonialism*, 2016.

54   Ministry of Social Affairs and Health, "Taking Wing Conference Report: Conference on Gender Equality and Women in the Arctic" (Helsinki: Ministry of Social Affairs and Health, 2002).

55   Larsen and Fondahl, *Arctic Human Development Report*.

56   Marjo Lindroth and Heidi Sinevaara-Niskane, *Global Politics and Its Violent Care for Indigeneity: Sequels to Colonialism* (London: Springer, 2017).

57   Pankaj Mishra, *Age of Anger: A History of the Present* (New York: Farrar, Straus and Giroux, 2017), 27–8.

58   P. Owens, "'No Farther West': The Mobilization of Collective Ethnic Violence against Indigenous Peoples in California, ca. 1850–1865," PhD diss., University of California – Irvine, 2015; L. Kingston, "The Destruction of Identity: Cultural Genocide and Indigenous Peoples," *Journal of Human Rights* 14, no. 1 (2015): 63–83.

59   Larsen and Fondahl, *Arctic Human Development Report.*

60   Lindroth and Sinevaara-Niskane, *Global Politics,* 18.

61   B.T. Godal, G. Hoogensen Gjørv, K.B. Harpviken, G. Nystuen, S. Rynning, A. Surhke, R. Tamnes, T. Wimpelmann, P.S. Hilde, E. Eikås, H. Høiback, A. Røe, E. Svendsen, and H.F. Widerberg, *NOU: En god alliert- Norge i Afghanistan 2001–2014* (NOU: A good ally – Norway in Afghanistan 2001–2014) (Oslo: Departementenes sikkerhets- og serviceorganisasjon, 2016).

62   See Security Council Report, http://www.securitycouncilreport.org /monthly-forecast/2017-09/afghanistan_22.php, for the September security forecast, as well as analyses from the Afghanistan Analyst Network (AAN) : https://www.afghanistan-analysts.org/the-humvee-bomb-series-the-october -wave-of-taleban-attacks-in-2017-context.

63   Ø.K. Landberg and O. Stokke (2016), "99 prosent av afghanske menn fikk nei. Her er grafene som viser at Norge er strengest i Europa" (99 percent of Afghan men received no. Here are the graphs that show that Norway is the most strict in Europe), *Aftenposten* (Oslo).

64   Amnesty International (2017), *Forced Back to Danger: Asylum-Seekers Returned from Europe to Afghanistan.* Amnesty International, https://www.amnesty.org /download/Documents/ASA1168662017ENGLISH.PDF.

11 Addressing Inequalities in the Arctic: Food Security in Nunavut

NATALIA LOUKACHEVA

Food security is a hot topic around the world and is of the utmost relevance in the Arctic, including Canada. It is a complex issue with multiple links – global, regional, national, and local. Often it is connected to sustainable development, economics, environment, health, trade, social wellness, politics, sovereignty, and law. The discourse on food security has been well covered in numerous reports, academic studies, and governmental and non-governmental recommendations for further action, all of which also concern Canada's North.[1] Numerous actors, including non-state stakeholders, representatives of the civil society, NGOs, not-for-profit organizations, Indigenous organizations, and regional and local actors, have been highly vocal about the state of food security in the North.

Although all aspects of food security discourse are important, this chapter focuses on food security in Nunavut, primarily through political and legal lenses. First, it explores the right to food and "food security" as a human rights issue. Using Nunavut as a case study, this chapter investigates why this issue is so crucial for all Nunavummiut (citizens of Nunavut) and why it has become so vitally important to the Indigenous residents of the territory. It also looks at the international dimensions of food security from perspective of the Inuit. It argues that food security is intertwined with a multitude of political and legal issues, including social justice, sovereignty, and Inuit rights.

As explained elsewhere in this book, the terms "security" (including "food security") and "sovereignty," while distinct, are closely linked. Despite the evolution in official thinking about food security since the 1970s, the concept is still flexible. Its most commonly accepted definition is the one put forward by the World Food Summit: food security exists "when all people, at all times, have physical and economic access to sufficient, safe and nutritious food to meet their dietary needs and food preferences for an active and healthy life."[2] Nutrition is the core dimension of food security, and the Committee on World Food Security, in developing a common terminology, has recommended the term "food and nutrition security."[3]

That term is often linked to the notion of "food sovereignty,"[4] which according to the Forum for Food Security is "the right of peoples to healthy and culturally appropriate food produced through ecologically sound and sustainable methods, and their right to define their own food and agriculture systems."[5] Clearly, the notions of "food and nutrition security" and "food sovereignty" are not the same, but they contemplate each other. The pillars of food security are food availability, accessibility, stability, and utilization or adequacy.[6] Currently, in the global context, there are many issues associated with national food security, such as the demand for food and its production and distribution. In the Arctic context, special considerations need to be taken into account, including: the limited feasibility of Arctic agriculture; the role of country foods and subsistence activities in northern communities; the cost of living, in particular high food prices; changes in the traditional diet (and health) of local residents; infrastructure limitations and restricted access to resources; and the impacts of environmental change.

In Canada's Central and Eastern Arctic, "food insecurity" has become an urgent matter. Geographically, Nunavut comprises one fifth of Canada, and it constitutes the largest Indigenous land claims settlement in the world.[7] Demographically, about 85 per cent of the 39,486 residents are Inuit.[8] Legally and politically, the territory of Nunavut is a sub-national unit of Canada with a system of public governance.[9] *De facto*, because of the Inuit majority and the fact that the territory was created as part of the Nunavut Land Claims Agreement (NLCA), Nunavut has a system of public governance with an "Indigenous face."[10] This factor is instrumental in Nunavut politics, in the composition and operations of governmental structures, and in policy-making. It is also important in understanding food security and sovereignty, which are linked to inequality and inadequate living standards relative to the rest of Canada. Ultimately, food insecurity in Nunavut is a human and Indigenous rights issue.

Nunavut and a Right to Food

The annual Nunavut food price survey indicates that food prices in Nunavut are far higher than the Canadian average.[11] Thus, in Nunavut, food insecurity has become an issue of social justice, poverty, and human rights. This raises questions about whether Canada has fulfilled its obligations under international law. It also points to the fact that in a country as wealthy as Canada, some residents still have standards of living typical of those in developing countries. According to the Inuit leadership, Inuit are suffering fundamental socio-economic distress (more than 70 per cent of households in Nunavut experience food insecurity), and Inuit "are living with great material deprivation in the midst of great resource wealth."[12] Indeed, "the enormous costs of imported food, combined with the high costs of hunting traditional country food have made hunger a major problem."[13] According to Statistics Canada, in 2011–12, at 36.7 per cent, Nunavut had the highest rate of food insecurity in the country, more than four times the Canadian average.[14]

It can be argued that Nunavut is an entity in transition, undergoing processes of reconciliation and territory-building. Too rapid a transition from non-industrialized traditional culture to modern democratic structures and economic development has seriously impeded socio-economic prosperity and well-being for Nunavummiut.[15] In terms of political development, Nunavut is experiencing something like a "voluntary" colonialism, with some suggesting that Nunavut is still a "colony."[16]

There are hopes that Nunavut will succeed in this transition and become self-reliant. That will depend on how the ongoing devolution process plays out. The existing culture of welfare dependency and 90 per cent reliance on federal transfers makes greater self-reliance problematic. Nunavummiut have long hoped that devolution will remedy some of the territory's economic and fiscal problems, and bring them opportunities and a quality of life similar to what southern Canadians enjoy.[17] But devolution in itself may not be a panacea. Ultimately, "the success of reconciliation and devolution in Nunavut is connected to the capacity of the Inuit and all Nunavummiut, in practice, to achieve sustainability."[18]

At present, the array of social ills, issues with the implementation of the NLCA, and limitations imposed by the existing legal and political structure have all compromised self-sufficiency, economic development, and the legitimacy of Nunavut's land claims and governance institutions. One serious impediment relates to social issues, which include growing poverty and lower standards of living than elsewhere in Canada. In this context, food insecurity has become a measurement of poverty and an indicator of unhealthy communities. Notably, it is a human rights issue, as Nunavummiut, like all other Canadians, have a right to food, which implies a right to *adequate* food.

The human right to food is recognized in several instruments of international law; of these, the International Covenant on Economic, Social and Cultural Rights (ICESCR) addresses it most comprehensively. Canada is a party to the ICESCR and thus has a duty to implement it in all parts of the country. In Article 11, the ICESCR talks about the right to food, which means that Canada should "recognize the right of everyone to an adequate standard of living for himself and his family, including adequate food, clothing and housing, and to the continuous improvement of living conditions" (Art. 11(1)). Furthermore, Canada "will take appropriate steps to ensure the realization of this right" (Art.11 (1)) and recognize that certain measures may be needed to ensure "the fundamental right to freedom from hunger and malnutrition."[19]

The ICERSCR's monitoring body – the Committee on Economic, Social and Cultural Rights – in its General Comment no. 12 lays out what the right to adequate food means as a human right.[20] It is inseparable from social justice, which demands the adoption of proper socio-economic and environmental policies targeting the "eradication of poverty."[21] The right to adequate food is strongly related to all other human rights, in that the root of this problem is "not the lack of food but the lack of access to available food, inter alia because of poverty."[22] Furthermore, "the right to adequate food is realized when every man, woman and child, alone or in community with others, has physical and economic access at all times to adequate food or means for its procurement."[23] In that respect, the concept of adequacy is of great importance to the right to food, and "the notion of *sustainability* is intrinsically linked to the notion of adequate food or food *security*, implying food being accessible for both present and future generations."[24] According to the committee, the core content of the right to adequate food implies "[t]he availability of food in a quantity and quality sufficient to satisfy the dietary needs of individuals, free from adverse substances, and acceptable within a given culture; The accessibility of such food in ways that are sustainable and that do not interfere with the enjoyment of other human rights."[25] The right to food implies adequacy – food security and accessibility. Like any other human right, the right to adequate food imposes on Canada, as a party to the covenant, obligations to respect, protect, and fulfil the realization of this right. The state must be proactive in strengthening citizens' "access to and utilization of resources and means to ensure their livelihood, including food security."[26]

Canada is obligated to implement the ICESCR by ensuring that all its citizens, including Nunavummiut, have an adequate standard of living (i.e., food security). Currently, there is a gap between Canada's international human rights commitments and their domestic implementation, especially regarding the right to food. The national implementation of this right is an ongoing issue, and so is the need for an integrated national food security strategy.[27] The Report on Canada by the UN Special Rapporteur on the Right to Food has revealed shortcomings in Canada's protection of social and economic rights, including the right to adequate food. It has used the increasing food insecurity among

Nunavummiut as examples of this problem.[28] The report of the special rapporteur has helped draw public attention to the severe food insecurity in Nunavut, and this has helped make it an important political and public priority there.

Poverty is the key factor preventing the realization of the right to adequate food, but at the federal level "poverty and socio-economic status are not recognized as a prohibited ground for discrimination."[29] One way to address this gap is to develop and implement sub-national poverty reduction strategies; another is to pass legislation to ensure the right to food. In other words, the implementation of the right to food is a matter of both policy and legislation. How does this right materialize in Nunavut?

Nunavut's Policies and Action on Food Security

Food insecurity in Nunavut has been a focus of public protest and was even a campaign issue in the 2015 federal election.[30] The territorial government of Nunavut (GN), Inuit organizations (such as Nunavut Tunngavik Inc.; NTI), municipal bodies, NGOs and not-for-profit organizations, families, and the private sector have all tried to address the urgent issue of food security and poverty. The chronology of Nunavut's initiatives and programs and the mandates of stakeholders engaged in anti-poverty and food insecurity reduction measures can be traced through multiple strategic action plans, reports, recommendations, and scholarship.[31] Grassroots activists and movements like Feeding My Family have been particularly important in pushing the political agenda on food security in Nunavut. An integrated approach engaging all actors has been endorsed by the GN and Inuit organizations. The GN has been the key influencer in shaping related policies and legislation. Often it has worked in collaboration with NTI, which is a watchdog organization for implementing the NLCA and represents the interests of all Inuit.

The GN has always emphasized in its policy documents the need for self-reliance and for reduced dependence on external funding as preconditions for a prosperous Nunavut. It has called for action on food insecurity in several of its policy documents.[32] Its *Tamapta 2009–2013* action plan emphasized that all Nunavummiut deserve to have "affordable, healthy food, safe water, and a home."[33] That plan committed the GN to developing and implementing a poverty reduction strategy, which among other things would "examine the availability and adequacy of community supports for breakfast and lunch programs" and "identify ways for government to support these initiatives."[34] The GN's *Sivumut Abluqta: Stepping Forward Together* (2014–18) declared that "healthy families through strong and resilient communities" was one of its key priorities and that "adequate food and housing are fundamental to the health, education and well-being of Nunavummiut."[35] To that end, it would "promote and support the use of harvesting skills and community-based solutions to enhance access to nutritious food throughout the territory."[36] The GN has emphasized traditional country food as a solution. Its *Turaaqtavut* (2018–22) notes that Nunavummiut food and housing needs are not being met and are too expensive. This document focuses on self-reliance as the foundation of the Inuit way of life, "enabled by traditional knowledge and contemporary knowledge and tools. Individuals, families, communities, and government share a responsibility to encourage and support self-reliance."[37] To achieve this, the GN has prioritized "responding to the needs of Nunavummiut for safe and affordable housing and food security."[38]

In 2011 the Nunavut anti-poverty secretariat conducted community and regional consultations that led to the Poverty Summit, which helped generate insights into poverty in Nunavut. Out of that summit came the *Makimaniq Plan: A Shared Approach to Poverty Reduction*, adopted by both the GN and the NTI in 2012, which was later formalized by the Nunavut Roundtable for Poverty Reduction (NRPR).[39] The plan provided a strategic framework to address poverty in Nunavut, declared food security a key priority, and called for a collaborative, integrated, holistic, and culturally sensitive approach by all stakeholders (governments, Inuit organizations, communities, etc.). The GN and the NTI signed a memo of understanding to establish the NRPR,[40] which is responsible for implementing the plan; this was aligned with special legislation to ensure its implementation. The Collaboration for Poverty Reduction Act has affirmed in law "the commitment of the Government of Nunavut to participate as a partner with Nunavut Tunngavik Inc., Inuit organizations and other governments, non-governmental organizations and businesses on the Nunavut Roundtable for Poverty Reduction to implement *The Makimaniq Plan* and the five year poverty reduction action plan in a manner consistent with Article 32 of the NLCA."[41] Section 5 of that act reaffirms the GN's commitment to collaborate with the NRPR; Section 9 creates a poverty reduction fund to help implement the plan.[42]

The *Makimaniq Plan* identifies six priorities for alleviating poverty in Nunavut, all of which are connected. Three of them are food security, housing and income support, and community and economic development. Food security means "that all Nunavummiut at all times will have physical and economic access to sufficient, nutritious and culturally-relevant foods."[43] According to the framework, improving food security can be achieved through individual and family empowerment, community support, strengthened relations, cultural identity reinforcement, "supporting healthy living and encouraging literacy and life skills."[44] Several tools and programs have been developed to achieve these goals and strengthen community-driven food security initiatives. As well, the Nunavut Food Security Coalition was created in 2012 to develop a long-term food security strategy for the territory.[45]

This coalition, co-chaired by the GN and the NTI, engages other partners to identify the best practices to ensure food security for the citizens of Nunavut.[46] It publicly released the Nunavut Food Security Strategy and Action Plan (2014–16) in 2014.[47] That plan identified the complex factors impacting food security in the territory and its indirect consequences, which pose an overall threat to economic development, social stability, and cultural integrity. The coalition considered "availability (enough wildlife on the land or groceries in the store), accessibility (adequate money for hunting equipment or store-bought food, and the ability to obtain it), quality (healthy food that is culturally valued), and use (knowledge about how to obtain, store, prepare, and consume food)" as the main components of food security.[48] It suggested a collective approach to and responsibility for improving food security in Nunavut. It also stated that food security will exist when "all Nunavummiut will have access to an adequate supply of safe, culturally preferable, affordable, nutritious food, through a food system that promotes Inuit Societal Values, self-reliance, and environmental sustainability."[49]

The strategy has also identified the following priority themes: country food; store-bought food; local food production; life skills; programs and community initiatives; and policy and legislation. Each of these is supported with further actions, and the action plan helps with their implementation.[50] The territory's legislative mission has been defined as building a strong social safety net that "promotes food security through relevant policy and legislative measures."[51] It supports the implementation of food-related legislation and regulations, such as the Donation of Food Act, which aims to encourage food donations and sharing and sets out the liability of the donor and the receiver;[52] this act is already "an integral part of Inuit culture."[53] The strategy also notes that food security is influenced by housing, income assistance, education, training, employment, and transportation policies,[54] and emphasizes the need "for territory-wide policy and legislation founded on Inuit Societal Values."[55] Those values – *Inuit Qaujimajatuqangit* (IQ) – have been guiding principles of the GN's policies and operations since the territory's founding and have been acknowledged in Nunavut's legislation.[56] The food security action plan was revised in 2018 to heighten the emphasis on issues related to climate change and to expand research on food security, monitoring, and evaluation.[57]

The GN has been supportive of intersectoral partnerships with the NTI, regional Inuit associations, communities, and others in tackling food security issues. It has also been advocating for policies and legislative measures for ensuring access to food at affordable prices. In this respect, the federal government's Nutrition North program, introduced in 2011 to replace the Food Mail Program dating back to the 1960s, has faced ongoing criticism. The UN Special Rapporteur on the Right to Food has outlined the program's shortcomings, which include a lack of transparency and weak monitoring and community participation.[58] For example, the Auditor General of Canada found several deficiencies with Ottawa's implementation of the program. Specifically, it aimed to make healthy foods more accessible and affordable in the North but did not take into account factors such as poverty, high costs of living, unemployment, and limited infrastructure.[59] Indigenous and Northern Affairs Canada accepted all of the AG's recommendations. In 2015, the new federal government promised to increase the program's funding by $40 million over four years; on 1 January 2019 the program received a $62.2 million boost from Ottawa.[60] The Nunavut Food Security coalition has issued recommendations for improving the program.[61] It remains to be seen how any of this may improve food security in the territory.

Inuit Rights, Food Security, and Sovereignty

Addressing food insecurity in Nunavut has variously been viewed as an anti-poverty measure and a matter of social justice (to achieve living standards on par with those of the rest of Canada). It is also part of efforts to re-enforce traditional activities so as to support Inuit skills, nutrition, diet, health, and social wellness. Thus, food security and sovereignty in Nunavut are closely linked to Inuit rights.

Inuit are protective of their "human right to access adequate food – whether traditionally harvested or obtained commercially."[62] The right to food is inextricably linked to Inuit culture, biodiversity and wildlife management, land use, and way of life. Thus, the protection of Inuit rights, especially harvesting rights (hunting, fishing, trapping, gathering), are considered by the GN, the NTI, Inuit organizations such as the Inuit Circumpolar Council (ICC) and Inuit Tapiriit Kanatami (ITK),[63] and regional Nunavut associations as an important step toward ensuring food security. These organizations address the issue in global, circumpolar, national, and local contexts.

Food security in Nunavut is influenced by global developments, including the pollution of country food by transboundary contaminants, the rising costs of food and fuel, economic vulnerability, climate change, animal rights movements, and increased shipping. Inuit have been vocal in their battles against climate change and other global developments in the environment, which are affecting their livelihoods. Defending their "right" to a cold,[64] clean, and healthy environment and to engage in harvesting activities that are essential to their cultural survival, in 2005 the ICC petitioned the Inter-American Commission on Human Rights seeking relief for violations resulting from global warming caused by acts and omissions of the United States.[65] In the process the Inuit showed how their subsistence culture might cease to exist because of the impacts of climate change and the resulting decline in their traditional resources. In 2015 at the UNFCCC COP 21 Paris negotiations on climate change, Inuit expressed concerns about the impact that climate change was having on their ability to sustain their culture, identity, and livelihood, including on the wildlife on which they depend for food.[66] In Paris, a joint statement on climate change released by the ICC and the governments of Nunavut and Greenland emphasized that "Inuit food security should be protected."[67] Clearly, for the ICC (as a transnational NGO representing the Inuit of four countries and four Canadian regions), the global issue of climate change is very much a food security issue.[68] In its 2018 Utqiagvik Declaration, the ICC stressed that "food security is central to Inuit identity and way of life; is characterized by a healthy environment and encompasses access, availability, economics, physical and mental health, Inuit culture, decision making power and management, and education."[69] The ICC offered an action plan to address food security and health issues.[70]

The ICC leadership promotes Inuit food security in all aspects of its work, including "community health and wellness, retention and transmission of Inuit traditional knowledge, use of Inuit management methodologies, improved co-management activities, sustainable utilization of wildlife, contaminants, biological diversity, climate change, and the availability of nutritious foods."[71] It pays special attention to improving access to sufficient Inuit traditional food sources – access that is often hampered by "changing economic and social conditions, contaminants, climate change and regulatory decisions taken by others on polar bears, seals, and other marine and terrestrial mammals."[72] These things threaten Inuit food security by endorsing policies and regulations restricting the species that Inuit can hunt, by limiting Inuit traditional management practices based on sustainable use (e.g., quotas), and by curtailing Inuit economic opportunities "from the bi-products of these food sources through trade restrictions."[73]

The 2009 EU trade ban on products originating from the seal hunt had a profound impact on Inuit economies and challenged Inuit identity and existence, given their continued reliance on traditional country food and their subsistence harvesting practices.[74] This ban has become a major political and legal issue and was challenged by the Government of Canada at the World Trade Organization[75] with support from Inuit organizations and the GN. In 2014, Canada and the EU came to an agreement that exempted Canadian Inuit from the trade ban, and in 2015 an amendment was made to the 2009 EU regulations.[76] Even so, irreversible damage had been done to Nunavut's fur industry and (closely linked) to Inuit health and diet.[77]

According to the Inuit, wildlife and harvesting are central to their subsistence, nutrition, and culture, given that "70% of Canadian Inuit households are active in wildlife harvesting and consume wild or country foods."[78] Country food is crucial for the Inuit not only because of its nutritional benefits but also because of the significance of hunting and harvesting in supporting Indigenous culture, knowledge, skills, and values. More than 90 per cent of households engaged in harvesting share these foods with the community.[79] As Inuit note, food security is a critical issue for them, as country food "sustains us, providing us with skills that we need in modern society, shaping our character, and teaching us strength and resilience."[80]

One solution to food insecurity would be to empower of Inuit to establish a "political, social and economic environment, grounded in Inuit way of life, that sets optimal conditions for Inuit food security."[81] According to the Inuit leadership, Arctic wildlife fuels their existence and "Inuit food security is dependent upon Arctic biodiversity and is our cultural identity."[82] Key challenges to food security are the high costs of traditional activities, coupled with economic vulnerability and the challenges of consuming country food.[83] For Inuit, "the ability to harvest country food is also an essential prerequisite in attaining the right to food."[84] Thus, they have argued, "the harvesting and consumption of country food must foremost be recognized as an essential pillar in the right to food for Inuit."[85] Inuit leaders have called upon various levels of government "to recognize the inherent rights of Inuit with respect to sustainable hunting, co-management, and other subsistence activities."[86] Legal protection of harvesting activities can be seen as a prerequisite for food security.

In Nunavut, several measures have been taken to ensure this protection both at the governmental level (e.g., the Country Food Distribution Program, which improves access to affordable and healthy country food via community harvesting funding and infrastructure funds,[87] and the Grants and Contributions in Support of Harvesters Policy, which helps hunters' and trappers' Organizations [HTOs] as described under the NCLA[88]), and at legislative levels (e.g., the Wildlife Act and new regulations that uphold Inuit harvesting rights[89]). All of these initiatives aim to improve access to country food and to protect and add value to the harvesting sector. The GN's programs support these activities; however, their exercise is being impeded by, for example, the loss of traditional skills and the staggeringly high costs of hunting equipment and commodities that support hunting and access to wildlife.

Inuit harvesting rights are key to addressing food insecurity. Subsistence activities are important to Inuit livelihood, and the NLCA recognizes this. Much of the NLCA deals with Inuit rights related to landowners, management of lands and resources, co-management, conservation and wildlife management, and harvesting rights; these encompass marine and offshore issues as well. Of the 42 articles in the NLCA, about one third are directly related to marine issues, including harvesting all marine mammals in open waters as well as from land-fast ice.[90] Inuit harvesting rights are also constitutionally protected by the NLCA via Section 35 of the Constitution Act, 1982.

Furthermore, Inuit harvesting rights have been re-enforced by the Nunavut judiciary in several cases. Notable examples include a Nunavut Court of Justice decision asserting the Inuit right to choose a hunting method (the *Polar bear hunt with traditional means case*),[91] the *Firearms case* (dealing with Inuit compliance with mandatory licensing requirements for firearms and ammunition for hunting purposes and the Inuit treaty right to hunt),[92] and the *Narwhal hunt case* (dealing with the Inuit harvest of narwhal tusks without a tag or licence affixed to them).[93] All of these harvesting right cases have a direct connection to the matter of food security in Nunavut, as an inability to hunt and limited access to traditional sources of food infringe on Inuit harvesting rights. For example, in the *Firearms case*, the plaintiff argued that his inability to access firearms would substantially impair his ability to harvest. This in turn "will mean less country food available to those Inuit hunters directly affected, and their families. This will mean less country food available for distribution to elders and extended family. This will mean less food available for distribution in the community generally."[94] In all of these cases, the courts have emphasized the importance of hunting traditions and activities for the preservation of Inuit culture, way of life, and identity as a people.

In Nunavut, food security and the right to food are connected to Indigenous peoples' rights more broadly, including the right to lands and natural resources as means of supporting their subsistence, the right to self-determination and participation in decision-making, the principle of non-discrimination and free prior informed consent, and meaningful consultation with communities on any resource developments that may affect their lands. Extractive resource developments can limit the exercise of subsistence activities and result in the loss of traditional food sources in Nunavut. For example, there have been tensions between the mining industry and Nunavut hunters over land use, as well as calls by Indigenous communities and hunters' and trappers' organizations for a ban on mining in caribou calving grounds under the Nunavut land use plan.[95] Another issue is seismic testing. In 2010 the Qikiqtani Inuit Association won an injunction from the Nunavut Court of Justice against seismic testing in Lancaster Sound, Jones Sound, and North Baffin Bay, all of which fall under the Nunavut Settlement Area (NSA). This injunction was granted on the grounds that testing safety was not guaranteed and that prior community consultations had not been meaningful enough. Inuit were concerned about the impact of seismic testing on the migration routes of marine mammals in traditional Inuit hunting areas. Thus, their right to harvest marine mammals was at stake. The court noted that the Inuit's inability to harvest those mammals would have implications not only for their diet but also for their cultural traditions of hunting, sharing country food, and making clothing – all of these fundamental activities for Inuit.[96] The court concluded that if testing took place as planned, the harm to the Inuit would be irreparable as "the loss extends not just to the loss of a food source, but to a loss of a culture."[97]

Since 2011, the Inuit of Clyde River, in an attempt to protect their culture of subsistence harvesting, have opposed a proposal by an oil industry consortium to conduct an offshore seismic survey in their area, which falls outside the NSA but is vital for the wildlife that Inuit depend on for income and subsistence. In 2014, the hamlet of Clyde River and the Nammautaq Hunters and Trappers Organization filed a claim in the Federal Court of Appeal (FCA) disputing a decision by the National Energy Board (NEB) to permit seismic testing in Baffin Bay and the Davis Strait.[98] The following year, the FCA dismissed the claimants' application for judicial review,[99] but by then the oil consortium had cancelled its plans to conduct seismic testing in the summer of that year,[100] and affirmed the same for 2016. The Clyde River group appealed the FCA's decision to the Supreme Court of Canada (SCC).[101] In 2017 the Court decided that "this testing could negatively affect the harvesting rights of the Inuit of Clyde River" and that the consultation and accommodation efforts by the respondents in this case were inadequate. The SCC allowed the appeal and quashed the NERB's authorization.[102] Interestingly, Shell Canada relinquished its exploration permits in Lancaster Sound in 2016, expediting the Government of Canada's creation of the Lancaster Sound National Marine Protected Area (Tallurutiup Imanga) to conserve natural and cultural resources on which Inuit depend.[103]

Finally, food security in Nunavut is connected to the matter of Canadian Arctic sovereignty[104] and "indigenous food sovereignty,"[105] which implies an Inuit right "to make their own decisions about food and define their own food systems."[106] For Inuit, "sovereignty begins at home" and its assertion requires healthy and sustainable communities.[107] Therefore, dealing with socio-economic distress in Nunavut, including food security, is also a way to exercise Canadian sovereignty in the Arctic.[108] Inuit also emphasize that the issue of sovereignty should be addressed in the context of respect for their rights, especially the right to self-determination and harvesting rights,[109] which are vital to food security in Nunavut. In a similar vein, "resource development must enhance, not detract from Inuit food security."[110]

Conclusion

Food security and the right to food in Nunavut extend far beyond the issues of accessibility and affordability. Both have significant cultural significance for Inuit, as their harvesting rights and sharing of country food are crucial for their identity and existence, as well as the socio-economic health of their communities. Thus, in Nunavut's context, food security is a matter of human rights, social justice, and due respect for Indigenous values, culture, and rights. This is a complex matter with multiple links that affect the Nunavummiut locally, nationally, regionally, and globally. As can be seen from other chapters in this book, it also has links to the ongoing Arctic sovereignty discourse and Indigenous "food sovereignty," in that the loss of traditional sources of food would mean the loss of culture.

The issue of food security is also closely intertwined with the issue of poverty in Nunavut. Therefore, dealing with food insecurity at the legal and political levels means addressing inequalities in this Arctic entity in transition. This process can succeed only as a collaborative effort engaging all levels of government agencies, Indigenous organizations, other NGOs and not-for-profit organizations, and all Nunavummiut.

NOTES

1 For a literature overview on this topic, see, for example, Council of Canadian Academies (CCA), *Aboriginal Food Security in Northern Canada: An Assessment of the State of Knowledge*, Expert Panel on the State of Knowledge of Food Security in Northern Canada [Report] (Ottawa, 2014); Canadian Polar Commission (CPC), *Food Security in the Canadian North: Recent Advances and Remaining Knowledge Gaps and Research* [Report, 31 March] (Ottawa, 2014).

2 UN Food and Agriculture Organization (FAO), *Rome Declaration on World Food Security and World Food Summit Plan of Action*, World Food Summit, Rome, 13–17 November 1996. This definition was reaffirmed in the *Declaration of the World Summit on Food Security*, FAO WSFS 2009/2, 16 November 2009. On the evolution of this concept since 1974, see, for example, UN FAO, *Trade Reform and Food Security: Conceptualizing the Linkages*, ch. 2, 25–30

(Rome, 2003); Committee on World Food Security (CFS), *Coming to Terms with Terminology*, Rome, 15–20 October 2012, CFS2012/39/4 CFS 2012.

3 On the nutritional dimension, see CFS, *Reform of the CFS*, 35: 2009/2 Rev. 2, October, 2009. The committee tried to avoid different uses of the terms "food security," "food security and nutrition," "nutrition security," and "food and nutrition security" and to standardize its official terminology. See CFS 2012/39/4, point 32.

4 Food Secure Canada advocates for food sovereignty. World Social Forum 2016: Let's Talk about Food Sovereignty, Montreal, 9–14 August 2016. It also endorses the global peasant movement La Via Campesina in its fight against injustice in the food system; see www.foodsecrecanada.org. See also Global Justice, "What Is Food Sovereignty?," www.globaljustice.org.uk.

5 Forum for Food Security, *Declaration of Nyéléni*, Sélingué, Mali, 27 February 2007, www.nyeleni.org.

6 CFS 2012/39/4, point 17.

7 Nunavut Land Claims Agreement Act, S.C. 1993, C. 29.

8 GN, Bureau of Statistics, 1 April 2020, www.stats.gov.nu.ca.

9 The territory was carved out of the Northwest Territories in 1999. *Nunavut Act*, S.C. 1993, C. 28.

10 Art. 4 of the NLCA and Natalia Loukacheva, *The Arctic Promise: Legal and Political Autonomy of Greenland and Nunavut* (Toronto: University of Toronto Press, 2007).

11 The 2015 Nunavut Food Price Survey, "Comparison of Nunavut and Canada CPI Food Price Basket Items," Nunavut Bureau of Statistics and Statistics Canada. GN, Nunavut Bureau of Statistics, 1 October 2015. In 2013 the estimate was that Nunavut food prices were 140 per cent higher than the average Canadian prices.

12 Mary Simon, "Inuit and Social Justice" [Speech], Ryerson University, Toronto, 24 May 2011.

13 Ibid.

14 Minister of Industry, Statistics Canada, Shirin Roshanafshar, and Emma Hawkins, "Food Insecurity in Canada" [Report], Cat. no. 82-624-X, 25 March 2015.

15 About these challenges, see, for example, Natalia Loukacheva, "From Recognition to Reconciliation: Nunavut and Self-Reliance – An Arctic Entity in Transition," in *Essays on the Constitutional Entrenchment of Aboriginal and Treaty Rights*, ed. Patrick Macklem and Douglas Sanderson (Toronto: University of Toronto Press, 2016), 399–422; Jack Hicks, "The Dissociative State of Nunavut," *Canadian Dimension* 47, no. 3 (2013), https://canadiandimension .com/articles/view/the-dissiciative-state-of-nunavut; Jack Hicks and Graham White, *Made in Nunavut: An Experiment in Decentralized Government* (Vancouver: UBC Press, 2016).

16 See, for example, Warren Bernauer, who talks about "extractive colonialism" with regard to uranium mining in Nunavut and argues with the 2014 op-ed by the editor-in-chief of the *Nunatsiaq News*, James Bell, in *The Globe and Mail*, saying that "Nunavut is no longer Canada's colony. It needs to end its own deprivation." Bernauer, "Nunavut Is Still a Colony: We Should Act in Solidarity to End Its Deprivation," *Canadian Dimension* 49, no. 1 (2015), https://canadiandimension.com/articles/view/nunavut-is-still-a-colony.

17 Loukacheva, "From Recognition to Reconciliation," 414–15.

18 Ibid., 402.

19 Art. 11(2)(a).

20 Office of the High Commissioner for Human Rights: "CESCR Comment No. 12: The Right to Adequate Food" (Art. 11), E/C.12/1999/5, 12 May 1999.

21 Point 4.

22 Point 5.

23 Point 6.

24 Point 7.

25 Point 8.

26 Point 15.

27 The special rapporteur concluded that "Canada does not currently afford constitutional or legal protection of the right to food." UN, Olivier De Shutter, *Report of the Special Rapporteur on the Right to Food*, Mission to Canada 6–16 May 2012, GA.A/HRC/22/50/Add.1 24 December 2012, points 10 and 16.

28 Ibid., Section VIII, Indigenous Peoples.

29 S. 7 of the Canadian Charter of Rights and Freedoms and its interpretation by governments, point 12. Quote from point 11.

30 Jim Bell, "Nunavut Demonstrators Gather to Protest Food Prices, Poverty," *Nunatsiaq News Online*, 9 June 2012; David Murphy, "Nunavut Food Security Protest in Iqaluit Focuses on Expired Foods," *Nunatsiaq News Online*, 16 June 2014; Thomas Rohner, "Nunavut Food Security Group Calls for One-Day Boycott," *Nunatsiaq News Online*, 21 January 2015; CBC Radio, "Nunavut's Food Crisis Is Becoming an Election Issue" [Transcript], 28 August 2015, www.cbc.ca/radio.

31 CCA, *Aboriginal Food Security in Northern Canada*; CPC, *Food Security in the Canadian North*; Impact Economics: *Understanding Poverty in Nunavut* [Report], prepared for the Nunavut Roundtable for Poverty Reduction, 31 August 2012; The Makimaniq Plan and regional reports for its implementation – *Kitikmeot Regional Gathering Report: Implementing the Makimaniq Plan*, Cambridge Bay, 12 June 2012; *Kivalliq Regional Gathering Report: Implementing the Makimaniq Plan*, Rankin Inlet, 31 May 2012; NTI, *Annual Report on the State of Inuit Culture and Society: The Nunavut Inuit Health Survey: Understanding its Influence and Legacy 2011–2013*; Hing Man Chan et al., "Food Security in

Nunavut, Canada. Barriers and Recommendations," *International Journal of Circumpolar Health* 65, no. 5 (2006): 416–43; James Ford, "Vulnerability of Inuit Food Systems to Food Insecurity as a Consequence of Climate Change: A Case Study from Igloolik, Nunavut." *Regional Environmental Change* 9 (2009): 83–100; Jennifer Wakegijig et al., "Collaborating toward Improving Food Security in Nunavut," *International Journal of Circumpolar Health* 72 (2013): 1-8; Hillary Fergurson, "Inuit Food (In)Security in Canada: Assessing the Implications and Effectiveness of Policy," *Queen's Policy Review* 2, no. 2 (2011): 54–79. There are also numerous NPOs and NGOs that deal with food security, such as the Feeding My Family Movement; see www.feedingmyfamily.org.

32 GN, *Nutrition in Nunavut: A Framework for Action* (Iqaluit: GN, 2007); GN, *Developing Healthy Communities: Public Health Strategy for Nunavut (2008–2013)* (Iqaluit: GN, 2008). Furthermore, the GN's Department of Family Services has a Poverty Reduction Division.

33 GN, *Tamapta,* "Building Our Future Together: Government of Nunavut Priorities 2009–2013" (Iqaluit: GN, 2009), 6.

34 GN, *Tamapta,* 11, 12.

35 GN, *Sivumut Abluqta – Stepping Forward Together 2014–2018* (Iqaluit, 2014).

36 Ibid., 14.

37 GN, *Turaaqtavut* (Iqaluit, 2017), 21.

38 Ibid.

39 Poverty Summit, Iqaluit, 28–30 November 2011; *The Makimaniq Plan: A Shared Approach to Poverty Reduction,* 30 November 2011, and 24 February 2012.

40 Memorandum of Understanding on the Nunavut Roundtable for Poverty Reduction entered into by the Government of Nunavut and Nunavut Tunngavik Inc., 24 October 2012.

41 S. 2. Consolidation of Collaboration for Poverty Reduction Act. S. Nu. 2013, c. 12. Art. 32, of the NLCA deals with the Inuit right to participate in the development of social and cultural polices.

42 The implementation of the *Makimaniq Plan* has been ensured by the adoption of the collaborative poverty-reduction action plan – *Makimaniq: Five-year Implementation Plan* – which was reviewed by the NRPR in 2014. The new version of the Five Year Poverty Reduction Action Plan was tabled in 2016. Furthermore, in 2017 the *Makimaniq Plan II* was introduced for 2017–22. This new plan follows priorities identified in the first plan. See Implementation Plan for Nunavut's Anti-Poverty Strategy, 9 August 2013; the Honourable Jeannie Ugyuk, Minister of Family Services, Minister Responsible for Poverty Reduction, *Minister's Annual Report on Poverty Reduction 2013–2014* (GN: Department of Family Services, 2014); *The Makimaniq Plan 2: A Shared Approach to Poverty Reduction, 2017–2022,* Nunavut Roundtable for Poverty Reduction 2017, at 9.

43 *Supra* note 42 (2013) at 23. The Makimaniq Plan 2, 9.

44 *Supra* note 42(2013), 8.

45 For the list of those tools and programs, see *supra* note 43 (2013), at 24–6.

46 The coalition was created on 26 June 2012. About its activities, see www.nunavutfoodsecurity.ca. Nunavut Food Security Coalition, *Annual Reports 2012–2013; 2013–2014,* and *2014–2015.*

47 The groundwork was done at the Nunavut Food Security Symposium, January 2013. Nunavut Food Security Coalition, Nunavut Food Security Symposium Record of Proceedings, 2013, www.makiliqta.ca; Nunavut Food Security Coalition, Food Security Strategy and Action Plan, 5 May 2014.

48 Strategy, 2014–16, 2.

49 Ibid., 4.

50 Ibid., 5.

51 Ibid., 12.

52 Consolidation of Donation of Food Act, S. Nu. 2013, c. 8; Action Plan, 22.

53 MLA Monica Ell, qtd in *Nunavut Food Security Coalition Annual Report 2012–2013,* 11.

54 Strategy, 12.

55 Ibid., 12.

56 *Sivumut Abluqta,* 2014–2018, and all previous GN's mandates since 1999. On IQ, see also ss. 8 and 9 of the Nunavut Wildlife Management Act, S. Nu. 2003, c. 26.

57 Nunavut Roundtable for Poverty Reduction, Spring 2018 Territorial Gathering, 17–19 April 2018, Rankin Inlet, Nunavut. Summary Report. Theme: Respite Spaces. TD 91–5(2), 7 November 2018. The Hon. Elisapee Sheutiapik, Minister Responsible for Poverty Reduction, GN, 12.

58 2012 report, *supra* note 27 at 17.

59 Report of the Auditor General of Canada, ch. 6, "Nutrition North Canada – Aboriginal Affairs and Northern Development Canada," Fall 2014.

60 One activity to improve the program is Nutrition North Performance Measurement Strategy, Indigenous and Northern Affairs Canada, January 2016. Irene Galfa, "Nutrition North Canada to Receive $62M Subsidy Boost for Better Access to Traditional Cuisine," *National Post,* 12 December 2018, www.nationalpost.com.

61 Nunavut Food Security Coalition, *The Nutrition North Canada Program,* March 2015.

62 ICC, *Food Security across the Arctic,* Background Paper of the Steering Committee of the Circumpolar Inuit Health Strategy, ICC-Canada, May 2012, 3. The Inuit have a "mixed economy" in which food is produced from hunting and the money but traditional sharing of country food is vital for subsistence. Miriam T. Harder and George W. Wenzel, "Inuit Subsistence, Social Economy, and Food Security in Clyde River, Nunavut," *Arctic,* 65, no. 3 (2012): 305–18.

63 The Inuit Right to food is ITK's priority. The ITK has formed the National Inuit Food Security Working Group, which works closely with the National Inuit Committee on Health and the ICC, www.itk.ca.

64 Watt-Cloutier was the ICC chair at the time of petition see: Sheila Watt-Cloutier, *The Right to Be Cold: One Woman's Story of Protecting Her Culture, the Arctic, and the Whole Planet* (Toronto: Penguin Canada, 2015).

65 ICC, Petition to the Inter-American Commission on Human Rights Seeking Relief from Violations Resulting from Global Warming Caused by Acts and Omissions of the United States, 7 December 2005.

66 ICC, J. Okalik Eegeesiak, ICC Chair, UNFCCC COP 21 Position Paper, "Inuit Call for Action from Global Leaders," UNFCCC COP21, Paris, France. ICC, 2014 at 1.

67 Joint Statement of Inuit Circumpolar Council, the Government of Greenland, and the Government of Nunavut on Climate Change, December 2015.

68 ICC, Food Security across the Arctic, n62; ICC, *Kitigaaryuit Declaration*, 12th General Assembly of the Inuit Circumpolar Council, 21–4 July 2014, Inuvik, s. 13 – "Inuit rights to manage migratory birds and other migratory animals in the interests of Inuit food security"; ss. 36–40 talk about Inuit food security from various angles. ICC Canada 2014–2015 and 2015–2016 operational plans also make food security one of their priorities. For example, the issue of food security has been addressed by the ICC and Inuit national organizations at other global and regional fora, including the UN (ITK and ICC [Canada], Inuit and the Right to Food, Submission to the United Nations Special Rapporteur on the Right to Food for the Official Country Mission to Canada, May 2012); International Whaling Commission (Report of the IWC Expert Workshop on Aboriginal Subsistence Whaling. IWC/66/ASW Rep 01, October 15, 2015), and the Arctic Council (see www.arcticcouncil.org).

69 ICC, 13th ICC General Assembly, *Utqiagvik Declaration: Inuit – the Arctic We Want*, Utqiagvik, Alaska, 16–19 July 2018, 1.

70 Ibid., Food Security, points 16–18 at 3–4.

71 *Kitigaaryuit Declaration*, s. 36.

72 Ibid., s. 37.

73 J. Okalik Eegeesiak, ICC Chair, Speech at CAFF Biodiversity Congress, Trondheim, Norway, 2 December 2014, 3.

74 Regulation (EC) No. 1007/2009 of the European Parliament and of the EC Council of 16 September 2009 on trade in seal products, OJL286. 31.10.2009. About legal issues, see Nikolas Sellheim, "A Legal Framework for Seal and Sealing in the Arctic," in *Polar Law and Resources*, TemaNord 533, ed. Natalia Loukacheva, 109–18 (Copenhagen: Nordic Council of Ministers, 2015).

75 WTO, "European Communities – Measures Prohibiting the Importation and Marketing of Seal Products" (WT/DS 400 and 401), 18 June 2014. The WTO upheld the discriminatory ban, which caused further frustration for Inuit.

Terry Audla, President of the ITK, "Inuit Decry WTO Appellate Decision to Uphold Discriminatory, Flawed Seal Ban" [ITK Media Release], 22 May 2014.

76 Regulation (EU) 2015/1775 of the European Parliament and of the Council of 6 October 2015 amending Regulation (EC) No.1007/2009 on trade in seal products and repealing Commission Regulation (EU) No. 737/2010. OJL 262, 7.10.2015.

77 GN, "Report on the Impacts of European Union Seal Ban (EC) No. 1007/2009," in Nunavut, Department of Environment, Iqaluit, 2 January 2012. See also WTO, "European Communities – Measures Prohibiting the Importation and Marketing of Seal Products," WT/DS400/16/Add.7; WT/DS401/17/Add.7, 16 October 2015; for campaigning by the Inuit Sila organization on this matter, see www.inuitsila.org.

78 Terry Audla, ITK Leader, "The Climate Change Bind for Inuit: The Double Burden of Impacts and Campaigns" [Speech], Canadian Climate Forum, Ottawa, 22 April 2015.

79 ICC, "The Sea Ice Never Stops: Circumpolar Inuit Reflections on Sea Ice Use and Shipping in Inuit Nunaat" [Report], December 2014; Audla, "The Climate Change Bind."

80 Ibid., 12.

81 Kitigaaryuit Declaration 2014, s. 39.

82 Eegeesiak, Speech at CAFF Biodiversity Congress, 2.

83 2012 ICC paper, n65. See also GN and NTI, "Country Food and Sustainable Community Initiatives Identified as Key to Food Security" [News Release], GN and NTI, 2013; Simon *supra* note 12.

84 ITK and ICC – Canada 2012, *supra* note 68 at 7.

85 Ibid., 10.

86 The Kuujjuaq Declaration, ICC, 9th General Assembly, Kuujjuaq, Quebec, 11–16 August 2002, point 13.

87 GN, Department of Economic Development and Transportation, "Country Food Distribution Program" [Policy statement], August 2015.

88 GN, Department of Environment, "Grants and Contributions in Support of Harvesters Policy," n.d.

89 Wildlife Act, *supra* note 56; GN, "New Wildlife Regulations Coming into Force" [News release], Department of Environment, 30 June 2015.

90 Art. 5 deals with wildlife, harvesting rights, hunters' and trappers' organizations, and regional wildlife organizations; Art. 6 – wildlife compensation; Art. 7 – outpost camps; Art. 8 – parks; Art.9 – conservation areas; Art. 15 – the key principles of marine areas management and the Inuit use of these areas for harvesting beyond marine areas of the Nunavut Settlement Area. On Inuit offshore rights, including harvesting rights, see Natalia Loukacheva, "Inuit Perspectives on Arctic Ocean Governance: The Case of Nunavut," *Ocean Yearbook* 28 (2014): 348–79.

91 *Noah Kadlak and NTI v. Minister of Sustainable Development* 2001NUCJ 1.
92 Firearms case, NTIv.Ca (Attorney General) 2003 NUCJ 01.
93 *R. v. Kooktook, Peetooloot and Tucktoo,* 2004 NUCJ 07.
94 *Supra* note 92, point 26.
95 Warren Bernauer, "'Mining in Caribou Calving Grounds': Can Nunavut Beat the Status Quo?," *Northern Public Affairs,* July 2014: 1–7.
96 *Qikiqtani Inuit Association. v. Canada (Minister of Natural Resources),* 2010 NUCJ 12, point 25.
97 Ibid., point 48.
98 Hamlet of Clyde River, Nammautaq Hunters andTrappers Organization – Clyde River, and Jerry Natanine and TGS-NOPEC Geophysical Company ASA (TGS), Petroleum Geo-Services Inc. (PGS), Multi Klient Invest as (MKI), and the Attorney General of Canada. FCA. Notice of Application for Judicial Review. Toronto: 28 July 2014.
99 Ibid., 2015 FCA 179.
100 CBC News, "Seismic Testing off Clyde River Cancelled for 2015," 27 May 2015. About seismic testing cases in Nunavut, see also Cécile Pelaudeix, "Governance of Arctic Offshore Oil and Gas Activities: Multilevel Governance and Legal Pluralism at Stake," *Arctic Yearbook – 2015,* 1–20 at 7–8.
101 They challenged it in October 2015 and in 2016 the Supreme Court confirmed that it would hold a hearing.
102 *Clyde River (Hamlet) v. Petroleum Geo-Services Inc.* 2017 SCC 40 1 S.C.R. 1069 July 26, 2017 paras 52–3.
103 ITK, "Inuit Leaders Welcome Lancaster Sound Announcement" [Media release], 8 June 2016.
104 Natalia Loukacheva, "Nunavut and Canadian Arctic Sovereignty," *Journal of Canadian Studies* 43, no. 2 (2009): 82–108.
105 Food Secure Canada, "Indigenous Food Sovereignty," Discussion paper no. 1, 2009, www.foodsecurecanada.org.
106 Lessee Paptsie et al., "The Right to Food Security in a Changing Arctic," Nunavut Food Security Coalition and Feeding My Family Campaign, 2013, 1.
107 ICC, A Circumpolar Inuit Declaration on Sovereignty in the Arctic, April 2009, point 3.12; Mary Simon, "Inuit and the Canadian Arctic: Sovereignty Begins at Home," *Journal of Canadian Studies* 43, no. 2 (2009): 250–60; Scot Nickels, ed., *Nilliajut: Inuit Perspectives on Security, Patriotism, and Sovereignty* (Ottawa: ITK, 2013).
108 For links with Canadian Arctic sovereignty discourse, see other chapters in this volume.
109 ICC, Declaration 2009, point 2.2.
110 ICC, A Circumpolar Inuit Declaration on Resource Development Principles in Inuit Nunaat, 2011, point 6.4.

12 The Transformative Power of "Security" Talk

FRANK SEJERSEN

The Arctic has its own history of challenges, problems, and predicaments, which have shaped the region as a particular place and been used to demarcate that space. Some of these problems have been framed by using the concept of "security." When security is introduced into the discussion, something happens. The concept gives weight, momentum, and direction to arguments, and certain referent objects, responsibilities, and avenues for action emerge. Increasingly, the concept of "security" seems to be a powerful and useful concept that is widely used to address a variety of questions.[1] This chapter sets out to discuss what may also be mobilized when security is evoked and when it takes centre stage in what we may term the "New Arctic." It argues that security thinking sets up a transformative space for society because it invites newness to enter the scene. Security discussions are conceptualized as acts of cultural translation where something may be lost and something gained. The chapter relates the idea of transformative space to issues related to climate change in Alaska and food security in Canada and Alaska.

The New Arctic

Since the end of the Cold War, environmental and climate change issues have been pivotal to the public's perception of the Arctic. That region is no longer viewed as a cold, marginal, military-strategic place; it is now seen as an open maritime space of global importance to our understanding of climate change dynamics. The Arctic is now viewed as a place of extreme physical and ecosystemic transformation, those changes having been set in motion by rising temperatures, among other factors, with severe consequences for the Arctic's inhabitants. A new landscape of risk and opportunity has been produced. Additionally, political changes with respect to the recognition of Indigenous peoples' rights have positioned these peoples as strong collective *rights-holders.* Various governments, treaties, land claims, and other political structures have led to Indigenous peoples' increased self-determination and changed the political *modus operandi.* The international cooperation that has developed under the auspices of the Arctic Council reminds us that rights-holders and stakeholders have been provided with new political arenas and tools to address and influence regional dynamics.[2] This landscape of risk and opportunity and these various partnerships, governments, and multi-level cooperative projects together comprise the "New Arctic."

To Think with "Security"

Security thinking is a particular kind of cultural and political act that makes it possible to transcend place and time while reproducing and reflecting on existing ideas of what constitutes stability and responsibility. Security thinking thus triggers a particular space-time and demarcates a space for agency, fear, hope, and promise. I argue that a security issue can be understood as a productive act of establishing a space for renegotiating causalities, subject positions, morality, and dominant ways of scaling (and is thus a little bit more than a reflection on a "referent object" and "agent of security," which are often referred to in security studies). Security is a powerful concept as it calls for moral action and can place human existence at the forefront in particular ways. This perspective, which I suggest here, is based on a post-structuralist approach to security and is inspired by the Copenhagen School of security studies.[3] Whereas the Copenhagen School focuses on the complexities of the securitization process, and thus primarily points to how security issues arise, I want to turn our attention to the productive potential of these securitization processes.

When we approach "security talk," "security thinking," and "security issues" as a transformative space, we may see not only different understandings of who/what is in need of being secured, from what threats, by what actors, and through what means, but also whom we become when secured. I see "security talk" not only as a conservative obsession with maintaining and protecting what is treasured from a perceived threat, but also as a *productive* and *creative* act of imagining and negotiating *who we are* and *who we want to become.* Security talk is thus also about the "future social." Basically, security talk can be seen as an act of future-making.[4]

This task of imagining the "future social" can be approached as a sociocultural action, where communities (at all scales) and individuals caught in fluid landscapes of (real or imagined) risks and threats mobilize new understandings of "community" and "personhood" – feared, anticipated, or desired. They may pursue what Homi Bhabha calls a "cultural translation,"[5] which he perceives as a process whereby people are compelled to *revise* their own reference systems, norms, and judgments when faced with other systems of significance. I propose to view the constructed images of the "future social" as an "other system of significance." When communities are attentive toward *other futures* – bad or good – people creatively try to establish a vision, to anticipate a storyline or a line of future development. Security thinking is thus able to evoke creative agency that brings the unprecedented into effect by way of imaginative power, thereby expanding the community's awareness of itself.

The transformative potentialities of security discussions can thus be conceptualized as an act of cultural translation where something is lost and something is gained. So when people engage in security talk they are not only lost in translation as they struggle to understand the times to come – they are also creatively producing something new. I thus see the translation as an activity inherent in any situation that relates to a security issue in which people have to imagine a "future bad." The idea of a "future bad" forces people to confront themselves with their own "future self" as "other," so to speak – one could see it as a "cultural encounter" with an imagined future self. The analysis of the construction of the "dangerous other" is often an inherent aspect of the study of security discourses.[6] Moreover, the processes of "othering" that I address are linked to how one's future self (as other) is negotiated, constructed, and imagined, as well as the productive aspects this entails. Images of "future bad" and questions of security and risk create a transformative space where people rethink and rescale constituent parts of society and identities. It is this process that can be approached as cultural translation.

I am *not* talking about cultural translation as a process taking place *between* closed and bounded systems where different perceptions of risk, threats, and security meet and are to be grasped through translation and negotiation (e.g., between local and state perspectives and concerns). I see cultural translation as a creative act of cultural production taking place in a carved-out transformative space where there is high attentiveness to the negotiated ideas of self and other.[7] Security thinking can be approached as an act of cultural translation where neither the original nor the translation are fixed and enduring categories because they do not have an essential quality, and both are constantly transformed in space and time.[8] In cultural translation neither "start" nor "target" is stable or entirely separate. Despite this uneasy but productive relationship between self and other, original and translation, start and target, the concept of cultural translation points our attention toward the high alertness of border-crossing in space-time and concerns about what such border-crossings may entail with respect to what is lost and what is gained. For Homi Bhabha, cultural translation is an attentiveness to hybridity. Walter Benjamin even argues that translation gives the "original" (which he sees as open, living, and unfixed) an afterlife or a prolonged life (*Fortleben*).[9] But *Fortleben* is, according to Bhabha, the essence of survival (in French *sur-vivre*). Bhabha applies Benjamin's ideas to his understanding of cultural translation in the following way: "If hybridity is heresy, then to blaspheme is to dream. To dream not of the past or present, nor the continuous present; it is not the nostalgic dream of tradition, not the Utopian dream of modern progress; it is the dream of translation as 'survival,' as Jacques Derrida translates the 'time' of Benjamin's concept of the after-life of translation, as *sur-vivre*, the act of living on borderlines."[10] This state of dynamic self-translation is essential in "security talk," where the "future bad" emerges as a border to apprehend and deal with.

What are the implications of seeing things as I propose here? If we, for example, look at climate-related security issues we quickly end up in the study of impacts, vulnerability, and resilience. I suggest, however, that it may also be productive to redirect our focus away from the usual question of "How do we deal with the risks?" toward the question of "Whom are we to become when dealing with the risks?"[11] The point of departure is that the question "Whom are we to become?" is tantamount to thinking of communities on another scale and to creating new images of social life. And if we ask this question, I think it has an impact on the knowledge regime we have established around security studies. In the following, I focus on two cases that have been demarcated as security issues. The first relates to the small Inuit community of Kivalina, Alaska, which is experiencing severe erosion to the point that the villagers need to be relocated. The second focuses on food insecurity in Alaska and Canada. In both security cases the Inuit enter into a productive reflection on the relationship between "contemporary self" and "future self" (as "other"), and in doing so carve out a space for newness.

Climate Change Insecurity: Kivalina

The small Inuit community of Kivalina, Alaska, is facing coastal erosion so severe that its inhabitants have been asking for relocation since 1910.[12] Storms are eating their way into the coast, and with each bite the waves take the village is undermined.[13] The increase in storms and the lack of protective ice are understood as linked to changes in climate.[14] These changes have left the village more exposed and vulnerable. According to Kivalina's attorney, "the village is being wiped out by global warming and needs to move urgently before it is destroyed and the residents become global warming refugees."[15] Furthermore, the changes in weather and ice have had an impact on subsistence activities and have made some forms of hunting more difficult.[16] Imaginaries of a future of uncertainty are dominant, and the inhabitants express little hope. Kivalina Tribal Administrator Colleen Swan[17] expressed the people's frustration and concern in this way: "Where will we go, and who will help us move?"

Kivalina is struggling to attract the attention of the authorities and make them understand the tremendous risks they are facing. The villagers, who have been called "America's first climate change refugees," fear for their safety and security.[18] The US Department of Homeland Security has been engaged in emergency plans for the community. A number of technical solutions have also been applied temporarily by the military to protect it, and possible new locations for it have been explored.

Seen from Kivalina, the erosion risk is an immediate security issue for the community. The inhabitants are being forced to imagine and scale themselves into a totally other future position. The translation and negotiation processes that I want to draw attention to are taking place not only between the community and the authorities, and among persons and families within the community, but also at an individual level, resulting in extreme personal distress and ambivalence. Each person has to establish and explore new narratives of being *Kivalinamiut* – those who see their identity as linked to Kivalina. Thinking about relocation can be viewed as a process of translation where those involved know that something personal and collective is being *lost* and that something *new* will emerge. Several relocation sites have been investigated,[19] with the site evaluations formulated largely in technical terms. The discussions centre on community and personal welfare, possibilities, and protection. The villagers have to translate technical language into future scenarios and evaluate the conditions for social and personal reproduction in a new site. Several referendums have been conducted so that community members can choose from different locations.[20] Many sites have been considered undesirable because they are too far from the coast, which would disrupt subsistence activities and make supply delivery difficult.[21]

In the relocation discussions, questions related to the process of cultural translation arise: If the community is relocated to another place, is it then the same community? And if not, what are the consequences for social reproduction? These are more than "questions"; they also amount to long chains of painful translations of personhood and community. The uncertain future, lack of foreseeable relocation, housing shortage, loss of traditional cultural knowledge, and poor living conditions,[22] "combined with feeling[s] of hopelessness could greatly contribute to social problems in the village."[23] To boost the imaginary power of Kivalina's residents in this process of translation, the organization Re-Locate (a collective of ethnographic artists and transdisciplinary partners) received funding "to further integrate arts and culture into the field of community planning and development. Re-Locate will work to co-create a village-based territorial planning process with individuals, families, and institutions in Kivalina that makes visible and brings action to their strategies and plans for relocation and for a world where particular subjectivities and cultural practices can endure and flourish."[24] This co-creation process can be seen as an act of cultural translation where ideas for the future are given space to grow. It is a process that will help the residents "visualize where we're at, where we can be, and how we can move in that direction," as formulated by Millie Hawley, president of Kivalina's IRA Council established pursuant to the provisions of the Indian Reorganization Act.[25] According to Colleen Swan, the process does more than boost the co-creation of future imaginaries; such projects also "empower the people to make the decisions."[26] The security situation has thus fostered creative community action to confront the "future bad" and has encouraged the exploration of alternative future selves as part of the conscious pursuit of fate control. This affirms and underscores the importance of self-determination as an Indigenous community.

Food Security

In the Arctic, the question of food security is often raised[27] as communities experience reduced accessibility and availability of food. Climate change is often pointed out as a major concern, and for good reason. Food security discourses pertain to access to and availability of country foods and the erosion of "traditional" subsistence hunting and gathering activities.[28] However, food security is a complex problem that cannot be reduced to climate change alone. Researchers estimate that 70 per cent of preschool children in the Canadian territory of Nunavut live in food-insecure homes.[29] The social, political, cultural, and economic sources that contribute to making the problem so massive are also identified.[30] How can "food security" be linked to cultural translation and the creation of a transformative space for newness?

Food Insecurity in Nunavut

Since 2012, the Inuit inhabitants of several communities in Nunavut have been protesting and demonstrating in the streets and in front of shops as well as boycotting stores, all to draw attention to high food prices and

their low income levels (see also Loukacheva in chapter 10). Despite
government subsidies, more and more people are struggling to make
ends meet, and the protesters point to the territory's rising cost of living,
low average incomes, insufficient social assistance, lack of employment,
and the federal government's failed Nutrition North subsidy program.[31]
To develop a long-term food security action plan, prominent Inuit con-
vened the Nunavut Food Security Coalition in 2011.[32] On a grassroots
level, by 2016 more than 24,300 people had joined the Facebook group
called Feeding My Family.[33] According to one protester, "they're just rob-
bing us, man! I'm a single individual and if I were to do my groceries
here all the time I'd have to spend most, if not all my income. And that's
just sick."[34] The food security problem in Nunavut is real, and people
interpret it as emerging out of a social, economic, and political context
that produces societal inequality, cultural disrespect, and resource in-
sufficiency. Thus, food insecurity is not just about food accessibility and
availability; it is being translated into issues of political failure, uneven
development, and companies' profit strategies, which have eroded a
healthy "future self."

The issue of food security in Nunavut has been used as a platform
for raising these issues and for drawing attention to how northern residents have been used, forgotten, and marginalized. One commenter
in the Facebook group explicitly draws the debate in that direction.
That person sees the protest strategy as aimed in the wrong direction:
"By boycotting NorthMart [the retail store in many northern Canadian
towns], we concentrate on the wrong end of the equation, let politicians off the hook and ensure people stay hungry."[35] The "future bad"
that is anticipated on the basis of the devastating contemporary food
problems invites reflection on the social context and the political institutions. Addressing food as a security issue calls for a certain collective
responsibility and action and also, in this case, points at how broken
promises and marginalization are deeply linked to the reproduction
of daily life.

The "transformative power of everyday life"[36] emerges when protesters in Nunavut argue for structural and political changes, pointing to
the inequality in the distribution of welfare accessibility and systemic
economic illogics. The everyday has been turned inside out so that
structural problems are exposed. The protesters shame and blame, as
well as criticize and hope. The protests (and thus the whole problem
of the collapse of food security in Nunavut) can be seen as the public arena of a social movement calling for a process of transformation
so that the "future bad" can be avoided through structural changes
and political action. Basically, the protesters are arguing for outside

intervention to remove food insecurity but have left a trail of structural and critical afterthoughts based on their experiences. Due to the structural aspects of production, distribution, and consumption of food, questions of "food security" are never just about getting proper food on the table; they always also reflect (and critique) the structural entanglements that emerge when imagining the "future bad." The public reflections on food insecurity in Nunavut bring the past, the present, and the future tightly together; this not only addresses the question of whom to become but also injects critical hope and newness into the discussion. "Yet Inuit remain confident that as a culture they will not only survive these changes but thrive," Lessee Papatsie and colleagues explain. "Local solutions to mobilise communities to address food insecurity are emerging."[37]

Food Security in Alaska

In Alaska as well, the question of food security is at the top of the agenda. There, Inuit communities are concerned, among other things, about the problems of climate change and its impact on the accessibility, stability, and availability of country food. They have experienced dramatic changes in the environment on which they base their livelihood.[38] The influence on accessibility, availability, and predictability of animals and plants important for their communities' food security is evident. To address issues related to environmental health, the Inuit Circumpolar Council (Alaska) has formulated the "Alaskan Inuit Food Security Conceptual Framework: How to Assess the Arctic from an Inuit Perspective."[39] ICC-Alaska argues that a paradigm shift is needed: "one must be willing to attempt to understand the Inuit culture to know what the Inuit mean when they talk about food security."[40] Besides pointing out how Inuit appreciate, depend upon, and use the environment, ICC-Alaska emphasizes how Inuit culture and social reproduction are intrinsically linked to a healthy environment.[41] The framework identifies a large number of problems, barriers, and concerns related to the maintenance of food security and puts forward a number of actions to be taken. The strong link that ICC-Alaska has forged between cultural and environmental integrity explicitly connects food security to food sovereignty. In this way, it also directly integrates Inuit control, involvement, and influence in, for example, environmental management structures and policies. Food sovereignty is also thought of as a conceptual way to expand (or confirm) the desire, need, and right to govern how food is obtained, managed, processed, stored, and consumed, and to have a decisive say in how this is prioritized.[42]

The "future bad" from this food security perspective is a future in which decision-making power lies *outside* Inuit communities and where their control/influence over their own fate is absent or diminishing. By making such a strong claim to their own right and responsibility to manage resources as part of reflections on "food security," Alaskan Inuit link self-governance and environmental management with everyday life. They infuse respect for Indigenous rights across all scales because environmental and community health is closely connected to dynamics outside the sphere of daily life (e.g., transboundary pollution and international trade bans). Self-governance is understood to include the capacity to decide on simple things such as what is to be sold in stores as well as on complex issues such as resource management policies.[43] The emerging "future bad" is one in which Inuit are marginalized and lack the power to influence daily life and the direction and momentum of societal and cultural change. The issue of "food security" condenses this Inuit concern for being able to pursue social and cultural reproduction with the desire to play a decisive role in deciding their own direction.

The issue of food security is perceived by Inuit as urgent and necessary; so is ICC-Alaska's proposal to use a food security lens defined by them: "There is no time to waste; we must begin to make changes today, not just for the sake of our culture but also for the sake of the entire Arctic ecosystem."[44] Inuit throughout the Arctic are experiencing rapid changes, and ICC-Alaska finds those changes to be accelerating, especially those related to climate change. It is pushing for change, and in calling for policy and structural changes through its own food security lens, it is positioning Inuit as in control of their own future. ICC-Alaska's recommendations are quite elaborate in terms of integrating Indigenous perspectives, knowledge, and ambitions. ICC-Alaska elegantly links its food security talk to food sovereignty. In doing so, it is not only linking security issues to sovereignty issues but also infusing a temporal dimension within a particular community (Alaska Native people) in an uncertain and unstable context. The entire framework is not set up to protect, preserve, and maintain Indigenous culture; rather, it is set up to allow them to influence the necessary newness that they hope will enter their world. In that way, they hope to influence whom they will become in a time of rapid change in which the "future bad" is deeply felt.

The Canadian food security case points our attention toward a security issue linked to immediate daily problems supposedly generated by the dynamics of particular postcolonial political and economic arrangements, whereas the Alaskan case underscores a long-term perspective where Inuit want to have a larger say in how resources are managed and for whose benefit. In both cases, security involves addressing existential threats to particular collectives of various orders and scales. As such security claims are made, the communities (and their right to social reproduction) are evoked simultaneously. Morten Axel Pedersen and Martin Holdbraad point out that we "need to ask what visions of the future and of time itself are at stake when security becomes an issue for people: what, and when, are *times of security?*"[45] In the Canadian and Alaskan cases, different temporalities emerge out of the security talk and different agencies are made possible. In both cases, however, food security talk comes to be about transformation and the infusion of newness.

Conclusion

Faced with "future bads," Inuit have to deal with enormous risks, dangers, and threats. They also need to negotiate and invent solutions in cooperation with authorities who often have different cultural and political ideas (and agendas) and thus subscribe to different programs for handling "future bads." I have argued that "security thinking" and "security talk" produce a transformative space in which it is possible for communities and individuals to translate themselves and their identities as communities and individuals. The concept of cultural translation also directs our analytical attention toward processes, politics, and meetings driven by this fundamental question: "Whom are we to become when dealing with "future bads?" In this way, translations of risk and security are deeply entangled in negotiations of future identities. If security talk is an act of cultural translation, newness is analytically infused. Security studies can then also focus on the highly difficult but productive tasks of negotiating the "future self" to come.

This take on security talk is based on an analytical attentiveness to discourses. It follows some of the ideas of *securitization theory* as developed by the Copenhagen School,[46] which invites new questions into security as a (political) discourse by asking who securitizes, on what issues, for whom, why, and with what results. However, the analysis in this chapter does not see "security" as a passing from one social order ("ordinary politics") to another (the extrapolitical realm of "emergency"), as the Copenhagen School does. Rather, it sees "security talk" carrying transformative and productive power to political and cultural projects at different scales as an act of infusing newness and change, here and now. In doing so, security talk creates room for individual and collective reflection driven by ideas of the "future bad." It is not about preserving a referent object, but about creating alternative futures to ensure durability over time (*sur-vivre*). One enters into a process of cultural translation where one's future self as the ultimate other in the "future bad" is the referent point.

Pedersen and Holbraad also underscore that it is "near-impossible to think of security without also imagining particular forms of reproduction, projection, and transformation of various units of life."[47] Thus, security talk is not only about what *may* happen but also about what *could* happen if something was done.

The question "Whom to become?" is imminent in issues we demarcate as "security issues" and is a pressing one to ask in "the New Arctic." It may be productive to integrate such questions as they open up for new voices, new perspectives, new narratives, and new encounters when we address issues demarcated as security issues. When new modes of description and anticipation come into being, new possibilities for action come into being in consequence.

NOTES

1 Lassi Heininen, ed., *Future Security of the Global Arctic* (Basingstoke: Palgrave Macmillan, 2016); Morten Axel Pedersen and Martin Holbraad, "Introduction: Times of Security," in *Times of Security: Ethnographies of Fear, Protest, and the Future*, ed. Martin Holbraad and Morten Pedersen, 1–27 (New York: Routledge, 2013).

2 Oran Young, *Creating Regimes Arctic Accords and International Governance* (Ithaca: Cornell University Press, 1998).

3 Barry Buzan, Ole Wæver, and Jaap de Wilde, *Security: A New Framework for Analysis* (Boulder: Lynne Rienner, 1998).

4 Frank Sejersen, *Rethinking Greenland and the Arctic in the Era of Climate Change* (London: Routledge, 2015).

5 Homi Bhabha, "Dialektal Kosmopolitism," *Glänta* no. 3 (2001): 20.

6 E.g., David Campbell, *Writing Security: United States Foreign Policy and the Politics of Identity* (Minneapolis: University of Minnesota Press, 1998).

7 Homi Bhabha, *The Location of Culture* (London: Routledge, 1994).

8 Boris Buden, Stefan Nowotny, Sherry Simon, Ashok Bery, and Michael Cronin, "Cultural Translation: An Introduction to the Problem, and Responses," *Translation Studies* 2, no. 2 (2009): 196–219.

9 Walter Benjamin, "The Translator's Task" [1923], in *The Translation Studies Reader*, ed. L. Venuti, 75–83 (London: Routledge, 2012).

10 Bhabha, *The Location of Culture*, 226–7.

11 Sejersen, *Rethinking Greenland*.

12 Glenn Gray, *Situation Assessment: Kivalina Consensus Building Project*. Report prepared for the City of Kivalina (2010), 2.

13 US Army Corps of Engineers, *Alaska Village Erosion Technical Assistance Program*, Alaska District (2006).

14   ACIA, *Arctic Climate Impact Assessment* (Cambridge: Cambridge University Press, 2004).

15   Cited in Rachel D'Oro, "Eroding Alaska Village Appeals Lawsuit's Dismissal," *JuneauEmpire.Com*, 29 January 2010, http://juneauempire.com /stories/012910/sta_556400655.shtml.

16   Gray, *Situation Assessment*, 22.

17   Cited in Christine Shearer, *Kivalina: A Climate Change Story* (Chicago: Haymarket Books, 2011), 12.

18   Anthony Bond, "America's First Climate Change Refugees," *MailOnline.com*, 30 July 2013, http://www.dailymail.co.uk/news/article-2381218/Kivalina -Americas-climate-change-refugees-Hundreds-forced-flee-Alaskan-village -disappears-underwater-decade.html.

19   Gray, *Situation Assessment*, 22.

20   Ibid., 29.

21   US Army Corps of Engineers, *Relocation Planning Project: Master Plan. Kivalina, Alaska*, Alaska District (2006b), 52.

22   Gray, *Situation Assessment*, 4.

23   US Army Corps of Engineers, *Relocation Planning Project*, 7.

24   Re-Locate 2015, "Re-Locate Receives 2015 ArtPlace America Grant," *Re-Locate*, 16 July 2015, http://www.relocate-ak.org/2015/re-locate-receives -2015-artplace-america-grant.

25   Cited in ibid.

26   Cited in ibid.

27   E.g. Gérard Duhaime and Nick Bernard, eds. *Arctic Food Security* (Edmonton: University of Alberta Press, 2008). See also Loukacheva, ch. 10 in this volume.

28   Daniel White, S. Craig Gerlach, Philip Loring, Amy C. Tidwell and Molly C. Chambers, "Food and Water Security in a Changing Arctic Climate," *Environmental Research Letters* 2 (2007): 1–4.

29   Grace Egeland, Angela Pacey, Zirong Cao, and Isaac Sobol, "Food Insecurity among Inuit Preschoolers: Nunavut Inuit Child Health Survey, 2007–2008," *Canadian Medical Association Journal* 182, no. 3 (2010): 243–8.

30   James Ford and Lea Berrang-Ford, "Food Security in Igloolik, Nunavut: An Exploratory Study," *Polar Record* 45, no. 234 (2009): 225–36. See also Gerard Duhaime, ed., *Sustainable Food Security in the Arctic: State of Knowledge*, Occasional Publication Series no. 52 (Edmonton: Canadian Circumpolar Institute, 2002).

31   Madelaine Chin-Yee and Benjamin H. Chin-Yee, "Nutrition North Canada: Failure and Facade within the Northern Strategy," *University of Toronto Medical Journal* 92, no. 3 (2015): 13–18.

32   Jennifer Wakegijig, Geraldine Osborne, Sara Statham, and Michelle Doucette Issaluk, "Collaborating toward Improving Food Security in Nunavut," *International Journal of Circumpolar Health* 72 (2013): 1–8.

33   Lessee Papatsie, Leanna Ellsworth, Stephanie Meakin, and Tiina Kurvits, "The Right to Food Security in a Changing Arctic: The Nunavut Food Security Coalition and the Feeding My Family Campaign" (2013), http://www.mrfcj.org/wp-content/uploads/2015/09/2013-04-16-Arctic.pdf.

34   Cited in Jim Bell, "Nunavut Demonstrators Gather to Protest Food Prices, Poverty," *Nunatsiaq Online*, 9 June 2012), http://www.nunatsiaqonline.ca/stories/article/65674nunavut_demonstrators_gather_to_protest_food_prices_poverty.

35   Cited in Thomas Rohner, "Nunavut Food Security Group Calls for One-Day Boycott," *Nunatsiaq Online*, 21 January 2015, http://www.nunatsiaqonline.ca/stories/article/65674nunavut_food_security_group_calls_for_one-day_boycott.

36   Cindi Katz and Andrew Kirby, "In the Nature of Things: The Environment and Everyday Life," Transactions of the Institute of British Geographers *16*, no. *3* (1991): 259–71.

37   Papatsie et al., "The Right to Food Security."

38   ICC–Alaska, *Alaskan Inuit Food Security Conceptual Framework: How to Assess the Arctic from an Inuit Perspective* (Anchorage: Inuit Circumpolar Council-Alaska, 2016), 65.

39   ICC–Alaska, *Alaskan Inuit Food Security*.

40   Ibid., 7.

41   Ibid., 13.

42   Ibid., 46.

43   Ibid., 71.

44   Ibid., 14.

45   Pedersen and Holbraad, "Introduction: Times of Security," 2.

46   Buzan, Wæver and de Wilde, *Security*, 1998.

47   Pedersen and Holbraad, "Times of Security," 23.

Afterword: Sovereign Futures in an Insecure Arctic

WILFRID GREAVES

At the start of 2021, much has changed and much remains the same with respect to the questions and challenges for sovereignty and security in the circumpolar Arctic. For better or worse, many of the old debates are alive and well: How should states exercise sovereignty in the Arctic? Will state practice remain law-abiding, or does it risk deteriorating into self-interest and national gain? Will the Arctic remain a zone of peace, or is conflict possible or perhaps even imminent? Are the Russians coming? What does climate change mean for this region of the world most acutely susceptible to its impacts, and what are its implications for both security and sovereignty as the ice melts, waters become more navigable, ecologies change, and human activities increase? Whose sovereignty should be considered? Whose security should be defended? Ultimately, the question at the very core of politics: who should decide all of the above?

There is no consensus on any of these questions within either academic or policy-making circles, nor, indeed, among a broader public with a still-nascent conception of what the Arctic is and what it means for global politics. Elsewhere, I have argued that the structures and institutions of Arctic regional security are straining, and perhaps fraying, as a result of the interrelated effects of geopolitical pressures and the prevalence of "pathological" conceptualizations of, and policy approaches toward, Arctic security. Derived from the Greek word *pathos*, for suffering, pathological is typically employed as a medical adjective to characterize that which deviates from a healthy, efficient, or sustainable condition.[1] Politically speaking, pathologies are practices that harm or undermine the interests of the actor responsible for the practice in question. With colleagues, I have argued that security in the Arctic suffers from three distinct pathologies: remilitarization of states' foreign and security policies in the absence of a clear military threat; hydrocarbon resource extraction in the context of human-caused global climate change; and the constrained inclusion of Indigenous peoples in regional governance.²

Each of these pathologies is still applicable, though each is also in flux as a result of factors both external and internal to the Arctic. The first pathology refers to the paradox that in the first years of the twenty-first century, Arctic states were investing considerable resources to remilitarize their Arctic regions and capabilities without a clearly defined military threat. In the decade from 2005 to 2015, circumpolar states reinvested in military capabilities and infrastructure to support Arctic military operations; renewed Cold War–era activities such as long range bomber patrols and the "buzzing" of neighbours' airspace; belligerently or inconsiderately asserted their territorial boundaries, including delimitation of the Arctic seabed and continental shelves; and sought to deter non-Arctic states from making claims in the region. While actual spending often fell short of rhetorical commitments, these developments fuelled widespread media coverage and public perceptions of a militarized race for northern territory and resources (as Mathieu Landriault discusses in chapter 3), including over the North Pole, the Northwest Passage, and the limits of states' extended continental shelves. All eight Arctic states have affirmed their commitment to a peaceful and rule-governed Arctic order based on international law and the peaceful negotiation of disputes, and their official policies all state that there is no prospective military threat in or to the region. Unfortunately, since I first argued that this remilitarization was pathological since it was occurring without a clear enemy, tensions among Arctic states have increased significantly, clarifying that this recent remilitarization does indeed reflect the long, now resurgent, tradition of enmity between Russia and the West (see also Huebert in chapter 4).

Since the popular overthrow (with US support) of the pro-Russian president of Ukraine in spring 2014, relations between Russia and Western states that happen to be its Arctic neighbours have continued their deteriorate. Russia subsequently invaded and illegally annexed the Ukrainian region of Crimea, then launched an unconventional conflict in eastern Ukraine that has led to the redeployment of NATO ground troops in Eastern Europe as a "tripwire" against Russian aggression. Relations between Russia and the five Arctic states that are NATO members (Canada, Denmark, Iceland, Norway, and the United States) are now the worst they have been since the end of the Cold War, with sanctions imposed on senior Russian officials and with Western companies prohibited from doing business within Russia. For its part, Russia has imposed reciprocal sanctions and threatened further escalation if the West does not refrain from encroaching on what the Kremlin continues to see as its rightful sphere of influence.[3] The causes of these tensions have nothing to do with the Arctic *per se*, but the seriousness of the deterioration has undermined further pan-Arctic cooperation, demonstrating its vulnerability to geopolitical developments exogenous to the region.

While it remains to be seen whether the effects of the conflict in Ukraine on Arctic governance and security will remain over the long term, a current result is that militarization in the region is now less ambiguous than it once was. Russia, NATO, and the European Union have all increased their military activities in the northern European theatre, and the five Nordic states have undertaken unprecedented military cooperation with one another and with the neighbouring Baltic states.[4] Norway has reinvigorated much of the northern defence apparatus that had become moribund after the Cold War, and Sweden, which remained neutral during the Cold War to preserve the strategic "Nordic balance" between the East Bloc and the West, has been contemplating NATO membership. Ominously, in 2018 the Swedish government even issued a manual to every household in the country with guidelines for how citizens should respond in the event of a national crisis, including war. Such preparations would seem extreme were it not for the recent strong escalation in military activities, in the European Arctic in particular. In October 2018, NATO carried out a two-week air, land, and sea training exercise called Trident Juncture to practise defending against an unnamed "fictitious aggressor" in the region spanning from the Baltic Sea to Iceland. Largely centred in northern Norway, where NATO and Russia share a land border, the exercise comprised 50,000 troops from thirty-one NATO members and partner countries; it was the largest NATO exercise since the collapse of the Soviet Union. For its part, in September 2018, the Russian military held its own exercise involving more than 300,000 personnel in the Far North and Far East regions of the Russian Federation. War games on such a scale, particularly between historical antagonists such as Russia and NATO, are a worrisome indicator for the future of security and conflict in the Arctic, even if the catalyst for such a conflict is unlikely to originate from within the region.

The second pathology of Arctic security is the continued search for fossil fuels, particularly the enthusiasm for offshore oil and gas drilling generated by the US Geological Survey's 2008 estimates that the region may hold up to 13 per cent of the world's undiscovered oil reserves and 30 per cent of its undiscovered natural gas (see Dolata, chapter 8). The revenues and jobs generated by fossil fuel extraction are central to the economies of many circumpolar states, notably Canada, Norway, Russia, and the United States. Notwithstanding some limited commitments to the international efforts to combat climate change, all four countries remained committed to their hydrocarbon sectors.[5] In the final weeks of his presidency, in December 2016, Barack Obama made two joint announcements with Canadian prime minister Justin Trudeau that appeared to signal a deeper commitment by both countries to act on climate change, including a near-total moratorium on new offshore oil and gas drilling in the waters of the North American Arctic announced in December 2016.[6] However, that moratorium was reversed soon after Donald Trump's accession to the presidency in 2017. Trump also withdrew the United States from the multilateral Paris Agreement on climate change. His executive order reversing the drilling ban was overturned by a federal court in March 2019;[7] even so, the US withdrawal from climate change mitigation efforts under his administration has been nearly total, and this has resuscitated the perennial debate over whether oil drilling should be permitted within the Arctic National Wildlife Refuge (ANWR).[8] In Canada, meanwhile, the debate over carbon pricing and the construction of new fossil fuel export pipelines had consumed national politics prior to the COVID-19 pandemic, with a wave of conservative governments elected provincially opposed to the federal government's adoption of a national price on carbon.[9] In Canada's federal election in 2019, the Trudeau Liberals were narrowly returned to power due, in considerable part, to voters' perceptions they were more committed to addressing climate change.

Elsewhere, Norway has opened new blocks of the Barents Sea to oil and gas exploration, and its coalition conservative government insists that fossil fuels will remain the backbone of the national economy. In April 2019, however, the parliamentary opposition surprised both the government and oil industry by refusing to support new exploratory drilling in the Lofoten region of northwestern Norway.[10] This move, taken by the opposition Labour Party over the objections of the Conservative government, was met with anger by Norway's largest energy labour union and risks replicating the pattern of division on the political left that has affected other democratic jurisdictions. For its part, Russia, though limited by the sanctions imposed since the start of the Ukraine conflict, also relies on fossil fuel extraction as the backbone of its economy, with oil and gas comprising 40 per cent of national revenues and a majority of Russian exports.[11] In December 2017, the $27 billion Yamal liquified natural gas (LNG) project in Siberia began exporting approximately 16.5 million tons per year of LNG to Europe and East Asia.[12] Even though the economic crisis caused by the COVID-19 pandemic has severely reduced global demand for LNG, further expansion in the Russian Arctic is scheduled to proceed.[13] Already among the largest emitters of greenhouse gases in the world, Russia has shown only pro forma interest in emissions reductions or in responding effectively to climate change.[14] In 2018, Greenland reopened bidding for oil and gas drilling on its western coast after a brief pause. Though there has been limited private sector interest in developing Greenland's oil reserves, the prospects for the self-governing Danish territory to achieve full independence have been widely linked to the increased revenues it would generate from fossil fuels. As private sector enthusiasm for new oil drilling has waned, so too has the movement for Greenland to pursue full independence from Copenhagen.[15]

These and other examples of Arctic states supporting, or even expanding, fossil fuel extraction are pathological with respect to Arctic security in at least two ways. First, they are at odds with the global political consensus that climate change must be limited to less than 2°C, as reflected in the multilateral 2015 Paris Agreement. The seriousness of the expected impacts of 2°C was reiterated by the Intergovernmental Panel on Climate Change in its 2018 report urging global policy-makers to limit warming to 1.5°C in order to avoid catastrophic environmental changes globally.[16] It is universally recognized that the polar regions are at acute risk of environmental collapse as a result of climate change, and that the current and future impacts of global warming will devastate communities, peoples, industries, and ecosystems across the circumpolar region.[17] The reality of Arctic warming was vividly demonstrated in 2019, which marked the fourth year in a row in which the circumpolar region experienced record-setting winter heat waves due to climate change.[18] The fact that the leading Arctic states are on track for warming of 4–5°C is therefore deeply alarming, for it will harm both themselves and the rest of the world.[19] It also contradicts the scientific assessment that to minimize future warming, "all Arctic [energy] resources should be classified as unburnable" and remain unexploited.[20] The current approach of Arctic states – to secure their interests through greater resource extraction – is thus inherently unsustainable and amounts to the prioritization of short-term financial benefit at the cost of long-term ecological and social catastrophe.[21]

The second way in which this is pathological is that it doubles down on a waning economic base, seemingly ignoring that private corporate actors are turning away from Arctic fossil fuels (for discussion of Arctic energy security see Dolata in chapter 8). During the boom in commodity prices prior to 2014, the Arctic was seen as the next global frontier for fossil fuels, and the energy sector as the answer to the question of how Arctic economies could modernize. However, the anticipated Arctic energy boom may prove illusory due to low oil prices, a low-carbon economy climate agenda, and technical challenges related to extraction.[22]

The collapse in the global price of oil from its high of more than US$140 per barrel to around $40 per barrel between 2014 and 2019 has cooled private sector enthusiasm for new conventional Arctic energy resources. Major energy companies have cancelled or suspended their Arctic projects,[23] and major reinsurers have signalled their growing unwillingness to finance Arctic oil and gas drilling, flagging their concerns over liability related to both local environmental impacts and possible litigation related to climate change.[24] While Arctic oil production has continued – and even expanded in parts of Russia[25] – changes to public policy in Arctic states and elsewhere around the world designed to curb greenhouse gas emissions and reduce fossil fuel consumption, such as Canada's federally imposed carbon tax, will further depress both private sector interest in Arctic energy investment and public demand for hydrocarbons. Overall, while large-scale resource extraction remains a central pillar of Arctic economies, the *Arctic Human Development Report* may have been correct to note, in 2014, that "high and rising prices of Arctic resources may not be a long-term phenomenon" and that "Arctic resources may face the long run pattern of resource prices declining in real terms."[26] This decline in investment in Arctic resources will pose real challenges to the political economies of many regions across the Arctic. The ideological or partisan pursuit of a fossil fuel–based economic future has exacerbated the degradation of the global environment; it has also heightened the reliance of Arctic societies on an increasingly unviable economic base.

The third pathology of Arctic security also persists, namely, the constrained inclusion of Arctic Indigenous peoples in regional governance arrangements and their contestation over how "Arctic security" should be defined and pursued. While a distinctive feature of modern Arctic governance has been the prominent role played by Indigenous governments and organizations, Indigenous peoples still struggle to have their views and interests reflected in the policies and practices of circumpolar states, and they remain marginal within settler and colonial political institutions. The establishment of self-governing regions and devolved Indigenous or Indigenous-majority governments in Greenland; Nunavut, Nunavik, the Inuvialuit Settlement Region, and Nunatsiavut in Canada; and Alaska's North Slope Borough; the creation of the Sámi parliaments as representative and advisory bodies in Norway, Sweden, and Finland; and the role of the six Permanent Participants representing circumpolar Indigenous peoples within the Arctic Council, are all important developments that underscore the considerable progress that has been made toward Indigenous political inclusion. But they do not alter the fundamental balance of power in the region, nor do they rectify the historical and ongoing processes of colonialism experienced by Arctic Indigenous peoples.[27]

Indigenous governments are limited in their authority and jurisdiction, human and fiscal capacity, and advocacy and governance effectiveness by the reality of colonially imposed borders that divide Indigenous peoples from one another.[28] Indeed, some scholars have lamented the shift in Arctic politics toward greater "Westphalianization," that is, the maintenance or imposition of state-centric forms of power and governance over Arctic policy and decision-making, notably within the Arctic Council.[29]

One consequence of this third pathology is the continued elevation of state-centric accounts of in/security in the Arctic, over and at the expense of those expressed by Indigenous peoples. As I and others have argued elsewhere, there is substantial evidence that Indigenous peoples' understandings of Arctic security have been marginalized or excluded within the policies of Arctic states.[30] Various Indigenous peoples, notably Inuit, have challenged states' militarized and economic conceptions of security and have sought instead to situate the social, political, economic, and cultural autonomy and well-being of Indigenous peoples at the centre of what "Arctic security" means.[31] Though they have been articulated publicly, repeatedly, and directly to powerholders and public officials, such Indigenous security claims have been structurally unable to achieve acceptance or recognition by state authorities and non-Indigenous majority populations.[32] Notably, Inuit have taken the lead in challenging assertions that state sovereignty holds precedence over the sovereignty of the region's Indigenous inhabitants.[33]

These three paradoxes of Arctic security are linked. They also bear on questions of sovereignty in the region. The (re)emergence of inter-state rivalries and the increasing (albeit still low) possibility of militarized conflict between Russia and other circumpolar states have legitimated state-centric and militarized accounts of security in the Arctic. National security and defence are core sovereign prerogatives of states; thus, responding to potential aggressors or rivals, including through economic activities that demonstrate effective control and use of Arctic territory (See Kikkert, chapter 1, and Lajeunesse, chapter 2), reinforces the underlying sovereignty claims of circumpolar states. But meanwhile, natural resource extraction and other industrial activities are contributing directly to human-caused climate change and other forms of environmental degradation that are undermining the health and integrity of Arctic and global ecosystems. Climate change and pollution, in turn, are contributing to the worsening environmental conditions across the circumpolar region, including the loss of sea ice that is driving inter-state competition in the region (see Huebert in chapter 4).[34] And it is Indigenous people, who are politically constrained and structurally precluded from "speaking security" to states, who have most consistently resisted industrialized resource extraction and other environmentally harmful practices as deleterious to their interests and prospects for survival. Indigenous well-being is intimately connected to the natural environment, and this directly implicates state inaction on climate change and support for resource extraction in the production of Indigenous peoples' insecurity. The second and third paradoxes of Arctic security are thus especially closely linked, since greater empowerment and authority for Indigenous peoples would result in greater action to mitigate the environmental changes that are drastically undermining their capacity to practise Indigenous lifeways on their traditional territories.

Conclusion

As the contributions to this volume demonstrate, sovereignty and security themes span vast geographies, long periods of time, and widely diverse areas of public policy, state action, and human life. Moreover, what these key concepts have long meant is being challenged and reimagined by new or resurgent phenomena in global politics, most importantly climate change, renewed geopolitical competition, and the growing indigenization of domestic and regional governance. The rate and scale of these changes appears to be greater than the speed at which Arctic institutions, and in some cases states' Arctic policies, can adapt, and this has generated a series of profound political, social, economic, and ecological challenges. As a result, the future of the Arctic(s) is not entirely clear, nor do we know which policies and practices will best produce "security" for states and peoples across the region.

I will, however, offer two qualified predictions for the Arctic region. First, in at least the near and medium term, the Arctic will remain a space defined largely in terms of state sovereignty, applied sovereign power, and, increasingly, the exercise of that power to support geopolitical competition between global powers and regional, circumpolar powers. This does not mean that violent inter-state conflict is inevitable or even likely. It also does not lessen the importance of other types of political actors, including Indigenous peoples and governments claiming their own exercise of sovereignty; sub-state and quasi-state actors exercising legal jurisdiction over large areas and substantial Arctic populations; and international governmental organizations, such as the Arctic Council, which will remain forums for diplomacy and negotiation. All of these and more will remain core elements in the complex architecture of circumpolar governance. But it seems clear – based on the contributions to this volume and the observations on recent Arctic politics noted in this conclusion – that Arctic states will insist on asserting their sovereign prerogatives and will employ their sovereign power, up to and including the use of force, to assert their perceived national interests. They also will guard their own privileged status in the region's "high politics." All indications are that the Arctic's future will continue to unfold within the legal and political framework of international legal sovereignty, disappointing those who had hoped that the unique qualities of Arctic governance and political cooperation might produce alternatives for transforming how political power and legal authority within the region are exercised.

The second prediction is, unfortunately, easier to make. In light of the evidence confronting us, it is likely that the Arctic's future will be an insecure one characterized by acute threats to state and human security across the region. Above, I outlined three pathologies of Arctic security policy is a result of which Arctic states will continue to undermine security in the region even while nominally seeking to enhance it. The likelihood of continued inter-state tensions among Arctic states is one dimension of this insecurity and is not to be underestimated. As many authors in this volume suggest, however, the greatest risk in the Arctic is not war or state conflict. Rather, it is climate change – already visible, certain to worsen, impossible to fully mitigate – that poses the greatest threat to security in the region. At the state and human levels, environmental changes will continue to upset the delicate balance that has sustained both past social conditions *and* geopolitical conditions conducive to maintaining (relatively) peaceful inter-state relations. Although some observers go to considerable lengths to note various benefits of climate change in the cold northern region of the world, it seems clear that any benefits will be either short-term or ephemeral, while the damage will be of sufficient magnitude that it will transform the basic fabric of human and non-human life. "The Arctic," as it has been constructed in the popular and political imaginaries of the past several centuries, is undergoing irreparable transformation, the site of ecological changes that are radically challenging ways of living in the Arctic and that are soon to affect those who live nowhere near the Arctic. It is little exaggeration to predict that survival – that conceptual cornerstone of what we mean when security is invoked – will become the locus of all policy and action in the Arctic and will become increasingly difficult over the coming century.

I expect that the Arctic's future will be a sovereign future characterized by profound human insecurities as well as growing challenges to states and their capacities to effectively govern their northern territories. This does not mean the end of the world, but it does mean the end of *one* world, an Arctic region constructed on the basis of an ecological system that is facing a transformative extinction event in the form of climate change.

Thus, as Sejersen prompts us to consider in chapter 12, faced with a "future bad" that is rapidly becoming a "bad" and dangerous present, the question that confronts peoples and states across the circumpolar world is "whom to become?" If the underlying conditions of the Arctic region that produced certain kinds of human and state behaviour are replaced by something new, then who must we become and how must we – as individuals, communities, and states – behave in order to make ourselves secure in this warm new world? We must reimagine the conditions of security in the Arctic, and if the future remains a sovereign one, then we must also reimagine how the use of sovereignty and the application of state power can be applied in order to enhance rather than diminish that security. The pathologies that produce Arctic *in*security must be overcome; if they are not, states will continue to undermine the conditions that support their own interests and the welfare of their citizens. Inuit leaders have long reminded Arctic scholars and policy-makers that sovereignty begins at home; so, too, must we remember that to be meaningful, security must apply at home. The security interests of states exist in relation to the needs and interests of their citizens. For a sovereign Arctic future to contribute effectively to conditions of Arctic security for people *and* states, the survival and well-being of people must be placed at the heart of Arctic security policy-making and practice. Only then will security in the Arctic be made sustainable, and sovereignty in the Arctic legitimized through securing the lives of the people who call the Arctic home.

NOTES

1 Merriam-Webster defines "pathology" as "1: the study of the essential nature of diseases and especially of the structural and functional changes produced by them; 2: something abnormal, a: the structural and functional deviations from the normal that constitute disease or characterize a particular disease; b: deviation from propriety or from an assumed normal state of something nonliving or nonmaterial; c: deviation giving rise to social ills." https://www.merriam-webster.com/dictionary/pathology.

2 Andrew Chater and Wilfrid Greaves, "Security Governance in the Arctic," in *Handbook on Governance and Security*, ed. Jim Sperling, 123–47 (Northampton: Edward Elgar, 2014); Andrew Chater, Wilfrid Greaves, and Leah Sarson, "Governance," in *Handbook on Arctic Security*, ed. Gunhild Hoogensen Gjørv and Horatio Sam-Aggrey (London: Routledge, forthcoming).

3 Henry Foy, "Russian Sanctions: Why 'Isolation Is Impossible,'" *The Financial Times*, 11 November 2018, https://www.ft.com/content/c51ecf88-e125-11e8-a6e5-792428919cee.

4   Tore Andre Kjetland, "The Nordic Countries Extend Military Cooperation," *Nora Region Trends,* 13 April 2014, http://www.noraregiontrends.org/news /news-single/article/the-nordic-countries-extends-military-cooperation/87.

5   See Lee Huskey, Ilmo Mäenpää, and Alexander Pelyasov, "Economic Systems," in *Arctic Human Development Report: Regional Processes and Global Linkages,* ed. Joan Nymand Larsen and Gail Fondahl, 151–83 (Akureyri: Steffanson Arctic Institute, 2014).

6   See Wilfrid Greaves, "Environmental Security, Energy Security, and the Arctic in the Obama Presidency," in *One Arctic: The Arctic Council and Circumpolar Governance,* ed. P. Whitney Lackenbauer, Heather Nicol, and Wilfrid Greaves, 101–25 (Ottawa: Canadian Arctic Resources Committee and Centre for Foreign Policy and Federalism, 2017).

7   Kevin Bohn, "Judge Rules Trump Executive Order Allowing Offshore Drilling in Arctic Ocean Unlawful," *CNN,* 30 March 2019, https://www.cnn .com/2019/03/30/politics/trump-offshore-drilling-arctic/index.html.

8   Stephen Mufson, "Trump Administration Takes Another Step towards Oil Drilling in Arctic National Wildlife Refuge," *Washington Post,* 20 December 2018, https://www.washingtonpost.com/national/health-science/trump -administration-takes-another-step-toward-oil-drilling-in-arctic-national -wildlife-refuge/2018/12/20/5fb93f40-0469-11e9-b5df-5d3874f1ac36_story .html?utm_term=.cb7e61e8d882.

9   Markus Hecker and Jackie Dawson, "Canada's Paris-Pipeline Paradox," *The Conversation,* June 2018, http://theconversation.com/canadas-paris-pipeline -paradox-97636.

10 Harry Cockburn, "Norway Refuses to Drill for Billions of Barrels of Oil in the Arctic, Leaving 'Whole Industry Surprised and Disappointed,'" *The Independent,* 9 April 2019, https://www.independent.co.uk/environment /norway-oil-drilling-arctic-ban-labor-party-unions-a8861171.html.

11 Ashleigh Garrison, "Russia's Achilles Heel: Putin Still Falling Short on Master Plan for Aging Oil Economy," *CNBC,* 19 July 2018, https://www.cnbc .com/2018/07/19/checkmate-putin-falling-short-on-master-plan-for-aging -oil-economy.html.

12 Henry Foy, "Russia Ships First Gas from $27bn Arctic Project," *The Financial Times,* 8 December 2017, https://www.ft.com/content/515d451c-dc11 -11e7-a039-c64b1c09b482.

13 Atle Staalesen, "Sharp Drop in LNG Exports, but Novatek Says New Arctic Projects Will Proceed as Planned," *The Barents Observer,* 13 April 3030, https://thebarentsobserver.com/en/industry-and-energy/2020/04/sharp -drop-lng-exports-novatek-says-building-new-arctic-projects-will.

14 See "Russia," *Climate Action Tracker,* 3 December 2018, https://climateac-tiontracker.org/countries/russian-federation; "Russian Ministry Warns of Coming Environmental Apocalypse Fueled by Climate Change," *The Moscow*

Times, 6 September 2018, https://www.themoscowtimes.com/2018/09/06 /russian-ministry-warns-coming-environmental-apocalypse-fueled-climate -change-a62804.

15 Page Wilson, "An Arctic 'Cold Rush'? Understanding Greenland's (In) Dependence Question," *Polar Record* 53, no. 5 (2017): 512–19.

16 IPCC, "2018: Summary for Policymakers," in *Global Warming of 1.5°C. An IPCC Special Report on the Impacts of Global Warming of 1.5°C above Pre-Industrial Levels and Related Global Greenhouse Gas Emission Pathways, in the Context of Strengthening the Global Response to the Threat of Climate Change, Sustainable Development, and Efforts to Eradicate Poverty* (Geneva: World Meteorological Organization, 2018).

17 ACIA, *Impacts of a Warming Climate: Arctic Climate Impact Assessment* (Cambridge: Cambridge University Press, 2004); J.N. Larsen, O.A. Anisimov, A. Constable, A.B. Hollowed, N. Maynard, P. Prestrud, T.D. Prowse, and J.M.R. Stone, "Polar Regions," in *Climate Change 2014: Impacts, Adaptation, and Vulnerability*, Part B: *Regional Aspects*, ed. V.R. Barros, C.B. Field, D.J. Dokken, M.D. Mastrandrea, K.J. Mach, T.E. Bilir, M. Chatterjee, K.L. Ebi, Y.O. Estrada, R.C. Genova, B. Girma, E.S. Kissel, A.N. Levy, S. MacCracken, P.R. Mastrandrea, and L.L.White. Contribution of Working Group II to the Fifth Assessment Report of the Intergovernmental Panel on Climate Change (Cambridge: Cambridge University Press, 2014).

18 Ian Livingston, "Alaska Is Baking in an Exceptionally Toasty March as Steep, Long-Term Warming Presses On," *Washington Post*, 28 March 2019, https://www.washingtonpost.com/weather/2019/03/28/alaska-is-baking -an-exceptionally-toasty-march-steep-long-term-warming-presses/?utm_term =.f7de9dfcaa9d.

19 Jonathan Watts, "Policies of China, Russia and Canada Threaten 5C Climate Change, Study Finds," *The Guardian*, 16 November 2018, https://www .theguardian.com/environment/2018/nov/16/climate-change-champions -still-pursuing-devastating-policies-new-study-reveals.

20 Christopher McGlade and Paul Ekins, "The Geographical Distribution of Fossil Fuels Unused When Limiting Global Warming to 2°C," *Nature* 517, no. 7533 (2015): 187–90.

21 Wilfrid Greaves, "Securing Sustainability: The Case for Critical Environmental Security in the Arctic," *Polar Record* 52, no. 6 (2016): 660–71.

22 Sarah Gulas, Mitchell Downton, Kareina D'Souza, Kelsey Hayden, and Tony Walker, "Declining Arctic Ocean Oil and Gas Developments: Opportunities to Improve Governance and Environmental Pollution Control," *Marine Policy* 75 (2017): 53–61.

23 Juliet Eilperin and Steven Mufson, "Royal Dutch Shell Suspends Arctic Drilling Indefinitely," *The Washington Post*, 28 September 2015, https:// www.washingtonpost.com/news/energy-environment/wp/2015/09/28

/royal-dutch-shell-suspends-arctic-drilling-indefinitely/?utm_term=
.aa299882a45e.

24 Miranda Green, "Barclays to Reject Most Financing for Arctic Drilling," *The Hill*, 14 January 2019, https://thehill.com/policy/energy-environment/425252-barclays-to-reject-most-financing-for-drilling-in-arctic.

25 Donald Gasper, "China and Russia Want to Develop Arctic Energy Resources Together, and US Disapproval May Not Deter Them," *South China Morning Post*, 12 September 2018, https://www.scmp.com/comment/insight-opinion/asia/ article/2163719/china-and-russia-want-develop-arctic-energy-resources.

26 Huskey, Mäenpää, and Pelyasov, "Economic Systems," 161.

27 Rebecca Lawrence, "Internal Colonisation and Indigenous Resource Sovereignty: Wind Power Developments on Traditional Saami Lands," *Environment and Planning D: Society and Space* 32, no. 6 (2014): 1036–53; Jerald Sabin, "Contested Colonialism: Responsible Government and Political Development in Yukon," *Canadian Journal of Political Science* 47, no. 2 (2014): 375–96; Frank Tester, "Colonial Challenges and Recovery in the Eastern Arctic," in *Inuit Qaujimajatuqangit: What Inuit Have Always Known to Be True*, ed. Joe Karetak, Frank Tester, and Shirley Tagalik, 20–40 (Black Point: Fernwood, 2017); Wilfrid Greaves, "Colonialism, Statehood, and Sámi in *Norden* and the Norwegian High North," in *Human and Societal Security in the Circumpolar Arctic: Local and Indigenous Communities*, ed. Kamrul Hossain, José Miguel Roncero Martín, and Anna Petrétei, 100–21 (Leiden and Boston: Brill, 2018).

28 Natalia Loukacheva, *Arctic Promise: Legal and Political Autonomy of Greenland and Nunavut* (Toronto: University of Toronto Press, 2007); Rauna Kuokkanen, "Self-Determination and Indigenous Women – 'Whose Voice Is It We Hear in the Sámi Parliament?,'" *International Journal on Minority and Group Rights* 18, no. 1 (2011): 39–62; Mia Bennett, Wilfrid Greaves, Rudolf Riedlsperger, and Alberic Botella, "Articulating the Arctic: Contrasting State and Inuit Maps of the Canadian North," *Polar Record* 52, no. 6 (2016): 630–44.

29 Jessica Shadian, "From States to Polities: Reconceptualizing Sovereignty through Inuit Governance," *European Journal of International Relations* 16, no. 3 (2010): 485–510; Shadian, *The Politics of Arctic Sovereignty: Oil, Ice, and Inuit Governance* (New York: Routledge, 2014).

30 Wilfrid Greaves, "Arctic In/Security and Indigenous Peoples: Comparing Inuit in Canada and Sámi in Norway," *Security Dialogue* 47, no. 6 (2016): 461–80; Wilfrid Greaves, "Environment, Identity, Autonomy: Inuit Perspectives on Arctic Security," in *Understanding the Many Faces of Human Security: Perspectives of Northern Indigenous Peoples*, ed. Kamrul Hossain and Anna Petrétei, 35–55 (Leiden and Boston: Brill, 2016); Kamrul Hossain, "Securitizing the Arctic Indigenous Peoples: A Community Security Perspective

with Special Reference to the Sámi of the European High North," *Polar Science* 10, no. 3 (2016): 415–24.

31 Scot Nickels, ed., *Nilliajut: Inuit Perspectives on Security, Patriotism, and Sovereignty* (Ottawa: Inuit Tapiriit Kanatami, 2013); ICC, *A Circumpolar Inuit Declaration on Resource Development Principles in Inuit Nunaat* (Nuuk: Inuit Circumpolar Council, 2011), s. 5.1.

32 Wilfrid Greaves, "Damaging Environments: Land, Settler Colonialism, and Security for Indigenous Peoples," *Environment and Society: Advances in Research* 9 [Special Issue on Indigenous Resurgence, Decolonization, and Movements for Environmental Justice] (2018): 107–24.

33 Terry Fenge, "Inuit and the Nunavut Land Claim Agreement: Supporting Canada's Arctic Sovereignty," *Policy Options* 29, no. 1 (2007/2008); ICC, *A Circumpolar Inuit Declaration on Sovereignty in the Arctic* (2009); Natalia Loukacheva, "Nunavut and Canadian Arctic Sovereignty," *Journal of Canadian Studies* 43, no. 2 (2009): 82–108; Mary Simon, "Inuit and the Canadian Arctic: Sovereignty Begins at Home," *Journal of Canadian Studies* 43, no. 2 (2009): 250–60.

34 Scott G. Borgerson, "Arctic Meltdown: The Economic and Security Implications of Global Warming," *Foreign Affairs* 87, no. 2 (March–April 2008): 63–77; Scott G. Borgerson, "The Coming Arctic Boom," *Foreign Affairs* 92, no. 4 (July–August 2013): 76–89.

Contributors

Petra Dolata is an associate professor of history at the University of Calgary.

Wilfrid Greaves is an assistant Ppofessor of international relations at the University of Victoria.

Gunhild Hoogensen Gjørv is a professor of critical peace and conflict studies at UiT, the Arctic University of Norway.

Rob Huebert is an associate professor of political science at the University of Calgary.

Peter Kikkert is the Irving Shipbuilding Chair in Arctic Policy and an assistant professor of public policy and governance at St Francis Xavier University.

P. Whitney Lackenbauer is a professor in the School for the Study of Canada and Canada Research Chair in the Study of the Canadian North at Trent University.

Adam Lajeunesse is the Irving Shipbuilding Chair in Canadian Arctic Marine Security Policy and an assistant professor of public policy and governance at St Francis Xavier University.

Mathieu Landriault is director of the Observatoire de la politique et la sécurité de l'Arctique at the École nationale d'administration publique.

Natalia Loukacheva is an associate professor of political science at the University of Northern British Columbia.

Andreas Østhagen is a senior fellow at the Fridtjof Nansen Institute and a senior fellow at the Arctic Institute.

Frank Sejersen is an associate professor of cross-cultural and regional studies at the University of Copenhagen.

Alexander Sergunin is a professor of international relations at St Petersburg State University.

Index

Printed and bound by CPI Group (UK) Ltd, Croydon, CR0 4YY

13/04/2025

14656521-0004